Cultivating Spirituality

Cultivating Spirituality
A Modern Shin Buddhist Anthology

edited by
Mark L. Blum
and
Robert F. Rhodes

This publication has been supported by the Shin Buddhist Comprehensive Research Institute at Otani University.

Cover art from the journal, *Seishinkai*, volume 11, no. 1, January 1911.

Published by State University of New York Press, Albany

© 2011 State University of New York

All rights reserved

Printed in the United States of America

No part of this book may be used or reproduced in any manner whatsoever without written permission. No part of this book may be stored in a retrieval system or transmitted in any form or by any means including electronic, electrostatic, magnetic tape, mechanical, photocopying, recording, or otherwise without the prior permission in writing of the publisher.

For information, contact State University of New York Press, Albany, NY
www.sunypress.edu

Production by Diane Ganeles
Marketing by Michael Campochiaro

Library of Congress Cataloging-in-Publication Data

Blum, Mark Laurence.
   Cultivating spirituality : a modern Shin Buddhist anthology / Mark L. Blum and Robert F. Rhodes.
     p. cm.
   Includes bibliographical references and index.
   ISBN 978-1-4384-3981-5 (hbk : alk. paper)—978-1-4384-3982-2 (pbk)
   1. Shin (Sect) 2. Religious life—Shin (Sect) 3. Pure Land Buddhism. 4. Japan—Religion. I. Rhodes, Robert Franklin. II. Title. III. Title: Modern Shin Buddhist anthology.

BQ8715.4.B58 2011
294.3'440952--dc22
                                                   2011009764

10 9 8 7 6 5 4 3 2 1

For Jan Van Bragt (1928–2007)

Contents

Foreword   ix
    Yasutomi Shin'ya

Abbreviations   xiii

Chapter 1   Shin Buddhism in the Meiji Period   1
    Mark L. Blum

KIYOZAWA MANSHI

Chapter 2   Kiyozawa Manshi: Life and Thought   55
    Mark L. Blum

Chapter 3   Why Do Buddhists Lack Self-Respect?   67
    Kiyozawa Manshi
    translated by Mark L. Blum

Chapter 4   Negotiating Religious Morality and
Common Morality   77
    Kiyozawa Manshi
    translated by Mark L. Blum

Chapter 5   The Nature of My Faith   93
    Kiyozawa Manshi
    translated by Mark L. Blum

SOGA RYŌJIN

Chapter 6   Soga Ryōjin: Life and Thought   101
    Robert F. Rhodes

Chapter 7 A Savior on Earth: The Meaning of Dharmākara Bodhisattva's Advent 107
Soga Ryōjin
translated by Jan Van Bragt

Chapter 8 Shinran's View of Buddhist History 119
Soga Ryōjin
translated by Jan Van Bragt

Chapter 9 Lectures on the *Tannishō* 139
Soga Ryōjin
translated by Jan Van Bragt

Kaneko Daiei

Chapter 10 Kaneko Daiei: Life and Thought 159
Robert F. Rhodes

Chapter 11 Prolegomena to Shin Buddhist Studies 173
Kaneko Daiei
translated by Robert F. Rhodes

Yasuda Rijin

Chapter 12 Yasuda Rijin: Life and Thought 217
Paul Watt

Chapter 13 The Practical Understanding of Buddhism 227
Yasuda Rijin
translated by Paul Watt

Chapter 14 The Mirror of Nothingness 233
Yasuda Rijin
translated by Paul Watt

Chapter 15 A Name but Not a Name Alone 239
Yasuda Rijin
translated by Paul Watt

Combined Glossary 267

Bibliography 279

Index 299

Foreword

Since its entry to Japan from the continent, Buddhism has flowed like a great stream through Japanese history. Within that stream, the most notable developments were made in the ancient capital of Nara and on Mounts Hiei and Kōya. Among these three centers, however, the most important was Mt. Hiei, the site of Enryakuji, the head temple of the Tendai school. We are all familiar with the great teachers of this stream, such as Ennin 円仁, Ryōgen 良源, Genshin 源信, Hōnen 法然, and Shinran 親鸞.

The chief objects of interest among scholars of Japanese religions in the West have included Zen Buddhism in the area of thought, Shinto and Shugendō in terms of folk studies, and the new religions inspired by Nichiren 日蓮 in the field of sociological studies. However, when looking at Japanese religions from the point of view of popular Buddhism, one cannot overlook the great influence that Pure Land Buddhism, especially Shin Buddhism, has had on the spiritual lives of the Japanese people. The fact that Pure Land Buddhism propagated by Hōnen and Shinran have, albeit slowly, begun to attract the attention of a growing number of scholars outside Japan, is to be welcomed.[1]

Despite this growing interest, however, the number of works about fundamental aspects of Pure Land Buddhism remains very small. Since Shinran's passing, Shin Buddhism has undergone three major revivals—in the late medieval period, in the Edo period and again in the modern period—but only a few studies published in English deal concretely with the content of the revivals between the medieval and modern periods. In an attempt to fill this gap in studies on Pure Land Buddhism in the West, the Shin Buddhist Comprehensive Research Institute of Otani University published a collection of articles about Rennyo 蓮如, who greatly contributed to the development of Shin Buddhism in the medieval period, in commemoration of his 500th memorial service.[2]

In the meantime, the International Buddhist Studies Research Group of the Shin Buddhist Comprehensive Research Institute had embarked on a project to select and translate some of the important works by Shin Buddhist thinkers of the modern period, that have been little known in the West. Although the work on this project had frequently been interrupted, we have finally been able to complete these translations, the result of over a decade of painstaking work.

The Meiji period, when Japan's modern period began, was a time when Western civilization surged over Japan like a tidal wave. It was an age in which the dramatic encounter between the cultures of East and West began. Within this encounter, all of Japan's traditional values were subjected to a complete and relentless critique. Buddhism was one of the value systems brought into question. Along with the persecution of Buddhism after the Meiji Restoration, the influx of new ideas and technologies from the various countries of the West and the spread of Christianity within Japan threw the Buddhist world, which had until then lolled comfortably under the protective policies of the Shogunate, into a state of crisis never known before.

This crisis posed the gravest threat to Shin Buddhism. To respond adequately to this crisis, it was necessary for Shin Buddhism, which had transmitted Shinran's teachings through the ages, to provide a spiritual foundation that would adequately meet the needs of the people coping with a period of intense change—a heavy burden indeed. Unfortunately, in reality, the intellectual vitality of Shin Buddhism had by then degenerated to the point where it was scorned as "the religion of foolish people."

We must remember the work of our forerunners who, through their own struggles in this period of intense change, were able to rediscover Shinran's fundamental message and open up a new frontier where Shin Buddhism could again flourish. Their labors pioneered the recovery of the dignity and prestige of Śākyamuni's religion in the modern period.

Our group decided that it was necessary to introduce readers outside Japan to several of the historical figures who, from the midst of the suffering and confusion of modernity, took refuge in the three treasures of the buddha, dharma, and sangha and contributed greatly to the rebirth of Shinran's faith and thought. After a careful discussion, four outstanding scholars were selected: Kiyozawa Manshi 清沢満之, who took the first steps toward the revitalization of Shin Buddhism in the modern period, Soga Ryōjin 曽我量深, who, as a disciple of Kiyozawa, played a pivotal role in the development of modern doctrinal studies, Kaneko Daiei 金子大栄, who clarified the fundamental stance of Shin Buddhist Studies as an academic discipline, and Yasuda Rijin 安田理深, who, in the postwar period, developed a new perspective on Shinran's thought and the Shin fellowship through his study of not only Buddhism, but also a wide variety of Western philosophical works.

To introduce the thought of these scholars, it was decided to translate of some of their most representative works. The problem then became which of these scholars' works to translate, and whom to ask to do the translations. Fortunately, four extremely capable scholars agreed to help us with our project.

Mark Blum, one of the editors of this volume, had been engaged in research into Shinran's *Kyōgyōshinshō* 教行信証 as well as Shin thinkers in the modern period since he was a graduate student at the University of California. He came to Otani University to look into the life and thought of Kiyozawa Manshi, while also preparing an article on that subject for publication in *The Eastern Buddhist*.

The late Jan Van Bragt, a Catholic priest who resided in Japan and served at the Nanzan Institute for Religion and Culture, was deeply impressed by modern Japanese thought, particularly the philosophy of religion developed by Nishitani Keiji 西谷啓治. His translation of Nishitani's seminal collection of essays, *Religion and Nothingness*, has had an enormous impact on the ongoing dialogue between Christianity and Japanese religions. At the same time, Van Bragt was, from very early on, also familiar with the writings of Soga Ryōjin, who had influenced the philosophers of the Kyoto School in some way.

Robert Rhodes, the other editor of this volume, is a scholar of Buddhist studies whose area of expertise lies in Japanese and Chinese Buddhism. He developed a strong interest in Kaneko Daiei's methodology for conducting Buddhist studies both during his time as a student at Otani University, where he came in contact with the academic tradition begun by Kaneko, and also while studying at Harvard University, where he became acquainted with Western academic methods.

Paul Watt, a scholar of Japanese thought specializing in Jiun Sonja 慈雲尊者, a Shingon monk active in the late Edo period, had often visited the Shin Buddhist Comprehensive Research Institute to conduct research since he was teaching at Columbia University. By chance, he happened to read one of Yasuda Rijin's works and was attracted to both Yasuda's thought and his way of life as a Buddhist.

When, at our request, Blum, Van Bragt, Rhodes, and Watt joined the International Buddhist Studies Research Group as guest researchers, we began holding meetings as often as possible to discuss the translations. Unfortunately, due to the busy schedules of the translators, we were not able to hold such meetings very frequently. However, these meetings were both stimulating and enjoyable. In particular, Jan Van Bragt's warm personality was always a source of inspiration for us. Deeply regretting his early passing, I cannot help but again feel awed remembering his many important achievements.[3]

After the careful editing of these translations by Professors Blum and Rhodes, this work has reached completion and we now have the opportunity to introduce one portion of the thought of modern Shin Buddhist thinkers to the people of the world. With a sense of respect for all of the hard work of the many people involved with this project, I want to express my deepest gratitude to those who have made this work possible.

In closing, I would like to thank the many people who made these translations possible. First and foremost, I must express my appreciation to the four chief translators who put so much time and effort into the project. I must also thank members of the working group that reviewed the translations and handled the countless odd jobs that helped to make the project proceed smoothly: Higuchi Shoshin, Inoue Takami, Inui Fumio, Ito Ejin, Kaku Takeshi, Kigoshi Yasushi, Kuroda Shinji, Minoura Akio, Miyamoto Hirotaka, Miyashita Seiki, Ogawa Naohito, Ozawa Chiaki, Saito Ken, Tamura Akinori, Watanabe Hiromasa, and Yamamoto Kazuhiko. Finally, special thanks is due to Michael Conway, who, besides reading the final version of the translation and making valuable suggestions, saw the anthology through the final stages of its production.

Yasutomi Shin'ya
Former Chief of the International Buddhist Studies Research Group
Otani University Shin Buddhist Comprehensive Research Institute

Notes

1. Andreasen 1998.
2. Blum and Yasutomi 2006.
3. Hase 2008.

Abbreviations

It is our policy at the Institute to allow translators to use their own voices and therefore not require them to adhere to our own notions of how technical terms should be translated. Due to this and the fact that the translators worked on their projects independently, the reader will notice some variation in the way terms are represented as well as some repetition of personal information such as the dates and Chinese characters for certain individuals.

Ch. Chinese

Jpn. Japanese

KDC Kaneko Daiei 金子大栄. 1977–1986. *Kaneko Daiei chosakushū* 金子大栄著作集. 12 vols. and 4 supplement vols. Edited by Terada Masakatsu 寺田正勝, Hirose Takashi 廣瀬杲, and Ito Emyō 伊東慧明. Tokyo: Shunjūsha.

KMZ Kiyozawa Manshi 清沢満之. 2002–2003. *Kiyozawa Manshi zenshū* 清沢満之全集. 9 vols. Edited by Ōtani daigaku 大谷大学. Tokyo: Iwanami shoten.

Skt. Sanskrit

SRS Soga Ryōjin 曽我量深. 1970–1972. *Soga Ryōjin senshū* 曽我量深選集. 12 vols. Edited by Soga Ryōjin senshū kankōkai 曽我量深選集刊行会. Tokyo: Yayoi shobō.

SSZ Shinshū shōgyō zensho hensansho 真宗聖教全書編纂所, ed. 1941. *Shinshū shōgyō zensho* 真宗聖教全書. 5 vols. Kyoto: Ōyagi kōbundō.

T	Takakusu Junjirō 高楠順次郎 and Watanabe Kaikyoku 渡辺海旭, eds. 1924–1934. *Taishō shinshū daizōkyō* 大正新修大蔵経. 85 vols. Tokyo: Taishō issaikyō kankōkai.
YRS	Yasuda Rijin 安田理深. 1983–1994. *Yasuda Rijin senshū* 安田理深選集. 23 vols. Edited by Yasuda Rijin senshū hensan iinkai 安田理深選集編纂委員会. Kyoto: Bun'eidō.

Chapter 1

Shin Buddhism in the Meiji Period

Mark L. Blum

Discerning changes in religion within a culture tells us as much about that culture as observing its political changes, if not more so, but unlike the latter that manifest in ways usually noticed quickly by public media, knowing how and when shifts in religious thinking occur can be immensely complicated. Although both stand on fundamental beliefs and values and express social realities as much as personal truths, religion is rarely explained by its leaders with the degree of explicitness that one commonly finds in political spokespersons, a fact that drives many to throw up their hands, yet motivates students of religion to probe deeper.

In this case, the complexity is deepened by the fact that the religious essays contained in this book also are reflective of Japan's encounter with "modernism" or "the modern world." The way in which the onset of "modern sensibility" is viewed today in hindsight differs enormously not only from nation to nation, but from viewer to viewer. Some people begin modern European history with the Spanish Inquisition, others with the American and French revolutions, to name only two perspectives. In the case of Japan, traditional views of history typically use the convenience of the Meiji Restoration in 1867–1868 to demarcate the transition from feudal to modern, but the prevalence of capitalism, the weakening of class distinctions, pervasive forms of public education, and so forth in the Edo period (1600–1867) argues against a facile "feudal" label for that era, which today is more commonly called "pre-modern," and some argue that Japan never had a true feudal period at all in the European sense of the word. But these arguments generally rest on political and economic grounds, whereas the focus here is on religion, philosophy, or "thought" (*shisō* 思想) as the Japanese like to call it, which follows a slightly different timetable and where the adjective feudal remains relevant but is used quite differently. Although these essays are exemplary examples of Japanese religion's encounter with modernity, the authors themselves do not explicitly frame their ideas as addressing the meaning of modernity, although the word for modern (*kindai* 現代) does occur in the sense of "today's society." But the reader will have no trouble discerning anxieties and problematizing that reflect not only modernism but postmodernism as well, such as Kiyozawa Manshi's reflections on the problem of locating moral authority.

I come back to the question of modernity later, but first it is important to make clear that these essays, some of which originated as public lectures, are of a particular type of discourse akin to what we would regard in a biblical context as theology. That is, although there is great depth of historical study of doctrine and philosophy evident in all of them, these authors are not writing as professional scholars but as professional religious. What ties these essays togther is an overriding concern within all four authors about the need to clarify not what Buddhism is but what Buddhism means, in their lives, at that moment. Although all were famed teachers associated with Ōtani University in one way or another, there is no pretense to "historical objectivity" here because they are speaking from inside their religious tradition, namely Jōdo Shinshū 浄土真宗 or Shin Buddhism. This does not mean these essays lack critical perspective. Quite the opposite, in fact. A critical stance toward *their own tradition* is clearly the engine that drives the motivation of all these authors. This orientation finds expression in the felt need to address the ambiguity surrounding nothing less than the biggest questions in Buddhism in the context of this particular tradition in the modern period. Namely, what is the nature of faith, karma, and history? How do we understand the religious symbols that stir us (such as the buddha's name)? What is the relationship between the authority of the received teachings in my tradition and the authority of my own experience? Are religious ethics and social ethics compatible in Buddhism or inevitably in conflict?

What also characterizes these essays is the assumed value of *subjective* understanding—another factor that removes them from the realm of historical scholarship that was practiced in their own time. Subjectivity is a slippery issue, for although we do not expect leaders of individual religious traditions to view their own denomination "objectively" vis-à-vis other traditions, when addressing their own they are expected to affirm common values and beliefs particular to that tradition, and this fact demands their rhetoric exhibit at least a nod toward objectivity in their own doctrines or dogmas. In the Shin Buddhist tradition, "other-power" (*tariki* 他力) represents the transcendent power of Amida Buddha to effect spiritual change within the individual, and forms a religious doctrine as central to their religious outlook as sin or grace in Christianity. Thus, when Christian theologians speak of original sin and Shin "theologians" speak of other-power, they must both at least begin from common, received understandings of these concepts that contain a strong impersonal dimension by dint of the fact that they represent and therefore belong to their community as a whole. But after launching from this common ground, the speaker may then shift direction in order to express entirely new and different meanings that he or she has unearthed in the investigation of seeking to uncover something like the archaeological creed lying at the base of their institution's heritage.

This is precisely the process found in these essays, and why they often are so provocative. At once traditional in terms of theme and topic, they are strikingly innovative in their interpretations. Often the authors will state that their perceptions are not new but merely corrections of contemporary misunderstandings, a move that allows them to remain orthodox, at least from their own point of view. The tension between normative doctrine and the abundant creativity in these essays was exacerbated by the very nature of the philosophical movement that formed the orientation of all the authors represented here, namely Seishinshugi 精神主義, translated here as "Cultivating Spirituality." As envisioned by its founder, Kiyozawa Manshi 清沢滿之 (1863–1903), Seishinshugi was the name given to a set of principles that prioritized personal, subjective experience as the basis for religious understanding, as well as the praxis that ideally brought about realization. Although the name Seishinshugi literally means something like "spirituality at the forefront," putting these principles into practice also was of central importance to Kiyozawa. To understand what Kiyozawa was trying to do and why, we need to consider both the objective and the subjective—Japan in the Meiji period when Kiyozawa lived, and Kiyozawa the individual.

Buddhism on the Defensive:
The Destabilizing Effects of Modernism on Shin Buddhism

Although the Seishinshugi movement may have been one of the most coherent responses to modernity within Japanese religion, overall Japan's emergence as a modern nation-state on its religion is dominated by the attacks first on Buddhism and Buddhist institutions from a variety of voices and then on the very value of religion itself. Even State Shinto as a modern creation is, from the Buddhist point of view, just one chapter in a litany of ideological moves designed to wean Japanese spirituality from its Buddhist moorings. But when we move into the late Meiji period, that is after 1895, religion as a whole is dismissed by leading intellectuals such as Inoue Tetsujirō 井上哲次郎 (1855–1944) as decidedly unmodern and thus feudalistic, a rhetoric that carefully does not include State Shinto because of its political implications.

The modern world's effect on Buddhist beliefs, values, practices, and institutions came very differently to each nation in Asia with a Buddhist history. In the case of Japan, attacks on institutional Buddhism brought on by the modernization of Japanese society came from three main sources: nativist and Confucian ideology, Western philosophy and religion, and political tensions arising from reform movements inside Buddhist institutions themselves. Seishinshugi grew out of a failed reform movement within the Higashi Honganji, or the Ōtani branch of the Shin tradition, but many of its ideas had an impact beyond that particular institution. Looking back on this movement from the twenty-first century, one cannot overlook the fact that among all sectarian religious forms in Japan in the Meiji period and beyond, no other school has produced so many towering intellectual figures. Beginning in the late Meiji period, Seishinshugi was thus more than a direct response to the unsettled nature of the Higashi Honganji organization in particular: it challenged Japanese Buddhism as a whole. To fully appreciate what Seishinshugi itself propounded in its historical context, we need to look in some detail at the nature of that historical context itself: that is, the external pressures on the Buddhist tradition in Japan and in this case the ways in which Shin Buddhism responded to them, both of which reflected the context within which the vision of Kiyozawa Manshi emerged.

The fall of the Tokugawa bakufu or military governing body and the establishment of the Meiji government in 1867 in effect meant the replacement of one group of samurai leaders with another, but this new oligarchy was inspired by an entirely different political ideology that had serious consequences for Japan, its neighbors, and relevent to the present study, for Buddhism and its institutions. Although there was an inherent nationalism in the *sakoku* 鎖国 policy of national isolation under the Tokugawa bakufu, the internationalization of Japan with the

Meiji Restoration resulted in a much more intense and violent form of nationalism. Although somewhat of a simplification, Christianity was the intended victim of the *sakoku* form of nationalism, and Buddhism was the intended victim of its modern form. But it was one thing to limit and eventually proscribe Christianity in the late sixteenth and early seventeenth centuries when it had only been in Japan for two generations. It was quite another to try to purge Buddhist belief from Japan in 1868 after its religious dominance of Japanese culture for more than a millenium.

The first cause of grief for Buddhist culture and institutions in Japan was not only an ancient one, but the most serious as well: xenophobia. I am referring to the rise of nativism throughout the nineteenth century that found nearly everything in Buddhist culture abhorrent. There were a variety of streams of thought in the Edo period that contributed to this sentiment, some emotional to the point of incoherence, some rationally pragmatic, and some so overtly political that there was no attempt to hide their ambition for wealth and power. The successful seizure of power by the Meiji leaders in the name of the emperor convinced those with nativist impulses of the righteousness of their cause like nothing else could. Legitimated by history, as it were, the ideological wing of the new government put Buddhism in the cross-hairs of their initial agenda of social and political reformation, one the one hand because it had been so closely aligned institutionally with the Tokugawa bakufu, and on the other because its foreign origin stigmatized it with an irreparable alterity.

Using the Spanish model of modernism alluded to above may be a useful comparison. In Spain at the end of the fifteenth century, the marriage of Ferdinand and Isabella unified enough of the peninsula to empower the court to drive out or force conversion of all Muslims and Jews, thereby defining a new "Spain" in terms of religious purity. "Modern" in this sense means using intimations of violence to define which persons, what social institutions, and most importantly what religious beliefs or affiliations were required for membership in the ethnic identity that defines a nation. The destruction of mosques and synagogues, the torture, and the ultimate exile of so many within a very short period of time was on a scale far worse than the persecution suffered by Buddhism in Meiji Japan. But there is a striking similarity with the impact of anti-Buddhist policies arising in the Mito 水戸 domain beginning in the seventeenth century, for example. To wit, such Spanish notions of the nation-state based on ethnic and religious identity over time spread to the rest of Europe, and these policies of the Mito domain, which aimed at defining Japan as a Shinto nation with Confucian social values, similarly spread to become a national movement in the nineteenth century.

Here it is worth remembering that "modern" does not necessarily imply democratic institutions of government or even support for such ideas as sovereignty residing in the populace or laws guaranteeing freedoms and rights. The nativist thinkers who led the ideological fight to "restore the emperor" to power in the Meiji period clearly believed in class divisions and the unassailable authority of kings. Their ethical values were expressly Confucian and, not surprisingly, they demanded *more* respect for hierarchy in society, equating hierarchy with social harmony and justice. The movements to strengthen Shinto and restore the emperor to power not only deified him in a way unprecedented but the various notions of nationhood (*kokutai, kokka, kunigara*) from this period also tended to locate national sovereignty in the person of the emperor himself rather than the national populace.[1] If these moves represented common ideological themes of what was modern in nineteenth-century Japan, they also represented the legitimacy of privilege. By contrast, at least on a doctrinal level, the most commonly accepted Buddhist teachings in Japan such as buddha-nature, karma, the availability of a positive vision of the afterlife for everyone, and even access to the power of deities like Fudō or Kannon instead all point unambiguously to themes that are universal.[2] By forcing the separation of Buddhism from native Shinto and working to shrink and discredit Buddhism, the nationalists spoke of egalitarian principles and values as part of a previously repressed Shinto culture while simultaneously demanding unquestioned obedience to the male sovereign in whose name they acted.

This form of anti-Buddhist rhetoric championed by the radical nativist wing of the late-Edo period imperial restoration movement and implemented in government policy in the early years of the Meiji period expressed a wholesale denunciation of Buddhism that typically was not, aside from the Mito example, a dominant or even viable political voice earlier in Japanese history. Nobunaga's attacks on Buddhist institutions, for example, had nothing to do with ideology. The one exception is the political turmoil surrounding Buddhism's formal arrival in Japan in the sixth century, but even that opposition was more about institutional rivalry than Buddhist thought. Unlike China and Korea, until the nineteenth century Japan never experienced periods of mass antipathy toward Buddhism in which Buddhist teachings, the clerical institution or sangha, and its societal practices were condemned out of fundamentalist tendencies within Confucian, Daoist, or nativistic intellectual movements. There was inevitable resentment among certain individuals toward the intimacy between Buddhist and governmental institutions that characterized Japanese political culture so thoroughly, but prior to the Edo period this was typically expressed in terms of personal retreat or reformist movements within Buddhism itself. People like Genshin, Kamo no Chōmei, Hōnen, Myōe, Ippen, Dōgen, Nichiren, and Ikkyū in some sense all represent this. Although undoubtedly well aware of the ideological shift among intellectuals away from Buddhism toward Neo-Confucianism and National Learning (*kokugaku* 国学)[3] from the Genroku 元禄 period (1688–1704) throughout the eighteenth and nineteenth centuries, the aristocratic elites—emperors, shoguns, daimyos, and their extended families—continued the ancient traditions of having Buddhist funerals and joining the Buddhist sangha when they retired from political life. This persistence of the old sociopolitical paradigm only made the impact of the early Meiji persecution all the more unsettling for the Buddhist professional community.

But of course doctrines are one thing and history is another. And even in the realm of doctrine, ideas are only accessible in specific historical contexts, within which they may emerge in unexpected, even contradictory forms, often contested by believers themselves. Among the many forms of Buddhism in Japan, the Shin tradition has a particularly rich and complex history on this point, if only because it began with the repudiation of monasticism and has developed into a tradition of factionalism, contestation, heresy, and excommunication like no other. The story of the Seishinshugi movement therefore suggests a form of that same individualistic seeking that has characterized Shin from its birth, but in this case it marks a particular type of response to the historical setting of Japanese Buddhism in search of a new identity in the modern era. The topic of Buddhism under seige during the Meiji period has already been discussed in elegant detail by James Ketelaar and Richard Jaffe, among others, and the reader is directed there for a more well-rounded picture.[4] Here I only focus on the implications of the historical processes in the middle to late Meiji period that provided both the stimuli and in many cases the materials out of which Seishinshugi was born.

Anti-Buddhist Rhetoric and Policy in the Tokugawa and Meiji Periods

As touched on earlier, one theme that runs down the center of Japan's entry in to the modern age is the prominence of nativist ideology. Although there was a steady growth in intellectual rhetoric attacking

Buddhism throughout the Edo period, for the first two centuries it was led by Neo-Confucians of either the Zhu Xi 朱熹 (Jpn. Shuki, 1130–1200) or Wang Yangming 王陽明 (Jpn. Ōyōmei, 1472–1528) schools, mostly the former. As hard as they argued for their philosophy being more appropriate for Japan than that of Buddhism, their source was still non-Japanese in origin and therefore whatever nativistic tendencies the Neo-Confucian writers held remained somewhat restrained. The real sting of nativist polemics begins with Hirata Atsutane 平田篤胤 (1776–1843). Hirata assumed the role of ideological heir to the scholar Motoori Norinaga 本居宣長 (1730–1801), although they never actually met, essentially exploiting Motoori's authority in pursuit of his own agenda. He urged a reconfiguring of Motoori's "school" of National Learning from something academic into a political action platform based on xenophobic religious values. Even though Motoori was passionate about bringing out native Japanese sensibility, famously rejoicing in such things as spontaneous expressions of emotion in ancient literature, he was primarily interested in poetry and philology, and his religious concerns were more about celebrating precontinental sensibilities in society and the natural world. He did not hold any overt antipathy toward Buddhism; in fact Motoori praised the linguistic studies of Buddhist monks like Keichū 契沖 (1640–1701) and Monnō 文雄 (1700–1763), and had a Buddhist funeral. If Motoori did have an ideological axe to grind, it was directed toward the overt stress on emotional self-control coming from the Neo-Confucianists, particularly the people promoting Zhu Xi.

Hirata, by contrast, was suspicious toward foreign systems of thought and regarded poetry as "an obstacle to understanding."[5] His project was to promote "Shinto" as the only proper religion for the Japanese people, and endeavored to realize this ideal by creating a model of Shinto that had a transcendent creator deity and a notion of the afterlife offering a positive alternative to the ancient conception of the "land of *yomi*,"[6] which was characterized by degeneration and pain. Hirata rejected both Buddhism and Confucianism, asserting that such external influences should be kept to a minimum; Japan was unique as a nation whose people are descended from the gods and must take care not to bespoil their native gifts. He even asserted that all gods throughout the world were born in Japan. He attacked the tradition of Shinto studies by court scholars, saying they had been corrupted by Confucian and Buddhist doctrines, and asserted his own definition of what Shinto was. There was thus a kind of messianism in Hirata, and as a result his polemics were often cruel, prompting the orthodox line of Motoori followers to reject him as a bona fide

National Learning thinker and refuting his scholarship as unsound. But many people found his cause contagious and in the end, Shinto studies were indeed altered by Hirata's views. Going into the Meiji Restoration, it was the disciples of Hirata who defined the nativist ideology of the new regime. As Hirata's critique broadened to include the Tokugawa bakufu and grew more popular in the process, his anti-Buddhist remarks grew more vituperative. The nativist attacks on the bakufu also implied an attack on Buddhism because of the cozy relationship the bakufu had with institutional Buddhism for most of the Edo period.

Part of Hirata's appeal in the nineteenth century resulted from a wave of insecurities that created a restless desire for change in society that eventually led to the fall of the central government itself. Inflation and natural disasters led to an unstable economy, and Westerners began to chip away at Japan's *de jure* isolation and even at its territory. The latter concern was forcefully presented by Fujita Yūkoku 藤田幽谷 (1774–1826), a central figure of Mitogaku,[7] the intellectual movement driving the leadership of the Mito domain that dovetailed with Hirata's agenda and figured so prominently in much of the ideology of at least the early Meiji regime. While serving as editor of the Mitogaku project of writing a massive history of Japan, Yūkoku decried the fact that Russia was taking control of the Kuril islands in the northeast of Japan in violation of Japanese declarations of sovereignty. He somehow combined an imperative of restoring the emperor to power with immediate action to restore Japan's rightful claim to the Kurils. By doing so, Yūkoku developed a stance that used strong anti-foreign fears to justify the need for restoring the emperor to power.[8]

The Confucian thinkers who dominated in the Edo period, unlike those of previous centuries, were generally either unsympathetic to Buddhism or overtly critical of it, especially those inspired by Zhu Xi. This trend can be seen as early as Fujiwara Seika 藤原惺窩 (1561–1619), the father of Zhu Xi studies in Japan (known as *shushigaku* 朱子学), who is quoted in a 1620 biography as having stated that Buddhism should be regarded as heresy because it eliminated any sense of humanity (*jin* 仁) or duty (*giri* 義理).[9] His disciple Hayashi Razan 林羅山 (1583–1657) and others complain that Buddhism disparages ethics in its search for truth, turning its back on not only family but all five of the core Confucian relationships. The other two lines of Confucian scholars in the Edo period—those following Wang Yangming, or *yōmeigaku* 陽明学, such as Nakae Tōju 中江藤樹 (1608–1648) and Kumazawa Banzan 熊沢蕃山 (1619–1691), and the old-school or *kogaku-ha*

古学派 people like Itō Jinsai 伊藤仁斎 (1627–1705), Ogyū Sorai 荻生徂徠 (1666–1728), and Dazai Shundai 太宰春台 (1680–1740)—did not see things much differently. Without delineating each position, what they shared in their complaints against Buddhism was that it failed society because of the weakness of its ethical imperative.

In short, Confucian thinkers in the Edo period no longer accepted the earlier paradigm wherein Buddhism formed Japan's central religious narrative while accommodating both Confucian principles and native kami cults as ethical, political, and magical supplements. Japanese *shushigaku* was based on Ming and Qing interpretations of *mingfen* 名分 *meibun*, a concept that stressed self-discipline, fidelity in one's social relationships, and the fulfillment of duty and obligation based on one's station in life. The underlying paradigm is that an individual's considered choices, if exercised properly, manifest principles of a cosmos naturally constructed as a rational and moral system. Accomplishing one's social duty was thus moral, ethical, humane, and affirming of life and the natural order all at the same time. Not surprisingly, proponents of these ideas were typically closest to bakufu policymakers. There also had been Buddhist efforts for some time at assimilating these Neo-Confucian feudal ethics into their religious systems: In *ōjōden* and other miracle texts,[10] for example, proper social behavior based on Confucian norms is part of what is karmically rewarded by the marvelous workings of Amida, Kannon, or Fudō, both in this world and the next. But intellectually, Buddhist traditional responses to Confucian presumptions of its own cosmological imperative were not as effective as in the past. Had the Japanese Buddhists any knowledge of Hinduism at that time, they would have noticed the similarity between *meibun* and the Hindu concept of *dharma*, and this might have provided them with better rhetorical means to argue the value of religion for a society conceived in Neo-Confucian terms.[11]

A second area of attack prior to Hirata in Confucian and nativistic movements expressed the perception that Buddhism was primarily oriented to the afterlife, whereas these competing ideologies were focused on achieving a reformation of the present world. They portrayed Buddhist thought as negative and world-denying, and their own stances as positive and world-affirming. The legal requirement of the bakufu that all families register with a Buddhist sect produced what is known as a "parishioner system," or *danka seido* 檀家制度, and as a byproduct, generations of family dead were now kept at cemeteries on temple grounds. This ensured continual ritual purification of the family dead for the parishioner and continual source of financial support for the temple. This setup, along with the formal legalization of main-branch temple networks (*honmatsu seido* 本末制度) from at least 1632[12] institutionalized a hierarchical structure within each Buddhist sect in Japan that is another Edo period legacy, which continues to this day.

To make matters worse, many Buddhist institutions in the Edo period were in a close administrative relationship with the bakufu and this also engendered resentment. When the *koseki* census was revived in the seventeenth century, the bakufu assigned this function to Buddhist institutions, requiring all families to register members' names and class status with their family temple. This also had the effect of certifying a fixed list of Buddhist schools as orders or sects (eleven in total), who became motivated by the social, political, and doctrinal rectification agendas urged by bakufu leadership. The bakufu also exploited temple networks by rewarding those temples that were geographically convenient for various monitoring functions in society, which in turn resulted in promoting what had been relatively insignificant temples to centers of administrative activities within the sects themselves. Once these "modernization" moves were institutionalized, they grew over time to become entrenched, ossified, and in some cases even reactionary, effects that were to a certain degree the result of bakufu hostility to anything new within the Buddhist world, including temple construction.[13] Because these newly configured Buddhist institutions were used by the bakufu to implement its policies of social control, a tight relationship developed between the two that only served to deepened the animosity toward what outsiders viewed as an institution deeply integrated into the political status quo in society. A third aspect of Buddhist-rejectionist ideology emerged in the second half of the Edo period when an economic argument was added. In language similar to that found in Chinese persecutions of Buddhism, monks, nuns, and their monasteries were decried as drains on societal wealth. It was demanded that the ordination of monks and nuns and the number of temples should be significantly reduced and held in check by a regulatory mechanism similar to the Ritsuryō system of the Nara period.[14]

Kashiwahara Yūsen, a specialist in early modern Japanese Buddhism, feels a strong sense of individual self-assertion pervaded Japanese society at the end of the Sengoku 戦国 period (1467–1568), pushing Japan toward a modernist condition of human-centered ideologies.[15] This tendency only grows throughout the Edo period, resulting in a valorization of pragmatic values that is exploited by the Neo-Confucian and National Learning movements who, by labeling Buddhism "other-worldly," use this shift to justify their anti-Buddhist attacks. But it is not until the nineteenth century when frustration over bakufu policies seen as unfair and contradictory combine with xenophobic sentiments to produce the toxic mix that ultimately explodes in the form of wholesale persecution of Buddhism in the early Meiji period. Kashiwahara points out that as early as the 1660s the Mito, Okayama, and Aizu domains had to some degree already begun to implement policies of destroying Buddhist temples, but it was not until the middle of the nineteenth century when policies to shrink the number of Buddhist temples by people such as Tokugawa Nariaki 徳川斉昭 (1800–1860), daimyo of the Mito domain, had noticeable effect.

The early Meiji period was dominated by social upheaval and the need for all social institutions to transition to a new political ideology, but it was particularly trying for Buddhism. Many people who study Meiji-period religion follow the model devised by Yoshida Kyūichi of dividing the experience of Buddhism in Japan during the Meiji reign into three periods: 1868–1885, 1886–1899, and 1900–1912.[16] But in a description of events written in 1921, Shimaji Daitō 島地大等 (1875–1927) separates off the first five years of the Meiji period as a unique period of "Shinto tyranny" toward Buddhism,[17] today referred to as *haibutsu kishaku* 廃仏毀釈, or "drive out Buddhism, destroy Śākyamuni." It began with the order to force a separation between Buddhism and Shinto known as *shinbutsu hanzenrei* 神仏判然令, initiated on the twenty-eighth day of the third month of 1868 (Keiō 4). Buddhist rituals were abruptly ended in the imperial palace and the Buddhist statue that had been enshrined there was moved to Sennyūji 泉涌寺 in Kyoto. Begging and cremations were forbidden, legal restrictions forbidding women from monasteries and preventing monks from eating meat, marrying, or wearing regular clothes were eliminated. Temples were forcibly "merged" in a process called *haigōji* 廃合寺, which actually began in the Mito domain during the Edo period. The regions where the most damage occurred were Toyama, Kagawa, Matsumoto, Kagoshima, and Sado island. It is recorded that in only the first year of Meiji, for example, the number of Buddhist temples on Sado was reduced from more than five hundred to a mere eighty. The extreme nature of this *shinbutsu hanzenrei* edict can be seen in the fact that the Nichiren sect was forbidden from conducting their traditional ritual prayer to Amaterasu and Hachiman, who are included in their *daimandara* 大曼荼羅, because they are Shinto deities in origin. Certain governors endeared themselves to the new government by adding yet more oppressive interpretations to the law, giving themselves the power to not only reduce the number of Buddhist temples within their political purview, but destroy texts and images as well.

In 1870, the Office (later Ministry) of Shinto created a system called *daikyō senpu* 大教宣布 to grant official titles to "national teachers" of Shinto empowered by the state in a national campaign to spread the religion. But by 1872, the separation policy was abandoned as too divisive and its jingoist advocates were pushed out of the ruling Meiji clique. It was replaced by a newly conceived fusion policy wherein centers were to be constructed to train priests in one common national religion that would blend Buddhism and Shinto together. Regional centers were established around the country for this purpose, but the main training ground for these new "evangelicals" (*kyōdōshoku* 教導職) was the Daikyōin 大教院 (Abbey of the Great Teaching), a school built on the grounds of Zōjōji, the regional headquarters for the Jōdoshū in Tokyo and the temple of personal refuge for Tokugawa Ieyasu (1542–1616). This was funded and controlled by the newly formed Ministry of Teaching, which was in effect nothing more than a new moniker for the Ministry of Shinto. In practice the Daikyōin proved immediately insulting to the Buddhists who were forced to participate. It took over most of the space inside the main worship hall at Zōjōji where a new altar was set up that removed the four Buddhist statues that had served as central images (*honzon* 本尊), for centuries and replaced them with four Shinto deities. The curriculum centered around revering the kami, promoting the ethics of loyalty, and protecting the state, three principles that were entirely devoid of Buddhist doctrine and whose connections to Buddhism reflected only its previous political accomodation with secular authority.[18]

Defying government requirements, in February 1875 all branches of Jōdo Shinshū—who in combination represented the largest religious population block—walked out on the Daikyōin and later that same year the enterprise itself was abandoned, a dismal failure. Although the promotion of what came to be called State Shinto continued, heavy-handed attempts to force a new relationship between Buddhism and Shinto, be they separation or fusion, were no longer seen. Instead the government found a willingness to negotiate with the major Buddhist institutions and, as calmer heads prevailed, discovered it was more profitable to enlist their support for its policies than to overtly suppress the faith as whole. Buddhist institutions, for their own part, remained happy to see this change because the core values their leadership had forged in the Edo period were essentially intact. In other words, they were only too happy to return to some semblance of the feudalistic king's law–buddha's law (*ōbō-buppō* 王法仏法) paradigm that allowed for mutually supportive public personas for both institutions. The middle years of the Meiji period were thus characterized by a political and ideological rapproachment wherein Buddhist institutional leaders generally endorsed the "enrich the nation and strengthen the military" (*fukoku kyōhei* 富国強兵) rhetoric that had become such an often heard slogan at the time. Many Buddhist leaders also found their voice again in the 1870s and 1880s by expressing strong anti-Christian feelings that allowed them to side with xenophobic sentiment while simultaneously creating an opportunity to make their case that Japanese culture was inconceivable without Buddhism, so deeply was it engrained in its language and customs.

Religion and Philosophy in the Meiji Period

Although it is obvious that the persecution of Buddhism in the first years of the Meiji period was a political act by a new oligarchy demonstrating it power, it also reflected broader changes in the nature of Japanese religion and society. The rhetorical attacks on Buddhism by Neo-Confucianists and nativists always reflected deeply held beliefs about the nature of mankind within larger conceptions of reality that fundamentally differed from the Buddhist view, but even these conceptions were overtaken by the impact of capitalism and materialism on society. Atsutane was perhaps the first nativist to see the possibility of replacing the Buddhist worldview with something more "modern," but arguably the most coherent fusion of religious and occupational obligations appropriate to the new market economy emerging in the middle Edo period began in the popular Shingaku 心学 movement founded by Ishida Baigan 石田梅岩 (1685–1744).[18a]

A century later as Atsutane and his followers worked to transform the National Learning movement into a Shinto revival ideology that demanded the political rehabilitation of the emperor, new religions that repackaged traditional kami cults into formalized "Shinto" sects also were emerging. Those we know most about from the nineteenth century are noteworthy for being dedicated to saving Japan. They were "universal" in the sense that their gods spoke through their mediums not only for their local communities but for the entire nation. This reflected a new understanding of something called "Shinto" as a national religion whereby local kami develop national profiles, akin to Weber's term *henotheism* to describe a similar development in Hinduism. The rise in popularity of shrine pilgrimage, especially to Ise, beginning in the eighteenth century no doubt contributed to this perspective. Best known of these Shinto-derived new religions dating from the end of the Edo period were Kurozumikyō 黒住教, Tenrikyō 天理教, and Konkōkyō 金光教, the former having spread among the samurai class, and the latter two succeeding primarily in rural areas among farmers.

After the Meiji Restoration, new religions continue to sprout up and, as is well known, the trend continues to this day. There is much good scholarship on this phenomenon, but there are a couple of points to keep in mind relevant to the specific movement of Seishinshugi under discussion here. First is the development of a national religious consciousness of Shinto mentioned earlier. Here it should be pointed out that although the invention of an institutionalized nativist religion by the Meiji government drew on that emerging consciousness, these efforts were widely seen as more political than religious. Second is that the enduring nature of the syncretic quality of Japanese religion runs very deep and did not suddenly disappear in the nineteenth century. Even the so-called Shinto-based new religions all incorporated some degree of Buddhist religious culture. Local kami cults, even in the context of their instantiation in shrines, were rife with Buddhist language, iconography, and ritual. Buddhists temples typically employed symbolic representation of a protecting kami somewhere on their property, and there were of course a great many fusion examples such as the various cults surrounding the god Hachiman who, although originating in Korea as a local deity, became tranformed in image and name as a bodhisattva by the major temples of the Nara and Heian periods, and then morphed into a Shinto god of war in the Kamakura period. The extreme rhetoric of some of the Atsutane-inspired leaders of the Meiji government reflected in policies that criminalized this kind of centuries-old fusion sewed deep seeds of doubt about religion and its role in society in general. Thus, the overt anti-Buddhist policies of the early Meiji regime were not only profoundly disruptive to an ancient religious paradigm about which the vast majority of Japanese felt comfortable, but to many became symptomatic of the passing of the "old" order of things as well.

The success of the new religions also revealed a profound crisis within institutional Buddhism itself which, for at least the first three years of Meiji rule, had to worry about its very survival. Of course there were (and are) Buddhism-dominated new religions as well, and relative to the identity crisis going on within the traditional, sectarian sanghas, it is no accident that the most famous new Buddhist religion, Sōka Gakkai, has always been essentially a lay movement. Japan was fast becoming a society dominated by materialistic values, and the government was quickly trying to fashion a national identity based on a kind of faux religious ideology that affirmed this new outlook as a source of national pride. The Buddhist tradition was ultimately called to redefine its own relevance to this new Japan, and all of the essays contained here may certainly be read as contributions to that collective effort.

The Impact of Christianity and Western Philosophies of Religion on Buddhism in the Meiji Period

One important change in Japanese Buddhism in the Meiji period is that its intellectuals could no longer ignore Christian theology and history. Christianity is present explicitly and implictly to various degrees in these essays, and ideas from Western philosophy are even more prominent. Thus, even while the number of Christians in Japan has remained small, its impact on Japanese religion, especially Buddhism, has been significant since its arrival in the sixteenth century, and there is ample evidence of Buddhist influence on Japanese Christianity as well. Western philosophy first came into Japan within Christianity in the late sixteenth century, but its impact was minimal due to the suppression of Christian and Western learning throughout the Edo period. But in 1862, even before the Meiji Restoration, Tsuda Mamichi 津田真道 (1829–1903) and Nishi Amane 西周 (1829–1897) managed to get on a boat to Holland where they studied philosophy at Leiden for four years. It was Nishi who coined the word *tetsugaku* 哲学 to represent Western philosophy, which became a popular subject in universities in the second half of the Meiji period. But although it fascinated Japanese intellectuals, especially the thought of Hegel, Marx, and Mill, prior to the 1950s *tetsugaku* did not penetrate into public education and had minimal impact on Japanese society as whole.

By contrast, although the number of Japanese converts to Christianity prior to its proscription in 1638 remained relatively small, rhetorical clashes with Christian missionaries did shake up the somewhat complacent Buddhist world just as sectarian institutions were beginning to restructure themselves with the outbreak of peace brought by Tokugawa Ieyasu. Kashiwahara even goes so far as to state that the ensuing institutional changes in Edo-period sectarian Buddhism were the direct result of its encounter with Christianity and the challenges it posed, and points out that the sect most affected was Jōdo Shinshū. Even after the banning of Christian activities, Christian attacks on Buddhist cosmology may have inspired a similar critique by Tominaga Nakamoto 富永仲基 (1715–1746) in his *Shutsujō kōgo*

出定後語 (Words Spoken after Meditation), a work used by Hirata Atsutane and his followers in their much more overtly aggressive anti-Buddhist attacks. After the Christians were free to proselytize again in 1875, they immediately began to publish works insisting Buddhist notions of heavens, hells, and pure lands were false. Christian writers and their ideas were in turn attacked in print by such well-respected Buddhist intellectuals as Inoue Enryō 井上円了 (1858–1919) and Shimaji Mokurai 島地黙雷 (1838–1911), to name but a few. But these responses were ultimately tinged with the same defensiveness and smugness that, like the missionaries, assumed the righteousness of their own positions. In short, there was no real dialogue until the mid-1890s when Buddhist intellectuals attained enough understanding of Western philosophy to appreciate its underpinnings within Christian thought. And one of the first persons to realize that his own understanding of Buddhism might be deepened from a study of both philosophy and religion in European history was Kiyozawa Manshi.

One could even argue that Seishinshugi thinkers did alter their conception of the ultimate as a result of their study of Western thought. For example, Kiyozawa often employs a writing style that uses Western terms or categories for religious concepts, and by the very nature of that language he poses a new kind of question for Japan. In some contexts he may use traditional Buddhist vocabulary and in others he may use Japanese translations of Western terms. In fact, determining, for example, if he means the same thing by the terms *buddha*, suchness (*shinnyo* 真如, Skt. *tathatā*), or *dharma-ness* (*hosshō* 法性, Skt. *dharmatā*) in one context and *the infinite* (*mugensha* 無限者) in another, can be difficult. But when Kiyozawa asks how the finite self can know the infinite and comments on the imperative nature of this self–other relationship not as a philosophical but as a religious question, we are in a new form of discourse that presages Nishida Kitarō 西田幾多郎 (1870–1945), who had some personal contact with Kiyozawa. On a purely conceptual level, Soga Ryōjin 曽我量深 (1875–1971) similarly ponders the meaning of history for religion in a way that was never part of traditional Buddhist hermeneutics. It is not that Buddhism had no notion of infinity or history, but the way these questions are asked often reflects Greek or Judaic ways of thinking about religion and philosophy that developed over the course of the Abrahamic religions. Similarly, Kaneko Daiei 金子大栄 (1881–1976) argues that the Pure Land itself is best understood, that is, functions best religiously, when it is understood as something like a Platonic ideal that impacts those who ponder it now, rather than as an actual physically existing place where one aims to be reborn after death. Kaneko further draws from the *Avataṃsakasūtra* (*Huayan jing* 華厳経 *Kegonkyō*) in using the concept of *dharmadhātu*[19] to explain his Platonic understanding of the Pure Land as nirvana, or as the sacred nature of everything beyond discrimination and description. Such ideas were highly innovative and yet upsetting to many at the time, particularly in the context of their religious institution, Shinshū Ōtani-ha, who expected these men to be futhering the cause of *shūgaku* 宗学, the academic study of scriptures based on established sectarian interpretation that continued (and continues) as a legacy of Edo-period orthodox doctrine. Kiyozawa, Soga, and Kaneko all had to undergo a period of expulsion from their institution for ideas that, as time passed, grew to gain recognition as some of the most interesting and inspirational of their time.

Thus, what distinguishes these Seishinshugi thinkers is their willingness to use European religious and philosophical concepts to deepen their personal understanding of Buddhist truth at a time when the study of Western philosophy and what came to be called "Buddhist philosophy" remained more or less distinct. Notice the commonality with Nishida's approach of using Western philosophical categories to explain Buddhist experience. Why the use of non-Buddhist ideas would prove so influential particularly in the Ōtani branch of Shin in the Meiji and Taishō periods is one of the enigmas of this history, but it established Ōtani University as arguably the leading intellectual Buddhist institution in Japan during the first half of the twentieth century.[20]

It all started with Kiyozwa Manshi, and at least part of the explanation for this freedom of inquiry within what was essentially a modern seminary was the nature of Kiyozawa himself as a religious thinker. A student in the Philosophy Department at Tokyo University in the 1880s when Ernest Fenollosa (1853–1908) was teaching, Kiyozawa's core interests seem to have been Kant, Hegel, and Schelling, but he also read John Stuart Mill and Herbert Spencer. Most of Kiyozawa's personal collection of Western language books are kept at Saihōji 西方寺, his temple in Mikawa. Among his books, there are many by Mill and Spencer, which reflect the interest in Utilitarianism in Meiji-period thought. Kiyozawa's time at Tokyo University also coincided with the tenure of Katō Hiroyuki 加藤弘之 (1836–1916) as its president. Katō is famous for ceasing the publication of his earlier works that argued for the belief in the inherent rights of man so that he could advocate for the doctrines of Social Darwinism, which is itself a theory of social conflict and resultant hierarchy based on the ideas of Spencer. Katō's "conversion" became public with his publication in 1882 of *Jinken shinsetsu* 人権新説 (New Explanation of Human Rights) during Kiyozawa's time at the university. Kiyozawa is unflinching in his abhorrence at Japan's general fascination with Spencer and Mill, which he understood as resulting from the popular embrace of the government's policy goals of increasing materialism and militarism. The worldview of the expansionist Meiji regime, based on the idea that man's natural state was one of conflict and violence, is echoed in their decision to launch a war with China just before Kiyozawa arrived at his conception of Seishinshugi. One can only wonder what he thought of Katō who, with age, seems to have sacrificed his empathy at the altar of ambition.

Katō's ideological reversal is a reflection of the society's ambivalence about how it needed to redefine itself and reposition itself within the international community. Obsessed with instilling the value of loyalty, when the Meiji government finally enacted its constitution in 1889, which it called "The Great Japan Imperial Constitution" (*Dainihon teikoku kenpō*), it made history by explicitly granting freedom of religion for the first time, but it also made it equally clear that the country was to be ruled by the emperor, that he was sacred (*shinsei* 神聖), and that no one was allowed to act in violation of either principle. The following year, the Imperial Rescript on Education was announced: a short, general aphorism, which implied quite clearly that each citizen's ethical duties are defined in part by demonstrable loyalty to the sovereign. Here is part of that text:

> Our subjects, ever united in loyalty and filial piety, have from generation to generation illustrated the beauty thereof. This is the glory of the fundamental character of our empire, and herein also lies the source of our education. . . . Should an emergency arise, you must offer yourselves courageously to the State, and guard and maintain the prosperity of the Imperial Throne.[21]

As Sueki Fumihiko notes, taken together these two documents liberally guarantee freedom of religion on the one hand but on the other lay down stringent ethical requirements within a clearly defined political context, in effect implying that ethics is much more important than religion.[22] Considering the intense concern with religion in the early Meiji period, what we see at this juncture, some twenty years later, is that a compromise has been reached in which the Shinto–Emperor paradigm is still central to government propaganda but it has now been reclassified as an ethical rather than religious concern. The creation of a jingoistic notion of Shinto at this point becomes an ethical ideology for ordering society based on a newly politicized myth of an ancient past when the ancestors lived their lives in perfect sacrifice for the very same goals of prosperity and military strength.

Although government and educational leaders used idealistic moral rhetoric in placing high value on ethics and ethics education, their use of the term *dōtoku* 道徳 to mean correct behavior was filled with a politically charged subtext that implied submission to authority. Ethics was a major focus for a wide variety of writers in the middle and late Meiji periods because the term brought forth one of the central conundrums of the age: for all the modern advances in "individual liberty" such as the legal elimination of classes and freedom of religion, why did it seem that everyone's sense of duty and obligation had become so heavy that as individuals they felt so constricted? In this context intellectuals used the concept of ethics as the framework to launch their own theories or advocacies. For example, Inoue Tetsujirō, chairman of the Philosophy Department at Tokyo University published a well-read treatise in 1902 entitled *Rinri to shūkyō to no kankei* 倫理と宗教との関係 (*The Relationship of Ethics and Religion*) in which he argued that religions had value only insofar as they could be turned into ethical systems.[23] And Katō's agenda promoting the natural selection of humans was further elaborated in a 1912 publication entitled *Shizen to Rinri* 自然と倫理 (*Nature and Ethics*).[24]

Another important ideological milestone during Kiyozawa's student years was the *lèse majesté* offense that ruined the career of the famous Christian convert Uchimura Kanzō 内村鑑三 (1861–1930). The Imperial Rescript on Education was issued on October 30, 1890, when Uchimura was teaching at the prestigious First Higher School (Daiichi Kōtō Gakkō) in Tokyo, which served as a kind of undergraduate training academy for Tokyo University. At the opening ceremony for the new school year held the following January, the Rescript was read aloud; after which everyone bowed in respect, but Uchimura refused, feeling it violated his Christian beliefs. The press, including Buddhist newspapers, reported the incident as scandalous and Uchimura was put under enormous pressure to recant and apologize. By April, he had resigned his post and two months later his wife died of influenza. The incident made plain the fact that when religious freedom ran up against ethics construed as political loyalty, ethical duty was paramount, even if it meant ruining a respected teacher's life merely for abstaining from a ritual. But just as Katō's newfound strength in Darwinian social values led him down the path of ultranationalism, Uchimura's life-changing event of asserting his right not to express loyalty to a divine authority he did not accept later brought him to embrace pacifism. Today, Uchimura is regarded as one of the great tragic heroes of Japan's turbulent modernization.

Responding to Meiji Policies

In response to this ideologically oppressive climate, a variety of reform movements were initiated within the Buddhist world in hopes of restoring its lost vitality and prestige. All the authors represented here were part of that process. To put their concerns in context, I would like to suggest some general observations about the common motivations behind these activities in the modern period.

First of all, it is worth keeping in mind that the internal structure and doctrinal orthodoxy of Buddhist institutions defined and redefined over the course of some two hundred years of Edo-period systematizing had become deeply entrenched when the Meiji period began. Most of the major Buddhist organizations put considerable effort into academic programs to define their sectarian doctrines and create official canons that put limits on which scriptures they held authoritative. The official doctrines of sectarian Buddhism became central to each sect's identity, and in the Meiji, Taishō, and early Shōwa periods those doctrines were not substantially changed from how they had been defined in the Genroku period (1688–1704). Insofar as these models seemed to have satisfied the vast majority of the population, it remains an issue of some debate as to whether Buddhism had thereby degenerated into a moribund social institution under the Tokugawa bakufu. But no one doubts that it had grown conservative. Thus, although it is true that Buddhist institutions were aware of the potential for political trouble even before the Meiji Restoration, they were slow to react both ideationally and institutionally. Two centuries of sectarian academics had created religious conceptions that had become highly rationalized and standardized; some Shin scholars today even say that Shin doctrine had become unassailable dogma. This inherited legacy made it particularly difficult for these large sects to absorb criticism and constructively engage with it in the Meiji period. This is reflected in their often reactionary responses on the one hand to nationalistic and Christian anti-Buddhist rhetoric of the period, and on the other to intellectual challenges to *shūgaku* doctrine from within the Buddhist denominations themselves.

Buddhist rhetoric went through essentially four stages in response to the denigration of its value for Japanese society in these first fifty years of Japan's opening to the world.[25] Early Meiji Buddhist statements reflect the imminent crises of violent government policies against all aspects of Buddhism; they show deep concerns for protecting the political, spiritual, and material capital of the established sects and minimal interest in embracing the changes afoot in society and the nation. Public statements in this first stage are marked by an certain defensiveness, such as asserting the time-honored king's Law–buddha's Law doctrine of mutual dependence of government and Buddhist sources of power mentioned previously. Another expression of what I call *defensiveness* is the frequent reference to the need to keep Christianity from penetrating Japan. Still negotiating its freedom to proselytize in the first decade of the Meiji period, Christianity often is identified by Buddhists in this period as the real foreign danger. This is an attempt to deflect the xenophobic anti-Buddhist ideology of the nativists in the direction of Christianity. Shinshū played a central role in this first anti-Christian effort, and from the first year of Meiji the seminaries of both Higashi and Nishi Honganji taught courses on Christianity so its priests could better refute its doctrines.

In the second phase, beginning about 1875, government-sponsored violence against Buddhist temples has ceased. Buddhist understanding of Christianity has deepened considerably, and now Buddhist authors typically trumpeted how philosophically sophisticated Buddhism was by comparison. This is the time when Buddhist scholars were motivated to study the history of Indian Buddhist thought because of the introduction of South Asian Buddhist language materials to Japan. They were especially interested in what they called "primitive Buddhism" (*genshi Bukkyō* 原始仏教), that is, the time of the founder Śākyamuni and shortly thereafter, hoping it would enable them to produce universal statements of Buddhist doctrine that represented the religion as a whole. This notion of reducing Buddhism to its lowest common doctrinal demoninator fit well with the aims of the Theosophist movement, founded by Henry Steele Olcott (1832–1907) and Helena Blavatsky (1831–1891) in New York also in 1875. It is no accident that many Buddhist intellectuals in Japan were initially taken with Theosophy during their own discovery of early Buddhism. From the limited amount the Japanese knew about Theosophy, its embrace of Buddhist esotericism looked like it might become a European form of Buddhism fashioned with a healthy dose of modern scientific rationalism. It thus seemed for a time to provide a possible solution to their political troubles because it was an avenue for them to be both pro-Western and pro-Buddhist. Olcott and Blavatsky moved to India and Ceylon in 1879 where they cultivated Buddhist contacts and eventually settled in Adyar near Madras where they worked to create a pan-Buddhist movement. Based on their search for a common Buddhist creed, Olcott audaciously published his Buddhist Catechism in 1881, which was initially well received around the world. It was first translated into Japanese in 1886 by Imadate Tosui 今立吐酔 (1855–1931), who grew up in a Nishi Honganji temple in Fukui, studied in America, and would later publish the first English translation of the *Tannishō* together with D. T. Suzuki.²⁶ Thereafter, Theosophy enjoyed a very brief period of fascination for Japanese Buddhists, during which many people connected with Shinshū actively participated. Olcott was first invited to Japan in 1889 by Hirai Kinza 平井金三 (1859–1916), who attended the World Parliament of Religions in Chicago to speak about Rinzai Zen, but whose mother grew up in a Shinshū temple.²⁷ Olcott's arrangements during this trip to Kyoto were largely sponsored by both Honganji, and during his second trip he labored hard, albeit unsuccessfully, to convince Shin leaders to approve his fourteen points of common Buddhist belief.

The third stage is characterized by a deep concern with ethics, coming in response to the debate that ensued after the Constitution and Rescript on Education were made public in 1888–1889. As one might expect, this rhetoric was not about debating universal or even Buddhist ethical norms, but was focused on demonstrating how Buddhist values and practices were not subversive (i.e., they showed respect for the imperial institution and held value for society as a whole). It should be mentioned that in the overt political resistance to the Daikyōin event, that is, as early as 1875, there were prominent Buddhists who refused to sacrifice their freedom of thought on the altar of ethical nationalism. Led by Shimaji Mokurai, these voices came to be called the Freedom of Belief (*shinkyō jiyū* 信教自由) movement.²⁸

In the fourth stage of Buddhist modernity, these politically charged responses finally gave way to a search for genuine spirituality. Beginning around 1894, we see the simultaneous launching of various intellectual Buddhist associations that published journals. The earliest publication was probably the magazine *Bukkyō* 仏教 (Buddhism), which ran between 1894 and 1899, and was supported by the Kei'i'kai 経緯会, a group led by Furukawa Yū 古河勇 (1871–1899). The journal was famous for stating "we have entered an age of doubt." Most likely the second Buddhist journal after *Bukkyō* was *Seishinkai* 精神界 (*Spiritual World*), an effort put out by Kiyozawa Manshi and his group of followers known as the Kōkōdō 浩々洞 (*Capacious Cave*). The disbanded Kei'i'kai then regrouped in 1899 under the name Bukkyō Seito Dōshikai 仏教清徒同志会, and began publishing a new journal

Shin Bukkyō 新仏教 (*New Buddhism*) in 1900.[29] From the second half of the 1890s we thus see an abrupt change of attitude whereby the search for public acceptance is abandoned, at times even disdained as an impediment, in what amounts to a private and public search for true religious insight.

Internally, the major Buddhist sects had to face the difficulty of reforming institutional models that had served them well for the better part of the Edo period. By the end of the seventeenth century most had established sectarian canons, training centers, and institutional rules that regulated the relationship between main and branch temples, and had put the entire institution on firm financial footing. This was particularly true for the Shin, Jōdo, Sōtō, and Nichiren sects, all of which were very strong at the time of the Meiji Restoration. But this very strength made it even more painful to consider and implement fundamental changes in structure and the way monks were educated. Financially speaking, the income from land holdings was an important part of whatever financial security had been established for many temples, and as noted previously this is precisely what the *haigōji* policy in late Edo and early Meiji aimed at disrupting.

As we saw in the example of the Daikyōin, the group that put up the greatest resistance to these forms of oppression was Jōdo Shinshū. Shin was unusual in that it was not dependent on extensive land holdings but had many temples, and all its clergy were already married,[30] so the elimination of large numbers of temples would have meant the collapse and ruination of the sect itself. That is why it did not flinch from opposing the *haigōji* movement as a matter of institutional policy. Another reason why Shin reacted more intensely than the other sects was that it had very strong support from its rural power base for this kind of action. In this way the resistance of Shinshū opened up an opportunity for Buddhism as a whole to reemerge late in the nineteenth century with its confidence intact.[31]

Here it is worth remembering that there are ten different branches of Jōdo Shinshū. Each operates independently in its financial operations, educational and doctrinal policies, internal structure, and in its political relations with different levels of government. What unites them under the rubric of Shin is their common linkage to the founder Shinran 親鸞 (1173–1262), their reverence for Shinran's writings, and government policies that at different times treated the branches as one body. Since one dimension of the Seishinshugi movement involves structural and ideological reform of their religious institution, it is important to clarify that in this case the institution in question is only the Ōtani branch, or Higashi Honganji. But in general all four of the writers represented here have simply been read as Shin thinkers, and in their time they did not represent Higashi Honganji for the most part.

From the outset, the Nishi and Higashi branches had different relationships with the new Meiji government. The reasons for this stem from developments that took place within the two branches during the Edo period, a topic beyond the confines of this study. Suffice it to say there was only one Honganji until Tokugawa Ieyasu. Conflicts had arisen within the hereditary leadership family of the Honganji during negotiations in 1580 to end Oda Nobunaga's (1534–1582) ten-year siege of the Honganji complex in Osaka, a battle known as the *Ishiyama gassen* 石山合戦. Kennyo 顕如 (1543–1592), the abbot of Honganji during this struggle, decided to accept a negotiated settlement but the son who had been leading the fight to defend the temple, Kyōnyo 教如 (1558–1614), refused to accept the surrender. His father thereupon removed Kyōnyo as his designated heir and appointed his fourth son Junnyo 准如 (1577–1630) in his stead. In 1591, Toyotomi Hideyoshi (1536–1598) awarded Junnyo a site in Kyoto to rebuild the Honganji. But Ieyasu saw an opportunity to divide the most powerful religious institution in the nation and in 1602 he awarded land in Kyoto to Kyōnyo to build another Honganji temple but under Kyōnyo's own leadership. The result was two rival Honganji institutions who divided the Honganji subtemple network and were subsequently never able to rejoin as a single organization. By the time the Japanese nation entered the international community 260 years later, the two branches had developed somewhat different doctrines and political outlooks. As it turned out, the Higashi branch was much closer to the Tokugawa bakufu, and sided with them in the ensuing military conflicts of the 1860s preceding the Restoration, while the Nishi threw its weight behind the revolutionary "reformers." The fledgling Meiji government, in dire need to distance itself from everything the bakufu had stood for, was therefore naturally more hostile to Higashi branch.

Despite the somewhat hysterical dream of eliminating Buddhism from Japanese culture altogether embraced by the more fervent "fundamentalist" Atsutane believers within the new government, both Honganji institutions (who changed their official names in the Meiji period to Jōdo Shinshū Honganji-ha for Nishi, and Shinshū Ōtani-ha for Higashi) gained some respite when the new government came to them for financial assistance. Having nearly run out of money early in the Meiji period, the government succeeded in securing loans from both, but its ties to the Nishi branch were more extensive. There is little evidence that this produced much in the way of tangible results for either, but at the very least it introduced an element of realpolitik into the circles of power in the Meiji government, and by the fifth year of Meiji the overtly harsh anti-Buddhist policies were no longer being enforced.

Internally, Meiji-period Buddhist dialogue concerning its mission reflected four general areas of concern. These issues became crystallized by the 1890s and continued well into the postwar period.

First was the identity in the new Japan of the sangha, or religious community. Of the so-called Three Jewels, it is the sangha where the traditions of practice and understanding, where the teachings themselves, and where the meaning of buddha are expected to be preserved.[32] The sangha is thus the locale where the message of the religion is to be found, where interpretations of that message are contested, and where the flame of truth is kept. But as a social institution, the sangha also has its own political, societal, and economic identity, and in that period of political hostility, self-preservation was its immediate goal. Survival required adaption to the new social realities, and accommodation of demands for change within. For, in addition to demonstrating their ideological acquiescence to the ever rising nationalism within the government, all Buddhist institutions in the first generations after the Meiji Restoration also needed to modernize internally. Shin Buddhism was somewhat of a special case because the religious paradigm that became orthodox in the Edo period stressed faith at the expense of practice. That is, it was taught that Shinran's understanding of "other-power" meant that believing in the value of practice too strongly signified a lack of faith in other-power itself. What is important here is that the usual Buddhist model that states that study and practice lead to understanding was replaced by one in which practice is de-emphasized such that study may lead directly to understanding. As such, Shin Buddhism became highly scholastic and highly doctrinal, and both Honganji institutions had colleges for training monks in the seventeenth century that continued into the Meiji period. But the curricula at both schools did not appreciably change despite the enormous advances in scholastic Buddhism at this time. Therefore, both branches of the Honganji internally faced frustration and demands from their own intellectuals for "modernization" of traditional interpretive models of the Buddhist teachings. One response was the creation of colleges open to the public that also served as academic seminaries for future priests, leading to establishment of Shinshū University in Tokyo by Higashi Honganji, which later became Ōtani University in Kyoto, and Ryūkoku University by Nishi Honganji, also in Kyoto. Both absorbed their earlier Edo period *gakuryō*-style seminaries, but because they combined traditional *shūgaku* with modern academics, there would always be an inevitable tension regarding curriculum, as seen in the expulsion of Soga and Kaneko from their posts as professors at Ōtani University.

This brings us to the second issue faced by Buddhists at this time: the felt need to reassess the content of the teachings themselves. In addition to the external attacks, the modern period also brought a host of new challenges within Buddhist thought itself. Although the philosophical challenge of Western ideas was not insignificant, much more important was the opening up of the canon to non-Chinese materials. Until the Meiji period, Japan had only known Buddhist scriptures in their Chinese form; there had been no direct contact with the Indian subcontinent. There was, oddly enough, a significant quantity Sanskrit-language materials that been brought from China in the Nara and Heian periods that was collected in Japan by the Edo period Shingon monk Jiun 慈雲 (1718–1804),[33] but no one was able to read them as no tradition of Sanskrit language study ever developed in Japan, or China for that matter. With the opening to the West, Japan learned of the active Sanskrit- and Pāli-based Buddhist studies being carried on in Europe. Scholars such as Nanjō Bun'yū 南条文雄 (1849–1927) journeyed to Oxford to study with F. Max Müller (1823–1900), famed philologist and editor of the *Sacred Books of the East*. Until this time, it had been assumed that when the Japanese received "the complete canon of scriptures" (*issai kyō* 一切経) it had meant just that. Japanese scholars now learned to read Buddhist scriptures in Sanskrit, Pāli, and Tibetan. Although there was no extant Sanskrit canon as only a few individual texts had been discovered at that point, entire canons in Pāli and Tibetan became available. They soon learned that although they had many scriptures in common with those traditions, there were a great many others that appeared only in those canons, and vice versa. The problem of apocryphal or indigenous sutras, something Chinese catalogers had pointed out many centuries earlier, now loomed much larger, as many of the most influential sutras in the standard canons of East Asia were found nowhere else, setting off a long period of textcritical scholarship in the hope of settling the question of which sutras were of Chinese and which of Indian origin.

The most immediate impact of the new textcritical scholarship was the unexpected appreciation of pre-Mahāyāna scripture, where a rational, worldly Śākyamuni Buddha was depicted that contrasted sharply with his image in most Mahāyāna literature. A theory first advanced by Tominaga Nakamoto—over a century before any actual reading of Indian materials—that the Mahāyāna sutras could not be the words of Śākyamuni, came under serious consideration in the Meiji period, now stripped of its polemic context. Although the methodology of Japanese Buddhologists closely paralleled their European counterparts, their goals were radically different—no less than a radical reassessment of the Chinese Buddhist canon and its traditional forms of hermeneutic exegesis. In Kiyozawa's writings, for example, we see an example of one of the most significant influences of the new scholarship: the dropping of traditional bias against the early, so-called Hīnayāna teachings that had deeply colored the Chinese Buddhist tradition by the time it had arrived in Japan. Suddenly the presumed inevitability of the Mahāyāna view of things was no longer a given, lending credibility to Nakamoto's thesis. This new perspective exploded into the public domain with the publication of *Bukkyō seitenshi ron* 佛教聖典史論 (*Essays on the History of Buddhist Scriptures*) in 1899 by Anesaki Masaharu 姉崎正治 (1873–1949), which argued in favor of the Nakamoto thesis, followed by *Bukkyō tōitsuron* 佛教統一論 (*Essays on a Unified Buddhism*) in 1901 by Murakami Senshō 村上専精 (1851–1929), which took the same position. These works reflect the strong interest in the beginnings of Buddhism in India mentioned earlier that depict an idealized notion of the religion as a small movement of religiously dedicated men and women before it became a social institution in Indian society. Another influential legacy from this period has been a reassessment of the life of Śākyamuni based on the new sources that became available, including inscriptions and archaelogical finds, producing something akin to the search for the "historical Jesus" in the West.

As the Japanese began to study India through Indian rather than Chinese sources, they increasingly gained appreciation of Buddhism as a product of Indian culture. And if Indian religion is rich in anything it is myth, an evaluative category absent in traditional Buddhist or Confucian thought. As scholars began to learn about comparative myth, it raised the question of whether the narratives in the Pure Land sutras or the *Lotus Sutra* were intended to be read as myth. If the Pure Land is myth, for example, then what does "birth in the Land of Bliss" (*gokuraku ōjō* 極楽往生) actually mean? If one were to argue these are narratives and not myth, how should that be done? Or, if one accepted the interpretation that the concepts of "Pure Land" and "birth" are myth, how does that change what these notions mean to us? Should it change the practices and rituals done in this context?

The question of myth led to the third problem of Buddhist thinkers at this time: how should Buddhism respond to the challenges posed by the flood of new ideas coming from the West and the internal critique of Buddhism as anachronistic? After moving beyond their initial polemic against Christianity, Buddhist thinkers began to compare the implications of monotheism with the nontheism (or for some, pantheism) of Buddhism. Did the scientific advances in the West suggest the religious traditions in Western cultures and societies compared more favorably with those of technologically backward Japan and China? While government persecution of Buddhism may have ended early in the Meiji period, there was no let up in the criticism that Buddhism held the nation back from materially progressing more quickly because it stressed inward reflection rather than outward action. Were the critics correct? What is the Buddhist argument against the overt material bias of Utilitarianism, Social Darwinism, and Communism? Or, should Buddhism position itself in support of Japan's headlong rush to define happiness through materialism? Can the Japanese people excel at science, technology, and trade in a way commensurate to the West without becoming Christians?

The final question reflects dialogue within the denominations about the need to redefine sectarian identities and how to teach those identities to future generations of priests and lay believers. To what degree was the Edo-period *shūgaku* legacy that defined a sect's beliefs, doctrines, and practices still relevant in the modern world? Given the new perspectives on the history of Buddhism, how should it be taught to future clergy in the colleges and seminaries which had been set up or reconfigured in the Meiji period by most of the traditional Buddhist sects? How much had society actually changed? Were the needs of the lay supporters and the clergy different from what they had been? Could Buddhism be appreciated and serve the spiritual needs of Japan if it were taught and practiced in the same way it had been a century earlier? The fact that the legal ban on Buddhist monks taking wives and eating meat was lifted in the Meiji period was in some sense a major change for the sangha in Japan, with the exception of Shin. Questions still remained as to how far Buddhist institutions should assimilate government policies; to what degree should they resist those policies when they appear morally wrong or intent on harming the sangha itself? It was well known that Shinran had no sympathy for local kami worship, and along with Nichiren-shū, Shinshū had a long tradition for distancing itself from state authority in the past. Should all Buddhist monks teach the divinity of the emperor? To what degree should they incorporate the Imperial Rescript on Education into their educational policies? Should they support military expansion by sending chaplains to accompany troops going abroad for such adventures?

Among the variety of responses that emerged as answers to the first question of how the sangha should reform itself, one of the most important was the urging of a return to monasticism, also echoed in Seishinshugi. In the early Meiji period, the monk Unshō 雲照 (1827–1909) of the Shingon school felt the sangha could save itself only by returning to its original commitment to monasticism, and he created a school for studying the precepts. Fukuda Gyōkai 福田行誡 (d. 1888) of the Jōdo school also stressed the importance of the precepts, but he chose to work for transsectarian collaboration and better scholarship to create new understandings common to all schools. Unshō took the position that intimacy between the sangha and the government was the norm in Japan and urged a return to that condition, whereas Fukuda saw the sangha as always having been independent and advocated that it should remain that way.

One of the more interesting doctrinal shifts that occurred at this time within Shin thought was the ideological strategy of refiguring the Mahāyāna doctrine of two truths. Instead of the traditional Mahāyāna notion of worldly and absolute truth as they pertain to the Buddha's teachings since the time of Nāgārjuna, the two truths were reconceived as social or *political* truth, and private or *religious* truth. The religious truth, called *shintai* 真諦, was accommodated in individual experience as *shinjin* 信心, the Shin ideal of faith and realization. By contrast, the political or "worldly" truth, called *zokutai* 俗諦, was now defined as moral and ethical norms based on loyalty to the emperor. As Fukuma Kōchō has shown, this was enshrined in 1871 in a final statement to his successor made by Kōnyo 広如 (1798–1871), head of Nishi Honganji, uttered when bedridden at the end of his life.

> As people born in the land of the emperor, none of us are not under obligation to the emperor. Particularly now when the rule of the excellent government of the Restoration has taken control, preserving the populace, and aiming to confront foreign nations, applying their intelligence day and night. Whether religious or lay, who would not assist the beneficence of the king and serve to illuminate his imperial prestige? How much more so when it comes to spreading the buddha's law (*buppō* 仏法) in the world! It is because of the protection of the sovereign and his ministers that those who believe the buddha's law are also given to dedicating their humanity and duty to the king's law (*ōbō* 王法) at the center [of their lives], to revere the kami, and to protect morality. . . . Thus our Great Reformer (Rennyo) said, "Touch the king's law to your forehead and store the buddha's law in your heart." What we want is for all priests and lay in our denomination to attain proper understanding

of our tradition and not to confuse the teaching of the two truths: to be loyal to the emperor and the state, responding in kind to the unlimited debt we owe to the court, and to achieve birth in the Western [Pure] Land in the next life where you become someone who will escape suffering forever.[34]

The institutional stand or policy of Nishi Honganji toward the new government is clearly laid out here, and it is worth noting that its recipient, his successor Myōnyo 明如 (1850–1903), decided to print and distribute the statement throughout the country among all their branch temples. Myōnyo added a colophon to the effect that this statement on the two truths was the final message of Kōnyo and should be respected as orthodox doctrine. But Kōnyo's stance also came to form the underlying position of the Higashi Honganji as well, suggesting that although Nishi Honganji may have been closer to the new regime, on the fundamental question of the government's demand for overt political loyalty from Buddhist leaders, the two branches of Honganji did not hold views that were appreciably different. To sum up, the Kōnyo statement clarifies the following:

1. The ancient principle of the mutually dependent and mutually supportive relationship between the norms of society and the principles of Buddhist doctrine was still relevant.

2. Shin Buddhists, both lay and clergy, should embrace the new government regardless of its policies toward Buddhism or the outside world. This means they should gladly accede to public expectation that they bow before the emperor and observe all required rituals directed toward the court as the symbol of the state.

3. The two levels of truth that characterize Mahāyāna Buddhism have now been invested with a political dimension wherein the mundane truth has been redefined as sociopolitical normative behavior, or "ethics."

This, then, was the direction that the institutions of Buddhism were headed. But not all Buddhists were in agreement. Let us now turn to the Seishinshugi movement as an example of stern resistance to defining Buddhism in Japan by its social policies.

A Return to Practice: Seishinshugi

As mentioned earlier, the name "Seishinshugi" was coined by Kiyozawa Manshi and discussed or alluded to in a series of articles appearing in a journal called *Seishinkai* published by a splinter group of Ōtani branch Shin priests from 1901 to 1919. Seishinshugi has many faces; that is to say, even today it means different things to different people. As a particularly creative and influential "Buddhist revival movement" (*bukkyō fukkō undō* 仏教復興運動) or a "new Shinran-ism" (*shin Shinran shugi* 新親鸞主義) of the Meiji period,[35] it is usually studied academically within Japan by students of Japanese thought, Japanese religion, or Buddhism in the modern world. Indeed it would not be difficult to argue that the twentieth-century vogue of interest in Shinran, spurred by the writings of people like Miki Kiyoshi 三木清 (1897–1945), Kurata Hyakuzō 倉田百三 (1891–1943), and Ienaga Saburō 家永三郎 (1913–2002), and which has transcended sectarianism, actually began with the pan-Buddhist appeal of Seishinshugi thought appearing in *Seishinkai*. Within the institutional context of Shin Buddhism as well, it is probably not an exaggeration to say that Seishinshugi is the most important new conception of Shin thought since Rennyo reformed Honganji in the fifteenth century. This does *not* mean Kiyozawa Manshi and his followers were able to transform the hearts, minds, and institutional power structure of the preponderance of Shin believers in the twentieth century. Seishinshugi has been controversial from the start and remains so today. But Kiyozawa and the other thinkers represented in this collection succeeded so thoroughly in jarring the moribund intellectual tradition of Shin (if not Japanese Buddhism in general) awake and opened up so many new conceptual avenues that it is also probably fair to say that no Japanese religious thinker with an interest in Shinran has not been affected by their achievements, even if only to reject them.

Additionally, among all centers of Shin Buddhist Studies, as the founder of Ōtani University, Kiyozawa Manshi's intellectual legacy is naturally most prominent there. As a result, Seishinshugi remains influential in both Shin and Buddhist studies at Ōtani today. Its appeal has been limited by its radical claims, its disinterest in politics, and its often confrontational stance toward traditional Shin dogmatics. It has always engendered controversy, but there are few Buddhist intellectuals in Japan today who are not familiar with Seishinshugi and accord it at least a modicum of respect. At the same time, it has alienated a number of professional Buddhists, especially in Shin culture, and caused considerable consternation even within the Higashi Honganji to the point that, as mentioned previously, three of the writers included here were expelled from the church.

Within the pages of *Seishinkai*, a variety of opinions were presented about the nature of Buddhism in modern Japan, some even critical of Seishinshugi itself. Although it was read by a broad spectrum of people during its brief existence, to the leaders of the Ōtani denomination the journal was often seen as a public challenge to its religious authority and therefore to the identity of the church itself. In setting the pace for what needed to be done to bring back criticial thinking about religion regardless of how broadly jingoism, militarism, and materialism were sweeping society, the intellectual currents that sprung from its pages directly attacked long-established orthodoxies of understanding, practice, and education within all forms of Buddhism, but particularly within Shin. This was particularly stinging for the religious institution that had paid for Kiyozawa's education and entrusted him with the education of its future intellectual leaders in appointing him first as tutor to the future abbot of Higashi Honganji and then as first president of its new university. The anxiety caused by Seishinshugi within the Ōtani branch of Shin was so deep that in expelling Kiyozawa, Soga, and Kaneko, they effectively sidelined the most brilliant minds within their own tradition. Kiyozawa had his clerical status restored but he died in poverty, unrepentant. Soga and Kaneko were eventually reinstated as faculty at the university, and Yasuda Rijin, the fourth author here, avoided this problem altogether by living and teaching privately in Kyoto. In this volume, we have gathered representative examples of the writing of all four thinkers, beginning with three essays by Kiyozawa that have messages for Japanese Buddhism as a whole. What follows is a historical outline of the generation of the ideas within Kiyozawa that formed the "skeleton" of Seishinshugi; the reader is directed to Chapter 2 for biographical information on Kiyozawa himself.

In 1890, Kiyozawa resigned from his position as principal of a secondary school to devote more time to writing. Beginning in 1895, he and twelve other Shin intellectuals, including Nanjō Bun'yū, began a campaign to obtain the freedom to develop more modern curricula in the teaching of Shin thought that incorporated new perspectives stemming from strides in Buddhology and understanding of Western religion and philosophy. Despite a spirited effort, he was not successful, leading to a deepening of his tuberculosis and his turning from educational and social concerns to religious issues. Seishinshugi is the direct result of this transition within Kiyozawa himself.

The major educational struggle had been centered on overturning the entrenched, dominating nature of *shūgaku*. One studied *shūgaku* in order to acquire knowledge of the orthodox understanding of relevant scriptures according to founders, patriarchs, and subsequent institutional leaders. Thus, the Jōdo, Shin, and the Ji sects are all Pure Land sects[36] who uphold the same three Pure Land sutras as their scriptures of ultimate authority,[37] but they all have different *shūgaku* because they read those sutras differently. With the founding in the seventeenth century of the official seminaries known as *gakuryō* or *gakurin*, the infrastructure of both branches of Honganji shifted to a pattern where these intellectual training grounds served as official vehicles for dispensing the views of sectarian leadership.[38] This allowed for unprecedented political control of what was and was not to be considered the orthodox doctrine, and an eventual shift in emphasis on teachings (as opposed to practice) as the defining principle of the sect, a trend seen in nearly all Buddhist sects during the Edo period. The overall result was a rigid curriculum that taught prepared answers to anticipated questions, effecting a stifling of inquiry beyond the defined rubrics and a religious culture that valued scholastic precision over the mysteries of religiosity.

Kiyozawa skillfully argued that the central authority of the *honzan* 本山 (administrative center of the sect) was overreacting to new interpretations of Shin doctrine because it had blurred the traditional distinction in Buddhism between *shūgaku* 宗学 and *shūgi* 宗義. As he defined it, *shūgi* was the core truth of a Buddhist school established by its founder that should be accepted by all its believing adherents; this was non-negotiable and institutional leadership could reasonably expect compliance with it. But *shūgaku* represented a tradition of critical inquiry; that is, it was the process of how individuals made sense of this creed-like *shūgi*. Therefore *shūgaku* should be expected to foster discussion and debate, where opinions need not be uniform. Disagreement was in fact a healthy sign that genuine comprehension was taking place. Kiyozawa observed, however, that young priests were taught to *believe* in the traditional explanations of *shūgaku* scholarship about suggestive yet vague Pure Land doctrinal notions rather than encouraged to *debate* those interpretations and gain respect for their plausibility only after subjecting them to the students' own critical analyses.

Kiyozawa's rhetoric also included a more subtle but equally stinging critique of the lack of any serious commitment to praxis or training for young monks in the Shin of his day. Over the course of intellectualizing Shinran's doctrine for two centuries, significant distortions had taken place. For example, Shinran's notion of other-power was taught in rational dialogue, with students feeling they could grasp it merely by learning what was taught to them in lectures. But Kiyozawa insisted that Shinran's message on other-power was something existential rather than doctrinal. One has to awaken to *tariki*, and this only happens when one sees one's own mental and emotional limitations. To study "objectively" what other-power should mean rather than experience its significance personally in the context of one's own individual mental makeup stultifies it, reducing it from a dynamic religious concept into a "dead word," as such things are called in the Zen tradition.

In a move that suggests an interesting parallel to Gandhi—born just six years after Kiyozawa—the valorization of practice in Kiyozawa's thought grew out of a personal plunge into asceticism, and this in turn strengthened the authority of his efforts to reform his denomination and presumably all forms of Shin Buddhism. The principle of personal sacrifice proving political sincerity is universal, but the intentional self-denial of food and physical comfort as a daily routine for the purpose of attaining bodily purity and mental power is particularly characteristic of the Indic/Buddhist religious paradigm. Although the Shin tradition is not without persons who saw rigorous discipline as conducive to deepening their faith and understanding of the Pure Land religion taught by Hōnen 法然 (1133–1212) and Shinran, as mentioned above during the Edo period the religion had moved away from faith based in disciplined practice to faith based on intellectual assent, and this fact made Kiyozawa's asceticism all the more startling. Through his writing of this period we see the critique that other-power had been so thoroughly reified into dogma that devotion to praxis came to be seen as indicative of a lack of faith. Kiyozawa raged at the normative Shin position that belief in the value of practice was labeled pejoratively as self-power (*jiriki* 自力), which itself had been reified in *shūgaku* as a heretical denial of other-power force and therefore taboo. Kiyozawa's theological point was that Shinran's teachings on other-power could only be appreciated in the context of traditional self-power praxis, and subverting this process amounted to not only removing the centrality of Shinran for Shin Buddhism, but weakening the religious import of the Shin tradition as a whole.

By March 1898, when his institutional reform journal *Kyōkai jigen* 教界時言 (*Timely Words for the Religious World*) had ceased publication, Kiyozawa's interest returned to the philosophy of religion. Most notably Kiyozawa turned to the study of the early Buddhist Āgama scriptures that give a much more realistic portrayal of Śākyamuni's experiences and motivations than the Mahāyāna descriptions he was familiar with. Here he found confirmation of the value of his natural inclination toward self-denial and self-discipline and the importance of personal insight through religious experience. He then turned to the writings of the Greek Stoic Epictectus (c. 55–c.135 CE), a crippled ex-slave who was relentless in his pursuit of insight and an ethical lifestyle through self-discipline and philosophic inquiry. In Epictetus he saw a similar perspective to his own view of self-power and other-power wherein it was believed by the Stoics that in order to attain happiness one must use reason to analyze the limits of one's power. It was during this period of study that Seishinshugi was born. In 1900, Kiyozawa formed a kind of communal study group that came to be called Kōkōdō after someone hung a sign with that name on the house they rented from Chikazumi Jōkan 近角常観 (1870–1941) near Tokyo University and by September of that year there were more than ten people living there. One of them, Akegarasu Haya 曉烏敏 (1877–1954), suggested they publish a journal, and in January 1901 the first volume of *Seishinkai* was released with an editorial statement by Kiyozawa's entitled "Seishinshugi," which explained the philosophy of the group. The journal contained an announcement inviting anyone, regardless of gender or education level, who would be interested in "cultivating the path" (*michi o osamemu* 道を修めむ) to come to open Sunday study sessions. During this same period, Kiyozawa was formally named founding president of the newly constituted Shinshū University. He insisted the school be located in Tokyo, away from Kyoto's conservative religious base, but it was moved down to Kyoto after his death in 1911, and renamed Ōtani University in 1922.

One of the longest lasting impacts of the Seishinshugi experiment was the attention it brought to the *Tannishō* 歎異抄 (*Tract Lamenting Differences*), a small text containing short aphorisms spoken by Shinran that were collected by a disciple named Yuien 唯円 (n.d.). Today, the *Tannishō* has become one of the most influential Buddhist texts in Japan, and it is largely due to the other-power perspective in this work that Shinran has emerged as one of the most attractive religious thinkers for educated Japanese regardless of sectarian affiliation, especially in the postwar period. But this was not always the case. Although appreciated by Rennyo, serious study of the *Tannishō* only began in the latter Edo period with an extensive commentary by the great scholars Kōgatsuin Jinrei 香月院深励 (1749–1817) and Myōon'in Ryōshō 妙音院了祥 (1788–1842), but it remained outside the traditional sectarian curricula of all branches of Shin in the Meiji period. During this Kōkōdō period, Kiyozawa had come to the conclusion that for himself the three most important religious texts were the Āgamas, the *Discourses of Epictetus*, and the *Tannishō*, and urged his student Akegarasu to study the *Tannishō*. From the January 1903 issue to 1911, Akegarasu published a series of articles on the *Tannishō* in which he quotes a portion of the text and discusses its meaning. Perhaps also inspired by Kiyozawa, his colleague Chikazumi Jōkan began to give public lectures on the *Tannishō* at this time, leading to his own publications of an annotated text of the *Tannishō* with exegesis as an appendix in 1905 and again as a separate book in 1906.

Turning back to Seishinshugi what did this name mean to Kiyozawa? Kiyozawa states in a general way that it denotes the essential importance of pursuing a spiritual path for oneself that would by extension lead to social harmony. In this sense, Seishinshugi reflects a traditional Buddhist approach to defining a particular religious *gestalt* of values, beliefs, and practices within the conception of what are called *mārga,* or paths to liberation. These range from the relatively concrete, such as the eightfold path that names professions (such as dealing in weapons) that are deemed counterproductive to spiritual progress, to the relatively abstract, such as the Pure Land path that is only defined as a commitment to seek birth in Amida's Pure Land.

Kiyozawa, Akegarasu, and others discuss Seishinshugi frequently in the opening volumes of *Seishinkai*. Insofar as the name of the journal mirrors the name of the movement and Kiyozawa discusses the name in the inaugural volume of the journal, we may conclude that the journal was created for the precise purpose of publicly discussing his ideas. Kiyozawa had of course participated in other such specialist journals, but as mentioned previously that the very phenomenon of public Buddhist journals serving as a medium for advancing the religion was something new to this period, reflecting a new awareness of Buddhism not only as an integral part of Japan's common heritage but as something that can be objectified for purposes of analysis in the public sphere. Here are two excerpts from these early volumes, beginning with Kiyozawa's explanation of why he coined the term as a way of describing his personal religious perspective.

> It is imperative that we find one complete place to stand while we are in the world. If we do not, then we will go through life doing things as if we were standing on a cloud giving a performance. One does not need any more explanation to understand that this need is simply to avoid falling over. As such, how do we gain a complete place to stand while going through life? In all probability it can only be through the power of something absolutely infinite. And the road to the mind that will obtain this state is what I am calling "Seishinshugi." In other words, Seishinshugi is the principle of putting things into practice while coursing through the world, the first of which is the search for a complete sense of fulfillment within one's own mind.[39]

Among the variety of themes associated with Seishinshugi, many are contained within this initial statement, such as the importance of working to clarify one's personal identity, the fact that this can only come from personal, inner experience, and that attaining this reflects a process of self-fulfillment.

The language is inspiring, but there is also some ambiguity in what Kiyozawa means by the term *Seishinshugi* itself when he speaks of "the road to mind that will attain [the infinite]." The definition of Seishinshugi here is rife with symbolic language, and so we must seek clarification in his reference to it in other contexts. Part of the problem for us today to understand him is that symptomatic of language usage at that time when so many new philosophies and systems of thought came into Japan so quickly, Kiyozawa developed his own personal style of expression that is not always clear today. He uses a great many words that end in *shugi* 主義, for example, akin to the suffix -*ism* in Romance languages. Even today the suffix *shugi* incorporates a range of meanings, from a formal theoretical system such as *marukusu-shugi* マルクス主義 (Marxism) to a set of values or a stylistic approach such as *shizen-shugi* 自然主義 (naturalism), *kokka-shugi* 国家主義 (nationalism), or *jitsuyō-shugi* 実用主義 (utilitarianism). Kiyozawa freely affixes this form to nouns to express abstract principles, such as *shukan-shugi* 主観主義 (subjectivism), *zensekinin-shugi* 全責任主義 (total responsibility-ism), *sekinin fubunkatsu-shugi* 責任不分割主義 (undivided responsibility-ism), or a system of thought or philosophy as in *tariki-shugi* 他力主義 (other-power-ism). The result is a host of abstract word-formations functioning as abstract principles in places where one might otherwise use adjectival forms, and nearly all are used within Kiyozawa's writing as synonyms of Seishinshugi, standing as representative flags for a variety of his philosophical positions. Included are such terms as *anjū-shugi* 安住主義 (peaceful resolution-ism), *funrei-shugi* 奮励主義 (encouragement-ism), *katsudō-shugi* 活動主義 (activism) and *jissai shugi* 実際主義 (realism). One of the most influential Kiyozawa neologisms is the term *naikan-shugi* 内観主義, which describes the process of finding the source of truth for oneself through introspection and using it as the basis for external action, a key principle in Seishinshugi. This expanded meaning would be much harder to communicate if he had used the available adjectival form *naikan-teki* 内観的, for whereas *naikan-teki* describes an attitude or viewpoint based on self-reflection, *naikan-shugi* implies a system of philosophical thought and personality development based on the valorization of inner experience. It would appear to be somewhat synonymous with Western notion of subjectivism, and is thus contrasted with *gaikan-shugi* 外観主義, which represents a value system based on holding empirical evidence as primary. Similarly, *tariki-shugi* takes the traditional term other-power, otherwise restricted to faith in birth in the Pure Land as the immediate goal of religion, and adds to it a dimension of reasoned understanding that may be applicable to many questions in life. As the father of all these new formations, *seishin-shugi* was itself coined to communicate Kiyozawa's standpoint wherein religious practice leading to religious experience must be the "first philosophy" of any modern system of values, ethics, or social activism.

The implementation of this view is expressed in one of the most intriguing aspects of Kiyozawa's thought: his emphasis on asceticism.

> When I look at the way things actually are, I inevitably think that if someone wants to enter into religious faith, the first thing they need to do is abandon all thoughts of appealing to anything outside of religion. You cannot allow yourself to rely on your material wealth, your wife, children, or friends, your parents or siblings, your status, your abilities, your scholarship or knowledge, or your nation. . . . If you do not pass through the gate of world-rejection wherein you put aside your family and abandon your wealth—and not look back upon these things—it will be extremely difficult to reach a place of true religious faith. . . . As the saying goes, a loyal minister does not serve two sovereigns, a faithful wife does not look upon two husbands. If you are passionately focused on something, you do not take notice of anything else. And it is true that if you chase two rabbits you will not catch even one. . . . Therefore the person who is sincere about entering the divine ground of religion should follow what is taught in Śākyamuni's biography; namely, he must abandon his parents, he must abandon his wife and children, he must abandon his wealth, he must abandon his country, and he must advance to the point he can abandon himself. To put it another way, a person who is sincere about entering the divine ground of religion must abandon such concrete things as filial piety and patriotism. In addition, duty and sympathy, ethics, science, philosophy, all of these become invisible to him. . . . I am not saying that at least once everyone needs to follow Śākyamuni's example and run off to live in the mountains. You can be in business, selling fish, teaching school, or serving in the military [and still pursue this]—any work you do is fine.

> My point is that in your mind you need to stop relying on family, friends, career, nation, scholarship, knowledge, or indeed anything else. Instead you need to turn all your attention to taking refuge in the Buddha.[40]

Religion for Kiyozawa is thus not simply one concern of many held by adults. If religion is to be meaningful to an individual, it must be pursued as a personal quest. Institutional concerns and personal concerns on the level of what Kiyozawa calls "religion" are inherently mutually exclusive, a stance reminiscent of Kierkegaard.[41] Anyone who truly wants to experience religious faith must be prepared to give up all contingencies in life and devote himself to this special goal, or he will never achieve his goal. This means giving up all that society tells the individual to hold dear: family, country, wealth, knowledge, and religious affiliation as well. This is not a path that seeks negotiated compromise.

These are extremely renunciant tones for a Shin Buddhist priest. As I have mentioned, Shin evolved through the Edo period in a way that was rather extreme in its devaluation of practice. As a result, Seishinshugi created and still brings criticism for stressing self-cultivation to the point of ignoring social obligations. But this view ignores the deep roots of Buddhism as a world-renouncing religion, whose code of behavior did not preclude work in society but tended to focus on teaching and taking care of the spiritual needs of individuals. Here we recall Kiyozawa's turn to the Āgamas, the earliest of the Buddhist scriptures, in response to his frustrating efforts toward reforming society and his own denomination. Although Japanese Buddhist intellectuals were drawn to this early period of Buddhist history in general, as mentioned earlier, Kiyozawa's interest was not in history but in the Buddha's ability to leave behind everything (even his family) in pursuit of enlightened wisdom. What Kiyozawa is doing in the above quote is merely stating in more modern, rational language what the historical Buddha's life story suggests to all believers: everything an individual knows about himself that normally would be used for personal support and protection must be set aside if he is to go beyond that known identity for a new one grounded in religious truth. Kiyozawa showed his motivation to seek liberation through self-deprivation earlier in life in a period that he called "minimum possible," discussed in the introduction to the Kiyozawa translations.

A variety of scholars have constructed lists of the central tenets or concerns of Seishinshugi by alluding to the different forms of these *shugi* or *-ism* word formations used by Kiyozawa to represent principles of the movement. It would take considerable space to compare their lists, so instead I will sum up the research by distinguishing three aspects of Seishinshugi thought that generally covers its core issues: internal–personal, external–religious, and external–social.

To address the internal–personal question, we need to first examine the central importance of critical internal reflection and meditative understanding as expressed in the word *naikan*, which we saw previously in the terms *naikan-shugi* and *naikan-teki*. This notion functions to represent Kiyozawa's belief that for two basic reasons we must first seek to define who we are through meditation: We can only know the world in terms of how our minds process what we perceive, and most human suffering stems from internal causes. This is basic, traditional Buddhist psychology, but not the kind of rhetoric one normally sees in a Shin thinker. It should be noted that Kiyozawa also takes pains to point out that he rejects the argument that the outside world does not exist as expressed in the extreme interpretations of the Yogācāra school and some of the German idealist thinkers. One important aspect of this *naikan*-orientation is the value placed on subjectivity; in essence *naikan* means subjectivity clarified by reflective meditation. Kiyozawa seems to reject the authority of any ethical and political system when it is justified as objective truth without subjective confirmation. This reflective, self-oriented *naikan* position is also referenced by the terms *jiyū-shugi* 自由主義 (freedom), *shukan-shugi* (subjectivism), and *kojin-shugi* 個人主義 (individualism), all terms that reflect the same values but express changes in perspective from an individual looking inward to an individual standing among other individuals in society.

The external–religious dimension is how *naikan* individualism is balanced by two religious perspectives about the relationship of the individual to the cosmos. One is something very much like the interdependence doctrine of *dharmadhātu* found in the Huayan or Kegon tradition. Labeled by Kiyozawa as "the truth of the unity of all phenomena" (*banbutsu ittai no shinri* 万物一体の真理), he understands this to mean not only that he as an individual is utterly dependent on all sentient beings for his very existence, but also that he has responsibility for all sentient beings as well. In his words,

> Now, the myriad things in heaven and earth are my wealth, all life forms are my children. I cannot help but maintain and preserve the myriad things, and love and respect life forms. . . . I cannot allow them to suffer or experience anguish.[42]

For Kiyozawa, this is the basis of morality *and* religion, but his personal sense of that reponsibility is through the buddha Amida. This conclusion is the outcome of facing the reality that he is incapable of protecting all sentient beings as his children, and manifests as a kind of conversion moment, when he turns to Amida Buddha and asks him to take up that responsibility for him. This, then, is the second religious principle in Kiyozawa, a doctrine that scholars have labeled "absolute other-power" (*zettai tariki* 絶対他力). In Kiyozawa's explanation, this organic unity of life, what he calls the *hontai* 本体, allows freedom for the individual to think and act, but it also demands obedience of him at the same time because this *hontai* is the one and only reality. *Hontai* is also understood as buddha, another reference to buddha as impersonal *dharmadhātu*. But at the same time, the personal buddha manifest as Amida is also critical because of his vow to accept everyone, regardless of their karmic record. Liberation or the elimination of personal suffering thus has both a general, impersonal aspect and a particular, personal aspect, if we can refer to a particular buddha as something "personal." Taking refuge in the buddha and the world as buddhaness is the basis of morality and ethics for Kiyozawa; as such this act must be based on the Buddha's doctrine of egalitarian acceptance. In Kiyozawa's words:

> Spurred on by the sound of virtue coming from the focused thoughts of the one-mind of Amida Buddha, focused thoughts of one-mind begin to move within myself. This is true essence of religion, the fountainhead of morality.[43]

The third issue of concern is the Seishinshugi position concerning the relationship of the individual to society. Kiyozawa's statements in this area are utterly religious, generally both idealistic and vague in terms of what actions or even policies they suggest. It is in the area of the individual's obligations to society that Kiyozawa's statements have generated the most controversy and the most biting criticism.

It appears that Kiyozawa is adamant that truly religious persons must not lose their spiritual balance when society becomes twisted or oppressive to the individual. One salient aspect of this perspective is his deep mistrust of ethical systems. Indeed, Japanese society could hardly have been more oppressive to the individual at this time, and Kiyozawa himself suffered for it. It is worth mentioning a powerful event that happened in May 1903, the last year of Manshi's life. Fujimura Misao 藤村操 (1886–1903), an eighteen-year-old student at the elite First Higher School in Tokyo (where Uchimura had taught), felt the hopelessness of his situation so acutely that he committed suicide by jumping off the top of Kegon-no-taki, a large waterfall in Nikkō. Fujimura had been an extremely promising student of philosophy and in his suicide note alluded to a insurmountable pessimism he felt toward the world, a mood that so many other young people shared at this time that a number of them followed him in ending their life. The novelist Natsume Sōseki (1867–1916) had been Fujimura's English teacher at the school and years later wrote that Fujimura's suicide had been one of the causes of his own depression. Kiyozawa's health had already deteriorated significantly by this point, but it is commonly inferred that his physical condition was not the only reason why Kiyozawa's "discovery" of the power of equanimity by Śākyamuni Buddha and taught to his early disciples is of cental importance in Seishinshugi thought, as is the imperative of attaining *anjin* 安心—deep faith and doubt-resolving awareness of the power of Amida Buddha. For these served as a bulwark against a terribly stressful society, and in discussions about society Kiyozawa often resembles a reclusive arhat more than an engaged bodhisattva. In the essay entitled "Seishinshugi to kyōdō sayō" ("Seishinshugi and Common Action"), he argues against the criticism that Seishinshugi was antisocial in this way:

> Our Seishinshugi truly centers on introspection (*naikan-shugi*), but as I have said many times this does not mean that we reject the external, objective viewpoint of things. Thus when we say we do not obsess over things in the external objective world, it means that we do not agonize or get upset over the forms that these objective phenomena take.[44]

But at the same time, Kiyozawa remained defiant in his priorities.

> Seishinshugi is not for this or that society; it is not for making the state (*kokka*) the first priority. Any "system of thought" (*shugi*) that does not understand the importance of the self cannot possibly bring us the peaceful resolution we seek.[45]

Critiques of Seishinshugi

Let us now move to consider more directly the complaints and criticims of Seishinshugi from Kiyozawa's contemporaries and voices still heard in the present day. Seishinshugi engendered public criticism almost immediately. One of the most consistent came from the pages of the rival journal *Shin Bukkyō* which, as mentioned earlier, also began publication in the later Meiji period, that is, after the successful conclusion of the Sino-Japanese War in 1895. Between 1895 and 1900 government policy becomes even more supportive of both capitalism and imperialism, the country grows economically, and the mood of the nation brims with a new sense of faith in materialism and nationalism. The intellectual Buddhists who launched *Shin Bukkyō* initially envisioned an idealistic journal similar in outlook to *Seishinkai* in that it called for freedom of religious thought and freely criticized problems with institutional Buddhism. But it developed into a forum that sought to redefine Buddhism as merely an intellectual set of ideas without monks, monasticism, temples, or institutions. In putting its weight into socially and politically liberal causes while riding the wave of nationalism, *Shin Bukkyō* begins to take on something of a nationalist-Marxist polemic against Buddhist forms of mysticism, such as the *naikan-shugi* advocated by Kiyozawa. In the same volume of *Shin Bukkyō* published in 1902, Sakaino Kōyō 境野黄洋 (1871–1933) and Hanada Shuho 花田衆甫 both have articles attacking Seishinshugi.[46] Sakaino somehow links it with the thought of Nietzsche, writing that both are having a negative effect on society. He titles his essay, "Ruijaku shisō no ryūkō [Niitche-shugi to Seishinshugi]" (The Popularity of Weak Thought: Nietzsche-ism and Seishinshugi), complaining that both weakened the nation by urging an emotional faith. Taking an indirect swipe at Kiyozawa who was extremely ill at this time, Sakaino says "the religion that we advocate is not a religion of the sick but a religion of normal people" and "religion that cannot follow along with the general education of the times is religion that is confrontational and unhealthy." He labels Seishinshugi and Nietsche's ideas as "religions for the weak and ignorant," and as "resignationism" (*akirame-shugi* アキラメ主義), a reference to the fact that Kiyozawa himself used the term *akirame-shugi* to describe his attitude toward past events. Kiyozawa is allowed to respond in the same journal, and two months later counters that while both Seishinshugi and the Shin Bukkyō movement may state that equality and social discrimination exist simultaneously, Seishinshugi puts their weight on equality and Shin Bukkyō puts theirs on discrimination.

In effect, Kiyozawa was critcizing the Shin Bukkyō group for affirming social inequalities, but the nature of the Seishinshugi movement was such that it repeatedly found itself confronting the same rhetorical outcry. Complaints like those of Sakaino are often reflected in later critical assessments of Seishinshugi, yet one is nevertheless struck by the fact that Kiyozawa's approach is still debated in Japan today and has thus remained compelling among students of religion and philosophy in today's very different societal context. While some criticism may be associated with sectarianism, the complaints that Seishinshugi abrogates its social obligations do have weight and are worthy of serious consideration. Indeed some members of the Seishinshugi movement itself have voiced similar concerns.

Consider the following passage by Kiyozawa from *Seishinkai:*

> When one interacts with things and people outside oneself, he should seek to increase the happiness of both self and others. This is not rejected by Seishinshugi, but rather something we welcome. Seishinshugi thus is not a practice of renunciation and escape. Nor is it a diffident practice. Cooperating to aid the happiness and welfare of society and the nation is encouraged within Seishinshugi. . . . The sufferings that I endure do not come from the actions of others, but from illusions within me. . . . [Thus] the first issue in the functionality (*jikkō shugi* 実行主義) of Seishinshugi is believing in the importance of searching for full satisfaction within one's own mind. And this begins by not suffering as a result of having to follow things or people outside oneself, and [continues in] the interaction and work done together with people to increase the happiness of mankind. One carries with them both complete freedom and absolute submission; this is how one can sweep away his pain and suffering.[47]

Although he does not explain what he means when he speaks of "absolute submission" and with this line he ends his statement, elsewhere he uses the same word for submission or obedience, *fukujū* 服従, to indicate the decision to give in to society's pressures, as in the case of the Imperial Rescript on Education. For example, the following editorial statement by his staff in the second issue of *Seishinkai* has often been cited by Kiyozawa's critics.

> Recently there have been calls here to recall the Imperial Rescript on Education. These have arisen among one group of educators. But this would truly be inconvenient at the moment.[48]

It is Kiyozawa's acceptance, or more accurately his lack of resistance, to politics and social demands that some see as an abrogation of any social responsibilty to take a stand against immoral public policies. But such a reading reflects a misunderstanding about Kiyozawa's mission. As in his statement above about the need to abandon all known relationships, Kiyozawa is nearly always speaking on the level of what he calls "the first issue in the functionality" of Seishinshugi; that is, to clarify one's own personal religious stance toward oneself and the world. This is not a plea for Shin Buddhism to turn its own *raison d'être* on its head and demand all its clergy become lifelong anchorites. He is simply saying that every religious person has an obligation to clarify his or her own spiritual stance before they can expect to be functional in any meaningful capacity in the world. It is the *seishin*, the mind, that first needs to be put in order; hence the name Seishin-shugi.

This same attitude can be seen in his rather extreme inference about the significance of the impossibility of ethical correctness, represented here in the translation in Chapter 4, "Negotiating Religious Morality and Common Morality."[49] It is a radical conclusion similar to that of Kierkegaard that the pursuit of ethics leads to religious awakening, not through success but through failure. But although his argument is compelling for its spiritual honesty, because his concerns remain limited to religious matters, it leaves undone the work of developing ethical values after religious awakening. Freely admitting that one is incapable of fulfilling his obligation to care for other life forms remains a religious statement, but that leaves out the question of how to behave properly in a social sense. Here Kiyozawa is silent, disturbingly silent for many. Even on the question of what ethical guidelines one should use when he has already completed the quest for personal spiritual confirmation, Kiyozawa tends to pull back. Thus, we have also essays with titles such as "Rinri ijō no an'i" 倫理以上の安慰 ("Peace Beyond Ethics"),[50] "Rinri ijō no konkyo" 倫理以上の根拠 ("Authority Beyond Ethics").[51] Among all his writings on ethics, however, it is "Negotiating Religious Morality and Common Morality," which most often is cited for his ethical viewpoint, for here he takes the remarkable position of accepting our inability to either discern or implement proper moral choice, and therefore the entire purpose of all moral schemes is to lead us to the path of other-power, that is, the acceptance of the power of the infinite. As many have pointed out, it is important to keep in mind that in taking this radical stand and refusing to indulge in any principled discussion of a philosophical basis for ethics or morality, Kiyozawa reflects the intense politicization of ethics and religion at the time, as stated above. Sueki has suggested that Kiyozawa was directly (and perhaps adamantly) responding to Inoue Tetsujirō's ideological campaign to valorize only religions that contributed to proper social ethics *as defined by the government*.[52] Inoue's position represented both an assertion of the politicization of ethics as natural and therefore normative as well as the denegration of religion into a tool for implementing social policy, even social engineering. In effect, Kiyozawa is saying "I answer to a higher power."

It is true that Kiyozawa did not openly oppose the implementation of the Imperial Rescript on Education. But to read into this any insincerity or lack of concern about proper behavior and its link to education policy is unconvincing. One need only recall the fact that at one point he threw himself so totally into precisely this kind of institutional reform that he ruined his health, his tuberculosis ultimately causing his death at the young age of forty-two. To the complaint that Kiyozawa was too accepting of society's ethical status quo, one can counter that his refusal to engage in any dialog on this issue was his own way of maintaining a subversive stance toward that very ideology. Reading any of Kiyozawa's later essays on the subject of morality and ethics, such as the one included here, reveals his consistent refusal to accept the authority of any ethical system, implicating the ethical systems in his own surroundings, both in secular society and in contemporary Buddhism. Sueki correctly identifies this move as anything but escapist, characterizing it instead as a successful reversal of roles for Buddhism that enabled it to go on the offensive after years of oppressive victimization at the hands of the Meiji government.

But the resultant lack of formulation of any ethical value system or principle of engagement with society remains a problem for Seishinshugi. In the absence of any concrete critique of inequity and injustice, Seishinshugi could easily be read as an affirmation of those very problems. Indeed Kiyozawa did write that "if something happens to one's country, one may march to war with a rifle on his shoulder," expressing a *Bhagavadgītā*-like acceptance of every aspect of the human condition. This limitation is significant, and calls for a new response from within Shin, if not all of Japanese Buddhism, to face the fact that religious institutions are also political institutions, and that even the model of "king's law–buddha's law" never absolved them from political responsibility. It has been just over a century since the death of Kiyozawa, and the legacy of Seishinshugi has produced some breathtaking results directly within Shin thought and indirectly within religious discourse in Japan as a whole over that century. We look forward to the next movement that will stand on the shoulders of the freedom of thought engendered by Kiyozawa's approach and make a similar contribution in the next century.

Writing in 1921, Shimaji Daitō, a scholar associated with the Nishi Honganji branch of Shin, declared that the two most important new movements in Japanese Buddhism in the modern period were

Seishinshugi and "Nichirenshugi 日蓮主義" as seen in Takayama Chogyū 高山樗牛 (1871–1902). By the term *Nichirenshugi* he meant a modern adaptation of the thought of the thirteenth-century monk Nichiren and his interpretations of the *Lotus Sutra*. Shimaji pointed to this because Nichiren's religious values influenced the formation of a host of new religious movements in the twentieth century, the most famous being Sōka Gakkai. Both Shin and Nichiren Buddhism are known for their relatively strong sense of sectarianism *and* their fierce political independence from the state. The leaders of Sōka Gakkai are famous for going to jail to resist government policies during World War II, yet the intensity of its sectarianism is also legendary. Although Seishinshugi has drawn criticism today for not advancing an antigovernment agenda in the face of rising fascism, on the other hand there is ample evidence to suggest that the countersectarian streak in Seishinshugi provided a major impetus for expanding the appreciation of Shinran as a religious thinker outside Shin circles, as well as opening the door to bringing nontraditional religious texts and ideas (*geten* 外典) not only into sectarian Shin Studies but into Buddhist Studies as well. A recent discovery that the idealistic teacher called simply "K" in the novel *Kokoro* by Natsume Sōseki, published in 1914, was probably based on Kiyozawa Manshi is yet another confirmation of how wide the impact of this movement was among the educated in Japan just as the country was painfully modernizing.[53] Although Japan is now well into its postmodern condition, the host of new writing on Kiyozawa and other Seishinshugi thinkers shows that many of the issues discussed in these essays are still thought-provoking in Japan. It is our hope that this volume will contribute to a consideration of them outside Japan as well.

Notes

1. There are various studies on the religious role of the emperor in the construction of Japanese nationality in the nineteenth century. Among others, see Maruyama 1974, and Yasumaru 1988.

2. Is it possible that the shapers of the "modern" policies of the early Meiji government envied the egalitarian, even democratic, values that pervaded Buddhist philosophical rhetoric and were thus looking for a way to usurp those values by recasting them as "Japanese" while denigrating Buddhism as outdated and non-Japanese?

3. The *kokugaku* or National Learning movement was a nativist study with aesthetic roots that later blossomed into full-blown political ideology. See Nosco 1990, Harootunian 1988, etc.

4. Ketelaar 1990 and Jaffe 2001.

5. Totman 1993, 462. Totman is following the research of Harootunian (1988), and in his summary of Atsutane's views and influence, does not even mention his stand against Buddhism.

6. The "land of *yomi*" or *yomi no kuni* (黄泉国), also *yomotsu kuni* were names for the land where the dead reside in pre-Buddhist Japanese religion. It appears in both the *Manyōshū* and the *Kojiki*.

7. *Mitogaku* refers to the intellectual culture formed in the Mito domain from the time of Tokugawa Mitsukuni (1628–1700). It developed a somewhat materialistic approach to education and social policy that sought to improve society by reducing the presence of Buddhism. In the course of the Tokugawa period, the vast majority of the approximately 2,400 Buddhist temples in the Mito domain in 1666 were destroyed, sold, or converted to private use. See Ketelaar 1990, 46–54, who draws on Koshmann 1987.

8. Discussed in Totman 1993, 457–60. See Fujita Yūkoku's essays *Kannō wakumon* 勧農或問 and *Chishima ibun* 千島遺文.

9. Paraphrased from *Fujiwara Seika sensei gyōjō* 藤原惺窩先生行状, of unknown authorship, as quoted by Kashiwahara 1995–2000, 3:304–05.

10. Ōjōden 往生伝 are collections of stories of individuals who achieved rebirth in the Pure Land as a result of piety, obervances, or disciplined praxis. See Blum 2007.

11. Coming from Mencius's take on Confucius, Wang Yangming stressed an innate understanding (*ryōchi* 良知) in mankind and the value of its expression in each individual through spontaneous action (*chigyō gōitsu* 知行合一). Japanese *yōmeigaku*, or studies of Wang Yangming, followed the interpretive line taken by Li Zhi 李贄 (Jpn. Rishi; 1527–1602), who attacked the Zhu Xi thinkers for stifling desire. In Japan, this position blended with the National Learning stance that affirmed the value of emotion that included desire as natural and good, resulting in a doctrine of morality of emotion. Nakae Tōju, for example, resigned his position in Iyo (Ehime Prefecture) on the pretext that he needed to see his mother in Ōmi (Shiga Prefecture), and lost his official rank for it. He then spent the rest of his life studying the Confucian classic on filial piety, and was known for his assertion that "filial piety is illuminated by divine light." As Buddhist doctrine doubts the validity of any form of knowledge or emotion because it may be tinged with desire for self-aggrandizement, on an intellectual level these differences were significant.

12. There had been some degree of administrative structure along these same lines for some time, particularly in the Shinshū and Nichrenshū in the medieval period. But this became codified in stages through the use of legal documents beginning from the ninth year of Kan'ei 寛永 (1632), when the Edo bakufu promulgated a decree in which all sects where instructed to list in a record book (*matsuji chō*) which temples were to be considered administrative centers, or honzan 本山, and which temples were to be considered branch centers, or matsuji 末寺, under their own administrative control. See Ishida 1984, 258. Tamamuro Fumio sees this process beginning within the bakufu

as early as the Genna era (1613–1616); see Tamamuro 1987, 40–51, where he gives some detail on the major sects.

13. The exception to this was the Jōdo-shū, which, as the personal faith of Tokugawa Ieyasu, succeeded in skirting the rules and built more than 1,150 new temples in the seventeenth century alone. See Ishida 1984, 258.

14. Ritsuryō 律令 refers to a legal code borrowed from China that the Japanese government used to regulate, among other things, Buddhist monks and temples.

15. Kashiwahara 1995–2000, 3:306.

16. Yoshida 1992.

17. Shimaji 1969, 387. Shimaji was and still is a respected scholar of Japanese religious history and Jōdo Shinshū in particular. He was ordained in the Nishi Honganji tradition, the son of the progressive thinker Shimaji Mokurai.

18. See Sekimori 2005.

18a. In *Tokugawa Religion* (2nd ed., 1985), Robert Bellah examines the modern dimensions of Ishida Baigan's thought and compares it with Weber's study of the role of Protestantism in the modernization of Europe.

19. The *dharmadhātu* refers to all existence, the entire universe, both as a unity and in all its multiplicity.

20. As James Dobbins has pointed out, the concept of "religious studies" in Japan prior to World War II was basically "modern" Buddhist Studies, meaning traditional Buddhist Studies with the addition of using Sanskrit and Tibetan materials to augment the Chinese canon for the first time. See Dobbins 2006.

21. *Kyōiku chokugo* 教育勅語, translation by Dairoku Kikuchi, *Japanese Education* (London: John Murray Publishers, 1909), reprinted in Earhart 1997, 237.

22. Sueki 2004a, 28.

23. Contained in Inoue 2003, volume 1.

24. Contained in Ueda 1990.

25. See Honda 1995, 228–30.

26. Imadate Tosui 今立吐酔 was one of the first Japanese to graduate from an American university, in his case the University of Pennsylvania in 1879. His translation of Olcott's *Buddhist Catechism* was called *Bukkyō mondō* (Buddhist Dialogs). In collaboration with D. T. Suzuki, he produced the first translation of the *Tannishō* in 1928, published by the Eastern Buddhist Society in their journal.

27. Hirai eventually ended up associate with Unitarianism and leading his own meditation seminars. For the most detailed study of Hirai and his role in the attempted globalization of Japanese Buddhism, see Yoshinaga 2007.

28. Kashiwahara 1995–2000, 3:400–01.

29. The name was changed again in 1903 to Shin Bukkyōto Dōshikai 新仏教徒同志会. See Kashiwahara 1995–2000, 3:416–18.

30. The Shin sect was unusual in that it publicly recognized married clergy as the norm, except during training, from its inception in the thirteenth century.

31. Kashiwahara 1995–2000, 3:391–92.

32. The Three Treasures 三宝, or *triratna,* defined as buddha, dharma, and sangha, or the founder, his teachings, and the religious community, was a common way in which the religion identified itself.

33. Known as the *Bongaku shinryō* 梵学津梁, this collection totaled one-thousand fascicles.

34. From a document entitled *Kōnyo Shōnin goikun gyosho,* in SSZ 5:777a. Quoted in Fukuma 1986. Fukuma gives a detailed description of the roots of this idea in Shinshū writings from the first half of the nineteenth century.

35. *Shinshū shinjiten,* 312.

36. These are three traditions or "schools" of religious practice and study that all stem from Hōnen and for that reason follow his hermeneutic of selecting the three sutras in the subsequent note as the most authoritative. The Jōdo 浄土 school or sect takes Hōnen to be its founder, and dates itself from his "conversion" to the Pure Land religious perspective in 1175. The Shin 真 school or sect takes Shinran as its founder, and the Ji 時 school or sect was founded by Ippen 一遍 (1239–1289).

37. There are hundreds of sutras that mention Amida Buddha, but the three that have held orthodoxy in Japan since they were identified by Hōnen are the *Muryōjukyō* (*Wuliangshou jing; Larger Sukhāvatīvyūhasūtra*), the *Amidakyō* (*Amituofo jing; Smaller Sukhāvatīvyūhasūtra*), and the *Kanmuryōjukyō* (*Guanwuliangshoujing*)

38. The *gakuryō* 学寮 were essentially boarding schools for novices. The *gakuryō* of the Nishi Honganji was officially disbanded in 1655 by the *bakufu* who intervened because a serious conflict had developed within the school, and thereafter the Nishi Honganji seminary was instead called a *gakurin* 学林. In Higashi Honganji, the name *gakuryō* remained, but the school was renamed Takakura Gakuryō after it moved to a street in Kyoto called Takakura. See *Shinshū shinjiten,* 72, and 347.

39. KMZ 6:3.

40. KMZ 6:76–78.

41. For a detailed look into the similarities between the thought of Kierkegaard and Kiyozawa, including consideration of evidence to suggest that Kiyozawa may have been influenced by Kierkegaard, see Blum 2003.

42. KMZ 6:12.

43. KMZ 6:13–14.

44. 精神主義と共同作用, at KMZ 6:97.

45. KMZ 6:92.

46. *Shin Bukkyō* 3:2, published in February, 1902. Hanada's title was "Hai-Seishinshugi: 'Seishinshugi' wo nanjite Kōkōdō shoshi no kotae wo nozomu 排精神主義:「精神主義」を難じて浩々洞諸氏の答を望む" (Disposing of Seishinshugi: Criticizing "Seishinshugi" and seeking answers from the members of Kōkōdō). See Serikawa 1989, 205–11. Kiyozawa uses the term *akirame-shugi* to mean his group does not cling to the past; see *KMZ* 6:91. It is also worth noting that Uchimura Kanzō, Takayama Chogyū, and Kimura Takatarō were also categorized with Kiyozawa for advocating "sick religion." It is also interesting that while Sakaino equates Kiyozawa with Nietzsche,

Shimaji Daitō (1969, p. 388) sees an affinity between Nietzsche and Takayama Chogyū, and sees instead something of Tolstoy in Kiyozawa.

47. KMZ 6:5.

48. *Seishinkai* 1:2, 1901, from the "Tōkyō-dayori" (Report from Tokyo) section.

49. KMZ 6:148–58.

50. KMZ 6:121.

51. KMZ 6:132.

52. Sueki 2002, 16–18.

53. "Sōseki no *Kokoro:* K no moderu" in *Mainichi shinbun,* August 18, 2006, Osaka edition, p. 7.

Kiyozawa Manshi

At age 29 (Courtesy of Saihōji, dated 1892)

Chapter 2

Kiyozawa Manshi
Life and Thought

Mark L. Blum

Kiyozawa Manshi 清沢満之 (1863–1903) lived a short life of only forty or forty-one (in Japanese counting) years, and lived it at a time of tremendous upheaval in Japan and especially within Japanese Buddhism. A deeply religious individual, he appears to us today as a natural leader who responded to the confusion of his age with energy and daring, attempting to carve out new expressions of Buddhism that would ensure its survival in an often hostile political environment.

He was born into a low-ranking samurai family as Tokunaga Mannosuke 徳永満之助, intially shortened to Tokunaga Manshi. His father had been the leader of a platoon of foot soldiers (*ashigaru*) but lost that position when the Meiji Restoration of 1867 eliminated privileges for samurai. In 1888, Manshi married Kiyozawa Yasu 清沢やす. Because the Kiyozawa family lacked a son, Manshi was adopted into his wife's family and took their surname, a common practice in Japan. His father was an admirer of the Zen school, particularly its disciplined approach to practice, but his mother was equally devoted to Jōdo Shinshū or the Shin school of Buddhism as a member of the Ōtani or Higashi Honganji branch. Ordained as a priest at the age of fifteen, Kiyozawa received financial support from the Honganji both for his high school studies in Kyoto and then at Tokyo Imperial University. Faced with two experiences of local school closings as a teenager, he later admitted that his chief attraction to joining the priesthood was the scholarship money the branch supplied to its dedicated students.

Kiyozawa entered what is now the University of Tokyo in 1882, and the next year moved from the Preparatory Division to the College of Letters, majoring in Western philosophy. He studied under Ernest Fenollosa (1853–1908), a scholar of Asian art from Salem, Massachusetts who nevertheless taught politics, philosophy, and business at the University of Tokyo from 1878 to 1886. Kiyozawa was initially devoted completely to philosophy and was accepted into the graduate program after graduation in 1887, intending to become professor of philosophy at the University of Tokyo. But only one year later he was asked by Higashi Honganji to leave school and become principal of their middle school in Kyoto, and he complied. Prior to this time he served as secretary of the Tetsugakkai 哲学会 (Philosophical Association) founded by Inoue Enryō 井上円了 (1858–1919), a fellow recipient of an Ōtani-branch scholarship five years his senior who studied in the same department. Kiyozawa also edited the first five issues of its journal. These are among the very first Japanese writings on Western philosophy, and Kiyozawa's 1892 monograph *Shūkyō tetsugaku gaikotsu* 宗教哲学骸骨 (Skeleton of a Philosophy of Religion), reflects the trend among his fellow students to blend Western and Buddhist philosophy by arguing for a rationalized view of Buddhist thought. This work was translated into English and distributed at the World Parliament of Religions held in Chicago in 1893, and predates Inoue's own similar attempt, Bukkyō tetsugaku keitōron 仏教哲学系統論 (Treatise on the Lines of Buddhist Philosophy), published in 1899.

Scriptural Orientation

Kiyozawa returned to Kyoto in 1888 at the age of twenty-six as a brilliant and confident young scholar in his new assignment as principal. That year he married and quickly established himself as a rising talent in the Buddhist world. But only two years later, after witnessing the depressed mood pervading Higashi Honganji and the psychological weakness of the students in his school, he resigned as principal. His response to the sense of despair in that environment was to throw himself into a lifestyle of extreme asceticism, which he labeled "minimum possible," using the English term. Spending less and less time with his family, Kiyozawa embarked on a path of self-discipline that limited his diet to a mixture of pine resin, buckwheat flour, and water. Soon thereafter he contracted pulmonary tuberculosis, from which he never fully recovered.

Throughout the 1890s, never fully in good health, Kiyozawa found himself attracted most profoundly to three works that are highly unusual for someone of his background, that is to say, as a priest in the Shin tradition, because by the end of the Edo period both the Higashi and the Nishi Honganji had established a rather extreme doctrinal position for a Buddhist order in claiming that liberation comes only from reliance on the intervention of Amida Buddha, not from personal spiritual achievement. Unprecedented in choosing works outside the Mahāyāna Buddhist canon, Kiyozawa made the unexpected choice of these three works to define his religious perspective: (a) the Agongyō 阿含経 (Skt. Āgama), or the scriptures of early Indian Buddhism, (b) the *Discourses* of the Greek philosopher Epictetus, and (c) the *Tannishō* 歎異抄 by Yuien, a disciple of Shinran. Any critical study of Kiyozawa would demand a detailed look at the religious and philosophical thought in all three of these works, a task that will have to be deferred to another venue. But a few words about each are in order, both because they were an inspirational source of Kiyozawa's faith and because in finding inspiration in them he was departing from tradition. When we remember that Kiyozawa's project was, at its core, an attempt to reinvigorate Shin Buddhism, the choice of these particular works is remarkable in that it shows that he was seeking a paradigm entirely different from the way Shin Buddhism was taught in the seminaries.

Agongyō

The Agongyō (Ch. *ahan jing*, a transliteration of the Sanskrit term *āgama*) are Chinese translations of the earliest strata of sutra literature traditionally ascribed to the Sarvāstivāda school, much of which corresponds to what is found in the Nikāyas of the Pāli canon used in the Theravāda school. Extant only in Chinese and Tibetan translation, this Sanskrit-based sutra material had long been a part of the Chinese canon, but largely ignored in East Asia due to the overwhelming influence of Mahāyāna Buddhism there. The Mahāyāna sutras frequently refer to the beliefs and practices of non-Mahāyāna monks as misguided or even shallow, and these Agongyō are the scriptures from the pre-Mahāyāna period. Thus, early in Chinese Buddhism the texts in the Agongyō corpus were designated as only of a preparatory nature, of interest only to scholars. As mentioned in Chapter 1, however, Kiyozawa lived at a time when the Japanese Buddhist tradition was rocked with a new appreciation for the early Buddhism represented in the Agongyō that previously had been dismissed as primitive and inferior. The Shin tradition was certainly no different in this, and thus Kiyozawa's embrace of early Buddhism was not something he would have learned from Honganji religious education or culture.

In this reverence for the Agongyō, Kiyozawa seems particularly impressed with three things: the psychological insight into the core Buddhist problem of *avidyā* (spiritual ignorance), the personal relationship between the Buddha and his disciples, and the commitment of the disciples to sacrifice nearly everything that is otherwise dear to them for the sake of pursuing the path: family, patriotic duty, ethical standards, even philosophy itself. There also is a concreteness typically missing from Mahāyāna texts in these early sutras, wherein the Buddha addressed everyday problems and psychological doubts expressed by his students, which are resolved through dialogue and reflection.

Epictetus

Already holding a strong respect for the intellectual honesty of Socrates, particularly his fearlessness in the face of death, Kiyozawa was strongly moved when he read the Stoic Epictetus. Epictetus (~50–~135 C.E.) had been a slave as a young man and was physically handicapped from the experience, and yet he was undaunted by those limitations in his dogged pursuit of truth, something that appears to have been particularly appealing to Kiyozawa. Epictetus firmly believed that pain has its origins in the unenlightened aspect of the self, and only can be relieved by a corresponding growth in the enlightened aspect of the self. According to the *Discourses* of Epictetus, the responsibility for doing so rests with the individual. This position is of a piece with the approach to *avidyā* presumed in the Agongyō and later elaborated in the early Buddhist commentarial literature known as Abhidharma. Many see Kiyozawa's esteem of Epictetus to be representative of his study of Western philosophy as a whole, but it also should be noted that like the Agongyō, Epictetus's Discourses represents a powerful affirmation of the values of cultivating discipline and personal responsibility.

Tannishō

The *Tannishō* is the only work among the three to come from the Shin school of Buddhism. This text appears to have languished in the storehouse of the Honganji until the fifteenth century when Rennyo (1415–1499) made a personal copy and brought it into Shin discourse. Indeed Rennyo's copy is the oldest extant manuscript of the *Tannishō*. Rennyo famously added a colophon to his copy of the text in which he wrote that the *Tannishō* was a most precious text of the Shin tradition but those who are not "karmically ready" should not be allowed to see it. Some have inferred from this statement and Rennyo's stature that the *Tannishō* enjoyed only limited circulation in the Sengoku and Edo periods, and was only studied by Shin clergy, but this is far from certain. In fact, two major studies of the *Tannishō* were published in the late Edo period.[1] There are indications, however, that the *Tannishō* was generally unknown in Japanese society, even to most Shin believers, at the start of the Meiji period. Kiyozawa's turn to the *Tannishō* as the representative work for knowing Shinran's doctrine signaled in some sense a rejection of Shin thought as defined by the Honganji seminaries, which had built their curricula around the study of the Pure Land patriarchs, Shinran's *Kyōgyōshinshō*, and Rennyo's letters. Kiyozawa was so convinced of the crucial relevance of the *Tannishō* that he decided to have it published it serially in the journal *Seishinkai* (see below), creating discussion of its ideas in the general public for the first time.

Like the Agongyō, the *Tannishō* often takes the form of a dialogue, which is largely missing from the *Kyōgyōshinshō*. And again, like the Āgamas, it reflects a religious attitude where people are expected to practice, not in monasteries, but as individuals. Because Shinran's magnum opus, the *Kyōgyōshinshō* is written in kanbun 漢文 (classical Chinese) and filled with doctrinal jargon, throughout the Edo period, Shin was learned primarily through the letters of Rennyo, which were written in Japanese. Through the efforts of Kiyozawa, which were continued in the next generation by preachers like Chikazumi Jōkan and Akegarasu Haya as well as philosophers like Soga Ryōjin, the *Tannishō* came into such prominence that it eventually replaced Rennyo's letters as the core Japanese-language text for transmitting Shin thought.

Finally, a word is in order about the similarity and symbolic value of these three texts. All three works reflect an eminently pragmatic or praxis-centered approach to religion. That is, they employ a dialogic rhetorical style in which specific problems are addressed, giving them a concreteness often missing from the Mahāyāna sutra literature. This shows Kiyozawa's turn away from the mythical and metaphysical in religion to the psychological, and may be seen as reflecting a kind of modernism about his thinking that parallels a similar move in Kierkegaard.[2] It also is clear that these three works in some way represent the three geographies of religious authority for Kiyozawa: the Āgamas, being the bedrock scriptures on which all forms of Buddhism stand, represent Buddhism as a whole; the *Discourses* of Epictetus stand for the truth embedded in Western philosophy; and the *Tannishō* is Kiyozawa's representative text for Shinran and the Shin tradition. Looked at even more broadly, in these three works we have the religious cultures of Asia (the East), Europe (the West), and Japan.

Educational and Church Reform Efforts

Kiyozawa embarked on two publishing efforts in the late 1890s that were to have far reaching influence in Japan as a whole. First is a journal he launched in 1896 called *Kyōkai jigen* 教界時言 (*Timely Words for the Religious World*), which was dedicated to educational reform in general and educational reform of the Higashi Honganji specifically. Supported by Inoue Enryō, Nanjō Bun'yū, Inaba Masamaru 稲葉昌丸 (1865–1944), and Murakami Senshō, he created a national sensation by first submitting a petition to the denomination's administrative officials demanding openness and freedom in their curriculum, and then encouraging students at Ōtani-sponsored schools throughout the country to circulate their own petitions in support of his goals of democratically electing administrative officials and the promotion of objective, "scientific" principles in the study of Buddhist doctrine and culture. At one point, 2,500 supporters attended one of Kiyozawa's lectures in Kyoto. Many who were working in the Higashi Honganji administration quit their posts to join Kiyozawa's movement, further weakening the position of the temple authorities. Kiyozawa published a remarkably forthright piece in the journal at this time that lambasts monks for their obsequiousness before officials in the government and in the temple hierarchy, called "Bukkyōsha nanzo jichō sezaru ya" 仏教者盍自重乎 and is translated here under the title "Why Do Buddhists Lack Self-Respect?"

Needless to say, the journal was read by Buddhists in all denominations, and elevated Kiyozawa's celebrity. I think it is fair to say that the *Kyōkai jigen*, despite its short life, signaled an important turning point in what we might call the "modernization" of Japanese Buddhism. That is, it provided a public forum for protest and negotiating power set up outside a political structure that appealed to the populace as a whole to support and justify its pursuit of reform. And not only were these reform efforts based on essentially Western ideals of freedom of religious expression and academic freedom in the study of religion, they also presumed the Western notion that this kind of "scientific" study of religion would only strengthen it.

Ultimately, Higashi Honganji responded by sacking its head administrator, who had long resisted Kiyozawa's reform program, and then by dismissing Kiyozawa and a number of his supporters from the clergy. Physically weak and psychologically depressed from the ordeal, Kiyozawa retreated to his home temple in November 1897, although the journal continued until April the following year. Over the next two years he continued his study of the three writings mentioned above.

Two-Truth Theory (真俗二諦論)

Between 1899 and 1901, Kiyozawa undertook four projects that also proved to be of lasting significance: He became the private tutor to the future abbot of Higashi Honganji, he was asked to create and head the new Shinshū University, he took up leadership at a dormitory called Kōkōdō for students of his who wished to follow his values and lifestyle, and he began his second major publishing effort by launching a new journal called *Seishinkai* 精神界 to propagate the values of a "movement" he called Seishinshugi 精神主義 (see Chapter 1). There is a host of intriguing ideas associated with this movement, but basically it is defined by Kiyozawa's religious orientation derived from his three scriptural sources discussed above. Kiyozawa and his disciples lived in their "cave" (Kōkōdō literally means "capacious cave") in a rented house in Tokyo in a disciplined manner with meager physical comforts, working hard to follow his commitment to a humble, dedicated religious existence that is nonetheless dominated by critical readings of texts. They hung a sign that read "Without bitterness toward heaven, without seeking from people" (ten o uramazu, hito nimo motomezu 天を怨まず、人にも求めず),[3] and they struggled for personal liberation through meditation and study. Best known of the committed followers were Akegarasu Haya, Tada Kanae 多田鼎 (1875–1937), and Sasaki Gesshō 佐々木月樵 (1875–1926), with Soga Ryōjin joining after Kiyozawa had left. Many more young intellectuals of the day participated in their activities on a limited basis, such as Nishida Kitarō 西田幾多郎 (1870–1945), Tokiwa Daijō 常盤大定 (1870–1945), Akanuma Chizen 赤沼智善 (1884–1937), and Yamabe Shūgaku 山辺習学 (1882–1944).

The content of the journal proved extremely lively and was an instant success among intellectuals in Japan. It did not express only one point of view, and there are many instances of difference of opinion among its contributors, such as the rift that evolved between Kiyozawa and his elder brother in religion Inoue Enryō when the latter began to argue for the acceptance of nationalism and nationalistic notions of ethics. It is precisely in the area of ethics that I will present one of Kiyozawa's most famous and certainly his most controversial position, a position that we might call a "religious deconstruction of ethics."

As any student of Buddhism knows, since Nāgārjuna, Mahāyāna Buddhism has based itself on the doctrine of two truths, although the basic concept predates Mahāyāna. In this theory, Nāgārjuna's transcendent mystical realm of truth is labeled as *paramārtha-satya* (Jpn. *shintai* 真諦), or ultimate truth, represented by *nirvāṇa* and *śūnyatā* (emptiness) and essentially unknowable by the normal consciousness of sentient beings. Instead what we can know is the *saṃvṛti-satya* (Jpn. *zokutai* 俗諦), the worldly or accessible truth, which includes the Buddhist teachings. The Dharma itself is both, and in that sense, the two truths are not separate, but ultimately one and the same. But as we tend to think we know things rationally, we can only be expected to know the aspect of this single truth that is rationally comprehensible, and that is defined as worldly truth. This hermeneutic was used by many Shin thinkers in the early to middle Meiji period as a way to rationalize their religious beliefs with the demands of Meiji society, specifically the government push to have everyone commit to strengthening Japan in the face of foreign invasions, both political and cultural. The standard view, however, was to assert that the Mahāyāna truth represented the highest truth and the political demands of society represented the worldly truth.

But Kiyozawa instead saw things in religious terms. The politicized government push for ethics instruction is the background to his discussion here on the instructional value of considering the Buddhist teachings on worldly truth in the context of ethics or morality. In his unique perspective, far distant from his contemporaries, Kiyozawa identifies man's relationship to the ultimate truth as one of faith, or in Pure Land rhetoric, tariki (other-power). He then identifies what he sees as two stages in the operation of worldly truth: prior to faith and after faith. Taking a hermeneutic position very close to that of Nāgārjuna, Kiyozawa asserts that seen from the perspective of tariki or faith realized, the worldly truth of Buddhism prior to the "attainment" of faith is only meaningful as a means to realizing tariki.

Critiques of Kiyozawa's Ethical Standpoint

Kiyozawa's ethical position has been criticized from a variety of standpoints both during his life and after his passing. Shigaraki Takamaro, for example, views Kiyozawa as irresponsible regarding the demands of society. He is particularly critical of a statement by Kiyozawa who, in explaining his view that ultimately the value of worldly ethics lies in their impossibility of compliance, uses the phrase "it does not matter what" (*nan demo kamawanu*) in regard to the origin or system of ethics involved. Shigaraki points out that this ignores the particulars of the situation for the individual, and insists that even in the service of attaining liberation through a breakthrough religious experience, that such moments of faith always occur within the context of history and are shaped by social forces. He asserts that in fact such moments of epiphany must come as the result of a cold, hard look at the particulars of one's value system in its social context, as it is only through the tension between the individual and society that such breakthroughs occur. Based on that presumption, Shigaraki concludes that Kiyozawa only held an idealized view of the moment of liberation that the Shin school calls *shinjin*.[4]

Shigaraki's critique, however, suffers from the fact that he does not attempt to fathom any understanding of Kiyozawa's intentionality when he said that it did not matter what an ethical system was based on. Even the mystic whose epiphany came from standing in the precise moral dilemma prescribed by Shigaraki would, at the point of transcending his conflict, jettison the constraints of whatever social system binds him. Moreover, to presume that Kiyozawa's religious awakening is somehow not orthodox Shin Buddhism because it is not contextualized in an ethically correct way, or that Kiyozawa was somehow bereft of concern for social ethics despite that fact that he lived at the politically charged time that he did, is unconvincing on its face, especially after the enormous energy and political risk he put into his reform program for the Honganji.

A more troubling criticism of Kiyozawa's stance made by Sueki Fumihiko and others is not directed at his religious understanding but instead arises from worries over the implications that others might draw from his words.[5] These writers allude to a lecture by Kiyozawa in support of the Imperial Rescript on Education. But although the views contained in that talk easily could be construed to amount to an affirmation of the various nationalistic policies of the new imperially formed government, the attribution of the Rescript-affirming statements Kiyozawa has been shown to be false by Hisaki Yukio, a writer who otherwise is quite critical of Kiyozawa on other issues.[6]

The Legacy of Kiyozawa's Educational Reforms

Jōdo Shinshū, particularly the Higashi Honganji or Ōtani branch, had a particularly pronounced effect on the modernization of Buddhist

Studies in Japan in the late ninteenth and early twentieth centuries, and Kiyozawa was instrumental in conceptualizing this new view of Buddhism as an academic discipline and its value for Japan and for Buddhism as a whole. As discussed in the previous chapter, like most Buddhist sects in Japan, the Higashi Honganji branch had been running a seminary with a fairly set curriculum since the seventeenth century that spawned, under Kiyozawa's leadership, a modern Buddhist university in 1901. Whether one regards this as the founding of a new institution or merely the reformulating of an old one, the intellectual climate at Shinshū University (later renamed Ōtani University) was significantly impacted by Kiyozawa's perspective on what would later be called the philosophy of religion.

The thinking of many of those who participated with Kiyozawa in setting up Shinshū University may be accessed through their writing in the journal Seishinkai founded by Kiyozawa, as discussed in chapter one. Many of the leading contributors to the journal, such as Nanjō Bun'yū and Sasaki Gesshō, were also on the faculty of Ōtani University. Another active contributor to the journal, Inoue Enryō, founded of what became one of the leading secular private universities in Japan, Tōyō Daigaku 東洋大学 (University of the East). It is for this reason that the writings of Kiyozawa and others in Seishinkai are also appreciated for their impact in the field of education.

Translations

The three Kiyozawa essays translated here were chosen both because they have been influential and because they each represent different aspects of his career. The first, "Why Do Buddhists Lack Self-Respect" was published in 1898 in *Kyōkai jigen* and, as discussed earlier, is an example of his efforts at institutional reform. The other two were written during the last year of his life as his health was deteriorating, and are generally viewed as something like concluding statements about topics that he had discussed numerous times earlier.

"Negotiating Religious Morality and Common Morality" came out in the May 1903 edition of *Seishinkai*, the same month that Soga Ryōjin joined the Kōkōdō and three months before Kiyozawa died. It is the last in a series of essays he produced in an attempt to clarify the ethical imperative of religion, and Shin in particular. Knowing he had little time left, it is almost entirely devoid of political compromise, despite the political climate of a time when the Buddhist community was struggling to regain its social legitimacy after decades of attenuation at the hands of the Meiji political oligarchy. By this time, the ideological war with Christianity had largely been set aside by Buddhist leaders, as both traditions faced similar pressures to conform to political demands for their compliance with the nationalistic goals of the new nation-state. Kiyozawa's radical stance asserting that the only genuine goal of religious morality must be religious understanding, and insisting that teaching secular morality and ethics was not within the purview of what made Buddhist clergy what they are was quite radical at the time, and in direct opposition to the leadership of his own sectarian institution.

Finally we have included my rendering of what is arguably Kiyozawa's most well-read religious statement. Written one week before his death in July 1903, the title he gave the piece was "This is How I Believe in the Tathāgata," but the editors of *Seishinkai* decided to rename it *Waga shinnen* 我信念, and its impact has been such that that title is still retained in parenthesis in the recently published complete works of Kiyozawa in which all original titles have been restored. This remains a signature statement of Kiyozawa today, both for its sincerity and for its human-centered, existentialist view of the religious imperative, a position many have found particularly inspiring and appropriate in postmodern society. It is another example of how deftly Kiyozawa was able to bring his personal vision and religious sensibility to the problem of the meaning of Buddhist faith in a world where Buddhist truths can no longer be taken for granted.

Notes

1. Among the surviving Edo period commentaries, most influential have been the *Tannishō kōgi* 歎異抄講義 by Kōgatsuin Jinrei 香月院深励 (1749–1817), reprinted by Gohōkan (later Hōzōkan) in 1899 and 1907, and *Tannishō monki* 歎異抄聞記 by Myōon'in Ryōshō 妙音院了祥 (1788–1842), published by Hōzōkan in 1909, both appearing around the same time as the Seishinkai discussion of the text.

2. See p. 74n41.

3. Based on a similar but slightly different line in the *Analects* of Confucius (14:37): 不怨天、不尤人, "do not resent what is natural, do not blame others."

4. Shigaraki 1998, 108–10, etc.

5. See Sueki 2002, reprinted in Sueki 2004a, and for a later treatment of Kiyozawa, see Sueki 2004b, 110–37. Cf. Fukushima 1986.

6. Hisaki 1995.

Chapter 3

Why Do Buddhists Lack Self-Respect?*

Kiyozawa Manshi

Translated by Mark L. Blum

Though a day has never passed without someone disrespecting a Buddhist monk, the situation has never been as bad as it is today.[1] While it may be true that the main cause of this is the clergy's ignorance and lack of study, it may also stem from the paucity of self-respect in their own minds.

Today's Buddhist clergy are well aware of their original responsibilities; that is, in addition to funerals and memorial services. But they avoid consideration of those duties by rationalizing that such things are beyond them. This view has twisted them such that they have become accepting of their state of lowliness and triviality. When people look down on themselves, then it follows that others will look down on them as well. Has the present situation come about purely by accident?

In the past, there were Buddhist monks who did not bow to kings.[2] And if they did not bow to kings, they would hardly feel the need to do so to lower officials. Why should the situation be any different today? How did we get to the point we are today with our clergy? When they see governors, they bow; when they see county chiefs, they bow. They bow to policemen, they bow to village leaders,

---

*This is a translation of "Bukkyōsha, ikanzo jichō sezaruya," based on the text in KMZ 7:139–44. The article was originally published in *Kyōkai jigen* 教界時言, No 15, January, 1898. Some of the paragraphs in the original are extremely long, so many of the paragraph breaks used here have been added by the translator. All notes are by the translator.

they bow to nearly anyone considered a gentleman or businessman by society. They are extremely polite, even obsequious. But they are not polite to everyone equally. The higher the status of the official, the lower their head goes. The more money someone has, the more reverential their manner. We must recognize the fact that these people are not paying respect to what is ethically proper in someone but to the person's wealth, they are not paying respect to the abilities of someone but to the person's power. How much lower can one get? In general, a mutual respect for self and others leads to politeness in human relations, and in such people there is nothing to criticize. But internally deficient in knowledge and virtue yet externally replete with the most cordial politeness, who could show admiration for the Buddhist clergy today? If [the rule that should guide them] is that one can never be too humble, where did they learn their arrogance?

These people are obsequious without being humble. Although the appearance of humility and obsequiousness may be quite similar, their essence is radically different. In contrast to a gentleman of humility who is equally humble toward everyone, the obsequious type is always markedly presumptuous toward a certain class of people. Let us imagine how we might expect a member of the Buddhist clergy to interact with his peers, for example. If someone receives a [high] rank from the administrators in the sect's headquarters, for example, he would regard it as an immeasurable honor. When clergy of such stature see other [clergy] ranked below themselves, regardless of the other's age or virtue, are there not many who treat these individuals as if they were slaves? Indeed such people are often haughty toward particular segments of society. It is important to realize that those who act servile toward one group do so because they will suddenly turn around and become insolent toward another. For that reason, [we know that] arrogance and obsequiousness spring from the same source; they only have different names. It is like the two sides of a scale: the higher one rises, the lower the other falls. The two sides move in opposite directions but their point of support is the same.

There is no comparison between people [who value such distinctions] and the humble gentlemen whose calm attitude of acceptance is displayed in lowering their heads before the wise and intelligent and their absence of arrogance toward the foolish and ignorant. Educators only respect what the world thinks of as knowledge and morality. But [traditional notions of] what we consider to be accomplished in wisdom or commendable in virtue, these are the things that we [Buddhists] should be striving for. What could possibly be the religious value of wealth and power, or the titles of nobility? [Today the clergy] lowers the dignity of the disciples of the Buddha, seeks pity from those in secular society, goes to astonishing lengths of flattery to impress others, and basically will do anything to gain someone's favor. Ah, do these saviors of the world desire to be its beggars? Do the leaders of the world want to be its slaves? Is this not an extreme lack of self-esteem? With behavior like this, what they say may sound beautiful but of what value is it? Whether the Dharma is taken seriously or disregarded depends on the person preaching it, and when these people sing the praises of Buddhism, it is tantamount to slandering it. If the way we viewed the relative importance of the Dharma had no relation to the dignity of the person [representing it], then we could put professional storytellers and actors in charge of propagating the faith. What need, then, would there be for this social class we call monks? Should we expect today's clergy to continue without reflecting on this, even a little?

But I am not yet finished. Lest my readers misunderstand me, allow me to explain further. At this point those reading this essay should be clear about the fact that my lamentations over the obsequiousness I see in the Buddhist clergy and my attempts to boost its self-respect do not in any way stem from a desire to promote a greater sense of pride or self-importance. However, arguing as I do here that it is wrong for our clergy to become too intimate with the world does not mean that I advocate that they should instead pursue the practice of focusing their minds on the contemplation of suchness and or the nature of reality while sitting in some idyllic setting enjoying moonlight drenched ivy or wind-rustled pine trees. In other words, I am not affirming a practice that has no correlation to worldly events, while remaining aloof from the world itself. This point requires some clarification.

As point of fact, Buddhists are required to live in two different worlds at the same time. What are these two worlds? One may be called the mundane, where the worldly truth (*saṃvṛti-satya*) operates. The other we may call the supramundane, the realm of the ultimate truth (*paramārtha-satya*). One is absolute, the other is relative. One is finite, the other infinite.[3] There are other ways to express this split but what matters is that one grasps the fact of this crucial distinction itself. The work of Buddhists is to benefit sentient beings in service of universal salvation, and they do this by means of transcending the worldly "dust" in their minds to view discriminations from the standpoint of equality. At the same time, they also place themselves within that worldly thinking so as to see how this equality appears from a standpoint affirming discrimination. In seeing discrimination from the standpoint of equality one therefore partakes in the enjoyment of the oneness of the *dharmadhātu*, and yet one recognizes the obvious separation existing between individual nations and societies, indeed in all human relations. How could one even compare this to a cosmopolitanism without distinctions? Therefore we must also view equality on the plane of difference. But although one may indeed recognize the reality of the myriad differences of this world, it is nonetheless imperative to rid oneself of attachments to any of them, to put aside greed and desire, and to love all people in all parts of the world. Yet this position is not an imperative arguing for an individualism that precludes equality either. Residing in equality but not being attached to it; residing in distinctions, but not being attached to them; although one may be there, he has not forgotten this world; although one may be here, he does not indulge in fame and fortune. When wisdom and compassion work side by side [in this way] without contradiction, this can be called the home ground of the Buddhist.

This may seem severe, but if one approaches things in this way, what is it that one would be unable to do? One could still bow to governors, county chiefs, policemen, village leaders, gentlemen, or businessmen—I do not see anything inappropriate in this. Bowing to such people is simply a ritual way of showing respect that is part of social discourse. One is not bowing to show respect for that person's wealth or power. And in any case, the interaction that one has with such people is only for the purpose of aiding one's efforts to benefit sentient beings in service of the goal of universal salvation. It must not be to serve one's desire for profit and renown. [The correct attitude] is thus compared to the lotus standing in muddy water, or a jewel found in the water. The more soiled the mud, the purer the flower; the dirtier the water, the brighter the jewel.[4] This is not the way things are today. Today [the Buddhist clergy] enter the soiled world soiled themselves, they throw themselves into dirtiness already dirty. And as the days grow increasingly defiled, the purity and light [within the Dharma] ultimately become impossible to see. Ah, is there someone who could throw a scoop of antiseptic on the pollution of this world of religion and thereby put an end to it? We have been waiting for quite some time for someone like this.

This disease affecting the clergy has entered a serious phase, and the great mass of monks are looking into the face of death. Could there be a simple way out of this? How regrettable that even those [in the clergy] with a modicum of learning are unable to throw off this defect, and one finds those in the world of Buddhist study and practice no less able to cast off this attitude of servility. Although they expound the lofty teachings of Kegon or Tendai, they do not attempt to cultivate those practices, assuming that those forms of praxis are impossible.[5] Although they may pick up a brush and write on the depths of Esoteric Buddhism or Zen, they do not actually engage in such contemplation, because they maintain an attitude that the mind cannot really comprehend these things. In this alienation between teachings and self, this separation between doctrine and mind, there are many whose views have become so twisted such that they accept their lowliness and triviality [as inevitable].

But although these ideas of Kegon and Tendai may be sublime, what could they be apart from our original nature? Although the meaning of the teachings in Zen and Esoteric Buddhism may be profound, what could they be apart from the One Mind?[6] If one looks for it, it is very close; but if one does not, it may be a thousand miles away. The difference between close and far is all within oneself. We can assume that when Śākyamuni was instructing someone, if the person went too far he would have restrained them, and when they had not gone far enough, he would have urged them forward. Thus, if you label something as difficult, then it will be characterized as difficult to comprehend, difficult to enter; but if you label it as easy, will it not be [similarly] characterized as easy to practice or easy to cultivate? If one affirms a [process of awakening] that is gradual, one can speak of a [bodhisattvas career] that requires three *asaṃkhyeya* (uncountable) kalpas to complete the six perfections or one hundred kalpas to acquire the marks of a buddha; yet if one affirms a [process of awakening] that is sudden, we can quote words to the effect that [enlightenment happens] in the instant of one moment of thought.[7] Seeing things as difficult today, people do not see what is easy; they understand [enlightenment] as gradual, and not as sudden. When people become pointlessly desperate like this, Buddhism is reduced to something useless, akin to offering a painting of a rice cake to someone hungry. Nothing could be more sad.[8]

Even though the number of people who study Buddhism is gradually increasing, the fact that the vitality of Buddhism is weakening day by day, month by month, can only be the result of an overall decline in the energy put into practice. In the end, truly living religious wisdom and virtue can only flow from the head and belly of someone engaged in practice.[9] There will always be some people, armed with the doctrine of the three time periods [of the Dharma], who will assert the impossibility of practice [leading to] realization. However, the doctrine of the three time periods of the Dharma is only a provisional distinction.[10] If I were a person of inferior nature, then even if I [lived in] the Age of the True Dharma it would still seem like the Age of the Latter Dharma to me. And if someone of a superior nature were [living] during the Age of the Latter Dharma, can we really say the True Dharma would be [categorically] unavailable to that person? An attachment to the three periods of the Dharma that leads to despair is certainly not the true intent of Buddhism.

I direct the above remarks not only to those affiliated with established schools such as Kegon, Tendai, esoteric Buddhism, and Zen, but for anyone who is serious in their study of Buddhist doctrine, regardless of whether they are formally ordained in any school or sect. I firmly believe in the importance of attempting to cultivate in practice that which you have studied. Otherwise, we cannot truly master the teaching and therefore cannot put it into effect. One may view this practical approach to the study of Buddhism as something like research into science by means of experimentation. Progress may seem slow, but the thoughts and imagination of such people are full of life. The [gain] may seem trivial, but there is an active functionality to it; it may seem small, but it will give you power. One can expect this kind of outlook to develop day by day, month by month, and if one takes advantages of these opportunities [for practice], the flower of the mind will slowly expand until one attains an unlimited vitality. For those who see nothing beyond research into individual words and phrases as part of an overall effort at analyzing dead words—how different is that [approach] from Zhao Kuo 趙括 (d. 260 BC) reading the books of his father?[11] I do not see one iota of pragmatic value in this.

In summary, this all-too-common shortcoming of the Buddhist clergy has unnecessarily pushed the Buddhist path to a position lofty and remote, while bringing people to a state where they conceive of themselves as obsequious creatures, all resulting in a state of even greater retrogression [for both]. This is the situation we are in, both in our attitudes toward our own practice and in what we do to assist others. One sees it in our elder clergy, one sees it in our younger clergy. The stain of this noxious attitude can be seen in a variety of different phenomena throughout the Buddhist world. The decline in Buddhism we see today stems from this problem. Looking back in time, the Buddhism of the last three hundred years has been almost a dead Buddhism. At the very least, outside the Pure Land path Buddhism [in Japan] has been dominated by interest in research and textual study. But the fact that Buddhism became this way is in no small part a result of the influence of the bad habits of Shinto and Confucianism during this same period. The level of learning in our country over the past three hundred years is beyond anything ever seen before. In Confucianism, there were people like Fujiwara Seika 藤原惺窩 (1561–1619), Hayashi Razan 林羅山 (1583–1657), Itō Jinsai 伊藤仁齋 (1627–1705), and Ogyū Sorai 荻生徂徠 (1666–1728), who dominated Confucian thought with their studies of China's classics, as well as its history and literature.[12] Their work led to the formation of interpretive schools, the banners of their learning flying in their respective directions. The major figures in Shinto learning were Yamazaki Ansai 山崎闇齋 (1618–1682), Iwagaki Matsunae 巖垣松苗 (1774–1849),[13] and Hirata Atsutane 平田篤胤 (1776–1843), and their influence can be seen throughout the land.[14] But when these teachers of Shinto and Confucian thought were not focused on poetry and literature, they emphasized philological studies, and those among them who put their energies into practice were as scarce as stars at dawn.

Most Buddhists were also seduced by this trend. They put their energies into writing and lecturing, externally debating with the Shintoists and Confucianists, internally trading arguments with Buddhists in other sects or in other branches of their own sect. The enormous effort put into this type of investigation has produced a remarkable level of precision in doctrinal research, but rarely has it meant anything beyond a rather complex probing. One sees very little creative insight into the issues considered. This is particularly obvious with regard to practice. This is why not one Kūkai 空海 (774–835), not one Saichō 最澄 (767–822), have emerged over the past three hundred years.[15] And in this period after the Meiji Restoration, when we are all in shock from political upheaval and enormous changes in the world, passing the years twisting to the left and stumbling to the right, this degenerated state of practice continues to worsen daily, now having reached the sorry state we find ourselves in today.

However, as a rule, things change after reaching a low point of decline. The type of complex religious research I have described has gradually become anathema to people in general and within some quarters of the religious one can even find conspicuous signs of a tendency to emphasize the practical aspects of Buddhism. This is precisely why we should not lose hope for the future of Japanese Buddhism, but continue to look forward to a time when a great light could shine forth again.

But whether this time [of renewal] comes sooner or later entirely depends on whether or not Buddhists today align themselves with this trend in order to confirm its future direction. How can a Buddhist not be inspired into action? May you reflect on your original duties, throw off all thoughts of servility, and make a major effort to put your teachings into practice!

The world has completed another cycle and a new year is upon us. Signs of spring are in the rivers and mountains, and the birds are returning to the tall trees from their remote abodes. I beg of you to seize the time and invite like-minded friends to join hands with us to move down the path further and further. Would that not be incredible?

> Sing with loud voice,
> warbler!
> The peak of the plum blossoms
> at my dwelling
> will not last forever[16]

Notes

1. There was a slow erosion of respect for Buddhist monks throughout the Edo period (1600–1867) as institutional Buddhism became transformed into semi-governmental bureaucracies under prodding from the Tokugawa bakufu who relied on temples for census taking and other administrative functions. Those temples that served as organs of the central government were paid a stipend for their efforts, leading to the development of a class of administrative monks within the clergy who had minimal devotion to practice. At the same time, this financial stability led to deeper integration of local temples into the communities around them and lives of their parishoners. But the legacy of this long period of the sangha's intimacy with the government was more public expression of disrespect.

2. The sociopolitical position of the sangha in its original conception was that of an institution outside society. Communities aimed at being self-sustaining, and monks were chastised for talking about politics or business. In this view, kings bow to monks, rather than vice-versa. In China, this tradition continued for some time in the south, but eventually the sangha lost its sovereignty. In Japan, the Shin and Nichiren traditions in the medieval period often ran into trouble for expressing a degree of political autonomy.

3. This distinction is based in Buddhist doctrine, where truth that we know on the basis of rational thought or insight is considered "worldly" in the sense that it is relative. The truth of the Buddhist teachings as understood through study are no less part of the realm of worldly truth. By contrast the ultimate truth is irrational, nondualistic, and counter-intuitive for ordinary people, and often is described as reflecting the world as buddhas see it. Kiyozawa's particular way of talking about the two truths usually involves his use of the terms finite and infinite as something he has brought in from Western philosophy, and those terms are generally not found in Buddhist discussions of this problematic. It also should be mentioned that at this time, the leadership of both Honganji institutions had taken a politically pressured

position that redefined "worldly truth" as including the ethical and political norms of contemporary Japanese society.

4. These are traditional metaphors for the way in which genuine spirituality emerges more easily from difficult circumstances. These are more commonly used to encourage practitioners not to let themselves be emotionally drained by difficult circumstances, but here Kiyozawa is using them self-referentially to refer to the power of humility.

5. Kegon and Tendai refer to more "mainstream" forms of Buddhism in East Asia where, in comparison with the Pure Land tradition of Buddhism, the clergy was always expected to be just as devoted to practice as to study. Indeed the model was study and then practice so that the content of one's study could be realized personally or existentially.

6. The term One Mind (*isshin* 一心) can mean different things in different contexts in East Asian Buddhism, but generally it either refers to a transcendent or cosmic reality, as found in the Zen tradition based on the *Awakening of Faith in the Mahāyāna*, or focused, single-minded practice.

7. Following Chinese precedent, most explicit in the early Chan school, all of East Asian Buddhism developed hermeneutic categories that divided whole sets of teachings as pertaining to a "gradual" or "sudden" path to liberation, with the former reflecting earlier Indian mythic presumptions that a great many lifetimes devoted to cultivating religious virtues were necessary before one could become a buddha, the latter expressing later doctrines of an inherent spiritually pure nature within each individual that could be realized without this long period of assiduous practice.

8. This is a strong criticism of the Shin tradition for not requiring a commitment to practice among its clergy. The word *gabyō* 画餅 in this metaphor of a rice-cake painting is used as in the Zen tradition for the uselessness of learning about liberation without experiencing the truth of the teaching through practice. Dōgen uses it in the *Shōbōgenzō*, for example, citing a line from Xiangyan Zhiguan 香厳智閑 (d. 898), who was renowned for his learning but could not answer difficult questions about himself from his master.

9. The words rendered here as "head" (*atama*) and "belly" (*hara*) reflect a slightly different relationship than our notion of "mind" and "body." Rather than a strict dichotomy, this is something more akin to intellectual knowledge and existential knowledge.

10. From the sixth century in China, it was understood that history meant decline in Buddhism, and although the scriptures were not in agreement on this, the general hermeneutic move was to affirm three time periods: True Dharma, Semblance Dharma, and Latter Dharma.

11. Zhao Kuo is an infamous general who lost a vast army in battle during the Warring States period (475–221 BC). He liked to speak abstractly with his troops rather than provide them with concrete instructions for battle, and is said to have spent more time reading his father's books than actually engaging in preparations for war. He skillfully talked about soldiering but failed in actual soldiering, resulting in his city state of Zhao being overrun in battle.

12. These are all influential leaders of the movement to spread traditional Confucian and Neo-Confucian learning in the seventeenth and early eighteenth centuries. Some of them, such as Hayashi Razan served in the Tokugawa bakufu as advisors on policy. See Nosco 1984.

13. The Hōzōkan edition of this text had this name written 松菌, but the new Iwanami edition of KMZ corrects the characters as 松苗, which enables us to identify the individual as Iwagaki Matsunae, also known as Iwagaki Tōen 巌垣東園.

14. Yamazaki Ansai ran a school and published on Confucianism and Shinto. Iwagaki Matsunae is a relatively obscure figure from Kyoto who was a scholar in the *kogaku* 古学 movement, best known for his writings on Japanese history, such as *Kokushi ryaku* 国史略 and *Tōen hyakuzetsu* 東圓百絶. Hirata Atsutane claimed the mantle of *kokugaku* leader but took that philosophy into a decidedly nationalistic, even xenophobic, direction. It is worth noting that among the seven influential non-Buddhist figures named in this paragraph Fujiwara Seika and Yamazaki Ansai began as Buddhist monks. Keichū (1640–1701), founder of the *kokugaku* movement, was also a Buddhist monk.

15. Kūkai and Saichō are two of the most creative and influential thinkers in the Japanese Buddhist tradition. Their legacies of founding the Shingon and Tendai schools in Japan had a formative impact on subsequent developments in Japanese religious thinking.

16. The images of plum blossom and warbler (*uguisu*) reflect a traditional trope of transition, particularly the seasonal change between winter and spring. This stems from the ancient belief that the warbler is unable to distinguish between snow and white plum blossoms.

Chapter 4

Negotiating Religious Morality and Common Morality*

Kiyozawa Manshi

Translated by Mark L. Blum

Recently, some people have asked why it is that even though morality is said to be the most important issue in the world of man, we do not pay respect to it in the pages of *Seishinkai* and even show a tendency to dispense with it. Other people argue as follows: Even though the Buddhist doctrine of the two truths, "absolute" (*paramārtha*) and "conventional" (*saṃvṛti*), as used in Shin Buddhism reflects an attitude whereby conventional truth is none other than the teachings of ethics and morality,[1] some authors writing in *Seishinkai* not only refuse to accept that view and fall into the error of partiality in advocating only for the value of absolute truth, but also cause Shin to be remiss in bringing benefits to the state and society. In the following pages, I present my feelings about the issue of morality and the Buddhist concept of conventional truth.

In general, the teaching of the two truths is extremely deep and subtle, and yet it also reflects a common, everyday attitude. One result of this fact is that there are people who have somehow only heard about the popular side of the issue and thus understand little of its profound implications. Although it is difficult to treat exhaustively the details of this matter in this space, I shall attempt to outline it briefly.

---

*KMZ 6:148–58. Originally published in the May 1903 issue of *Seishinkai*. "Shūkyō-teki dōtoku (zokutai) to futsū dōtoku to no kōshō" 宗教的道徳 (俗諦) と普通道徳との交渉.

Buddhism begins from humanist considerations and proceeds to develop a plethora of doctrines, all of which have been classified as either Hīnayāna or Mahāyāna, exoteric or esoteric, and so forth. Beyond that, for those who are spiritually unable to enter into any of those systems, there is one final path that saves all sentient beings without exception by means of a single Dharma teaching: namely, the teaching of the two truths, conventional and absolute, which exhausts the full extent of the Buddha's great compassion. For this reason, it goes without saying that the teaching of the two truths transcends the so-called ethics and morality of this world but, in addition, the sublime message embedded within the gate of conventional truth is itself truly astonishing.[2]

Whether ethical or religious, in general any teaching circulating in the world is based on thoughts of good and bad that exist in our minds.[3] These teachings all endeavor to encourage the good and control the bad; by doing so the goal is to bring us to attain peace of mind. Spoken of from another point of view, we are trying to release ourselves from dissatisfaction and obtain contentment. But within this suffering and joy,[4] it is the suffering and joy as it relates to the issue of good and bad that is indeed the predominant concern [in this context]. What we call teachings are attempts to enable us to reach a place where we can remain with confidence.

Now with regard to the issue of precisely what is good and what is bad, [we can say that] although all ordinary people feel this is perfectly obvious, looking at the research of scholars we find that things are in fact not at all clear. What is considered good in Country A may be considered bad in Country B, and the reverse may also be true. Moreover, what was [considered] good during a former time may be seen as bad in later time [within the same country]. The converse also occurs. This being the situation, there are inevitable doubts about what is truly good and what is truly bad. When people speak of a morality or religion that is relevant and practical, however, they have little interest in such debates or doubts. When practical morality or religion is the basis of one's concern, prevailing conceptions in other countries or in previous eras are simply not considered. The crucial point is now, directly before us—deciding what action we should take. At such moments, nothing else matters. [For most people, their approach is simple:] in their heart of hearts what they feel is good is good, what they feel is bad is bad. Were it possible to always do what one thinks good and never do what one thinks is bad, all systems of morality and religion would affirm this position.

On the other hand, if we turn to the question of why morality and religion are so difficult [to practice], we must first recognize the fact that when each individual tries honestly to base their actions on what they feel is good and bad, things just do not happen as he thought they would. In fact, the harder one strives the more one will realize how problematic the situation is. And as understanding of the difficulty progresses, concern only grows. From this corresponding growth in concern comes a variety of arguments on the subject of good and evil.

The present situation in Japan is exactly at this stage. From the desire to advance the practice of morality, we have today a blossoming of academic discussions on the subject of ethics. Some say that if one's motivation is good, then, as a result, one's behavior must accordingly be good. Another position states that regardless of one's motivation, if an individual's actions are evil, then this is [unambiguously] evil. The various positions put forth are interesting and, for the purposes of research, these [views] are all worthy of note. But in the end, this is merely debate or research.

When we come to the actual *practice* of morality, however, debate or research makes little difference. Individually, every person need only do precisely what they think is right and not do what they think is wrong. But carrying out exactly what one thinks is good and completely refraining from what one thinks is bad has its own difficulties, and this kind of "difficulty" is completely different from the "difficulty" that arises in current debate or research [on what constitutes proper morality or ethics]. If the situation were such that we could not get to the level of practice until these troublesome investigations into the nature of ethics were resolved first, then we would have to say that today we are not yet at a time when [ethical] praxis can take place. The actual practice of morality, however, is not at all dependent on the former issue being resolved. This has been the state of things since ancient times [regardless of the state of debates over what constitutes good and evil]. And there is nothing to prevent one from beginning ethical [practice] today as well. In fact, if we do not begin [our ethical behavior] today, moreover, when could we hope to? For the time when [debate over the content of morality is concluded] might never come. Hence, the practice of morality should not be linked to any debate or research. They are entirely separate issues.

The experience of difficulty in the execution of moral behavior will lead certain individuals to examine the relevant research and debate into the matter but here, too, they encounter a variety of problems that cannot easily be resolved. When this becomes clear, they feel unusually stimulated to redouble their efforts in execution. Now, once again, with an even deeper zeal than before, people will return to the path of single-minded cultivation of practice. It is interesting that at this stage many who are either well grounded in scholarship or possess strong intellectual leanings will spend long periods of time, even decades, in intellectual debate. Among those with little academic training or relatively weak intellectual inclinations, however, there are many who easily succeed in breaking away from this labyrinth of argument and investigation. There are also many who, from the outset, have never engaged in debate or research; their concerns are entirely focused on performance. In any event, in the end no one can avoid experiencing problems in the execution of moral behavior. Those people who have heard the teaching of the two truths according to *tariki* Shinshū and feel they are capable of easily putting into practice the conventional truth teaching have simply not reached this point yet. They are of a like mind to those researching and debating the question of morality.

There is something else I want to say concerning the fact that it is not easy to do what is right and abstain from what is wrong. This notion [of doing good and avoiding evil] is a basic idea expressed in all teachings; but from one perspective, we can say that, in fact, rather than calling them "teachings," they should be seen as natural desires. Even without relying on any discussion of teachings, we are naturally endowed with desires motivating us to do good and avoid doing bad. Therefore, if it were truly possible to act on [these inclinations] without difficulty, then we should still be able to do what is morally correct. But things do not really work in this way and, in fact, even when [ethics] are taught with extreme care, still no one can fully put into practice what they are taught. To the practice of morality applies the saying: a three-year old can speak of it but even an eighty-year old cannot do it. Accordingly, for anyone who thinks the practice of Shinshū conventional truth is easily accomplished, it has to be said that this a misapprehension of the situation.

Some people will say that Buddhist conventional truth according to Shinshū is different in its intent than ordinary ethics or morality. They will say that since the usual sense of ethics or morality has been separated from religion, those ideals may not be possible to put into practice but because Shinshū conventional truth is a morality that flows from absolute truth, and so long as the attainment of faith in the form of *shinjin*[5] is definite, its practice will be natural and inevitable. Though it seems there is an element of truth in this, there is another aspect that requires some care. And that is distinguishing between things that occur naturally and inevitably from things that are carried out intentionally and deliberately. Something that occurs naturally and inevitably need not be taught. The necessity of "teachings" lies in the attempt to enlighten our intentional actions by means of those teachings. Therefore, if the practice of conventional truth in Shin terms were accomplished naturally and inevitably, so long as the ultimate truth teaching exists, there should be no need for conventional truth teachings in the first place. In light of the fact that the conventional truth is taught nearly shoulder-to-shoulder with the absolute truth, however, it is clear that the practice of conventional truth is in fact not something that manifests naturally and inevitably following the attainment of *shinjin* of absolute truth. Instead, what is gained naturally and inevitably from the *shinjin* of absolute truth is the so-called "ten benefits gained in the present life" (*genshō jisshu no yaku* 現生十種の益).[6] Because these are obtained naturally and inevitably, there is no teaching regarding them that admonishes us to "do this and do not do that," or insists "one must do this and must not do that." There is no hint of any teaching here that tells us to ask the gods for protection or pray to be endowed with blessings of virtue. This is because even without such requests or prayers one naturally and inevitably obtains the benefits of protection from the gods and blessings of virtue. Among the ten benefits [attained when faith is realized], those like the transformation of evil into good and the recognizing and repaying one's debt of gratitude, are concerned with good/evil and gratitude. But like the benefits of divine protection and blessings of virtue, these accrue naturally and inevitably, and therefore there is no [accompanying] teaching of "For this reason, do this and do that."

As stated earlier, because the Shin conventional truth is expounded as a teaching equally majestic with the absolute truth, it should be understood that it does not express something that naturally and inevitably manifests from the experience of faith; rather it exists in order to edify our volition. Seen in this way, there is no problem affirming that the difficulties in implementing the conventional truth of Shin are not particularly different from the difficulties in implementing ordinary, common morality, and ethics. In other words, it must be that the perfect practice of Shin conventional truth is [also] something not easily to put into practice.

Although the perfect practice of both conventional truth in Shin and common ethics or morality may be difficult, some degree of success is possible. If one gradually cultivates oneself, in fact, one can increasingly draw closer to perfection [in praxis]. The teachings [of any moral system], though they may be vexing, are therefore most important in this respect. It is a frequently presented argument, moreover, that [moral] practice is an urgent imperative. This position also has some truth to it. But strictly speaking, on this point we must draw a distinction between conventional truth in Shin tradition and common morality. The general attitude toward common morality is that we really have no other way to proceed: one way or another our moral progress must proceed on track. For, regardless of whether or not it is actually possible, we have no choice but to commit ourselves to carry out [these ideals] one step at a time. Even if one's resolve is firm, however, when it comes to the point of the actual implementation [of the morally ideal act], one gradually falls into a state of anxiety. In the end, the individual will either turn to religion or become hopelessly despondent about his or her own future. Originally, the conventional truth as expounded in Shin stands together with the absolute truth, [and we must bear in mind that] future events will all be accomplished by absolute truth. From the outset, therefore, there is not the slightest imperative to seek one's own progress in terms of conventional truth.[7] Especially in terms of praxis, one will encounter troubles, as mentioned earlier, so no matter how hard we strive, there is simply no means by which we can do something laudable. Moreover, the ability or inability to [successfully] carry out these ideals depends on one's current karmic situation or innate make-up.[8] If one's karmic or natural design is inferior, no matter how much effort that person may make, he is simply at a stage where he is unable to produce anything superior. Therefore, for Shin, conventional truth does not aim at the usual goal of competency in the implementation [of its teachings]; its efficacy lies elsewhere. It is not about training us to be able to performing admirable deeds. Accordingly there is a great difference in the tenor of Shin conventional truth and that of common morality, which is aimed at producing commendable behavior. Put another way, it does not really matter whether one does something splendid or something wretched, the goal of the conventional truth teaching in Shin Buddhism lies elsewhere.

One may wonder, then, what the actual purpose of conventional truth is for Shin Buddhism. The answer is that its aim is to lead the individual to the perception that it is difficult to carry out that conventional truth. Although there may be differences between those who have attained faith as it relates to absolute truth and those who have not, in either case the aim of enabling someone to appreciate the *impossibility* of moral praxis is identical.

By way of explaining the profound beauty of this, let us first turn to those who have not yet attained faith. Having perceived the difficulties in moral practice, such people enter the religious [path] and thereby proceed down the road to the attainment of faith. At first glance, this may not seem like much, but in fact it is not a simple matter. The basic impediment blocking the entrance to other-power faith is the conviction that one is capable of practicing self-power discipline. Although there are many forms of self-power praxis, its most ordinary form is ethical or moral behavior. As long as someone thinks proper moral action is indeed possible, that person can never enter into other-power religion. Thus to seriously try to put into practice [the ideals of] morality and ethics, only to recognize that in the end the results do not accord with the dictates of morality and ethics, is in fact an indispensable condition for becoming religious. In this case, the focus is on overcoming the deluded reliance on self-power, so whether it be the Shin teaching of conventional truth, the morality and ethics common in society, the five precepts,[9] the ten kinds of good behavior,[10] or the attempt to do good in every action, it does not matter. The teaching of conventional truth in Shin is the most favorable, however, because it is constructed in a way that directly opens the door to absolute truth.

Next we consider someone after he has obtained faith. Although we attain "the great settled mind" (*daianjin* 大安心)[11] as a result of other-power faith, the habitually deluded mind of self-power still continues to arise in us. Then, when we hear teachings on conventional truth, because those teachings are directed precisely at this deluded mind, our reaction is to immediately attempt to put those ideals into practice. Then we engage in such practice, but we eventually perceive how truly difficult this is, whereupon we turn around and rejoice [once again] in our other-power faith, returning to the attitude embodied in the phrase, "In our sincerity and joy of faith, we forget the self and return to the ocean of the buddha's vow, where there is no practice that has not been completed."[12] In other words, in the case [of one who has attained faith], because practice that aims to implement the conventional truth teaching is so difficult, [it becomes clear that] its purpose is to deepen one's personal thoughts of gratitude toward the infinite compassion [of the Buddha].

Of these two approaches to the conventional truth teachings, the first is an example of the principle of taking a teaching from one context and applying it to another. When people hear that in Shinshū there is the idea of a conventional/absolute doctrine of two truths or a mutually dependent two-truth doctrine, they may think this reflects a religion that has not forgotten about the state and society, and that those who have yet to attain faith should indeed make every effort to practice Shin conventional truth because it will eventually become a guide that leads them to attaining faith based in absolute truth (*shintai no shinjin*). Yet the true meaning of the traditional doctrine of mutually dependent two truths is expressed in the second example given earlier [i.e., after one has attained faith]. It is precisely because someone has reached faith based in absolute truth that he is not surprised by his inability to put into practice [the norms of] conventional truth. And because he fails at this, his sense of thankfulness toward his absolute truth-supported faith only deepens, and he feels even more vividly the exquisite beauty of the mutual dependence and mutual support [of the two truths].

The practical value of the essential message of the conventional truth lies, therefore, in its fundamental meaning for those in the second group [i.e., those who have attained faith], but I would also like to add something about the progression of this. Although the utility of the conventional truth manifests in the beginning by means of the difficulty of its implementation, with the passage of time this becomes apparent even without sensing the difficulties involved in its application. Finally, one reaches the point where simply hearing words such as "conventional truth" or "morality," enables that person to savor the true implications of the fact that the two truths are mutually dependent. Or, seen from another perspective, I cannot actually practice according to [the dictates of] of conventional truth and morality, but it is only natural that I cannot. This self who is stymied in moral practice is embraced by an infinite compassion that will never yield. Truly the only emotion here is gratitude—expressed in a surge of humility and joy. This state of mind may not readily arise in the beginning, but in the end it appears instantly whenever one hears about "conventional truth," morality, and so on.[13]

There is also a contrary proof of this. When observing someone who looks upon the Shin approach to conventional truth as if it were no different from common morality, we will see how that person is attached to their ability to do the right thing, how he anguishes[14] over questions like "Should I abide by this or not?" or "Can I do without this or not?" We will feel pity for the error of that person's attachments, but we also delight in the fact that our own situation is peacefully resolved. Indeed, questions of responsibility or obligation as in "should I . . ." or "can I . . ." occupy a predominant share of the anguish in our lives; their influence is simply enormous. Although the

Shin form of conventional truth does contain elements of a command idiom expressed in terms of "Do this" and "Don't do that," generally speaking, however, in its core it does not approve of such exterior pressures as "You should do this" and "You must not do that." Even in cases where anguish is created from the use of such [enjoining language], it is not comparable to the anguish experienced under the deluded thinking associated with common morality. In other words, when arbitrary notions of "You must do this" and "You must not do that" are added to the delusory abstractions of common morality wherein one is ordered to "Do this . . . Do not do that," the situation [may escalate to where] it seems a solemn command has come down from God or the Buddha saying, "You absolutely must do this," or "It is strictly forbidden for you to do that." People accordingly come to think that the crucial matter of their salvation will depend on their ability or inability to implement so-called proper moral behavior, consequently feeling "If I do not do this, I will not be saved," or "If I do that I will not be saved." When things reach this level, people feel extremely anguished regarding their capacity to behave appropriately. Whether or not one is able to implement the conventional truth as taught in the Shin tradition of other-power Buddhism, however, has not the slightest relation to the most important issue of one's salvation. Although there may be some anxiety over one's ability to implement it, not only is this incomparable to the agony arising from the delusory abstractions of ordinary morality, but the nature of this agony is completely different. One is like the agony of being tormented by demons, the other is like feeling shameful before the great compassion of the Buddha. In one there are tears arising from fear of the intense anger of [the demon who] never forgives, whereas in the other there are tears that come from being touched by the depth of compassion and mercy encompassing us anywhere, anytime.

Given this situation, we know that outside of the issue of *shinjin* faith in the absolute truth, the Shin teaching of conventional truth is not something that sets out to impose rules and regulations on human behavior. If it were offering regulations for our actions, we would expect its principles to be definite and precise. In fact, whether it be simply restrictions on behavior, duty to the laws of the state, or the five [Confucian] virtues of benevolence, justice, politeness, wisdom, and fidelity, [in Shin] such matters are decidedly vague. Even in the basic formula of the "five good acts and five bad acts"[15] or the phrase, "excluding those who have committed the five grave offenses or slandered the true teaching,"[16] the intent is, again, somewhat different. Of course if one were seeking to reconcile these formula with each other, he could say that they all may be implying the same thing. But it is better not to force such an accommodation. Why? Because just as we have said, the conventional truth teaching of Shin is not aimed at its implementation; if anything, it is aimed at arousing the perception that its implementation is impossible.

There is no need to enumerate every instance of this in detail, just as there is no need to settle on what it means. It applies to whatever approach one takes: it is therefore acceptable to see this as either imploring one to practice what is said to be good or urging one not to do what said to be bad. In either case, the individual will reach the point where he awakens to the fact that the perfect practice of either cannot be possible. This awakening is none other than the essential point of the conventional truth. Reaching this point and gaining this awakening becomes the elation of faith based in absolute truth. The conventional truth teaching is thus nothing less than the means to perceive the faith of absolute truth from behind it. That is to say, whereas the absolute truth tends to be positive, conventional truth tends to be negative. For that reason it is a great misperception to think the conventional truth teaching exists in order to actively lead people to uphold standards of human behavior or to benefit the state and society. Of course there may indeed be some areas in which the conventional truth teachings are expounded as a basic duty to the laws of the state or pertain to humanistic concerns, in which case they are carried out to some degree. But these are things that have appended [to the original]—that which cannot be carried out is its principal element, as explained previously. But though the secondary aspects of conventional truth may bring a degree of efficacy in their implementation and are therefore respected instead of its principal notions, this serves no purpose at all. Despite the fact that the essential message of the doctrine is religious, it is its appended moral elements that are valued most highly; an odd form of reasoning indeed!

In general, when one brings together the ideas of Buddhist conventional truth and morality, or Buddhist conventional truth and the state (*kokka*), one should take care to explicate the qualifications of each. Looking first at how conventional truth and morality relate to one another, our primary need is to know what is meant by conventional truth. And if one looks into this, what becomes immediately apparent is that conventional truth stands alongside absolute truth in the doctrine of other-power Shin. In other words, Buddhist conventional truth is teaching of religion rather than a teaching of morality. It is not a humanist teaching but a Buddhist teaching.[17] Seeing it in this way, it goes without saying that this so-called conventional truth is something to be explained by religious persons and that its goal is to produce religious results. Morality, on the other hand, is morality—it is not religion. It is a humanistic teaching, and has nothing to do with the way of buddhas. Hence, it should be expounded by specialists in morality with the goal of producing moral accomplishments. Although politicians do not hesitate to speak about commerce, politicians are not merchants. And although merchants do engage in business activities involving grain, merchants are not farmers. In that we differentiate between religion and morality, there is no need to confuse their domains. If one does not recognize the distinction between religion and morality, such as taking the stance that religion is none other than morality and morality is none other than religion, then any discussion of the relationship between Buddhist conventional truth and morality is pointless. When that happens, one feels no compulsion to separate conventional truth from absolute truth in order to talk about morality, for both Buddhist truths are reduced to teachings on morality.

Let us now consider Buddhist conventional truth's relationship to the state and society. Because in general the notion of conventional truth is a religious teaching, it should go without saying that its contribution to the state and society is its contribution of religious achievements. So while already [recognizing that] propounding the teaching on absolute truth in Buddhism contributes religiously to society, to then reproach Buddhists for not preaching the conventional truth [in a prescribed fashion] because it means no benefits for society is pulling out keys to a different gate. If absolute truth and conventional truth taught things that were separate and distinct, then it would be acceptable to say there is an insufficiency if we teach one and not the other. But in fact, absolute truth and conventional truth only differ insofar as they approach things from the front or from the back; seen from the position that their teachings express exactly the same truth there should be nothing lacking if we teach only one. In any case, there should be no argument against the fact that the contribution to state and society of affirming Buddhist conventional truth lies in its religious impact, and when the absolute truth teaching is expounded, this is already in effect.

There is an argument in which it is claimed that although it may be acceptable to draw a distinction between religion and morality such that religious people preach religion and moralists preach morality, the preaching of religion itself has the effect of destroying morality and is therefore problematic. Raising this problem may give one pause, but there is nothing that can be done about it. If morality is that weak, then its dissolution may not be such a bad thing. It is, after all, the duty of a religious person to teach religion. But he fulfills that duty for its religious effect, certainly not because he intends to do away with morality. Thus if morality were destroyed [in the process of religion being taught], it would be a case of morality destroying itself.

One wonders, however, how relevant such vague arguments are to the reality of our situation. Just what is the professional religious supposed to teach? He is in no position to choose between someone who has killed another human being and someone who has not, or to be concerned over whether or not the person in front of him is a thief, or whether or not someone who wants to commit adultery should be allowed to do so. Speaking from the religious point of view, he or she has no choice but to stress that infinite compassion [embodied in the Buddha] does not alter its salvific intent based on whether or not someone has committed murder, theft, adultery, or any other sin.

How does the specialist in morals hear this? Is this something that he feels will destroy morality, something that will vitiate humanist values? If there are people who assert such things without hesitation, they do so rashly. Because anyone who clearly understands why religion and morality are distinguished would have to say this: "Not scolding someone for having committed murder, theft, adultery, or lying is truly what religion is supposed to be about." Nevertheless, from a humanistic, moral point of view, murder and theft are heinous crimes; licentiousness and falsehood must not be allowed. The people who commit these offenses are all transgressors against humanity and, in a moral sense, depraved individuals. [It is thus without denigrating morality that we advocate that] professional religious should expound their teachings from a religious standpoint and specialists in morality should preach about their moral concerns. Standing separately, there should not be even a hint of any conflict of interest.

[Consider the mind of] someone who has murdered, stolen, had improper sex, or lied. If his moral concerns came before his religious concerns, he would repent and thereafter devote himself to a moral path. If he gave precedence to religion over morality, he would rush at once to a portal of religion. If he were someone who needed both religion and morality, then after repenting his sin, he would simultaneously commit himself to the paths of both. If he were someone who did not reflect upon either religion or morality, he would wander in the dark night of his crime just as he is. We can also use this model to understand people who have not committed crimes like murder, theft, and so forth.

In conclusion, we must recognize that vague arguments about religion being harmful to morality, or that promulgating

Buddhism means the destruction of humanistic values only invite misunderstanding. Issues such as these demand precision. The distinction between religion and morality should now be clear: namely, religious advocates uphold the religious dimension of life and moral advocates maintain the moral dimension of life. If each works to his full capacity, then each will contribute his own meritorious services to the state and society.

I have expressed my understanding here by letting my brush run freely on how the conventional truth in Shin and the so-called ethical and moral issues of the world should be negotiated. This being a work written after I have become ill, I would like to express my apologies for it being at a stage where a certain carelessness has been unavoidable.

Notes

1. Only implied in the earliest sutras, it is the commentarial and Abhidharma literature, both Pāli and Sanskrit, that two contrasting levels of truth become a hermeneutic tool for Buddhist intellectual discourse. This was greatly expanded in the Mahāyāna, most famously by Nāgārjuna, but sutra discussions are not uncommon as well. The so-called worldly or conventional truth (*saṃvṛtisatya*) in a strictly Buddhist doctrinal context denotes the teachings of the Buddha presented in worldly or everyday language, but even the Buddha noted that his teachings employ conventional names and concepts that may be misunderstood. The higher or ultimate truth (*paramārthasatya*) marks truth that can only be seen by those who have awakened to the truth of the Dharma. Although not originally discussed in ways relevant to secular problems of ethics or morality, in East Asia the understanding of conventional truth was deeply influenced by statements in the *Nirvana Sutra* where it is also described as commonsense knowledge based on worldly experience. All major schools of Chinese and Japanese Buddhist thought took positions on how to interpret conventional truth and its relationship both to worldly knowledge and wisdom. During the later Edo period in Japan, undoubtedly influenced by increasingly anti-Buddhist rhetoric in *kokugaku, kogaku*, and certain Neo-Confucian thinkers, a number of Shin Buddhist leaders begin to redefine both truths, speaking of conventional truth only as social morality and ethical obligation, stripping away its religious purpose and transferring that dimension to absolute truth. This strategy weakened the xenophobic arguments of the nativists, but in affirming status-quo notions of social and political obligations by adding a Buddhist veneer to them, it raised new questions for devout Buddhists about the relationship between the two truths. In Kiyozawa's jingoistic age, some Shin Buddhist leaders went as far as asserting that obedience to the emperor fell within the rubric of conventional

truth, so we can safely infer that this essay was written with the Shin clergy in mind, if not directed solely to them.

2. Kiyozawa's position is that recognition of the existence of the ultimate truth does not require abandoning the worldly truth; instead the latter is embraced as provisional but indispensable. See the discussion of the five evils in the second fascicle of the *Wuliangshou jing*.

3. The terms *zen* 善 and *aku* 悪 have very broad usage in Japanese, particularly in a Buddhist context, and encompass such contrasting moral pairs as "good and bad," "good and evil," "right and wrong," "wholesome and harmful," "supportive and deleterious," and so forth. Kiyozawa never clarifies in which sense he is using the terms and, presuming this is reflective of the fact that he did not want to exclude any dimension of meaning embedded in either word, the way I have rendered them into English may vary depending on context.

4. Suffering and joy are standard Buddhist terms for the two poles of how we process sensation: we are either repulsed by what perceive as leading to suffering or anxiety (*duḥkha*) or attracted to what we think will bring us joy or happiness (*sukha*).

5. Shinjin 信心 denotes attainment of religious liberation as defined in the Jōdo Shinshū tradition, and is left untranslated here. In this context, Kiyozawa appears to be referring to an assumption that those who have attained this awakening are de facto capable of proper moral discernment and successful praxis in moral terms, or as he puts it, "perfect praxis."

6. This refers to the ten kinds of benefits said to accrue to the nembutsu practitioner during this lifetime as mentioned by Shinran in the chapter on Faith in his *Kyōgyōshinshō*: protection by gods and spirits, supreme merit, turning evil into good, protection by buddhas, praise from the buddhas, protection by the light of the buddha-mind, joy of attaining faith, repayment of gratitude to the buddha, practice of compassion, entering the group destined for buddhahood. For a full discussion on this topic, see the *Bukkyo Daiji'i* 2:1099–1101.

7. This section can be read as an expression of anger directed at the Honganji for its moral directives issued at this time which, in accommodation to the anti-Buddhist sentiment within the political establishment, included honoring parents and the state as a religious obligation.

8. The term *karmic situation* translates *gōhō* 業報, which specifically refers to the resultant karma or karmic fruition from one's past actions that inform and to a degree determine the spiritual capacity one has in this lifetime. *Innate make-up* translates *tenpu no moyō* 天賦の模様, which seems to indicate some notion of patterns of thought and/or behavior that one is born with. This latter term may be a reference to genetic coding.

9. *Pañcaśīla*. These are prescribed for all Buddhist laymen: no killing, stealing, illicit sex, lying, or drinking of intoxicants.

10. *Daśakuśala*. These are a number of lists of ten forms of bad behaviors to be avoided in the Buddhist tradition: no killing, stealing, illicit sex, lying, disrepectful language, slander or abusive language, dissension-causing language, covetousness, anger, and false views.

11. In general, *anjin* is taken as a synonym of *shinjin* in Shin doctrine, with some leaders such as Rennyo preferring this term. With this term, "great *anjin*," Kiyozawa seems to make it clear he means a determinant, if not ultimate religious attainment.

12. SSZ 1:541.

13. Note Kiyozawa's use of the passive action of "hearing." Because all praxis directed toward personal liberation, not only that of morality or worldly truth, is considered futile in Shin doctrine, Shinran's emphasis on hearing (*mon* 聞) the Dharma has held special religious significance in Shin. Distinguished from merely listening, the technical term *mon* refers to discerning or encountering the truth through hearing the preaching of the Dharma. Although Kiyozawa's use of hearing is somewhat different here as it includes ordinary social morality, it similarly implies a religious affirmation.

14. The word translated here as "anguish" (*hanmon* 煩悶) has political associations because of the situation in Japan at the turn of the century when the nation was directed into wars against both China and Russia, and young people were under enormous pressure to conform to the new imperialist model for Japan created by its leaders, often supported by Buddhist clergy, including the leaders of both Honganji. The suicide of Fujimura Misao, a prominent philosophy student at Tokyo University, at this time expressed the anxiety of this generation and led to many copycat suicides.

15. This phrasing comes from the standard translation of the so-called *Sutra of Immeasurable Life* by Saṃghavarman, the *Wuliangshou jing*, an early work where the Sanskrit term *pañcaśīla* (see n.5) is rendered as "five good acts" (*gozen* 五善), in contrast to its more common translation as "five precepts" (*gokai* 五戒). Not observing these five precepts was then termed the five "bad acts" (*goaku* 五悪).

16. This phrase is added as a disclaimer in the famous eighteenth vow of the *Sutra of Immeasurable Life*, wherein these transgressors are excluded from this promise to all sentient beings by Amida Buddha to guarantee birth in his Pure Land. The *Guanwuliangshoujing* seems to make up for this lapse in universality by including even transgressors in its definition of who can enter Amida's paradise, and Shinran took this phrase in an admonitory rather than a proscriptive sense.

17. Here *humanist* translates *jindō* 人道, a word with Confucian roots that was transformed in the modern period to represent humane, humanitarian, and so forth, essentially anything human-centered. In the Confucianist education received by Kiyozawa when growing up, *jindō* would have expressed Confucian moral principles as the basis for individual values. But when Kiyozawa was at university studying philosophy, he would have studied ideas like "humanist teachings" as a form of religion, as in the phrase *"la religion d'humanité"* coined by Auguste Comte (1798–1857), and often translated into Japanese as *jindōkyō* 人道教. The language used by Kiyozawa similarly contrasts *jindō no kyō* 人道の教 with *butsudō no kyō* 仏道の教. As Comte was arguing for a new form of religion based on ethics, it is entirely possible that Comte is the reference here, rather than Confucius.

Chapter 5

The Nature of My Faith*

by Kiyozawa Manshi

Translated by Mark L. Blum

As is my wont, I frequently speak about such things as "faith" (*shinnen* 信念) or "tathāgata" (*nyorai* 如來). But what do I mean by "my faith"? What is this tathāgata to which I profess my faith? Here, I will try to answer these questions.

It should be obvious at this point that faith for me refers to how I believe in the tathāgata. This, then, calls forth two issues: believing and tathāgata. The two may appear to be completely separate things but as far as I am concerned, they are absolutely indivisible. On the question of what my faith is about, the answer is that it is about believing in the tathāgata. On the question of what this tathāgata is, the answer is that it is the fundamental basis of what I believe in. If we divide them, we could call one believing and the other what is believed in. In other words, my believing is precisely my faith, and that which is believed in by me is the tathāgata. Another way of putting it is to use the traditional categories of the individual who believes (*ki* 機) and the Dharma which is believed in (*hō* 法). But if we insist on only using traditional categories such as believer and what is

---

*Original title, *Ware wa kono gotoku nyorai wo shinzu* 我は此の如く如来を信ず, but when it appeared in print posthumously in the journal *Seishinkai,* the original title was replaced with *Waga shinnen* 我信念. This is arguably the most well read of all of Kiyozawa's writings, thus to this day is best known by *Waga shinnen*. In the newly edited KMZ 6:330, both titles appear. Cf. previous translations by Kunji Tajima and Floyd Shacklock (1936), Bandō Shōjun (1972), and Nobuo Haneda (1984).

believed, and so forth, we run the risk of losing our understanding of what is in fact understood, so I will not pursue this line of thought.

What is it that I believe in, and why do I do this? What sort of effects are produced by such a thing? There are various points to consider here. Let me look at effects first. This believing that I do has the primary effect of removing distress and pain from my life. One could call this the salvific effect. Whatever it is called, I can say that during those moments when I have feelings of anxiety or even agony, emotions that can be brought on by a variety of different causes and conditions, if this faith should manifest in my heart I suddenly feel calmed and even joyful. The way it happens is that when my faith becomes manifest, it takes over my mind completely such that there is simply no place left for deluded perceptions or deluded thoughts to settle [and play a role in my consciousness]. At that point, no matter what [potentially disturbing] influence or situation may occur, as long as my faith is present such things will not be able to provoke feelings of distress or anxiety within me. Particularly for someone hypersensitive like myself, and especially now when my emotional state is aggravated by illness, if this thing I am calling faith were not there, it would be impossible to avoid extremes of distress and anxiety. I think, however, that such faith is just as essential for a healthy person as it is for someone who frequently suffers the debilitations of sickness. When I speak of a religious sense of gratitude, what I am referring to is the elation that comes from having my agonies actually swept away by my faith.

The second question concerns why I believe in the tathāgata. As I stated earlier, this [situation] is the result of the effects [of my faith], but there are other reasons as well. Saying one benefits from the effects is only relevant after this believing has begun, for before believing one has no idea what the effects will be, if any. Of course, one hears of the effects from others and at that point one may have no reason not to believe them, but the impact of what amounts to hearsay never really goes beyond supposition. It is only through personal experience that one can truly know the presence or absence of the benefits of faith.

But my belief in the tathāgata is not just the result of seeing the effects of this faith. It has another important basis. My belief in the tathāgata occurs at the limit of everything that I know. Aside from a time in my life when I lacked real concern for human affairs, once I seriously began to take even the slightest interest in the human condition I felt obsessed with the question of the meaning of life. And when I reached the conclusion that the meaning of life is incomprehensible, it was at that point that my faith in the tathāgata arose. Gaining faith probably does not require that one go through such a lengthy process of inquiry, so the course of events that led me to this conclusion may indeed seem accidental. But in fact in my case, it could not have been any other way.

Within my faith there is an element that believes in the ineffectiveness of my own efforts.[1] And to believe in my own ineffectiveness, it was necessary first to exhaust my entire range of intellectual faculties to the point where I could not longer even raise my head. This effort involved an incredible ordeal. Before I finally reached this limit I speak of, time and again I concluded that religious truth must be such and such, only to have that conviction destroyed by subsequent experience. As long as one attempts to establish their religious grounding by means of logic or research, such upheavals are inevitable. What is good, what is bad? What is truth, what is falsehood? What is happiness and what is unhappiness? One cannot possibly understand any of these. When I stood on that ground of understanding nothing, I threw up my hands and came to trust in the tathāgata, and this became the focal point of my faith.

The third question queries the nature of my faith itself. The answer to this is that my faith believes in the tathāgata. The tathāgata is the embodiment of the sacred (*hontai* 本体) that I am able to believe in and, moreover, cannot help but believe in. Faced with the truth of the powerlessness of my own efforts, I [know I] lack the ability to stand on my own, but this tathāgata in whom I am able to believe as the fundamental embodiment of the sacred has the power to make me what I am. Faced with a world filled with good and bad, truth and falsehood, happiness and unhappiness, and yet personally lacking the ability to know one from the other, I am unable to move right or left, forward or backward [to accommodate these things]. This tathāgata in whom I am able to believe as the fundamental embodiment of the sacred is capable of enabling such a person as myself to course through this world calmly, without malice.[2] Without believing in this tathāgata, I would neither know how to live nor how to die. I could not exist without believing in the tathāgata. This tathāgata is a tathāgata that I am incapable of not believing in.

This, then, is a summary of my faith. In terms of my first problem [of anxiety], the tathāgata for me is infinite compassion. In terms of my second problem [of ignorance], the tathāgata for me is infinite wisdom. In terms of my third problem [of practice], the tathāgata for me is infinite power. As such, my own faith believes in the reality of infinite compassion, infinite wisdom, and infinite power.

Because the tathāgata is infinite compassion, from the time when my faith was resolved the tathāgata enabled me to immediately gain peace and tranquility. The tathāgata in whom I believe did not wait for the next world, but brought me enormous happiness here and now. I am not saying that I have not gained various degrees of happiness from other things, but none surpass the joys of this faith. For that reason, the happiness of my faith is my greatest happiness in this world. This happiness is something that I experience every day and every night. As I have not experienced happiness in the next life yet, I cannot comment on that.

Because the tathāgata is infinite wisdom, I receive its illuminating protection and am liberated from the delusions that stem from wrong understandings and wrong views. Almost unconsciously I find myself drawn into inquiry and research by force of habit, and easily fall into a host of useless arguments. There are times when I have even attempted to prove the existence of infinite compassion by means of finite, inelegant speculation. Thanks to the establishment of my faith, however, were I to fall into such illusory thinking for a period of time, it would be easy for me to reflect upon the imprudence of this activity and abandon such theorizing. The aphorism, "To admit to what you do not know, this is to know,"[3] may be the apogee of human wisdom, but we have a hard time accepting this. I used to hold truly presumptuous opinions about things. But now I appreciate expressions like "ignorant Hōnen," or "foolish and bald Shinran,"[4] for I, too, have learned to be truly content with ignorance. In the past, although I described [my tools] as finite and imperfect, I still had a hard time freeing myself from the mistake of using that limited and imperfect human knowledge to pursue a perfect standard or the reality of the infinite. In the past I, too, feared that if we did not clarify the norms for judging truth or good and evil, that heaven and earth would crumble and society would become unmanageable. But now I have reached the conclusion that human knowledge could never create standards for truth or goodness.

Because the tathāgata is infinite power, my faith grants me great power. Under normal conditions our own considerations and discriminations lead us to determine how we will respond to things, but when things become even a little complicated that same ability to consider and discriminate easily becomes indeterminate. That is why these inquiries and researches gain momentum. But when, as mentioned earlier, we seek out standards or search for reality, then the difficulty of deciding how to act mounts precipitously and we become nearly completely nonplussed. One should carefully choose their words, one should conduct oneself properly, one must not break the law, one must not violate the codes of morality, one must not breach the rules of propriety, one must not go against accepted modes of behavior. There are obligations to oneself, obligations to others, obligations to family, obligations to society, obligations to parents, obligations to one's lord, obligations to one's husband, obligations to one's wife, obligations to siblings, obligations to friends, obligations to good people, obligations to bad people, obligations to the old, obligations to the young, and so on. Such duties and obligations that arise out of the teachings of so-called ethics and morality are exceedingly difficult to carry out. If one is serious about fulfilling these obligations, in the end he or she will only end up faced with the depressing truth of the impossibility of the entire enterprise. When I ran up against this impossibility it distressed me immensely. If I had thought that there were no alternative but to agonize interminably over the reality of this impossibility, I would have ultimately killed myself. But through religion I have shed this anguish and now feel no need for suicide. In other words, through my belief in the infinite compassion of the tathāgata, today I have gained peace and calm.

How has the tathāgata of infinite compassion enabled me to gain this peace? [The tathāgata] has saved me by taking responsibility for everything that is not external. No matter what sins I may have committed, before the tathāgata such things matter not a whit. I no longer have any need to discern good from bad, right from wrong. In whatever I do, I simply follow my inclinations and act according to what my heart dictates, without hesitation. I have no concern whatsoever as to whether or not my behavior is in error or in sin. The tathāgata graciously takes responsibility for all my actions. Simply by believing in this tathāgata I am able to live in continual peace. The power of the tathāgata is infinite. The power of the tathāgata is unsurpassed. The power of the tathāgata is ubiquitous. The power of the tathāgata pervades every direction in its unrestricted, undefiled activity. Entrusting myself to this miraculous power of the tathāgata, I gain a great calm and a great peace. Entrusting my very life to the tathāgata, I feel no anxiety and no unease. It is said, "In life and death it is destiny, in wealth and poverty it is ordained by heaven."[5] The tathāgata in which I believe is the sacred embodiment of heaven and of destiny.

Notes

1. This translation of 自力の無功 is actually reading the last character as 効 instead of 功. This is because I take this phrase to be in conscious contrast

with the phrase in the previous section 信念の効能. If in fact, Manshi is not contrasting the two notions, and wants us to read his text as written, then the phrase must mean rather "the lack of any accomplishments that came from my own efforts."

2. The phrase "calmly, without malice" renders *kyoshin heiki* 虚心平気, which expresses the notion of a clear state of mind without grudges, resentment, or prejudice.

3. 知らざるを知らずとせよ、これ知れるなり. This appears to be a rather free translation of Socrates' disavowal of knowledge, usually rendered as something like "The only thing I know is that I know nothing."

4. These are words used by the individuals themselves used as expressions of humility.

5. 死生命あり。富貴天あり. From the *Lunyu*, or *Analects* of Confucius.

Soga Ryōjin

Taken when Soga is around 30 (Courtesy of Sōō Gakusha, Kyoto. Photo not dated. Circa 1905)

Chapter 6

Soga Ryōjin
Life and Thought

Robert F. Rhodes

Soga Ryōjin 曽我量深 (1875–1971) was arguably the most innovative thinker in the history of modern Shin Buddhism.[1] Following in Kiyozawa Manshi's footsteps, he sought to express his teacher's insights in terms of traditional Shin Buddhist discourse. Soga was born as the third son of Tomioka Ryōdō 富岡量導, the head priest of Entokuji 円徳寺, a Shin Buddist temple in Niigata Prefecture, and his wife Tatsu. The temple was small and poor. But Soga was a brilliant child and he finished grade school in just three years, graduating before his elder brother. After studying the basics of Buddhism at Beihoku Kyōkō 米北教校, a Higashi Honganji school in Sanjō in Niigata, he moved to Kyoto at the age of eighteen to continue his studies. In 1897, he married Soga Kei and became the adopted son of Soga Enan 恵南, the head priest of the Jōonji 浄恩寺 in Niigata Prefecture.

In 1899, Soga entered the graduate division (*kenkyūka* 研究科) of Shinshū University, the Higashi Honganji seminary that had been created in 1896 from several departments split off from the Takakura Gakuryō. In 1901, when the school was reorganized as a modern university and moved to Tokyo under the under the leadership of Kiyozawa, Soga followed. In 1902, while still a graduate student, Soga published a series of article criticizing Kiyozawa's Seishinshugi as a form of passive acceptance of fate. Kiyozawa replied to Soga in an essay entitled "Seishinshugi to sanze" 精神主義と三世 ("Seishinshugi and the Three Periods of Time"), but Soga remained unconvinced.[2] However, Soga was soon converted to Kiyozawa's point of view and joined the Kōkōdō, the community of Kiyozawa's disciples, in 1903.

(By this time, Kiyozawa had already left Tokyo, and had returned to his temple, Saihōji.) The following year, Soga become a professor at Shinshū University, but resigned in 1911 when the school was moved from Tokyo to Kyoto.

After his resignation, Soga returned to the Jōonji in Niigata to devote himself to thinking and writing. It was at this time that he published the essay translated below, "Chijō no kyūshu: Hōzō Bosatsu shutsugen no igi" 地上の救主—法蔵菩薩出現の意義 ("A Savior on Earth: The Meaning of Dharmākara Bodhisattva's Advent"), in the journal *Seishinkai* in 1913. In this essay, Soga focuses on Dharmākara Bodhisattva (Hōzō Bosatsu 法蔵菩薩), a topic long considered marginal in traditional Shin thought, and interprets it as a symbol of the awakening of faith in human beings. This essay became a key work in the development of his thought. Dharmākara is, of course, Amida Buddha's name before he attained Buddhahood. According to the *Sutra of Immeasurable Life* (*Muryōjukyō* 無量寿経), the central text of Shin Buddhism, eons ago Dharmākara vowed to attain enlightenment upon encountering Lokeśvararāja Buddha. Dharmākara then made forty-eight vows outlining the kind of Pure Land he would create if and when he became a Buddha. After innumerable kalpas of arduous practice, he fulfilled his vows, and now presides over a Pure Land called Sukhāvatī (Jpn. *Gokuraku*) located far off in the west.[3]

At the beginning of "Chijō no kyūshu," Soga confesses that for a long time he considered Dharmākara Bodhisattva to be pure myth, something created simply to provide Amida Buddha with a plausible background story. However, he continues, through a series of insights he came to understand Dharmākara as the symbol of Amida's salvfic vows working within the human heart to lead all beings to enlightenment.[4] The arising of faith, he declares, is none other than the birth of Dharmākara Bodhisattva within the heart of us human beings. Formerly, Soga had understood salvation in a passive way, as the faithful acceptance of the fact that we are embraced by the saving light emanating from Amida Buddha residing in a other-worldly realm far up in the heavens. But now, he views faith dynamically, as the voice of Dharmākara calling to us from the depth of our being, urging us to awaken to our true selves. When we discover Dharmākara within ourselves, we can entrust ourselves in his power which, like a great ship, ferries us over to the Pure Land.

In 1916 Soga returned to Tokyo as professor at Tōyō University, and concurrently served as editor of *Seishinkai*. In 1922, he published *Kyūsai to jishō* 救済と自証 (*Salvation and Self-Realization*), a collection of his essays. Another important collection of essays entitled *Chijō no kyūshu* (*A Savior on Earth*) was published in 1924. The following year, he was called to Kyoto to become professor at Ōtani University. In 1927, he published *Nyorai hyōgen no hanchū to shite no sanshinkan* 如来表現の範疇としての三心観 (*The Three Minds as a Category of Tathāgata's Manifestation*), a transcript of a series of lectures he presented in 1926 under the auspicies of the Shinshū Kyōgaku Kenkyūsho 真宗教学研究所 (Research Institute for Doctrinal Studies) of Higashi Honganji. In this volume, Soga further extended his existential understanding of faith developed in "Chijō no kyūshu" and equated Dharmākara Bodhisattva with the *ālayavijñāna*, the eighth and deepest level of consciousness.

Soga's existential interpretation of faith proved extremely controversial. During this time, conservatives who supported the traditional interpretations of Shin Buddhist dogma were still powerful, both within the Higashi Honganji administration and the faculty of Ōtani University. Already in 1928, Kaneko Daiei, Soga's close colleague at Ōtani University, had been accused of heresy for his book, *Jōdo no kannen* 浄土の観念 (*The Idea of the Pure Land*), which had presented a radically new interpretation of the Pure Land under the influence of Neo-Kantian philosophy that was then in vogue. As a result, Kaneko was forced to resign his professorship and was expelled from the priesthood. At that time, Soga had tendered his own resignation in protest, but had been persuaded to remain at his post by the university president, Inaba Masamaru 稲葉昌丸 (1865–1944), one of Kiyozawa Manshi's close associates.[5] But when, in spring 1930, Soga's critics attacked his *Nyorai hyōgen no hanchū to shite no sanshinkan* as heretical, he felt compelled to submit his resignation once again. This time, Inaba passed it on to the Higashi Honganji administration, where it was accepted.

Soga's resignation sparked a period of crisis at Ōtani University. The students, who had earlier protested Kaneko's resignation, demanded a meeting with the director of education (*kyōgaku buchō* 教学部長) of the Higashi Honganji to express their disapproval. When the meeting was rejected, they began a nationwide campaign to criticize the denomination's handling of the Soga affair. The Higashi Honganji responded by drastically reducing the university budget and suspending several professors thought to be sympathetic with the students. As a result, the entire faculty and staff of the university resigned and the student body withdrew en masse from the university. However, a compromise was reached in June, in which the protesting professors were reinstated and the students returned to their classes.

But this was not the end of the matter. The following year, on

March 20 (the day after the graduation ceremony), Inaba was dismissed from his post and Saitō Yuishin 斉藤唯信 (1864–1957) was appointed in his place. Moreover, the university regulations were revised to read that only priests holding the high rank of Lecturer (*kōshi* 講師) could serve as president and that faculty members could not serve in administrative posts in the university. The latter rule implied that henceforth all of the university's administrative positions would be held by Higashi Honganji appointees. Once again a campaign in protest of the decision erupted, leading the Ministry of Education to intervene and hold hearings with the various parties involved. Finally, a compromise was reached at the Higashi Honganji assembly in June, in which the university regulations were revised again so that the post of president was not limited to priests having the high ecclesiastical rank of Lecturer. In August, Uesugi Bunshū 上杉文秀 (1867–1936) was appointed the sixth president of Ōtani University and things returned to normal.[6]

As this indicates, the controversy over Soga's *Nyorai hyōgen no hanchū to shite no sanshinkan* was not limited to disagreements over doctrine but ultimately developed into a struggle for academic freedom. However, after giving up his professorship in 1930, Soga did not return to Ōtani University for over ten years. After leaving the university, he established a private academy called Kōbō Gakuen 興法学園 (Academy for Raising Up the Dharma) with Kaneko, Yasuda Rijin, and other associates, where he passed his days writing and lecturing on Buddhist texts. *Hongan no butchi* 本願の仏地 (*The Buddha-Ground of the Original Vow*), published in 1933, was an important work treating the relationship between faith and the original vow. *Denshō to koshō* 伝承と己証 (*Tradition and Self-Realization*) published in 1938, and *Naikan no Hōzō* 内観の法蔵 (*Dharmākara of Introspection*) published in 1941, his third and fourth collections of essays, also date from this period of his life.

In May 1935, on the occasion of his sixtieth birthday Soga was asked to give a series of public lectures at a hall in Kyoto called the Yamaguchi Kaikan. These talks were later published as *Shinran no Bukkyōshi-kan* 親鸞の仏教史観 (*Shinran's View of Buddhist History*). In it, Soga criticizes what he saw as the shortcomings of positivistic Buddhist historiography then current in Japan. With the introduction of modern historical methods, a number of groundbreaking studies on Buddhist history had been written. Although Soga recognized the importance of these objective studies on Buddhist history, he was not fully satisfied with them, for he understood Buddhist history primarily as the history of the practice and actualization of the Buddhist path. Following Shinran's *Kyōgyōshinshō*, Soga argues that the 2,000-year long history of Buddhism is none other than the history of the religious tradition flowing forth from the *Sutra of Immeasurable Life*. In other words, it is the history of the transmission of nenbutsu and the history of the progress of Amida Buddha's original vow. Hence, Soga is critical of the evolutionary view of Buddhist history current in his day, which held that Buddhism was founded by Śākyamuni and developed in various ways over time. Soga questions whether such an interpretation can provide an adequate framework for explicating the spiritual dimensions of Buddhist history. Although not repudiating the view that Śākyamuni is, from the commonsense point of view, the founder of Buddhism, Soga here emphasizes that Śākyamuni himself was born from the history of the original vow. Buddhism does not begin with Śākyamuni, but is firmly rooted in the eternal Dharma that lies in Śākyamuni's background. In Soga's view, Śākyamuni arose from, and participates in, the history of the actualization of the Dharma that reaches back to beginningless time. Through our encounter with this tradition, we discover our true selves and are given the courage to live on the basis of the Buddhist teachings.

In 1937, Japan began a full-scale invasion of China. Ironically, the atmosphere of increasing crisis that the war created allowed Soga to be appointed Lecturer of the Ōtani denomination, and he was invited back to Ōtani University in 1941. The following year, he was asked to be the main speaker at the Ōtani denomination summer retreat for priests (*ango* 安居). The lecture was later published in 1947 as *Tannishō chōki* 歎異抄聴記 (*Lectures on the Tannishō*), a part of which is translated here. The *Tannishō chōki* has remained one of Soga's most widely read works.

In the meantime, Japan's increasing involvement in the war caused major changes at Ōtani University. More and more students and teachers were conscripted (deferment from military service for university students was abolished in 1943) and those that remained were all mobilized to work in factories and on farms. Because it proved impossible to hold classes under such circumstances, a research institute called Ōtani Kyōgaku Kenkyūsho 大谷教学研究所 (Ōtani Research Institute for Doctrinal Studies) was established so that professors could at least remain gainfully employed as researchers at the institute. Soga was appointed head of the Shin Buddhist Doctrinal Study Department (Shinshū kyōgakubu 日本教学部), one of the institute's four departments.[7] Even during the war years, when the total enrollment eventually dwindled to about five or six students, Soga continued to lecture on Shin Buddhism. However, as food and other basic necessities became increasingly scarce, Ōtani's athletic field was turned into a vegetable garden, and Soga, along with the other professors, was compelled to spend much of his time tending the field.

After the war, in 1949, Soga was purged from the Ōtani faculty by the occupation forces as being unfit as a university teacher. However, two years later, he was appointed professor emeritus of Ōtani University and finally became its president in 1961 at the age of eighty-six. Even at this advanced age, he continued to lecture and publish widely. Important works from the postwar years include *Bunsuirei no hongan* 分水嶺の本願 (*Original Vow of the Continental Divide*), published in 1954, the essay "Shin ni shishi gan ni ikiyo" 信に死し願に生きよ ("Die in Faith and Live in the Vow"), published in 1961, and *Kyōgyōshinshō shin no maki chōki* 教行信証「信巻」聴記 (*Lectures on the Chapter on Faith in the Kyōgyōshinshō*), published in 1963, a masterly account of Shin faith. He passed away in 1971.

Notes

1. The standard work on Soga's life is Itō 1993. An excellent presentation of Soga's thought is also found in Honda 1988.
2. At KMZ 6:91.
3. For the story of Dhamākara Bodhisattva as found in the *Sutra of Immeasurable Life*, see Gómez 1996, 161–75.
4. For Soga's views on Dharmākara Bodhisattva in English, see Soga 1965.
5. Inaba took part in Kiyozawa's attempt to reform the Higashi Honganji church, which led to his expulsion from the priesthood. Later, however, he was reinstated and went on to serve as president of Ōtani Middle School, director of the Higashi Honganji administration, and in 1928 president of Ōtani University. Inaba is also known as the editor of two collections of writings by and about Rennyo: *Rennyo Shōnin ibun* 蓮如聖人遺文 and *Rennyo Shōnin gyōjitsu* 蓮如聖人行実.
6. See Ōtani Daigaku Hyakunenshi Hensan Iinkai 2001, 347–57.
7. The three other departments of the institute were Japanese Doctrinal Studies Department (Nihon kyōgaku-bu 日本教学部) headed by Kaneko Daiei, Asian Development Doctrinal Studies Department (Kōa kyōgaku-bu 興亜教学部) headed by D. T. Suzuki, and the Humanities Department (Jinbun kagaku-bu 人文科学部) headed by Suzuki Hiroshi 鈴木弘 (1890–1956).

Chapter 7

A Savior on Earth

The Meaning of Dharmākara Bodhisattva's Advent*

Soga Ryōjin

Translated by Jan Van Bragt

I

Toward the beginning of July last year (1912), at the home of my friend Kaneko[1] in Takada,[2] it dawned on me that "The Tathāgata (i.e., Amida Buddha) is myself." Then, toward the end of August, this time at Akegarasu's[3] place in Kaga,[4] I was handed the phrase, "The Tathāgata becoming me saves me." Finally, around October, I realized that "When the Tathāgata becomes me, it signals the birth of Dharmākara Bodhisattva." This may not mean much to other people, but for me—who for twenty years had been plagued by sickness and

---

*This essay, *Chijō no kyūshu: Hōzō Bosatsu shutsugen no igi* 地上の救主—法蔵菩薩出現の意義, published in the journal *Seishinkai* in 1913 when Soga was thirty-eight years old, is one of his most important works. It was reprinted in 1924 in a collection of essays entitled *Chijō no kyūshu*. Throughout his life, the focus of Soga's thought lay in the question of how spiritual liberation is achieved through faith, and in this essay he argues that it is attained when we realize Amida Buddha manifesting himself in our hearts as Dharmākara Bodhisattva, the guise in which Amida appears in the world to work for the liberation of sentient beings. The translation is based on the text found in SRS 2: 408–21. Several passages dealing with technical matters of Shin Buddhist doctrine have been deleted in the translation. These sections are indicated by ellipses. All footnotes have been provided by the editors.

worldly worries, and who had not understood the meaning of the scriptures on this point, even though I made it my task to read from them daily—the insight I received made me feel as if I was handed a torch that all of a sudden lit up a room that had been kept in darkness for a thousand years.⁵ I lacked the capacity to express that feeling but could not keep it to myself either. Thus, from October of that year, I have set forth a part of it in a series of short pieces in *Bōfūshiu* 暴風駛雨 (Tempest).⁶ Also, in the January 1913 issue of the journal *Mujintō* 無尽灯 (*Inexhaustible Lamp*),⁷ I published an article entitled "Kuon no busshin no kaikensha toshite no genzai no Hōzō Bosatsu" 久遠の仏心の開顕者としての現在の法蔵菩薩 ("The Present Monk Dharmākara as the Revealer of the Eternal Buddha-mind"). I am overwhelmed by the many expressions of sympathy and demands for further explanation that I received from friends in the Dharma far and near, just as I am still surprised by the boldness and assertiveness of my own thought.

II

To be honest, this figure of Dharmākara Bodhisattva has for a long time been for me a big concept I did not know what to do with. Of course, I do not understand either the meaning of a Pure Land lying myriads of miles to the west but, as a person who cannot consider the present world as a Pure Land, I cannot but surrender to the idea of the western paradise. However, I could not believe, and did not think I had any obligation to believe, in the figure of Dharmākara Bodhisattva, the original vow he took after five kalpas of reflection, and the impossibly long period he is supposed to have devoted to ascetic practice in order to gather merits for the salvation of all. In my childhood, on hearing the passage about him in the *Shōshinge* 正信偈 (*Hymn of True Faith*),⁸ I was moved without really understanding. Indeed, simple believers are often moved to tears by the mere words "five kalpas of reflection."⁹ On reaching the age of discretion, I lost all interest in Dharmākara's practice as the causal stage of the vow.¹⁰ It was, then, simply the name "Unhindered Light in the Ten Directions" (*jin jippō mugekō nyorai* 尽十方無碍光如来)¹¹ that became attractive to me. Adducing meaningless categories such as the great law of causality, I reasoned that, because humans cannot think without basing themselves on causality, the Tathāgata, in order to make known to us humans his original vow, had revealed his will by way of the law of causality, which is the law of all human thinking. My true heart in all this was to do away with the causal vow-practice of Dharmākara, while yearning as before solely for the unhindered light.

Namely, while heralding my faith as being centered in the original vow, in fact the original vow was for me nothing but simply the great spirit of the enlightened Tathāgata. The monk Dharmākara was an illusory figure, a fictive name, and his five kalpas of reflection and innumerable kalpas of practice were nothing more than a theater act of the Tathāgata—or rather, a play of my own brain. Despite all the talk on Dharmākara, the savior was and remained for me the eternal Tathāgata of Unhindered Light.

III

However, the eternal Tathāgata of Unhindered Light stays on the level of an object of our yearning, in other words, on the level of our ideals, and as such cannot be our savior. Such a faith is indistinguishable from the "self-nature and mind-only" enlightenment[12] that is envisaged by "the path of sages."[13] Salvation, on the other hand, is a matter of manifest reality, the great problem of the self as subject of actual human life. We cannot be saved by a baseless ideal of the self. The gods, buddhas, and bodhisattvas of the ten directions[14] and the three periods of time[15] are all fragments of the human ideal. The name "Buddha of Unhindered Light" encompasses all these names of gods, buddhas, and bodhisattvas, and thus has the meaning of the sum and unity of all human aspirations. As such, we cannot but direct to it our deepest yearnings as to the greatest and highest human ideal. Yet, the mere ideal of light, while sufficing to be the light of wisdom that lights up the darkness of the long night of our ignorance—the antipode of our ideal world—could not be the active vessel that takes away the pain and suffering of the actual great ocean of *saṃsāra* (the cycle of transmigration).

Only when we are taken up into the vow-ark of great compassion,[16] the ideal becomes one with reality. Then the sea of human life itself, that is full of real suffering, interpenetrates unhinderedly with the light, so as to become itself a wide ocean of light. Away from the vow-ark of great compassion, human life remains a sea of suffering, sinfulness, and hindrance. Even supposing that the unhindered light illuminates the sea of suffering of actual existence, what benefit would that bring to the self that is drowning at the bottom of the sea? Indeed, what is truly demanded by actual present reality is not light in the sky but the ark of the vow on the sea of real human life. It is not the eternal *dharmakāya* buddha[17] who is the savior of the real self; the savior of the real world must be a human buddha who deigns to appear in the real world.

That Christianity speaks of a Trinity, posits Jesus as the mediator between God and human beings, and considers this God-man Jesus as the true and direct savior is undoubtedly for the sake of satisfying this demand. The Father, the Supreme God, being eternal light, is not a being to be in intimate contact with the real world. Even supposing that this world is among the works of the Supreme God's hands, from the moment that the real world has come into actual existence, the Supreme God and the world are totally separated and independent from each other. Thus, this Supreme God in his own primal nature has already lost the capacity to rule, elevate, and save human beings. It is for that reason that He conceived the plan to send his especially beloved Son Christ into the real world, to make him the savior of that world and the unifier of the spiritual world, and in that way to reunite himself above with human beings below, who had been alienated from one another for a long time.

Between the father, who is eternal light, and us human beings, who are floundering at the bottom of the ocean of *saṃsāra*, there is a distance as great as that between heaven and earth. The majesty of the father cannot reach us directly. That is why he, dimming his light and adapting to the dust (*wakō dōjin* 和光同塵),[18] deigned to appear as Dharmākara Bodhisattva, this savior who is a human buddha.

IV

If so, what kind of person is this Dharmākara Bodhisattva? Where did he appear, where did he make his vows, where did he engage in ascetic practice and where did he reach enlightenment? His enlightenment evidently points to the Pure Land in the west that lies infinitely beyond the realities of this world. The problem, however, is the place of the birth of this human buddha, Dharmākara Bodhisattva, namely, the causal stage of Amida Buddha.

In Christ's case, no matter how much he bathes in an ideal light, it is clear that he is after all one historical person. He owes his capacity of being the savior of the real world, for one, to the fact that he has a foundation in that real world. On the other hand, however, it is due to his being one historical person that he cannot perfectly fulfill the role of savior. No matter how superior a man one makes him out to be, he is after all a man, and must therefore be equal with us all in the point of needing salvation. And if one posits him between God and man as a mediator, he immediately loses the capacity of saving the real world. Moreover, he is and remains himself, while I am and remain myself. Thus, even while being a manifestation of a celestial world, from the moment he is one individual person he cannot be the savior of other individuals, such as myself. If in this way he cannot be near enough to us to be our savior, it follows that he is nothing more than a precursor in enlightenment, who shows us that the Supreme God is near to us human beings as a Father. Thus, while outwardly showing the appearance of a religion of salvation by other-power, Christianity ends up being in fact an idealistic doctrine of self-power effort when that mask is finally taken away. The Supreme God, who is the ideal world, by his light only makes clearer and clearer the depth and weight of the karmic hindrances of human beings; and to us nothing is left but to cry out the pain of vain effort, while yearning for the light of the Supreme God.

Dharmākara certainly did not appear as one historical human being. He deigned to be born directly in the heart–mind of us human beings. The calling voice directed at all sentient beings of the ten directions did not come from the high world of pure light, nor was it uttered objectively by one human person. This voice arose from the dark breast of suffering of each human being. That the original vow of Dharmākara Bodhisattva is called the ark on the great ocean of *saṃsāra* intimates that the calling voice arose from the depth of my soul, from right under my feet. While all of the world's idealistic religions are "religions of heaven," our religion of salvation by Dharmākara Bodhisattva has the honor of being the only "religion of the earth." There are many "religions of light" but our Shinshū is the only "religion of the ark." Only our Shinshū is a religion of the real world, a religion of true salvation. . . .

Why is it that there are so many people in the world who go to their perdition in the depth of the ocean of *saṃsāra*, while vainly praising and putting their trust in a future light? Truly, together with the many religions in the world that praise the light, our Shinshū too adoringly trusts in the light of the Tathāgata that penetrates all ten directions. But, we who praise the eternal and everlasting light do not reside in the sky. We find ourselves in the ark that sails the great ocean of reality, and there is not a single one in this ark who will perish forever. While being in the midst of the great ocean of life, the people in the ark of the great vow are far away from *saṃsāra*. When I forget that ark, I can no longer be a person who praises the light. For, my real self, weighed down as it is by aeons of karma, cannot but naturally drop down as far as it can. I am not a person floating in the sky.

The buddhas, bodhisattvas, and gods of the ten directions and the three periods of time all equally call out from heaven: "Come!" Each of them shines on us with its particular light. And Amida Buddha of the regally burning light, which unifies all these lights, is supreme among them. Still, yearning and salvation are not one and the same thing. It may be true enough that all gods and buddhas do not reject us but forever call and enlighten us, but when we, powerless beings, meet the problem of the salvation of the real self, when it comes to the matter of praxis, we must reject and do away with the gods and buddhas by ourselves. To speak plainly, in all these gods and buddhas we find an ideal calling voice but no original vow of real salvation. In its true sense, the original vow is limited solely to the forty-eight vows of Dharmākara Bodhisattva. We may speak lightly of salvation by other-power, but there is no true other-power besides the "original vow-power" of the Tathāgata that our founder Shinran has revealed to us.

But, what is this original vow-power? It is the power that saves the real self. But is this not a beautiful and idle thing like a painted dumpling? The power of the compassionate bodhisattva Kannon 観音 is, indeed, such a painted dumpling; it has no real basis anywhere. It is nothing but a beautiful metaphor. The original vow of Dharmākara Bodhisattva is totally different. As a human buddha, Dharmākara Bodhisattva is, as such, the eternally existent Amida Buddha; at the same time, in another aspect, he is the true subject of the self that seeks salvation. I have expressed this idea with the words "the Tathāgata is none other than myself," and again have sensed it as "the Tathāgata becomes me." In other words, as savior he is the figure of the unity of *ki* 機 (faith) and *hō* 法 (Tathāgata).[19] Or again, on the side of the human being to be saved, he is the figure of the unity of the buddha-mind (faith) and the mind of common mortals[20] (sinful karma).

In the single figure of Dharmākara Bodhisattva, we worship the majestic power of the eternal *dharmakāya* buddha and see the figure of the self that, awakened to its sinful self in the midst of evil karma, surrenders itself wholeheartedly. In him, while seeing the figure of the exalted parent, we discern, in another aspect, the figure of the favorite child. Dharmākara Bodhisattva is not a third person that stands as mediator between the Tathāgata, the eternal father, and us sentient beings; in his one person he is precisely the Tathāgata *and* us sentient beings. He is, at once, the first person and the second person; while being the object of our faith, he is at the same time the subject of our faith; he is the savior and the saved, the relier and the relied on, in one. He is, at once, a guest in the ark and its captain;

the master of the original vow and its intended object. When I start thinking of the person of this Dharmākara Bodhisattva, and the reason and meaning of his birth, I am overwhelmed by strong feeling and a sense of awesome wonder.

V

When I am struck with amazement at the inconceivable figure of this Dharmākara Bodhisattva, I feel awe before the inconceivable figure of the eternal Tathāgata and, at the same time, am amazed about my own inconceivable existence.

What, then, is this Dharmākara Bodhisattva? None other than the subject of the surrendering faith that is mindful of the Tathāgata. His eighteenth vow is the expression of the Tathāgata's loving experiment with the entrusting child-mind of the sentient beings. Our founder Shinran stated that the eighteenth vow realizes the faith of a beliver (ki 機), but what does it mean, after all, to realize the "entrusting person" (tanomu ki たのむ機)? What does it mean to say that the Tathāgata has deigned to realize or accomplish the faith that we were supposed to arouse? If it were said that the Tathāgata had realized the vow and practice that we were supposed to bring forth, we could still understand that in an objective way, since vow and practice are objective to some extent. It is a different matter with faith, however, since this cannot be conceived at all apart from the subject. What could it mean, then, that an objective Tathāgata has realized in the subject's place the one moment of real faith of the true subject, whereby the self entrusts itself intimately to the Tathāgata? Is not precisely faith the true life of our pure subjectivity? It would appear, therefore, that this at least cannot be realized on the side of the objective Tathāgata.

Indeed, Masters Shandao and Hōnen, in their interpretation of the three aspects of faith and the ten moments of invocation in the eighteenth vow[21]—an interpretation that asserts that faith, vow, and practice (nenbutsu) are the causes of birth in the Pure Land—make a distinction on this point: Of the three causes, faith as pertaining to the believing subject is detached from the original vow as the object of faith. They, then, consider the name, as endowed with both vow and practice, to be realized by the Tathāgata, and therefore call the eighteenth vow the "Vow of Birth by Nenbutsu" (nenbutsu ōjō no gan 念仏往生の願). Only our founder Shinran, experimenting with this vow in the depth of his own heart, and discovering the original vow of Dharmākara Bodhisattva in his own subject, resolutely called this vow the "Original Vow of Faith and Entrusting" (*shishin shingyō no hongan* 至心信楽の本願). Truly, in his self-awareness, Shinran was not only the "true guest" (object) of the original vow, but also its "master" (subject). At this point, for one, we feel that, when the doctrine of our founder is said to be directly transmitted by Amida, these certainly are no mere words of idle praise. For he discovered the great spirit wherein the vows of Dharmākara were made precisely in his own one moment faith. As our savior, Dharmākara is none other than the eternal Tathāgata but, when in his experiment with entrusting he is turned toward the eternal Tathāgata, he is none other than the faith, which is the subject's true self for us sentient beings.

Among the words of the eighteenth vow, the oath, "if there are sentient beings that are not born in my land, may I not attain the supreme enlightenment," presents Dharmākara Bodhisattva directly in his capacity of father of eternal light, and the summons, "with sincere mind entrust yourselves, aspiring to be born in my land, and saying my name perhaps even ten times," directly shows him as coming into the subject of the sentient beings of the ten directions and experimenting with the stirrings of the hearts of us children. . . .

Especially in connection with the very "subjective" act of faith, it is not fitting to speak of "the Tathāgata acting in my place." Instead, we better speak of "the Tathāgata directly becoming me." Precisely the true self of entrusting faith is the core of the eighteenth vow, and what is called "other-power salvation of the original vow" is ultimately nothing but the Tathāgata deigning to become the subject of the surrendering faith of the nenbutsu practitioner. As long as one places Dharmākara Bodhisattva or his original vow simply on the objective level, in the rank of object of faith, one cannot yet call him somebody who has experimented with the original vow and has entrusted himself to it.

As to why the Tathāgata made the oath of faith, how he made it, and why he did not simply pledge birth by the nenbutsu, those are profound questions that deserve further deep reflection. . . .

Precisely by experimenting with the true subject of the practitioner, which is entrusting, the Tathāgata fulfilled and revealed the parental heart that makes him pronounce the vow; at the same time, precisely through his parental heart, he experiences the children's heart of entrusting. Truly, the eighteenth vow attests to the fact that Dharmākara Bodhisattva is the unhindered unity of the children's heart of entrusting and the parental heart of the vow, and shows that his personality consists in the self-awareness of the unity of parent and child. Dharmākara Bodhisattva is the figure of the unity of Dharma and sentient beings, of the buddha-mind and the mind of the common mortal. He directly feels the karmic evil of all sentient beings as his own; he does not blame us, but only himself. By experimenting with the sinfulness of common mortals, he arouses the buddha-mind on the side of the children, which is entrusting; and by experimenting with that entrusting, he brings forth the eternal parental heart that prompts him to make the vow.

Dharmākara Bodhisattva is the *figure* of the Tathāgata deigning to become me; and, at the same time, he is the manifestation of the Tathāgata having become us sentient beings—as indicated in the eighteenth vow.

VI

In order to save me, who from time immemorial up to the very present has been tossing about in the ocean of *saṃsāra*, burdened with the weight of karmic evil, the Tathāgata who is the eternal father has projected himself into this ocean of *saṃsāra*, has become intimately my true and ultimate subject, and thereby has awakened me from the dream of the beginningless night of ignorance. On the surface, the Tathāgata has called me "Thou," but in his hidden depths he has deigned to consider me directly as "I."

In connection with Dharmākara Bodhisattva, the sūtra speaks of "five kalpas" [of reflection] and "innumerable kalpas" [of practice].[22] On hearing this, people are apt to consider this as an old tale that has nothing to do with their present self. In fact, however, the one moment wherein Dharmākara Bodhisattva evoked the faith of sincere entrusting is an absolute moment that embraces innumerable kalpas. And equally the first moment wherein we are made to experience faith is an absolute moment that covers innumerable kalpas. . . . The present of faith is the great present of immeasurable life. There are no later moments that can be added to this moment. . . . Apart from that first one moment there is no faith; the living reality of faith is only in the present. Why, then, view faith, which is the highest and only subject, as something in the past, as if it were a "thing" that has raised you once and for all to a peak of attainment, toward which only gratitude is in order. Faith is the ultimate subject, the true self. Therefore, when we distance ourselves from the one moment of faith, we are already far from the Tathāgata, away from the self, and are living in the sky of illusory dreams. . . .

When we consider the moment when, innumerable kalpas ago, Dharmākara Bodhisattva made his vow and the moment wherein we obtain faith as one absolute moment, the vow of Dharmākara comes to lie within our present moment of faith. Both these moments are the beginning and aftermath of the same one moment. The innumerable kalpas of Dharmākara's practice and the ten kalpas that already elapsed since he obtained buddhahood[23] [may seem to lie in between but we] cannot separate the two.

Truly, the five kalpas of reflection on the vow, the innumerable kalpas of practice, and the ten kalpas that have elapsed since obtaining buddhahood are all finally included within the one moment of faith of the great present. Dharmākara Bodhisattva is no ancient myth; he is a reality of present faith. If we conceive of him apart from the one moment of faith, he becomes a mere mythological figure. The other Pure Land sects are religions of childish myth, since they distanced themselves from the one moment of faith and became religions of idle yearning. In them, there is no real basis for the figure of Dharmākara and, consequently, for them the original vow, the bodhisattva's practice, his attainment of buddhahood, the Pure Land, even salvation and birth in the Pure Land, all become mere ideals. . . . In fact, the ten kalpas and many eons, and also the moment of death [which many tend to see as the real moment of salvation], do not exist apart from the self-awareness of the present one moment of faith. . . .

Dharmākara Bodhisattva's original vow of the realization of entrusting, while being a thing of the beginningless past, is totally embraced by the one moment of our self-awareness. The Bodhisattva first experiments with the eternally deluded heart of common mortals, directly brings forth therein the buddha-mind of entrusting, and from the midst of that mind of wholehearted surrender arouses the heart of the eternal Tathāgata that makes the salvation of all the condition of his own attainment of buddhahood.

VII

When all is said and done, the yearning for light is a common trait of all religions, not a characteristic of other-power religion. By truly returning to our self, we must turn away from a religion that praises light to a religion that takes us up into the ark. When we awaken to our present innermost reality and discover ourselves at the bottom of the ocean of *saṃsāra*, then, surprisingly enough, we find ourselves sailing on the ark. . . . The ark of the vow is really there in the present, and as long as there is this boat, the Pure Land of Bliss, while being far, is close at hand. The great and only problem is not whether the Pure Land and the Tathāgata are far or near, but whether we ourselves are aware of the ark of the vow or not. . . .

Notes

1. Kaneko Daiei.
2. Presently the city of Jōetsu 上越 in Niigata Prefecture.
3. Akegarasu Haya 暁烏敏 (1877–1954). Akegarasu was born in a Shinshū temple in Ishikawa Prefecture. Under his teacher, Kiyozawa Manshi, he assisted in the publication of the journal *Seishinkai*. In 1950, Akegarasu became the head of the administration of the Ōtani denomination. He is well known as the author of the *Tannishō kōwa* 歎異抄講話 (*Lectures on the Tannishō*). His writings are collected together in *Akegarasu Haya Zenshū* 暁烏敏全集 (*Complete Works of Akegarasu Haya*) in twenty-seven volumes.
4. Presently Ishikawa Prefecture.
5. This simile derives from Tanluan's *Jingtulunzhu* 浄土論註 (*Commentary on the Pure Land Treatise*). In this text, the recitation of the nenbutsu is likened to light shining into a room that has been dark for one thousand years. See Inagaki 1998, 199–200.
6. Refers to a column in *Seishinkai* where Soga published a series of short essays from 1908 to 1913. The essays can be found in SRS 4: 203–380. The word *"bōfūshiu"* (literally "violent winds and sudden rain") comes from Daochuo's *Anleji* 安楽集 (*Collection of Passages on [the Land of] Peace and Bliss*) (T 47: 13c), where deluded existence is likened to a storm fraught with violent wind and rain.
7. A journal published by Shinshū Ōtani University. It was published from 1895 to 1920, when its name was changed to *Bukkyō kenkyū* 仏教研究 (*Buddhist Studies*).
8. A hymn, written by Shinran, which is a compendium, as it were, of Shinshū doctrine. It is found at the end of the "Chapter on Practice" in the *Kyōgyōshinshō* and often is recited in Shinshū religious services.
9. According to the *Sutra of Immeasurable Life*, after arousing the aspiration for buddhahood under Lokeśvararāja Buddha, Dharmākara Bodhisattva reflected for five kalpas on the features of a perfect pure land. Subsequently, he set forth his forty-eight vows and embarked on his practice to construct his pure land.
10. Buddhist doctrines are often systematized by means of the categorical scheme: "causal stage" (*inni* 因位) and "resultant stage" (*kai* 果位). In this case, the same entity, in the causal stage, is called Dharmākara and, in the resultant stage, Amida Buddha.
11. An alternate name for Amida Buddha, frequently used by Shinran.
12. In the preface to the "Chapter on Faith" in the *Kyōgyōshinshō*, Shinran criticizes those Buddhists who attacked his teacher Hōnen's understanding of Pure Land Buddhism as "floundering in concepts of 'self-nature' and 'mind-only'." See CWS 1: 77.
13. The "path of sages," also called "the path of self-power," refers to the way for attaining buddhahood by practicing the arduous bodhisattva path in this world over a period of numerous lifetimes. This is contrasted to the "Pure Land path," also called "the path of other-power," in which one

strives to attain buddhahood by first attaining birth in Amida Buddha's Pure Land and undertaking bodhisattva practices there.

14. North, south, east, west, northeast, southeast, northwest, southwest, zenith, and nadir.

15. Past, present, and future.

16. Amida Buddha's saving power often is likened in Pure Land Buddhism to a ship that carries the believer across the ocean of transmigration to the Pure Land.

17. *Dharmakāya* (Dharma-body, Jpn. *hosshin* 法身) is the Buddha as absolute reality, identical with the Dharma-nature, in contradistinction with, mainly, the *nirmāna-kāya* (personified body, Jpn. *ōjin* 応身) or the Buddha appearing in the world.

18. A term originally taken from chapter 4 of the *Daodejing* 道徳経, which states, "[The Dao] dims its light and adapts itself to the dust [i.e., the world]." In Buddhism, it refers to cases in which buddhas and bodhisattvas, in order to undertake their task of saving all beings, transform and manifest themselves in a form that is most suited to helping the sentient beings in need of salvation. Soga argues that, because Amida, as the formless *dharmakāya* buddha, is beyond all conceptualization, the Buddha took the guise of Dharmākara Bodhisattva in order to manifest himself in a form understandable to us humans.

19. The Japanese term for "the unity of *ki* and *hō*" is *ki hō ittai* 機法一体. This is a concept used to explain the meaning of the six characters Namu Amida Butsu 南無阿弥陀仏 (I take refuge in Amida Buddha). The first two characters, "Namu," refer to the faith of sentient beings (*ki*) and the last four characters, "Amida Butsu," refer to the workings of Amida to save all beings (*hō*). In other words, faith and the Tathāgata's power become one through the act of calling out Amida's name.

20. Here, "common mortal" is used as a translation for "*bonbu*." *Bonbu* is used in contradistinction with "buddha" (enlightened being). It thus denotes an unenlightened being, with all the karmic burdens, passions, and sufferings this implies in the Buddhist worldview. In Shin Buddhism, where it is often used, it also connotes the idea of "being unable to gain salvation by one's own power."

21. The eighteenth vow reads, "If, when I attain buddhahood, the sentient beings of the ten quarters, with sincere mind entrusting themselves, aspiring to be born in my land, and saying my name perhaps even ten times, should not be born there, may I not attain the supreme enlightenment. Excluded are those who commit the five grave offenses and those who slander the right dharma" (CWS 1: 80). The three aspects of faith are the sincere mind, entrusting, and the aspiration to be born in Amida's Pure Land referred to in this passage. The ten moments of invocation refer to the act of "saying my [i.e., Amida Buddha's] name perhaps even ten times" mentioned in the vow.

22. According to the *Sutra of Immeasurable Life*, after enunciating his forty-eight vows, Dharmākara Bodhisattva practiced the Buddhist path for innumerable kalpas until he finally realized his Pure Land.

23. According to the *Sutra of Immeasurable Life*, ten kalpas have elapsed since Amida Buddha attained buddhahood. See Gómez 1996, 176.

Chapter 8

Shinran's View of Buddhist History*

Soga Ryōjin

Translated by Jan Van Bragt

Lecture I: What Is a True History of Buddhism?

To all gathered here to celebrate my sixtieth birthday by these three days of lectures my heartfelt thanks.

In case you are wondering what I meant by affixing the title "Shinran's View of Buddhist History" to these lectures, it has something to do with the founding of our Shinshū. Most people consider it only common sense to say that Shinran is its founder, that Shinran started Jōdo Shinshū (True Pure Land School). Still, there are people nowadays who doubt whether Shinran ever had the intention of founding Jōdo Shinshū. They ask where Shinran himself ever expressed that intention, and argue that Shinran always says that he wants nothing but to follow and believe the doctrine of his master Hōnen, and that therefore it is rather Hōnen who is the founder of Jōdo Shinshū. We must confess that these arguments sound reasonable enough. However, to discuss this question sensibly, we should first investigate what it means to establish Jōdo Shinshū and therefore what Jōdo Shinshū is all about, what its concrete content is.

---

*This translation is based on the text found in SRS 5: 385–471. Since the text is quite repetitious and difficult to read, a number of passages have been deleted in the translation below. The deleted sections are marked by ellipses. In addition, titles to each section were added by the translator to facilitate the understanding of the text. All the notes were added by the editors.

Recently, while studying the *Kyōgyōshinshō*, I came face to face with that very problem: What is this Jōdo Shinshū? Suddenly then I got the insight or inspiration: The thing called "Jōdo Shinshū" is the new view of Buddhist history experienced by Shinran, Shinran's grasp and clarification of what constitutes the true history of the Buddhist tradition, the true spirit of the Buddhist path. Thus, what goes by the name of "Jōdo Shinshū" represents the history of Buddhism as sensed by Shinran.

Shinran received the doctrine of the nenbutsu of the original vow from Hōnen. From that time onwards this original vow served him, be it only vaguely, as a principle for viewing Buddhist history, or as what could be called the basic spirit of the history of Buddhism. . . . By way of Hōnen, then, by way of the Buddhist path that flowed through Hōnen's personality and the doctrinal tradition he represents, Shinran quietly traced back far and deep to the background and root-source of that tradition. He traced back 2,000 years looking for the trunk or core of the long history of Buddhism. There he discovered Buddhist history with its profusion of forms, all vying with the others in beauty. What could be considered to be the trunk line in that 2,000-year long development of Buddhism? Through the beginningless interplay of factors by which the Dharma flourishes and benefits living beings, Shinran was finally afforded an insight into the unifying factor of that history; that is, his spiritual eye was made to open so that he could inwardly discern the main line of Buddhist history. This very view of Buddhist history is precisely what is called Jōdo Shinshū.

Modern Buddhist Studies, which have become influential in Japan in the last sixty years, tend to present the history of Buddhism as follows. First, there was the pure basic Buddhism as preached by the teacher Śākyamuni; after his passing, his disciples compiled the Tripiṭaka (the Buddhist canon) and developed the so-called Hīnayāna, an individualistic and subjective form of Buddhism that fell apart into many sects. Then, to offset this trend, a kind of unitary revivalist "return to Śākyamuni" movement, known as Mahāyāna Buddhism, arose. At the beginning, this movement was motivated by a desire to see the future savior of this world, Maitreya Buddha, appear on earth; next, belief in birth in the eastern Pure Land of Akṣobhya Buddha came into vogue; finally, then, there arose the faith in the western Pure Land of Utmost Bliss of Amida Buddha. Therein the aspirations of the Mahāyāna movement would have found their completion.

This is, indeed, one possible way of presenting the history of Buddhism, but I submit that it is a Buddhist history seen from the viewpoint of historical materialism, a materialism that negates the very spirit of Buddhism and leaves no room for any unified body of Buddhist truth, for any spirit pervading the whole of Buddhist history. . . . Moreover, in this view of Buddhist history, the truth that Buddhism teaches is thought not to have existed at all prior to Śākyamuni. Śākyamuni would then have been the absolute founder of Buddhism, who for the first time and all of a sudden discovered this truth. In a sense, of course, I have no gripes with this position. Śākyamuni was indeed the founder and patriarch of Buddhism, and in a way Buddhism could be called "Śākyamuni-ism." In this sense, "buddha" means simply Śākyamuni Buddha, and "Buddhism" means the doctrine taught by Śākyamuni.

However, in Shinran's view, Buddhism is not simply the doctrine which Śākyamuni realized and preached. For Shinran, Buddhism is the doctrine directed at the attainment of buddhahood, the doctrine that teaches about the buddha, the doctrine that teaches that which makes a buddha truly into a buddha and thus aims at making all sentient beings into buddhas. It is the doctrine *of* the buddha, both as subjective genitive (buddha as subject) and objective genitive (buddha as object). Buddhist scholars nowadays concentrate on the former with total neglect of the latter: the nature of a buddha and the way to become a buddha. In their study of Buddhist doctrine, they are therefore only interested in whether something has been really taught by the Buddha or not. They have thus eyes only for the doctrine and forget about the matter of practice whereby buddhahood is realized.

Still, true Buddhism is precisely the path to become a buddha. It is nothing but a doctrine wherein the unfolding of the buddha-path forms the silver thread. It is all about Śākyamuni Buddha, in the sense that it was Śākyamuni who, by his insight into how he himself became a buddha, made clear the path whereby all sentient beings can equally become buddhas.

Presently Buddhist Studies applies the law of evolution to the history of Buddhism and considers that thought develops from the simple to the complicated. Śākyamuni would thus have preached a sharp but simple path of inward practice, a simple and clear, practical and moral path, free from all theory and mysticism, and with which everybody who heard it could not but agree. This message was gradually turned into philosophy and mysticism, and so Mahāyāna Buddhism originated. In this view, there is no perspective of sentient beings becoming buddhas; this idea would have been absent from the beginning. Here Buddhist history is treated as a "thing," without any regard for the concrete nature and meaning of the thing. We are offered here a superficial and abstract picture; it is like beer that lost its fizz. . . .

The Buddhist path sought by Shinran, the history of the path as lived by the ancestors, was something completely different. It was the historical testimony of sentient beings, lost in delusion, staking their lives on the quest for the Buddha and finally finding him; it was history as the hall of Buddhist practice wherein our ancestors single-mindedly searched for the path and walked it with their entire being. It is far from a Buddhist history as a process of evolutionary development, as people are presenting it today, from a basic Buddhism to Hīnayāna, to Mahāyāna, and finally to the One Vehicle (*ekayāna*),[1] or from self-power Buddhism to other-power Buddhism. Such a history is not a history of Buddhism, but in its true sense a history of the negation of Buddhism. The true history of Buddhism is precisely the historical process of sentient beings becoming buddhas, and thus of bringing the Buddhist path to realization: the historical path walked for more than 2,000 years by buddhas and bodhisattvas since Śākyamuni. There can be no doubt about this. . . .

There is "Buddhist history" only where there is Buddhist reality. Where Buddhism has been reduced to nothing, "Buddhist history" is merely a subjective notion, a dream. After all, of what significance could it possibly be to construct a history of Buddhism, when one has done away with the fact of Buddhist experience? The method of approach to the history of Buddhism must grow out of the object: Buddhism as living in the experience of our ancestors, in the practice of peoples. In other words, Buddhism as the object and Buddhist history as the method must be one. The same phenomenon, which transcends time while caught in the flow of time, is called "Buddhist history," when viewed in its temporal aspect, and is called "Buddhism" when considered as transcending time. They are two only by the difference of viewpoint.

When speaking of Buddhist history, the presupposition has mostly been that Buddhism began with Śākyamuni. In my view, however, the position accorded Śākyamuni should be like that of Emperor Jimmu 神武 in Japanese history.[2] The history of Japan is often said to begin with Emperor Jimmu's ascension to the throne, but in fact the real beginnings of Japan go far back in time beyond that point. If we want to truly understand Buddhism, we must look for Śākyamuni's background. What made Śākyamuni truly into Śākyamuni Buddha? What is the basis on which Śākyamuni was not simply the human Śākyamuni? What was it that made the human Śākyamuni become a genuine buddha, Śākyamuni? Why was it that innumerable living souls could not but call out in reverence, "Homage to the Buddha!"

(*namu butsu*) when they came before Śākyamuni? These are the important questions.

Of the time before Śākyamuni's decisive appearance into the world, we have, as first "chronicles," the *jātakas* (birth stories) about the previous lives of Śākyamuni.[3] Are these purely fictive tales, such as bedside stories for children, or is there more to them? I think that we should quietly reflect on the significance they might possibly have. In later sutras, then, we find similar elements. In the *Huayan Sutra*, we encounter the legend of Sudhana's spiritual search.[4] What would be the meaning of the various spiritual teachers he meets in the course of his quest? In the *Lotus Sutra*, there is the episode of the bodhisattvas welling out from the earth[5] wherein the great earth splits open and out of it there springs forth an uncountable number of bodhisattvas. Again, what significance could this have? And in the *Larger Sutra of Immeasurable Life*,[6] we have the story of Amida Buddha striving toward the fruit of buddhahood kalpas ago, under the name of Dharmākara Bodhisattva. What does this story tell us? It might be worth our while to give these questions some serious attention.

However this may be, although it is correct to say that the history of Buddhism begins with Śākyamuni, it is also true that Buddhism has roots that go back to long before the history of Buddhism. To come back a moment to the earlier mentioned stories in the sutras, in their case we may have to distinguish between their form and content. In their written form they certainly originated after Śākyamuni's death, but what about their contents? Could it be, for instance, that the vast collection of *jātakas* was created in just a few hundred years after the Buddha's passing? Or do they represent a tradition handed down from several thousands of years before the Buddha's birth? . . .

Lecture II: Śākyamuni Buddha and His Background

Frankly speaking, my view about the origin or wellspring of Buddhism is that Buddhism certainly is not something simply begun by Śākyamuni. It is not easy to express this thing in a straightforward way, but let me say that, in my view, the Tathāgata Śākyamuni was born out of a legendary tradition that was already in place when he appeared. Such traditions have their roots in a long experience and practice of a people or, again, in the pure aspirations or feelings that lie at the bottom of such a practice. While originating out of that long and profound tradition, Śākyamuni selected from it and unified it, so as to make out of it a clear guideline to follow for us sentient beings in the future. Would not that be what Śākyamuni realized, the true position he occupied, the very meaning of his coming into the world?

The truth of Buddhism is not something produced by Śākyamuni. It is a truth without beginning or end. It existed long before Śākyamuni and is forever the same, not at all dependent on Śākyamuni's coming into the world. However, this truth had been molded into symbols from various viewpoints and had found expression in a rich profusion of legends. Śākyamuni's profound realization and mission consisted in making a judicious choice among, and steering in a right direction, these legends that symbolize and adorn the Buddhist path, in gathering them into a synthesis and thus pointing out the direction to be followed in the future.

Would this realization of Śākyamuni have found its true expression in the doctrines ascribed to him, such as the four noble truths and the chain of dependent co-origination? . . . It seems to me that with these doctrines alone the path to become a buddha does not truly come into relief. For these doctrines to become truly fitting to the Buddhist path, to constitute the bodhisattva path as the true gateway to buddhahood, they must be illuminated by and set within the background of Śākyamuni. Only then do they come to life.

Consequently, Mahāyāna Buddhism, far from being a Buddhism that originated centuries after Śākyamuni's passing—so-called as a result of a theorizing and philosophizing, or idealizing and mystifying of Śākyamuni's original message—rather represents the spatially and temporally boundless background that made Śākyamuni's self-realization into an authentic self-realization. It is only with this background in mind that we can truly speak of the Buddhist path. It was this background that was meant, I think, when the tradition spoke of "buddha lands," and it is there that we must first look when we reflect on the matter of Amida's Pure Land.

When we restrict our view to Śākyamuni's self-awareness in the present, we must say that, in that state, he saw before him (in the future) only emptiness of emptiness: an empty, signless, and desireless world. But, when we consider Śākyamuni's inner background, the womb of the past that gave birth to him as a buddha, we encounter the experiential world of all buddhas and bodhisattvas amassing merit and acquiring virtue. In that world there beats the pulse of an immensely wide and profound original vow, as attested to by the ancestors, who offered their lives for it and truly found eternal life in it. Śākyamuni arose with that immeasurable experience of the ancestors as his mother earth and took a stand on it as on his ultimate ground. Thus, he was able to adorn the empty, signless, desireless world, to make it concrete, to symbolize it, and to set it on a preordained course for thousands of years to come.

Buddhism is not something that Śākyamuni etched out in his head; it is a historical praxis that Śākyamuni sensed. It is precisely in the history of Buddhism that the true path resides. This history forever preaches the Dharma in the present. Śākyamuni as an individual human being with a life span of eighty years, no matter how outstanding he was, is and stays only a human being. . . . It is not imaginable that, in the fifty years of his public life, Śākyamuni would have preached that whole rich array of the Mahāyāna sutras. On this point, modern Buddhist Studies appear to be of the same opinion. But would it even be possible for those grandiose scriptures to have originated in the few hundred years after Śākyamuni's passing, as the same Buddhist scholars dogmatically maintain? This is a question we must pay sufficient attention to.

What, then, is the foundation or basis upon which Mahāyāna Buddhism came to life? This foundation is the earth, and that pure, unsoiled, and objective earth is what is called the Pure Land. Where is that Pure Land, by which Mahāyāna Buddhism is brought to life, to be found? If we read the sutras carefully, we can find it in the *jātaka* stories, these chronicles of Śākyamuni's former lives. These stories speak in symbols,[7] but symbols that offer true meaning, "symbols" in the sense the sutras themselves use the word: symbols that "adorn," or give form to, the Pure Land. To "adorn the Pure Land" means, basically, to give form to what lies in front by way of Śākyamuni's past background and to further adorn the past by way of what lies in front, by way of the future as illuminated by the past. It is to mirror the forms of the past in the future, to mirror the forms of the future in the past, and to unify past and future in the present. That is how I think we must conceive of it.

My talk today was not well structured and may have sounded like the report of a dream, but I have not the slightest doubt about its basic idea: that the root of Buddhism lies in the history of Buddhism, which is the foundation that made Śākyamuni into Śākyamuni Buddha. It lies in the pre-history of Śākyamuni that formed Śākyamuni's self-awareness.

When viewed in this way, the 2,000 years of Buddhist history appear in a different horizon. . . . People nowadays tend to propound a discontinuous view of Buddhist history. The different schools

Buddhism has developed in its history under the influence of karmic circumstances—such as Kegon (Ch. Huayan) Buddhism, Tendai (Ch. Tiantai) Buddhism, and Zen (Ch. Chan) Buddhism—then appear to have originated each by itself. . . . Is not there a way for present Buddhism to go beyond these divisions, and for Buddhist history to turn into a unified history of something that is free from such divisions? I think that Shinran's view of Buddhist history offers us precisely such a way.

Lecture III: The *Larger Sutra* as the Unifying Thread of Buddhist History

The history of Buddhism, as found in modern Buddhist Studies, presents an evolution from early Buddhism to Hīnayāna, and from Hīnayāna to Mahāyāna. I am not going to deny that, factually, Mahāyāna developed from Hīnayāna. However, the so-called evolution as presented there is in fact only a stitching together of different historical fragments that appear to be unrelated to one another. Indeed, to present a development without asking for its unity and sense, is to fall into a materialist view of Buddhist history. That presentation amounts only to the explanation of an empty shell, the mere outward appearance of Buddhism; the inwardly experienced reality of Buddhism, wherein its essence could appear, is not revealed therein.

How about, for instance, the origin of the Mahāyāna sutras? Could these immensely profound oceans of wisdom have been arbitrarily thought out by a single person or even a small group of persons? Let us think, for a moment, of the vast and infinite *dharmadhātu* depicted in the *Huayan Sutra*, the profound and mysterious state of wisdom developed in the *Perfection of Wisdom Sutras*, the unfolding of the true essence of the Buddha that illuminates the age-old darkness as found in the *Lotus Sutra* and, finally, the story of the fulfillment of the vow by Dharmākara Bodhisattva—which is central to the *Larger Sutra of Immeasurable Life*—whereby the nondiscriminating nature of suchness descends into a great compassion that embraces all equally. . . . Would all these be only disparate tales, arbitrarily thought out by some individuals? For common sense, it is only conceivable that the contents of these sutras had been transmitted and believed in for a long time by a people, and finally one or more redactors brought order into the tale, removed the contradictions from it, and rounded it out.

Suggestive on this point may be the aforementioned episode in the *Lotus Sutra*, whereby all of a sudden an innumerable host of bodhisattvas emerge from this very earth. These bodhisattvas are said to belong to Śākyamuni's past. They had never been seen before and are young, vigorous, even savage, as it were, without genealogy or tradition. But the light they radiate puts the individual venerable elders of Śākyamuni's assembly in the shadow. Indeed, the contents of the Mahāyāna sutras must have been transmitted for centuries, from before Śākyamuni's time. Against the background and out of the depths of that lofty and profound tradition Śākyamuni saw the light. . . . Only in this perspective can we, people of common sense, in all simplicity accept what is written in these sutras.

Let us go back now to Shinran's view of the 2,000 years of Buddhist history. In a word, for Shinran the root and stem of Buddhist history is to be found in the *Larger Sutra of Immeasurable Life*; the history of Buddhism is the history of the dissemination of the *Larger Sutra*. With this sutra as its root and stem, the Buddha's path, Buddhism's step-by-step historical development, has progressed. And by this process humankind has found self-awareness and salvation or liberation from *saṃsara*. Within this history, with it as their "earth" and haven, sentient beings have been joyfully born and have died in peace. . . . This is how the story of Buddhism sounded in Shinran's ears, I am sure.

What, then, about the myriad forms Buddhism has taken in its history? They are all branches and flowers on that trunk of the *Larger Sutra*. They have bloomed in wild profusion and will continue to do so, precisely because the life-giving trunk is there.

To think that Buddhism possessed no unity at all during the centuries of so-called sectarian Buddhism (*buha Bukkyō* 部派仏教)[8] is a superficial view. At that time, Hīnayāna Buddhism may or may not have been divided into more than twenty different schools,[9] but even then all Buddhism had the identical taste of Mahāyāna. In fact, that identical Mahāyāna taste has pervaded all Buddhism since Śākyamuni's time, and it is certainly not true that Mahāyāna Buddhism flourished, and was brought to unity, for the first time by such great masters such as Nāgārjuna. What they accomplished was only a renewed clarification, over against the divisions and struggles of sectarian Buddhism, of the principle of Buddhist unity. . . . From its very beginning onward, Buddhism has flowed in one unified stream. The outward divisions notwithstanding, the history of this unified Buddhist path has flowed quietly with the pace of an elephant king, while forever developing inwardly.

Where do we find the proof of this? Shinran found the testimony to this unity in the *Larger Sutra*, considered by him as the true teaching, the true explanation of Śākyamuni's coming into the world, and the final expression of the One Vehicle. Why did he consider the *Larger Sutra* to be the true teaching? Because this sutra opens and reveals the history of the one path of Jōdo Shinshū, while itself standing in the midst of that history. It is not so that the history of the *Larger Sutra* began only after a sutra, later called *Larger Sutra of Immeasurable Life* originated. It is proper to the *Larger Sutra* that it originated in the midst of the history of its path and clarifies that path. The *Larger Sutra* exists with the history of its path as a presupposition.

As he writes in the "Chapter on Teaching" of his *Kyōgyōshinshō*, Shinran discovered the central purport of the *Larger Sutra of Immeasurable Life* within the sutra itself, in the words:

> Amida, by establishing the incomparable vows, has opened wide the dharma-storehouse, and full of compassion for small, foolish beings, selects and bestows the treasure of virtues. [The sutra further reveals that] Śākyamuni appeared in this world and expounded the teachings of the way to enlightenment, seeking to save the multitudes of living beings by blessing them with this benefit that is true and real.[10]

Here, the sutra itself cries out its intent, and Shinran listened to that voice, without adding any personal views. In other words, in this sutra the path itself expresses the path with absolute authority, and utters the name of the path. It is an absolute command, a teaching in the imperative.

Shinran discovered the concrete and real principle of Buddhism in the original vow of Dharmākara Bodhisattva, as it is revealed in the *Larger Sutra*. The history of the *Larger Sutra* is precisely the history of the disclosure of the original vow. It is this original vow that proves that the *Larger Sutra* is the true teaching. . . . Seen in the framework of Buddhist history, the fact that there are people who reject this original vow shows that for the greater part the history of Buddhism has been a history of doubt and disparagement of the original vow. Outwardly, it is a history of doubt and slander, but inwardly it is a history of faith in and compliance with the original vow. The more doubt and disparagement befall it on the outside, the more faith and entrusting in it deepen inwardly. And the more reliance on the original vow deepens, the louder grows the chorus of doubt and slander.

Lecture IV: The *Larger Sutra* as Rooted in History, in the Great Earth

It will be said that my views run counter to the common sense or accepted opinions of the academic world. True enough, but what counts as common sense in the academic world is far removed from the common sense of the people, and I consider the common sense of the people as the true common sense. . . . Scholars only explain. But rather than explaining, I witness. I walk the path of witnessing, not by myself alone—that would be "self-nature and mind-only"—but together with and through all of you I witness first of all to myself.

The tradition of the *Larger Sutra*—with the legend of Amida's original vow and practice in his causal state as Dharmākara Bodhisattva—appears as one among the many intermingling Buddhist traditions, but, in fact, it is the wellspring and mainstream of all these legends and traditions. . . . Among these traditions some, as for instance that of the seven buddhas of the past,[11] may go back to Śākyamuni himself and may have been transmitted in the Śākya clan, while others, as for instance the many legends found in the *Lotus Sutra*, may have originated later. . . . But, it is not a question of which tradition came first and which came later. The question is: Which one is the concrete expression of the true and unadulterated religious aspirations of human beings? . . .

The real greatness of Śākyamuni lies in the greatness of his background. When you take this background away from him, Śākyamuni becomes nothing more than an outstanding scholar of the way, and his attainment merely an eminent example of "self-nature and mind-only." Buddhism would then be nothing but a kind of moral doctrine, something not too different from, for example, Laozi's *Daodejing*. If you consider Śākyamuni's thought to consist only of tenets like the four noble truths, it becomes something very abstract and nothing but a sort of idealism. . . . One then gets the picture of an arhat, and not that of a buddha or Tathāgata.

Let me take the noble truth of suffering as an example. The tenet that human life is suffering cannot be based simply on Śākyamuni's personal experience of hardships; there must be an inner basis by which it is self-attested. Wherein, then, does this real basis lie? It lies precisely in the historical background interiorized in Śākyamuni. It is this historical background that testifies to the noble truth of suffering.

The four noble truths, the twelvefold dependent co-origination and so on are all historical realities. It is the historical reality that made Śākyamuni speak out. Śākyamuni did not speak in an autocratic way. He spoke because he could not help but speak out. In the fact that he was made to speak out, his words became self-testifying. If it were only that Śākyamuni proffered these tenets as he formed them in his mind, we would have explanation, and all explanation is after all dogmatic. But, in the fact that he was made to speak out, the power itself of the truth that made him speak out was present, and thus his words became self-attesting. In that way, the past was authoritatively present, and a present thus backed by the past will never perish.

In my understanding, the tradition of Dharmākara Bodhisattva was, for Shinran, the pure background that gave rise to Śākyamuni. . . . The tradition in Śākyamuni's background, this true and unadulterated tradition, must have its origin in Amida Buddha. The Buddha called Amida is ultimately the ancestor that embraces Śākyamuni; Śākyamuni is a descendant bathing in the light of Amida Buddha. Furthermore, Amida Buddha is also the ancestor of our people throughout history, and we ourselves are descendants taken up in the ocean of his light.

The various other traditions that have developed out of Śākyamuni's message have all had their time; they came and went, blown by the winds of impermanence. At certain times, various buddhas have appeared, such as Maitreya, Akṣobhya, Mahāvairocana, the Bhaiṣajyaguru, and so forth; but they have all disappeared from the mainstream of Buddhist history. Their names are preserved as characters on the pages of classical texts but they are no longer alive. . . . However, all these buddhas obtain new and undying life by being taken up and unified in the history of Amida's eternal vow. Is not that one aspect of the seventeenth vow that speaks of all buddhas praising Amida Buddha's name? For this vow says:

> If, when I attain buddhahood, the countless Buddhas throughout the worlds in the ten quarters do not all praise and say my Name, may I not attain the supreme enlightenment.[12]

On hearing these bold words I have long contemplated this glorification of Amida by all the buddhas as happening in high heaven. In me, however, this evoked only a kind of mystical feeling without the voices of these buddhas becoming a roar to shake heaven and earth. No, the buddhas of the ten directions that praise Amida's name are not abstract notions situated in a celestial sphere. These are buddhas working actively on this very earth, buddhas that order the history of this earth and are walking on this earth in the present. After long years of meditation on the seventeenth vow, as presented by Shinran, I came to see that Shinran had a clear vision of this.

Many people before Shinran have envisaged that this seventeenth vow—and, in general, all forty-eight vows of Amida—was speaking about a mystical world in the remote past. For Shinran, on the contrary, these vows tell us about present history on this very earth. Indeed, all things on this earth are in the present. . . . Without this earth, there is no present. By having its feet firmly on this earth, each moment is eternal present. . . . In Shinran's view of the nenbutsu, all the events in the true history of Buddhism must relate to the "Great Earth." There must be footprints left where they walked.

The Mahāyāna sutras evince this very fact. They are not simply describing fantasies in the sky. If they can speak with great freedom about realities in the heavens, it is because they have a solid relationship with things on earth, because they have truly viewed on the Great Earth the flesh and blood of the heavenly ideals. A heaven unrelated to this earth has no meaning; a true heaven appears only after one has opened one's eyes to the earth. Heaven, namely, is the future that is present in the now, and the earth is the past that is present in the now.

There has been endless discussion on the question whether or not the Pure Land has form and whether or not it is located in a certain direction. And one speaks of a formless pure land and a pure land with form,[13] but of course there cannot be two Pure Lands. The formless pure land and the pure land with form are one and the same. This, however, cannot be explained; it can only be attested to by our praxis, our demeanor in the present. Therefore, we should think of Dharmākara Bodhisattva's praxis as a praxis on this earth. . . .

The light of Amida Buddha as such is not visible to the eye, but, embraced by that light, our ancestors have kept on walking step by step their long journey of human experience. When we hear the traditional expression about "a Pure Land lying billions of lands to the west," we may feel that this has nothing to do with the life of our people, but, as somebody who deeply feels his rootedness in the tradition of the ancestors, I am convinced that this must have a profound historical basis here on earth, as a chronicle of the experiences of the ancestors. It is only when we open our eyes to that earthly basis that we can boldly speak of heavenly reality.

It is because the pure and formless ideal world is symbolized on earth in these pure forms that this earth becomes formless and the heavens take on form. For this reason, heaven and earth are, in the final analysis, one. Heaven is fashioned after the earth, and the earth is fashioned after heaven. It is in such a perspective that expressions such as "a Pure Land lying billions of lands to the west" originate.

We should not claim that the world itself is bad simply on the basis of abstract speculation. The world as impermanence and a "burning house"[14] exists through defiled common mortals. Do we not often speak simply of the world as a burning house, while forgetting our own passions? It is, of course, also wrong, while equally forgetting our own passions, to view this world as the Pure Land in a complete affirmation of this world. On the other hand, some who simply claim that this world is a burning house and absolutely bad go on, with this as the only reason, to postulate a pure land existing somewhere far away and to believe that they will attain buddhahood there. Such people think of becoming a buddha completely apart from actual reality. What do they then become a buddha for? Does not the very spirit of the Buddha die in such a quest for buddhahood? All this may convince us that we must give the question of the Pure Land serious attention. . . .

I may seem to be speaking in riddles, but I am thinking here of our ancestors. The historical course walked by our ancestors is, after all, something material. A course is a thing. But, it is precisely through things that the supra-sensible takes form. The spiritual is symbolized through things. Things are symbols, forms and concrete expressions of the mind. The spiritual does not exist as an entity apart from and contrary to things; the mind exists only as in-formed by things. Still, even as in-formed by things, the spiritual is essentially eternally formless, going beyond things in a negation. But, precisely by the fact of always being formless and beyond things, the spiritual has the capacity of taking form in things. It is only in things with form that the formless mind is truly expressed and given to us. . . . It is in this sense that I see the Pure Land as the history of the Pure Land.

Let me summarize here what I wanted to convey in my rather confused talk today. Śākyamuni Buddha exists only by the grace of Amida Buddha's original vow. The core of the question is not whether that single great personality known as Śākyamuni has existed or not. That there has existed a buddha called Śākyamuni is a question of the historical background that made Śākyamuni into a buddha. The problem does not reside in Śākyamuni as a mere human person, but in the Buddhist path that brought the person of Śākyamuni Buddha into being. The true history of Buddhism, the history of Amida's vows, lies in the point that Śākyamuni was made to be a true buddha, an authentic Tathāgata. It is in the midst of the history of the Buddhist path that Śākyamuni was born and the attainment of buddhahood became a reality. In other words, Śākyamuni, while being a real existent, was a manifestation body of Amida Buddha. The great mission for the sake of which Śākyamuni came into this world is to be found only in his being a manifestation body of Amida's original vow.

Meditative reading of the *Larger Sutra* made it dawn on me that the roots of Buddhism are deep and solid, and the origins of Buddhism go back far and wide. In the midst of that historical path of profound self-awakening, the one who brought this whole to unity was Śākyamuni. Thus, through Śākyamuni, the world before Śākyamuni came to bathe in bright light. But, the eternally pure world brought to light by Śākyamuni is, in fact, the world of eternal light that brought Śākyamuni himself to light. In this way, the explicit history of Buddhism opened up for the first time. Since there are no direct reports from his time, we cannot even imagine what of all this was present in Śākyamuni's self-awareness or transpired in his words. Was there or was there not anything in the form of the forty-eight vows? We do not know, and it does not really matter whether such things were there or not. What counts is that for a very long time this primitive and pristine tradition lived on.

In a nutshell, the 2,000-odd year history of Buddhism is the history of the growth and transmission of the *Larger Sutra of Immeasurable Life*, and this is the history of the spread of the nenbutsu. Within this history of the nenbutsu, the *Larger Sutra* has gradually taken shape. The *Larger Sutra* marks the history of the nenbutsu; the nenbutsu is more fundamental than the *Larger Sutra*. In the beginning was the *name*. Before the *Larger Sutra* existed, the original vow of the Tathāgata was, and before the original vow existed, the name was. . . . The *Larger Sutra* did not originate all of a sudden; it came to be perfected in the history of vow and nenbutsu. The *Larger Sutra* grew up in history. What developed in the midst of history was the *Larger Sutra*.

Having already existed as spoken word and legend from the very beginning of the beginningless history of the Buddhist path, the *Larger Sutra* gradually took shape and, and, at the point where it reached completion, was finally written down. . . . The *Larger Sutra* is a growing thing. Today, the letter of the *Larger Sutra* is already fixed but its content is in an infinite process of inner deepening. It is not that we go on deepening it; it deepens by itself. We are only occasions or opportunities for the *Larger Sutra* to deepen itself.

It is within this history of the vow and the nenbutsu that we come into the world, live, breathe, and finally return to the earth as dry bones.

Lecture V: We Ourselves in the History of the Nenbutsu—By Way of the Patriarchs

What, then, about the different periods that have traditionally been distinguished in the history of Buddhism? From of old, Buddhists themselves have been speaking of a gradual decline of Buddhism over three periods: True Dharma, Semblance Dharma, and Latter Dharma.[15] Modern Buddhist Studies divide the history of Buddhism, for example, into early Buddhism, Abhidharma Buddhism, and Mahāyāna Buddhism. These periodizations are not mistaken, as long as one perceives that, with these as occasions and moments, the great spirit of Buddhism has continued as one pure whole, and has gradually developed in depth. . . . Throughout all the historical vicissitudes—such as, for example, the struggles among the many Abhidharma schools—the spirit of the Buddhist path has lived on in the breast of people, and has pervaded the soil they stood on, their very feet, their actions, and lives.

Current historiography of Buddhism speaks of a development of Buddhist doctrine. There is no doubt that such a development took place, but at the back of the doctrine there always was practice and a history of the practice. It is in the development of the practice that the development of the doctrine had its basis and content; it is therein that it finds its witness. It is only through this witness that the development of doctrine occurred. Without it we cannot speak of history in the so-called development of doctrine. Speaking of a development of doctrine may sound good, but without that background and foundation in the actualization of practice-faith, this so-called development is nothing but a design on a piece of paper.

Shinran clarified the explicit history of the nenbutsu in terms of the seven patriarchs of the three countries.[16] . . . In his *Kyōgyōshinshō*, he quotes many passages from the sutra. However, instead of taking these passages directly from the sutras, he takes them from the commentaries on the sutras by the patriarchs. . . . What does this mean? We can see herein how much he valued the historical transmission of the Buddhist tradition, and how highly he evaluated the fact that, in the patriarchs, the doctrine of the sutras is accompanied by practice. . . . Shinran, for example, quoted Tanluan's commentary on Vasubandhu's *Pure Land Treatise*, attributing the quotation to the *Treatise* itself. This does not mean that he made a mistake, mixing up these two different texts. Shinran deliberately did this because he considered that the very spirit of Vasubandhu had been transmitted to Tanluan. In that case, it is only natural to come truly into contact with the vitality of Vasubandhu's words through Tanluan. At that point, practice comes into the picture. If it were only a question of Vasubandhu's doctrine or reasoning, that could be grasped without passing through Tanluan.

Shinran finally found the wellspring of the history of the name in the seventeenth vow. It is in the "Chapter on Practice" of the *Kyōgyōshinshō* that he clarified the Jōdo Shinshū tradition by this "Vow of Praise of Amida's Name by All the Buddhas" (*shobutsu shōmyō no gan* 諸仏称名の願).[17] This vow is, indeed, the real principle behind the history of the Pure Land path, the real principle underlying all of Buddhist history. Shinran's view of Buddhist history is characterized first of all by the fact that he takes the seventeenth vow as its principle. As to the "innumerable Buddhas in the lands of the ten directions" of which the vow speaks, we are inclined to imagine them as constellations in the sky, but Shinran thinks of them as the real wellspring of the tradition that runs through Śākyamuni and the seven patriarchs. He sees it as the source of the continuous stream of the nenbutsu practice flowing forth here on earth.

We should also not forget that these patriarchs did not stand by themselves. They had the spirit and thought patterns of their age in their background, and in accordance with this, they promoted Amida Buddha's original vow. "To promote" here means to further clarify the spirit of the name and then to hold the name aloft to the people. Their destiny was, inwardly, to bring the name to life and, outwardly, to spread the name widely for the benefit of the deluded common mortals of their age. The patriarchs are only seven in number, but each of them is backed by innumerable people of his age. The patriarchs stand as representatives of these masses. The tradition of the seven patriarchs, the history of the nenbutsu: it is the process whereby, in the "Namu Amida Butsu," the original vows inwardly realizes themselves and outwardly goes on embracing its true recipients, all sentient beings. By outwardly saving sentient beings it realizes itself, and by inwardly realizing itself it saves sentient beings.

In that perspective, "all the buddhas" means first of all the seven buddhas of the past, of whom tradition speaks. But, for Shinran, the seven buddhas of the past are the seven patriarchs. Just like Śākyamuni, Shinran had his own seven buddhas of the past. . . . Here we must reflect anew on what a buddha really is. A buddha is someone born from the development of the original vow, a human being who entered into the stream of that history.

In his *Shōshinge*, Shinran calls the totality of the history of the nenbutsu simply "nenbutsu." "Namu Amida Butsu" does not originate for the first time by our reciting it. In Shinran's view, the totality of Buddhist history is "Namu Amida Butsu." The nenbutsu is not simply the nenbutsu as recited by us. Nenbutsu is the history of the original vow. Shinran calls the nenbutsu practice of an individual who disregards that history "self-power nenbutsu." The true nenbutsu of the original vow is the nenbutsu in the midst of history, the nenbutsu that flows through history, the nenbutsu that constitutes the unity of history.

In the "Chapter on Practice," Shinran explored the historical events of the disclosure of the name. In these historical events, however, he also saw the stages of his own living faith, the process whereby he himself realized his faith. That is what he shows, I believe, in his "Chapter on Faith." In other words, in his view, our true self-realization of the Buddhist path lies within the history of the nenbutsu and consists in our participation in that course of events. . . . Shinran discovered the "Namu Amida Butsu" of the pure and unadulterated vow-mind in the midst of the nenbutsu as the fulfillment of symbol and adornment. And in the midst of the history of the Dharma of "Namu Amida Butsu," he found the nenbutsu as the personal and transhistorical faith of his own heart.

True faith in the nenbutsu means to be born from the history of the nenbutsu tradition, and—transcending the history of the nenbutsu, while standing in the very world of the nenbutsu—to participate in the making of that nenbutsu history, and to attest to the undying light of that history. It does not mean, as happens in the nenbutsu of the Buddha visualization *samādhi* (*kanbutsu zammai* 観仏三昧),[18] to simply praise the perfected name, without reference to the historical fulfillment of the vow.

Truly, by the calling voice of Amida Buddha, which summons us to put our trust in the name, we are carried beyond the history of the ongoing and deepening nenbutsu tradition and, in a naturalness that negates history, we are made to take our stand in the initial moment wherein Dharmākara Bodhisattva made his vow. Therein precisely a new and true history of the nenbutsu begins.

Notes

1. One Vehicle indicates the ultimate Buddhist teaching in which all sentient beings become buddhas. This concept is explained in various Mahāyāna texts, most notably the *Lotus Sutra*.

2. Emperor Jimmu, the legendary first sovereign of Japan according to ancient chronicles such as *Kojiki* 古事記 (712) and *Nihon shoki* 日本書紀 (720). During the time of Soga's lecture, the idea of an "emperor-centered

historiography" (*kōkoku shikan* 皇国史観) was emphasized in Japan. Referring to this idea, Soga analogized Śākyamuni's position in Buddhist history to that of Jimmu in Japanese history and criticized the tendency in Japanese academia to relegate Śākyamuni to a mere historical figure.

3. The *jātaka*s are stories about Śākyamuni during his previous lifetimes, when he was still a bodhisattva striving to attain enlightenment and buddhahood. The stories focus on the numerous acts of heroic self-sacrifice he undertook in order to attain enlightenment.

4. Sudhana is the name of a youth who appears in the Gaṇḍavyuha chapter of the *Huayan Sutra*. This text describes in detail the story of Sudhana's pilgrimage to fifty-three "good spiritual friends" (*kalyāṇamitra*) in search of enlightenment.

5. According to the "Welling Up Out of the Earth" chapter of the *Lotus Sutra*, while Śākyamuni was preaching this sutra, the earth split open and innumerable bodhisattvas welled out from the earth to pay homage to the Buddha. See Hurvitz, *Scripture of the Lotus Blossom*, 225–36.

6. In this essay, *Larger Sutra of Immeasurable Life, Sutra of Immeasurable Life* and *Larger Sutra* are used synonymously.

7. Soga has a distinctive understanding of the concepts of "symbol" (*shōchō* 象徵) and "adornment" (*shōgon* 荘厳). Originally, adornment meant to decorate oneself and one's land. However, Soga redefined this concept, linking it to the word "symbol." He explained that adornment and symbol are the means of expressing and giving form to a spirituality that has no form or shape. As a concrete example to illustrate this, Soga points to the forty-eight vows of Dharmākara Bodhisattva in the *Sutra of Immeasurable Life* and the twenty-nine adornments in Vasubandhu's *Pure Land Treatise*. On Soga's distinctive use of "symbol" and "adornment," see his *Hongan no Butchi* 本願の仏地 (The Buddha-Ground of the Original Vow), found in SRS 5: 217–384.

8. A term often used in Japanese Buddhist scholarship, used to refer to the period soon after the Buddha's death (from around 200 BCE) in which Buddhism began to divide into different schools.

9. The East Asian Buddhist tradition holds that Buddhism divided into twenty schools after the Buddha's death.

10. Cf. CWS 1:7.

11. The seven buddhas of the past refer to Śākyamuni and the six buddhas who are said to have appeared before him.

12. Cf. CWS 1:13.

13. There is a traditional distinction between pure lands with and without form. The former, like Amida's Pure Land in the west, is given form through its direction and its lavish descriptions. The latter is suchness itself, beyond all distinction.

14. Here Soga quotes from the *Tannishō*. The parable of the burning house, which symbolizes a world full of suffering and anxiety, derives from the *Lotus Sutra*.

15. The Buddhist view of history holds that the world goes through three distinct periods of time after the demise of Śākyamuni Buddha. In

the first period of the True Dharma (*shōbō* 正法), the Buddha's teaching, its practice and attainment of enlightenment all exist. In the second period of the Semblance Dharma (*zōbō* 像法), the teaching and its practice remain, but there is no one who can gain enlightenment. Finally, in the third period of the Latter Dharma (*mappō* 末法), only the teachings remain, and there are neither people who practice the Buddhist teachings or attain enlightenment.

16. The seven patriarchs of the three countries refer to Nāgārjuna and Vasubandhu of India; Tanluan, Daochuo, and Shandao of China; and Genshin and Hōnen of Japan.

17. This is the name that Shinran gave to the seventeenth vow.

18. The Buddha visualization *samādhi* refers to the practice of continuously reciting Amida Buddha's name with the aim of entering a state of meditation and gaining a vision of this Buddha.

Chapter 9

Lectures on the *Tannishō**

Soga Ryōjin

Translated by Jan Van Bragt

Part I: The Problem of Good and Evil

With regard to good and evil, we usually imagine that they can be managed by our human free will. Good and evil would then be clearly delineated and human beings would be endowed from birth with moral reason. By means of that moral reason, given to us as lords of creation, we would possess the freedom to determine our own conduct. Even when ignorant of this kind of reasoning or theory, people have probably always felt that way, but nowadays they have also come to know the theory. People today are strong in reasoning and theory, but their intuitive powers have become blunted. That is how they came to the present theory. I call this idealism. In olden days, there may not have been idealists in this sense, but people showed a tendency akin to it. They thus thought already that people can do good, provided they want to. In the Buddhist tradition, we call this idealist way of thinking self-power in meditative and nonmeditative practices (*jōsan jiriki* 定散自力).[1]

---

*The following is a translation of two selections from Soga Ryōjin's *Tannishō chōki* 歎異抄聴記 (*Lectures on the Tannishō*) dealing with the topic of karma. The first selection translated here corresponds to section 2 of lecture 5, whereas the second selection consists of section 4 of lecture 10 and the whole of lecture 11. The Japanese text is found in SRS, 6:76–78 and 149–65, respectively. All notes were added by the editors.

We find a description of good people and evil people in the passage of the *Contemplation Sutra* concerning the nine grades of people who attain birth in the Pure Land (*kubon* 九品).² This passage lists exhaustively different sorts of people according to their attitude toward good and evil. As you may know, the upper level of the highest grade contains the people that practice all the meditative good deeds and also the most excellent of the nonmeditative practices. In the three levels of the highest grade we find the good people of the Mahāyāna school, and in the upper and middle levels of the middle grade the good people of the Hīnayāna school. The lowest level of the middle grade represents the good "people of the world." In general, thus, the upper and middle grades contain the good persons. It is then the three levels of the lowest grade that consist of evil persons. As evil persons they are all equal and there is no need to further distinguish among them, but the sutra divides them into three different levels according to the gravity of the evil deeds they commit. But, although there is the difference of good and evil among them, the people of the nine grades are all common mortals (*bonbu* 凡夫). Indeed, Shandao has the expression "nine grades, common mortals only."³

So, what is the meaning of the term common mortals? All people that live a life of karma (*shukugō* 宿業) are called "common mortals." One is a common mortal on account of karma. Among common mortals there are good people and evil people but, because good people as well as evil people are totally swayed by karma, they all are called common mortals. In contradistinction, a person who transcends karma and acts or behaves naturally without calculation (*jinen hōni* 自然法爾) is called a saint. He is a person whose actions naturally correspond to the Buddhist way. Such a person is also called a buddha. Roughly speaking, sentient beings who are not buddhas are common mortals. . . .

What, after all, is karma? Etymologically, karma might be said to be synonymous with "fate" (*unmei* 運命), but what many contemporaries understand as fate is different from the idea of karma in Buddhism. Fatalism is a theory that results from materialism. It is a sense of karma that leads to the view of karma; karma is grasped by a "sense" (*kankaku* 感覚). That is how I prefer to characterize it. Fate is not the content of a sense but of a theory. It is a conclusion drawn by intellectualists, a product of human reason; it exists only as a result of a specific kind of ratiocination. Karma could be called the sense of fate, and that is a completely different thing.

I had been dealing with the problem of karma for a long time until, some years ago, I all of a sudden got the inspiration that karma is grasped by a primal faculty or "instinct" (*honnō* 本能). Karma is not something discovered by human reason. It is a matter of an instinct given by birth. Even when trying hard, a human person could not get to know karma by reason. The human person as a whole, the self in its entirety is involved in karma; it is a subject of karma. Therefore, the self can be said to exist within karma. And, from the moment a person has received the gift of knowing karma, he is already within the original vow of the Buddha, inside the field of the great heart of compassion. It is not right to associate the feeling of despair with karma. The idea of fate is an expression of despair, but not so the feeling of karma. On the contrary, it is a matter of being made to know karma by the light of Amida's great compassion, and this means an "opening up of past good karma" (*shukuzen kaihotsu* 宿善開発) a kind of conversion, or conversion and contrition. In a word, karma is a gate that lies inside the heart of great compassion and, at the same time, manifests that great compassion.

Part II: Karma and Faith in the *Tannishō*

On the Third Chapter of the *Tannishō*

The third chapter of the *Tannishō* reads as follows:

> "Even a good person can attain birth in the Pure Land, how much more easily an evil person." But people of the world always say, "Even an evil person will be born, how much more easily a good person." At first sight, this view may appear more reasonable, but it is contrary to the intent of the other-power of the original vow. The reason is that as long as a people do good through self-power and are not fully relying on other-power, they are self-excluded from the original vow. However, by reversing their attitude of self-power and dedicating themselves to other-power, they attain birth in the true land of reward.
>
> It was solely in order to enable the evil person to attain buddhahood that Amida made his vows, out of compassion for those like us who, possessed of mental defilements, have no hope of liberating ourselves from *saṃsāra* through any form of practice. And so the evil person who relies on other-power is above all endowed with the true cause for

birth. Hence Shinran's saying, "Even a good person can attain birth born in the Pure Land, how much more easily an evil person."[4]

This third chapter of the *Tannishō* is especially relevant for our conception of the *ki* 機 aspect of deep faith.[5] It moreover shows that this deep faith in its connection with the idea that the evil person is the true recipient of Amida's compassion. "*Even a good person can attain birth in the Pure Land, how much more easily an evil person.*" These are famous words. They raise the banner of the nenbutsu Dharma—"just say the nenbutsu and be saved by Amida"[6]—in an uncommonly incisive way, and makes it clear that this Dharma takes the evil person as its true object.

Here, "good person" and "evil person" are defined by their own self-awareness. These expressions have nothing to do with calling somebody else good or evil; it is not a question of pointing out, somewhere beside oneself, good people and evil people, and then declaring that, among them, it is the evil ones that are the true recipients of Amida's vow. The expression, after all, has to do with the *ki* aspect of deep faith and, therefore, the "good people" intended are people who think of themselves as good and the "evil people" are people who are convinced that they do not possess any cause or means for birth, that they are "people incapable of any observance, and thus doomed to fall into hell." The passage calls "evil person" somebody who deeply believes that he himself possesses neither the power for enlightenment and liberation, nor the wherewithal for birth in the Pure Land.

Kōgatsuin,[7] in fact, recognized as much, but he added the reflection that it may have been especially important at the time the *Tannishō* was written to stress the privileged position of the "evil person," and that this was all right as long as it was applied to a person whose past good karma opened up, but dangerous to do this in connection with a person wherein this was not the case and that, therefore, the *Tannishō* should not be shown indiscriminately to ordinary persons. There may be something to be said for this. Ryōshō,[8] on the other hand, opined that one must make it clear that the terms "good person" and "evil person" are not used here in their ordinary sense and that, if they were taken in their ordinary sense, the alternative position, quoted by Shinran, would rather apply, namely "*Even a good person can attain birth in the Pure Land, how much more easily an evil person.*"

Expressions similar to this one are found in Hōnen. Hōnen used the terms "evil person" and "good person" in their ordinary sense. It is the meaning of the words from the standpoint of an observer.

But even though our founder Shinran used these words in a different sense, we must not necessarily conclude that Hōnen and Shinran contradict one another on this point. The words are the same but the contents are different. Hōnen speaks from his standpoint as a guide of other people; Shinran, on the other hand, simply bares his own self-realization, and then waits for people of the same conviction to come forward.

Of course, even in Shinran's case, it would be hard to imagine that he would have used that bold expression when writing things down in his own hand. It is an expression used by Shinran while talking freely, and to people whose good karma was opening up. Since that is the case, I believe that Kōgatsuin has good reasons for his concern. On the other hand, Ryōshō may be right in castigating Kōgatsuin on this point, but it remains true that we must pay attention to the fact that Shinran's expression belongs to the category of oral tradition. Oral tradition does not consider expediency, but speaks unadorned truth. When writing things down, on the other hand, one is sure to mix expediency with truth. The strength of the *Tannishō* lies in the fact that it has been written down in a straightforward way. On that point it is different from the *Kudenshō* 口伝鈔 (*A Chronicle of Oral Tradition*) by Kakunyo 覚如 (1270–1351),[9] who writes things rather selectively, out of fear that people might get mistaken ideas. The *Tannishō* does not concern itself with the possibility of being misunderstood. As a result, there are undoubtedly people who misunderstand it. But is it not true that words which are not subject to misunderstanding have no efficacy as medicine? It is with such thoughts in mind that I want us to read our present text.

"*At first sight, this view may appear more reasonable, but it is contrary to the intent of the other-power of the original vow.*" At a first hearing, it may sound reasonable, but on deeper reflection we must come to the conclusion that it does not correspond to the spirit or intent of Amida's original vow. The word "intent" (*ishu* 意趣) is also used in chapter 10, where it is said that the disciples who, according to the second chapter, came from afar to visit Shinran in Kyoto in order to hear his verdict on points of doctrine disputed among them, "received Shinran's intent." Also here it means the intent or true meaning of the original vow of other-power. And Shandao wrote, for instance, "Although the advantages of the two gateways of meditative and nonmeditative practices have been taught up to this point [in the *Contemplation Sutra*], in view of the intent of the Buddha's original vow, this is to bring sentient beings solely to wholehearted utterance of the name of Amida Buddha."[10]

Turning to the words, *"The reason is that as long as people do good through self-power,"* the "good persons" of the beginning are now called "people [who] do good through self-power." The people of the six higher grades in the *Contemplation Sutra* are precisely such people, whereas the people of the three lower grades are common mortals who do only evil and no good. However, the people who do good are also common mortals. Good or evil, people are all common mortals; good or evil, all is karma. While doing good or evil, as their karma dictates, people are not conscious of the fact that it is all karma. When they do good, they think they are good people; when they do evil, they think they are evil people. They imagine that they do good because their heart is good, and imagine that they do evil because their heart is evil. But that is not the case; good and evil are both [due to] karma. . . . All the people of the nine grades have a mind of self-power, a mind of calculation concerning good and evil. When dividing them nevertheless into good and evil people, we can say that those who belong to the category of the "good people"—the people of the six higher grades—in their particular situation, lack the mind of total reliance on other-power. Because good karma is at work in them, and they therefore think they are in a good situation and have no need of other-power, *"as long as people . . . are not fully relying on other-power, they are self-excluded from the original vow."* They are not in accord with the original vow.

For people of self-power good, it is not easy to overturn this mind of self-power. But *"by reversing their attitude of self-power and dedicating themselves to other-power, they attain birth in the true land of reward."* When people, who rely on self-power either in meditation or in nonmeditative practices, overturn their ego mind, their attitude of proudly relying on their own power and, throwing away all calculation, trustfully enter the wide path of the other-power of the luminous and true original vow, they too can attain birth in the Pure Land. Shinran thus envisages that there are people of self-power good who convert and obtain birth. However, he then turns to "those like us who [are] possessed of mental defilements." It is thus clear that, when he spoke about people of self-power good, he was referring to other people, not us. *"Those like us who, possessed of mental defilements, have no hope of liberating ourselves from* saṃsāra *through any form of practice."* We are among the people for whom Amida made the Vow.

"It was solely in order to enable the evil person to attain buddhahood that Amida made his vows, out of compassion. . . . And so the evil person who relies on other-power is above all endowed with the true cause for

birth." To be an evil person is thus the best condition for birth in the Pure Land. One might have expected Shinran to speak of "a faith that relies on other-power," but in fact he spoke of the "evil person who relies on other-power." It is the fact that a person is aware that he is an evil person who must rely on other-power, which endows him with the true cause (*shōin* 正因) for birth. Shinran here speaks of the "true cause" for birth, but I think it has the same meaning as the "true receptacle" (*shōki* 正機) of which he speaks elsewhere. Thus, the "evil person" of this third chapter can be said to be the true receptacle or object of the original vow. We should never forget, however, that "evil person" means somebody who is aware of being an evil person.

All in all, what is at stake in this chapter is the mind that is called "the *ki* aspect of deep faith" in Shin Buddhist doctrine. And the "good people" and "evil people" of this chapter must be seen in the perspective that good and evil are both karma. Seen from the Dharma, good people and evil people are equal, but seen from the side of *ki*, when it is a question of having the right disposition toward Amida's working, evil people are the right objects of the original vow. It is for their sake that Amida made the selected vow (*senjaku hongan* 選択本願) and went through unimaginable hardships during long kalpas for its fulfillment.

The Self-Awareness of Karma and the *Ki* Aspect of Deep Faith[11]

Yesterday, we analyzed the text of the third chapter of the *Tannishō*, and became aware of its connection with the *ki* aspect of deep faith. It appears, however that the idea of this aspect of deep faith invokes in most people the image of a very dark and gloomy world. The *ki* aspect of deep faith is not directly identical with the consciousness of karma. Rather, it can be said to be the fact of deeply believing in what the self-awareness of karma confronts us with.

> We should realize that in truth we are ordinary unenlightened beings involved in birth-and-death, who from the remotest past up to the present time have been forever floundering in *saṃsāra*, and that we have no way of freeing ourselves.[12]

These words by Shandao are a good expression of the self-awareness of karma. The *ki* aspect of deep faith means to deeply believe in this. It can, thus, provisionally be called the consciousness of one's karma, but it is more precise to say that it is deep faith with regard to this consciousness: to believe in it and to submit to it. It is true that consciousness without this deep faith is not real consciousness. Through this deep faith, the consciousness of karma reaches its full meaning and comes to show its concrete content as consciousness.

It is already more than thirty years ago that I first contended that this *ki* aspect of deep faith is, as it were, the self-awareness of Dharmākara Bodhisattva. I do not say that this pronouncement was the fruit of deep experience at the time; it was mostly the outcome of logical inference. I meant to say that, at the point of this deep faith, we open the eyes of Dharmākara Bodhisattva. The question is, then: How does the consciousness of being a common mortal, caught in evil and bound to the wheel of birth-and-death, signify the opening of Dharmākara's eyes? Is not Dharmākara Bodhisattva Amida Buddha himself in the causal stage, and does this fact not point in the opposite direction? Still, I think that I can stand by what I thought and discussed with people in my student days so long ago: namely, that the *ki* aspect of deep faith is Dharmākara Bodhisattva, and that by this deep faith we open the eyes of Dharmākara.

Indeed, it is in and through the *ki* aspect of deep faith that we "intuit" the figure of Dharmākara. This faith is the very sense of the existence of Dharmākara Bodhisattva, our parent, and for his parental heart. The consciousness of karma, the knowledge of being "a person of karmic evil, caught in birth-and-death," means for me: Oh Dharmākara, that you appeared as the parent who took upon yourself alone all the evil and pain of sentient beings!

Such, indeed, is the figure of Dharmākara Bodhisattva. Without the awareness of this figure, we would divide evil and responsibility among ourselves: this is my responsibility and that is yours. In so doing, we would make our own responsibility light and load the heavier part on the shoulders of the others. That is the natural tendency of the human ego. A human being now does good, and then does evil. So, although I am willing to take one part of the responsibility upon me, I am, after all, only one among innumerable sentient beings. Supposing the number of Japanese to be 100 million, I must take upon myself only 100 millionth of the responsibility, and can leave the 99,999,999 other parts to others.

As long as we reason in this way, arithmetically, there is no genuine consciousness of karma. Such consciousness implies the sense of being linked "by blood" to all others. We cannot literally say, however, that we are linked by blood to people of others races and countries, and even among the people of our own country there are only few that share the same blood with us. However, "blood" here does not simply mean a linkage among human beings; it extends to the very earth with its mountains and rivers. The root of this "blood" is the Great Earth, the soil, the land. Sentient beings and the land are one. When speaking of a collectivity such as a people, we usually think only of a kinship among people, but the Buddhist tradition sees things differently. For example, it habitually links together "recompense in the sentient beings" (*shōhō* 正報) and "recompense in the environment" (*ehō* 依報)[13]; it sees them as one. Each of us feels recompense not only in sentient beings (ourselves), but also in the environment.

Buddhism does not speak of giving birth to the land, but of "getting a feel for the land." The moment we are born, we get a feel for the earth with its mountains and rivers at the same time as we get a feel for ourselves. In the world of karma, nobody is an island by himself or herself; everybody is linked with everybody else. All sentient beings—and not only sentient beings, but all things in the world—are linked in mutual empathy. The world of karma is a world of mutual resonance and co-respondence (*kannō dōkō* 感応道交).

Many people appear to be thinking about karma more or less in the following way. Karma is a Buddhist doctrine. I do not really grasp its meaning, but doctrine is doctrine. It sounds a bit like an old wives' tale to me, and it appears to paint the human condition in very bleak colors. But all of this is off the mark. When we truly open our eyes to karma, all things in the world, and the very earth with its mountains and rivers, open themselves up to each other and become companions to one another. Let us consider Mount Hiei,[14] for instance. It does not rise up all of a sudden; it has been towering there for many millions of years. Still, it somehow is in empathy and co-respondence with me; it answers when I call. There is a communality between us. It is not indifferent to my calling; it always answers me, be it unwittingly. Although I feel the mountain consciously, the mountain answers me unconsciously. Sentient and insentient mutually resonate and co-respond.

If we do not know karma, we put our solitary ego forward against others. Even while living under the same roof with one's spouse for many years and having had several children together, we do not know our spouse's heart. How sad! Because of their ego-centered heart, people become insensitive to the feeling of karma. The more people engage in scholarship, the more they lose the sense for things. It makes me suspect that scholarship is there to make people lose understanding! It has been said, "those who do not know (the importance of) the afterlife are foolish, even though they may understand eighty thousand sutras and teachings."[15] The afterlife is a matter of "sense," the 80,000 things are objects of knowledge. Only when we become someone like a simple illiterate person will the world of pure sensation open up for us.

And through this pure sensation we shall be brought to aspire for the world of pure feeling and to know it at a deep level—namely, through the symbols that symbolize pure feeling in pure sensation. This is precisely the world of faith. It is in that sense that I said that the *ki* aspect of deep faith "senses" Dharmākara Bodhisattva. Whereas the *hō* (Dharma) aspect of deep faith senses Amida Buddha in his state of fruition, the *ki* aspect is the path that leads to a sense of Dharmākara Bodhisattva, the same Amida Buddha in the causal stage. Cause and fruit are one and not two. Through the cause we enter into the fruit, and by the fruit the cause becomes clear to us.

When we enter the world of karma in this way, we come to understand the moods of all kinds of people, and all human beings come to be linked with one another by "blood." Therefore, the deeds of all human beings become our own responsibility. We then take on our own shoulders the sins and pains of all sentient beings. On the surface, the *ki* aspect of deep faith does not appear to mean that we take responsibility for all evil. Yet it means that we obtain an intimate sense for Dharmākara Bodhisattva, the causal stage of Amida Buddha, who took on himself all sin and pain. Indeed, Dharmākara is no ancient myth; I sense him poignantly in my own body. And that is none other than the consciousness of karma. This does not mean, however, that we ourselves are Dharmākara; it means that we sense Dharmākara Bodhisattva beyond the distinction of self and other. That is the consciousness of karma, which is the content of the *ki* aspect of deep faith.

When speaking of "my own body," I do not want to "privatize" my body as a separate entity. If I could consider my body as mine from an egocentric standpoint, I would be free to do whatever I want with it. In the present context, however, the fact that my body is mine does not allow for such arbitrariness. My body is public property. Parents can call their children theirs, but that does not mean that they can do whatever they want with them. Their own children are public property too in that sense. But, calling my body public property should not be misconstrued as setting my body apart from me or throwing it away from me. Precisely by my consciousness that it is public property, my body becomes truly mine. At the very moment that I truly sense my body to be public property, I receive my body as entrusted to me. Only then it becomes truly mine. It is my body, not by deciding from the very beginning that it is mine, but by receiving it as mine in the consciousness of its preciousness as public property. In that vein, I can say that my body is Dharmākara Bodhisattva, the receptacle wherein to sense Dharmākara Bodhisattva. My body is precious as the vessel wherein to feel the same as what Dharmākara Bodhisattva feels.

When we Buddhists speak of our "karmic body," outsiders often get the impression that we despise our body. But not only outsiders, even we ourselves, who situate ourselves within Buddhism, are prone to thinking in that way. Since it expresses a tenet of our religion, we will defend it with our mouths, but in our hearts we feel it to be a deplorable tenet. The doctrine of karma is one of the targets of contemporary critique of Buddhism: that it considers our bodies to be results of karma and our country to be a defiled land (*edo* 穢土). There is no doubt that these two are connected. However, in the feeling that my country is truly a defiled land, there is the consciousness that I myself am responsible for it. It was not originally a defiled land; it came to be so as a result of my karma. Moreover, to be painfully aware that one's country is a defiled land signifies that one truly loves one's country and wants to purify it. Thus, love and high regard for one's country appear in the guise of that seemingly derogatory expression, "defiled land." People who from the beginning call their own country a pure land betray thereby an indifference to their country. Would those be the people that carry the country of Japan on their shoulders? There lies the crux of the problem. Personally, I think that the heart that feels an aversion for all defiled lands is precisely the pure heart that is truly concerned with all sentient beings and with the country.

It is in that sense that I intuit the Dharmākara Bodhisattva of flesh and blood in the consciousness of karma. I sense Dharmākara Bodhisattva in my whole body, in all my limbs and organs. While saying this, I know that there are persons among you who will misunderstand me, but this does not keep me from saying it. I am satisfied if one person out of ten hears me rightly, even if the other nine misunderstand me. Among one hundred blind people, it is enough that there is one who has his eyes open; that the ninety-nine others are blind does not matter then. The important thing is that there is one person who sees. It would be ideal, of course, if all one hundred of them had good eyesight, but as long as there is one who does, he can lead the ninety-nine others. I say things like the ones I just said in the hope of finding, be it only one, a person whose eyes are opened, so as to understand me correctly.

Dharmākara Bodhisattva and the Dharmākara Soul

When hearing the old tale of Dharmākara Bodhisattva, we are apt to experience it as a fairy tale. Indeed, as long as we do not sense it in our very body, all of Buddhism is nothing but a fairy tale. It is through the pores of our body that we have a vivid sense of Dharmākara and of karma.

Who is this Dharmākara Bodhisattva? He is the person who has a sense of karma, while taking upon himself alone the sins and pains of all sentient beings. And it is through the *ki* aspect of deep faith that we sense the Dharmākara of flesh and blood. I do not mean to say that I myself am Dharmākara. Even Dharmākara himself did not call himself by the name Dharmākara. There is, therefore, not a single person who calls himself by that name and says, "I am Dharmākara."

Nichiren declared that he was the Eminent Conduct Bodhisattva,[16] about whom the *Lotus Sutra* prophesied. Such was Nichiren's self-consciousness. I am not judging whether this is good or bad; I am only saying that there are such people. I think that, today, there are many "little Nichirens" around. People written about in newspapers and magazines are like little Nichirens who proclaim their name and think "I am it!" It is all right as long as there is only one Nichiren but, if too many people grow noses as long as that of a *tengu* 天狗,[17] the noses would get in each other's way!

Anyway, in the *Larger Sutra of Immeasurable Life*, Dharmākara Bodhisattva did not himself say "I am Dharmākara." When he asked Lokeśvararāja Buddha to teach him how to establish a pure land wherein to save all sentient beings, the Buddha answered, "You yourself should know." Thereupon Dharmākara replied, "No, that is too vast and deep for my comprehension."[18] He did not answer, "Yes, I know," and the Buddha did not tell him, "Indeed, you could not know." That would rather be the conversation that currently takes place nowadays: the individual saying of himself, "Yes, I know," and of the other, "You could not know." This is a scenario for a world of strife. On the contrary, the *Larger Sutra* presents a world of harmony, with the teacher saying, "You yourself should know," and the disciple answering, "That is too vast and deep for my comprehension."

Dharmākara Bodhisattva is a figure that appeared in the depths of human history, but there is not a single individual that claims the name for himself. This is a very good thing, a thing to be grateful for. In the case of Eminent Conduct Bodhisattva, it is possible to say, "I am he." But in the case of Dharmākara Bodhisattva, we cannot say this. Therein lies a basic difference between the *Larger Sutra of Immeasurable Life* and the *Lotus Sutra*.

What kind of person, then, is Dharmākara Bodhisattva? Nobody can say, "I am Dharmākara Bodhisattva." This bodhisattva is the subject of a deep self-awareness that one is an "ordinary unenlightened being involved in birth-and-death, who from the remotest past up to the present time has been forever floundering in *saṃsāra* and that one has no way of freeing oneself," who then became Amida Buddha. Somebody who has claimed the name Dharmākara for himself cannot become Amida Buddha. Dharmākara Bodhisattva is a person with a deep sense of responsibility, and having sufficient empathy to take the responsibility of all sentient beings upon himself alone; a person who does not get angry even when kicked and trodden upon by the feet of all. The unimaginably long kalpas of ascetic practice the sutra ascribes to him are precisely that.

I have spoken earlier about the five gates of mindfulness[19] and about "opening the three aspects of faith into the five practices of mindfulness."[20] Dharmākara Bodhisattva, who made the vow of the three aspects of faith, went on to devote himself for unimaginably long kalpas to the practice of the five gates of mindfulness. To endure in view of the future and not to be misled by people, that is precisely Dharmākara Bodhisattva, Dharmākara's very soul or spirit. To sense this spirit of Dharmākara Bodhisattva—that is Jōdo Shinshū or the True Pure Land path. People who have received the gift of living in Jōdo Shinshū must all sense the Dharmākara soul. And the path that leads to this sense is the twofold deep faith,[21] especially the *ki* aspect of deep faith. The consciousness of karma is the path to sensing Dharmākara's soul, to entering into and submitting in faith to that spirit.

It is said that the *ki* aspect of deep faith is a matter of rejecting (the contrivances of self-power), but it is not only rejecting; there is in it also the (positive) meaning of acceptance in faith. It is not so that acceptance in faith is to be found only in the *hō* aspect of deep faith; I am convinced that also the *ki* aspect embraces that positive element. Therefore, the awareness of oneself as an "evil person" discussed in chapter 3 of the *Tannishō*, namely, the consciousness of karma, means to shoulder the evil of all sentient beings. This "evil person" is the evil person, not of "that fellow is an evil one," but of "I myself am precisely an evil person." It is not your passion-riddenness but my own. The "I myself" points to self-awareness. Therein we truly intuit or sense Dharmākara Bodhisattva.

The consciousness of karma is thus the sense for Dharmākara Bodhisattva. Here, however, we better speak of sensing the actually living Dharmākara Bodhisattva than of sensing Dharmākara's mind. Dharmākara Bodhisattva is not dead, but eats, gets angry, and feels desire. When hearing this, you may think I am tricking you, but no, Dharmākara is factually living the life of an ordinary person or "householder." You may think of him as a very special person but, in fact, he is to be found everywhere. Provided attachment to the ego is taken away, Dharmākara Bodhisattva is present in any place whatever. He certainly is not present where there is self-centeredness but when we remove our ego attachment by the *ki* aspect of deep faith, everything that meets the eye is Dharmākara Bodhisattva. Not only human beings, but also the very earth with all the things on it, are his body. In that capacity, all things make the supreme vow, take on themselves alone the evil and pain of all sentient beings, and stand there solemnly without complaining. When we truly open our eyes, all that we see is Dharmākara Bodhisattva, and all things in the whole world are symbols of Dharmākara's spirit.

That is the Buddhist view of the world. It is not a theory or scholarly thesis. When quietly worshipping or giving praise, you must be sensing this Dharmākara. Our founder Shinran did not sense Dharmākara Bodhisattva in some far-off place. Vasubandhu called the acts of the five gates of mindfulness the practice of "sons and daughters of good families."[22] Shinran, on the other hand, called these acts the practice of Dharmākara Bodhisattva. Thus, through the acts of the five gates of mindfulness, we can sense Dharmākara.

Dharmākara Bodhisattva is not a mere tale; but his reality could be shown only by way of a tale. The world of symbols can be manifested only in the form of tales. That is why Dharmākara appears in the sutra as a story of the past. However, what was there in the past is still here in the present, and will be there in the future. Dharmākara is patiently continuing the practice of the five gates of mindfulness.

The Meaning of Deep Faith

It is the *ki* aspect of deep faith that is the way to come into contact with that exalted Dharmākara Bodhisattva. Why would it be called "deep faith"? Let us think for a moment of our founder Shinran. He must have worshipped Dharmākara Bodhisattva in his master Hōnen. A person who worships a bodhisattva is himself a bodhisattva; somebody who worships a buddha is himself a buddha. It is said from of old that a buddha is mindful of a buddha, that buddhas keep one another in mind. On the other hand, a person who considers a neighbor to be a demon is a demon himself. There is the old story wherein a man called a neighbor a dirty fellow because the paper on his sliding doors was torn, and it then turns out that the man himself had been peeping at the other person through the holes in his own sliding doors. The sliding doors of that man's heart were certainly in shreds.

It is in that vein that I say that we sense the figure of the causal stage of the Buddha—or, again, the *"namu"* of Namu Amida Butsu—through the *ki* aspect of our deep faith. It is only when we take things on this deep level that it can truly be said that "Even a good person can attain birth in the Pure Land, how much more easily an evil person." That is why one speaks here of "deep faith." The meaning of that term must be sought in this direction.

The only person who truly knows karma is the Buddha. We ourselves do not know karma, but we deeply believe in the karma that is known to the Buddha. The Buddha is aware of the karma of all sentient beings, and takes it all upon himself. When it comes to the world of karma, we may know perfectly well who did what, but after all it is all our own responsibility, for we are linked by blood to all sentient beings. It is a matter of sensing karma with a heart of humble great compassion. With a heart that truly bleeds for all sentient beings, loves them, feels their pains and joys, and truly embraces them all equally—we may think here of "the four immeasurables"[23]—one senses the karma of all sentient beings in one's own body. We can say that this body itself is a microcosm, a little "Great Earth."

We must sense sin on that deep level; it is not a matter of thinking it out with our heads. Deep faith is a deep feeling, a feeling wherein oneself and the Buddha communicate, but the body that is given us plays a special role therein, and that body is historical. Our physical body certainly finds its direct origin in our parents, but it is the fruit of a past tradition going back for thousands, even millions, of years. Therefore, the sensations that we feel in our flesh and bones do not deceive us; we can sense Amida's vow through our bodies.

A vow is an ideal, but this does not mean that Amida's original vow has no substance. It makes itself felt through this body, which is the subject of history and the subject of the nenbutsu recitation. From the moment that Amida made his vow long ago, that sense has lived on. We have died and have been reborn, but this sense has persisted unchanged as mindfulness-remembrance (*nen* 念). That is what is meant by tradition. Therefore, when we hear the old story of Dharmākara Bodhisattva, we intuit: indeed this is it! And this is because our body clearly recognizes it. In that sense, my body is my body, but it is not my exclusive possession. It is the body of the Buddha, and belongs to all sentient beings. While being a thing of the Buddha and of all sentient beings, it is at the same time truly mine. I have received it as mine.

These realities come into their own in the *ki* aspect of deep faith. In it, faith and mindfulness embrace: the faith of deep faith and the mindfulness of the consciousness of karma. When inner mindfulness and outer faith thus come together and respond to one another's call, I am made into the only child of the Buddha. It is precisely the passion-ridden common mortal that is the only child of the Buddha. This, I have been made to feel, is the profound basis of what we are told in chapter 3 of the *Tannishō*.

Jōdo Shinshū means to awaken to the spirit of Dharmākara Bodhisattva, and we awaken to this spirit when we become convinced of the powerlessness of our self-power, reject all the contrivances of self-power, and henceforth take our seat in the ark of Amida's vow-power. At that moment, the entire world becomes full of Dharmākara Bodhisattva. From this arises my conviction: since there are innumerable Dharmākaras found in it, Jōdo Shinshū will know a new heyday, provided all these Dharmākara join hands. Now is the time for it; we must not squander this moment of grace. All this may sound like day-dreaming, but it is not.

Notes

1. The *Contemplation Sutra* holds that we can attain birth in the Pure Land both through meditative and nonmeditative practices. The former refer to such acts as visualizing, in a state of meditative absorption, the various features of the Pure Land, as well as Amida Buddha and his attendant bodhisattvas. The nonmeditative practice refers to practices undertaken without entering into a meditative state, such as the recitation of the nenbutsu. *Jōsan jiriki* refers to the act of undertaking these practices in an attitude of self-power. It is contrasted to *gugan tariki* 弘願他力 (other-power attitude relying on the extensive vow), which refers to the act of undertaking these practices in an attitude of other-power. Here, however, Soga uses the term *jōsan jiriki*, not strictly in this technical sense, but to refer to the human attitude that one can determine the course of one's life through one's own efforts.

2. The *Contemplation Sutra* divides people born in the Pure Land into three grades, each of which is further subdivided into three levels, making a total of nine grades of birth into the Pure Land.

3. Found in the first fascicle of Shandao's *Guanjingshu* 観経疏 (*Commentary on the Contemplation Sutra*). See T, 37: 249a-b.

4. SSZ 2:775

5. Following Shandao, Shinran distinguishes two aspects of faith: the *ki* aspect of deep faith (*ki no jinshin* 機の深信), and the *hō* aspect of deep faith (*hō no jinshin* 法の深信). The first is to believe that one is a foolish being, caught up in *saṃsāra* with no prospect of gaining release, whereas the second is to believe deeply that the only possibility of liberation is reliance on Amida's vows. Shandao's statement on the *ki* aspect of deep faith is paraphrased in the afterword of the *Tannishō*, which is quoted below.

6. From chapter 2 of the *Tannishō*. See SSZ 2:774.

7. Kōgatsuin Jinrei 香月院深励 was a professor of the Takakura Gakuryō, the Higashi Honganji seminary. He was instrumental in systematizing the Shin Buddhist doctrinal system during the Edo period. Among his numerous works is the *Tannishō kōgi* 歎異抄講義 (*Lectures on the Tannishō*) in one fascicle.

8. Myōon'in Ryōshō 妙音院了祥 (1788–1842), a disciple of Jinrei, was a pioneer in the positivistic study of Shin Buddhist texts. In his *Tannishō monki* 歎異抄聞記 (*Notes on the Tannishō*), he first set forth the theory, now widely accepted but quite radical for his age, that Yuien 唯円 was the author of the *Tannishō*.

9. Kakunyo, Shinran's grandson, played an important role in the institutionalizing the Shin school. The *Kudenshō* is his outline of Pure Land teachings.

10. This passage is found in the fourth fascicle of Shandao's *Guanjingshu*. See T, 37: 278a.

11. This section marks the beginning of lecture 11.

12. Postscript of the *Tannishō* (Bandō and Stewart 1980, 77, slightly amended). This passage originally derives from Shandao's *Guanjingshu*.

13. The recompense of sentient beings refers to the physical body one receives as the result of past actions (karma), while the recompense of the environment refers to the physical setting one is born into as the result of past actions.

14. A mountain located to the northeast of Kyoto. It can be seen from anywhere in the city. On it stands Enryakuji 延暦寺, the head temple of the Tendai sect. Shinran studied as a Tendai monk on Mount Hiei before converting to the Pure Land teachings.

15. This passage derives from Rennyo's *Ofumi* 御文 (*Pastoral Letters*). See Rogers and Rogers 1991, 242.

16. According to the "Welling Up Out of the Earth" chapter of the *Lotus Sutra*, the Eminent Conduct Bodhisattva (Jōgyō Bosatsu 上行菩薩) is one of the four chief bodhisattvas that welled out from the earth to pay homage to Śākyamuni Buddha when the Buddha was preaching this sutra. See Hurvitz 1976, 225–36.

17. A long-nosed goblin who, according to Japanese folktales, is said to live in the mountains. A person who is overly proud of himself is often referred to as having a nose as long as that of a *tengu*.

18. Cf. Gómez 1996, 164.

19. The five practices that makes up the nenbutsu according to Vasubandhu's *Pure Land Treatise*. They are worship, praise, vow, contemplation, and transfer of merit. See Kiyota 1978, 278ff.

20. This is discussed in lecture 3 of the *Tannishō chōki*. See SRS 6: 52ff. The three aspects of faith refer to sincerity, entrusting, and desire to be born in the Pure Land mentioned in the eighteenth vow. In the *Tannishō chōki*, Soga states that sincerity corresponds to worship, praise, vow (the first three of the five practices of mindfulness), whereas the desire to be born in the Pure

Land corresponds to contemplation and transfer of merit (the last two of the five practices of mindfulness).

21. The twofold deep faith refers to two aspects of faith—*ki* and *hō*—discussed in note 5.

22. Kiyota 1978, 278.

23. *Shi muryōshin* 四無量心, also known as the four *brahmavihāras*: immeasurable compassion, immeasurable sympathy, immeasurable joy, and immeasurable detachment.

Kaneko Daiei

At age 54. (Courtesy of Sōō Gakusha, dated 1936)

Chapter 10

Kaneko Daiei

Life and Thought

Robert F. Rhodes

The Life of Kaneko Daiei

Kaneko Daiei 金子大栄 (1881–1976), an influential modern Shin Buddhist scholar, was born in Takada 高田 (now Jōetsu city) in Niigata Prefecture.[1] He was the eldest of nine children born to Kaneko Yūei 金子勇栄, the priest of the Shin Buddhist temple Saikenji, and his wife Tei 貞. After three years at the local Shinshū Beinan Chūgakuryō 真宗米南中学寮 (Shinshū Beinan Middle School), he transferred to the Shinshū Kyoto Middle School in Kyoto to continue his studies. Two years later, he entered the preparatory division (*yoka* 予科) of Shinshū University, the precursor to the present Ōtani University, which had been founded in Kyoto in 1896 to provide education in Western languages, philosophy, and science in addition to Buddhist thought. In 1901, the very year when Shinshū University was moved to Sugamo in Tokyo and reconstituted as a modern university under the leadership of Kiyozawa Manshi, Kaneko became a student in its regular division (*honka* 本科). It may be noted that Soga Ryōjin, who was to become Kaneko's lifelong friend and spiritual mentor, was a graduate student (*kenkyū-in* 研究員) at the school at this time. At the university, Kaneko studied Kegon 華厳 (Ch. Huayan) philosophy, and also came under the influence of Kiyozawa's Seishinshugi. Kaneko graduated in 1904. He submitted two papers for his graduation thesis: "Tariki ōjō ron" 他力往生論 ("On Birth in the Pure Land through Other-Power") and "Kegonkyō kakubon no kōyō" 華厳経各品の綱要 ("Summary of Each of the Chapters of the *Huayan Sutra*"). Following graduation, Kaneko returned to his temple in Takada where he worked to spread the Seishinshugi ethos through lectures and occasional writing. In 1915, he published his first book, the well-received *Shinshū no kyōgi oyobi sono rekishi* 真宗の教義と其の歴史 (*Teaching and History of Shin Buddhism*). In April of that year, he returned to Tokyo to become the editor of the *Seishinkai*, a journal that had been founded by Kiyozawa. His stay in Tokyo, however, lasted only a little more than a year, because in 1916 he was appointed professor of Shinshū Ōtani University in Kyoto. (This was the new name given to Shinshū University when it was moved to Kyoto in 1911.) There he lectured on Kegon philosophy and taught introductory classes on Buddhist thought. His *Bukkyō gairon* 仏教概論 (*Survey of Buddhism*), published in 1919, was based on his university lectures. It also was during this period of Kaneko's career that his *Shinshūgaku josetsu* 真宗学序説 (*Prolegomena to Shin Buddhist Studies*) appeared. The title alludes, of course, to Immanuel Kant's *Prolegomena to Any Future Metaphysics*. Kaneko was a popular teacher, with many students (even those not formally enrolled) attending his classes.

In 1925, Kaneko published a short book entitled *Jōdo no kannen* 浄土の観念 (*The Idea of the Pure Land*), in which he set forth a radical new thesis that the Pure Land is an Idea (*kannen* 観念).[2] This book was a transcript of a lecture he gave in October of the previous year. Kaneko amplified his views in *Higan no sekai* 彼岸の世界 (*The World of the Further Shore*) published in 1925, and *Shinshū ni okeru nyorai oyobi jōdo no kannen* 真宗に於ける如来及び浄土の観念 (*The Idea of the Tathāgata and the Pure Land in Shin Buddhism*). The latter work, based on a lecture given in October 1925, was published in 1926.

Traditionally, Amida Buddha's Pure Land is described in the sutras as a marvelous paradise existing far off in the west. Although Shinran, the founder of Shin Buddhism, does not reject such image of the Pure Land, he declares that it does not represent the true Pure Land. In his view, the true Pure Land is none other than nirvāṇa itself, a totally transcendent realm beyond all human conception. Although this realm can only be rendered metaphorically as a radiant realm of infinite light, in order to make it accessible to human understanding, it is described using concrete imagery, that is, as a delightful realm pleasing to the senses situated in a specific location far from this world.

Over the centuries, however, the popular view of the Pure Land as a blissful world lying in the west to which we go at death remained pervasive, even among Shin Buddhist believers. But eventually by Kaneko's time, such understanding of the Pure Land had become unacceptable to many, including those among the Shin priesthood and laity. In 1923, Nonomura Naotarō 野々村直太郎, a professor at Bukkyō University (now Ryūkoku University) and a priest of the Nishi Honganji branch of Shin Buddhism, published a book entitled *Critique of Pure Land Buddhism* (*Jōdokyō hihan* 浄土教批判). In this book, he attacked the popular understand of the Pure Land, as being backward and feudalistic and suggested that the notion of the Pure Land be expunged from Shin Buddhist discourse. Nonomura's volume immediately provoked a great controversy. Even though Nonomura's thesis gained widespread support (the faculty of Bukkyō University, for example, supported Nonomura), it was harshly criticized by many people within the Nishi Honganji. After about a year of fierce debate, Nonomura's thoughts were branded heretical. Consequently, he was expelled from the priesthood and was forced to resign from his professorship.[3] Kaneko's *The Idea of the Pure Land* was published just two years later and, like the earlier book, it too became the center of a heated debate. In this book, Kaneko (like Nonomura) argued that the naively realistic understanding of the Pure Land has become a serious impediment to accepting the Pure Land teachings. Indeed, Kaneko asserted that any description of the Pure Land as a postmortem paradise, despite its undeniable value as an expedient device, is ultimately a reflection of our worldly desires and does not represent the true Pure Land. However, unlike Nonomura, Kaneko did not propose to reject the concept of the Pure Land altogether. Instead he sought to reinterpret the Pure Land and argued (based on his reading of Plato, Kant and Neo-Kantian philosophers like Hermann Cohen) that the Pure Land is an Idea, the eternal realm beyond all human conceptualization.

What is meant by an "Idea"? As is well known, this term (also translated into English as "Form") goes back to Plato. As Masao Abe explains,

> According to Plato, beyond the realm of phenomena perceptible by our senses and subject to time and to change, there exists a realm of "Forms" which are immutable, timeless, and knowable only by the pure intellect. This realm exists independently and transcends the phenomena that participate in the Forms. Forms are realities and prototypes which make individual things what they are—the copies of the former.[4]

As Abe says (in the quote above, he uses the term "Form" instead of "Idea"), Ideas exist in an eternal and timeless realm lying beyond our world of everyday experience and serve as archetypes of all things that exist in our experiential world. Taking his cue from Plato, Kant, in *Critique of Pure Reason*, posits three "Ideas of Reason"—the soul, the universe in its totality, and God—which transcend all human experience and refer to what is perfect, unlimited, and unconditioned. They cannot be apprehended through ordinary perception and can be known only by the pure intellect. But these Ideas are of great practical significance, since they are regulative principles which serve as goals to which we must continually strive.

Following Shinran's position outlined above, Kaneko affirms that the Pure Land is, fundamentally speaking, "the world of the further shore" (*higan no sekai* 彼岸の世界), or the realm of nirvāṇa lying beyond the cycle of birth-and-death. It was in order to restate this traditional Shin Buddhist position in terms of the western philosophical vocabulary then current among Japanese academics, that he characterized the Pure Land as an Idea. In describing the Pure Land as an Idea, Kaneko sought to underscore the fact that it is a transcendental realm lying beyond the world of everyday experience. However, he also emphasizes that it is an ideal toward which we must continually strive, even thought it is ultimately "inconceivable and beyond apprehension."

But although Kaneko denies that the Pure Land is an actual place, he does not deny its reality. In fact, he argues that the Pure Land has for the believer a reality that is more real than anything we ordinarily experience. Furthermore, in the following passage in opening essay of *The World of the Further Shore* (*Higan no sekai* 彼岸の世界, a sequel to *The Idea of the Pure Land*, published in 1925), he describes the Pure Land as his spiritual homeland.

> "The world of the further shore"—it is the true land that we have yet to behold and, at the same time, the spiritual homeland (*kyōri* 郷里) for which we yearn. In contrast, the world of this shore (*shigan no sekai* 此岸の世界) is a hollow and false world in which we have become so accustomed to remaining, and, at the same time, a foreign land [in which we have lived so long that] we have forgotten when we began our peregrinations. Hence, the roots of what we call our religious life is to be found in our grief over [the fact that we exist] in the world of this shore and our desire to dwell in the distant world of the further shore.[5]

Here Kaneko argues that the Pure Land is to be best understood as a symbol of our deepest spiritual yearning: our elemental desire to live in a perfect world free from all the suffering and anguish to which we are daily subjected. Hence, the Pure Land is depicted as our spiritual homeland, a world from which we have become totally estranged but which still serves as the focus of our hopes and aspirations. In Kaneko's view, the importance of the Pure Land lies in its symbolic meaning that, when properly understood, remains significant for the people of the modern age.

But if the Pure Land is not an actual place, where is it to be found? Kaneko replies it is to be found in self-awareness (*jikaku* 自覚) of the believer. To explain this, he cites the famous opening lines from Vasubandhu's *Pure Land Treatise*: "World-honored One! I single-mindedly take refuge in the Tathāgata of Unhindered Light Completely Illuminating the Ten Directions and vow to be born in the Land of Peace and Bliss." This passage has long been esteemed as a paradigmatic expression of Shin Buddhist faith. In his analysis of this passage, Kaneko focuses on the relationship between the terms "I," "Tathāgata" (i.e., Amida Buddha), and "Land" (i.e., the "Land of Peace and Bliss" or Amida's Pure Land). It is commonly assumed that the Tathāgata and the Pure Land exist independently from "I," the believing person. However, Kaneko maintains that it is precisely in the self-awareness (or faith) of the person who has taken refuge in the Tathāgata, that the Tathāgata and his Pure Land manifest themselves and take on an irresistible reality.[6]

It may not be out of place here to mention that a similar view had already been espoused by Kiyozawa concerning Amida Buddha. In his celebrated essay, "The Nature of My Faith" he argues that the Tathāgata in which he believes is "the fundamental basis of what I believe in." In other words, Kiyozawa here understands Amida Buddha, not as an other-worldly supernatural being residing in a world far off to the west, but as the saving power that appears in the believer's faith. The analogous point is made by Kaneko in his description of the Pure Land: It too is not an actual place located somewhere in the universe, but a spiritual reality that appears in faith. This "subjectivist turn," which locates both Amida Buddha and his Pure Land in the self-awareness of the believer, is a major theme that underlies modern Shin Buddhist thought.

Kaneko's analysis of how the awareness of the Pure Land arises is ultimately derived from Shinran's distinctive dialectic of faith (ultimately derived from Shandao) known as the "two kinds of deep faith" (*nishu jinshin* 二種深信). As cited in the *Kyōgyōshinshō*, the two kinds of deep faith are as follows:

> One is to believe deeply and decidedly that you are a foolish being of karmic evil caught in birth-and-death,

ever sinking and ever wandering in transmigration from innumerable kalpas in the past, with never a condition that would lead to emancipation. The second is to believe deeply and decidedly that Amida Buddha's forty-eight vows grasp sentient beings, and that allowing yourself to be carried by the power of the Vow without any doubt or apprehension, you will attain birth.[7]

According to this passage, faith has two aspects, which, however, are experienced simultaneously. That is to say, the moment we truly realize that we are deluded, passion-ridden beings unable to save ourselves through our own efforts, we realize that it was precisely in order to save such beings that Amida Buddha made his vows. Through this realization, we are led to entrust ourselves completely to the saving power of the vows. Kaneko's argument above—that "I," "Tathāgata," and "Land" appear simultaneously in the self-awareness of faith—is based on this dialectic of faith. The moment we gain unerring insight into our own true natures as deeply deluded beings, Amida manifests himself to lead us out of the world of birth-and-death. At the same time, since, according to Buddhist mere consciousness philosophy, the world is a reflection of our inner mental states, the moment we discern our deluded natures, we also perceive our everyday world for what it is: a wretched world in which we are tormented by grief and profound disappointment at every turn. When we see our world mirrored in all of its imperfection in this way, there arises in us a profound desire to cast aside this world and seek the Pure Land in order to realize the life of perfect fulfillment that it symbolizes.

Predictably, Kaneko's view was quickly accused of heresy, inasmuch as it appeared to deny the existence of the Pure Land, relegating it to the status of a mental projection. In traditional Buddhist terms, Kaneko was accused of maintaining the position that "the Pure Land is mind-only" (*yuishin jōdo* 唯心浄土), that is, that the Pure Land is a mental construction devoid of real existence. In November 1927, Kaneko was summoned before the Jitōryō 侍董寮, an organ within the Higashi Honganji decided matters of orthodoxy, and was charged with heresy. Despite the fact that Kaneko enjoyed the support of a number of Ōtani University's professors and students (the students held protest meetings and eleven professors including Inaba Masamaru, the university president, offered their resignations [which, however, were ultimately not accepted] to express their solidarity with Kaneko), he was forced to resign from his professorship in 1928 and, the next year, to give up his Shin Buddhist priesthood.⁸ Subsequently, he spent nearly eleven years as a professor at Hiroshima Bunkyō University.

Despite the tragedy that befell him, Kaneko remained productive during his years away from Kyoto. Between 1938 and 1941, he published the *Kyōgyōshinshō kōdoku* 教行信証講読 (*Lectures on the Kyōgyōshinshō*), his monumental three-volume study of the *Kyōgyōshinshō*. In 1940 he published *Nihon Bukkyō shikan* 日本仏教史観 (*A History of Japanese Buddhism*) based on his lectures at Hiroshima. Kaneko was also a popular speaker, frequently sought out to give Dharma talks throughout Japan. In 1940, Kaneko was reinstated into the Shin priesthood and invited back to Ōtani University the following year. Opposition to Kaneko's interpretation of the Pure Land had gradually receded, but perhaps a more important reason was the fact that Japan had begun to mobilize for total war. As one of the foremost thinkers of Higashi Honganji, Kaneko was drafted into the denomination's efforts to cooperate with the government's wartime policies. Kaneko was an ideal candidate, since already during his Hiroshima years, he had written extensively on Shōtoku Taishi 聖徳太子, an imperial prince who played a major role in promoting Buddhism when it was first introduced to Japan, praising his role in spreading Buddhism. Although hardly a jingoistic nationalist, Kaneko took part in organizations and conferences supporting the government's policies and eventually published a lengthy paper entitled "Kōkoku Bukkyōgaku josetsu" 皇国仏教序説 ("Prolegomena to Imperial Buddhism").⁹ Consequently, after Japan's defeat, he was declared unfit as a teacher and was purged from the Ōtani University faculty in 1949. It is worth noting, however, that in 1947 he had published the *Shūkyōteki kakusei* 宗教的覚醒 (*Religious Awakening*), in which he declared the need for the Japanese people to repent for the suffering caused by the war.¹⁰

In 1952, when the purge was rescinded, Kaneko once again resumed teaching at Ōtani University as emeritus professor. His lectures continued until 1974, when he turned ninety-two years old. Kaneko remained a prolific author throughout the postwar years. In 1956, he published the masterly *Kyōgyōshinshō no kenkyū* 教行信証の研究 (*Study of the Kyōgyōshinshō*), and in 1961 he produced a modern Japanese translation of the *Kyōgyōshinshō*. He also continued to lecture widely throughout the country. Many of these lectures were transcribed and subsequently published, helping to make Kaneko one of the most widely known Shin Buddhist figures in Japan. He died in 1976 at the age of ninety-six.

Prolegomena to Shin Buddhist Studies

What follows is a translation of Kaneko's *Prolegomena to Shin Buddhist Studies*. With the passage of a new law on institutions of higher education in 1922, Shinshū Ōtani University was reorganized and renamed Ōtani University. To celebrate this event, in October 1922, Kaneko delivered a two-day series of lectures at the Yamaguchi Bukkyō Kaikan 山口仏教会館 in Kyoto under the title "Shinshūgaku josetsu" ("Prolegomena to Shin Buddhist Studies"). In these lectures, Kaneko attempted to describe how the study of Shin Buddhism should be pursued in the academic setting of a modern university. The lectures were published as a book under the same title in January 1923. Although brief, this volume had an enormous impact on the Shin academic community and has continued to influence Shin Buddhist studies until the present day.

The academic study of Shin Buddhism has its roots in the works of Kakunyo 覚如 (1270–1351), Shinran's great-grandson, and Zonkaku 存覚 (1290–1373), Kakunyo's son and the author of the *Rokuyōshō* 六要鈔, the first commentary written on the *Kyōgyōshinshō*. However, the study of Shin doctrines and texts reached new heights during the Edo period. During this time, the Tokugawa government encouraged scholarly activities by the Buddhist sects, mainly in order to divert the monks' attention away from political matters. As a result, the various Buddhist schools established seminaries for the specialized study of their doctrines. The Ōtani denomination's academy was called the Takakura gakuryō 高倉学寮. Its professors (*kōshi* 講師) included such renowned scholar-monks as Ekū 慧空 (1644–1712) who served as the first professor, Kōgatsuin Jinrei, Myōonin Ryōshō, and Enjōin Senmyō 円乗院宣明 (1750–1820). Their style of exegesis, called *kunkogaku* 訓詁学 (literally "study based on the interpretation of ancient words"), consisted primarily in providing detailed word by word exegesis on the authoritative texts of the Shin Buddhist tradition. This style of scholarship continued well into the modern age. A representative example of a study in this style is the *Kyōgyōshinshō kōgi* 教行信証講義 (*Lectures on the Kyōgyōshinshō*) by Yamabe Shūgaku and Akanuma Chizen, first published in 1913.[11] This work still remains essential reading for all students of the *Kyōgyōshinshō*.

Unfortunately, despite its many undeniable achievements, the *kunkogaku* style of scholarship frequently tended to fall into dry scholasticism. During the Meiji period, the Japanese educational system was reconstituted along Western lines. In keeping with the times, a new form of Shin Buddhist Studies was felt to be needed. Kaneko attempted to sketch out a new style of Shin Buddhist academics in the *Prolegomena to Shin Buddhist Studies*. In this volume, Kaneko argues for the need to establish Shin Buddhist Studies as a modern field of academic study. All academic fields of study, he asserts, are constituted by three fundamental questions: what, how, and why. In other words, all academic disciplines must have their object of its study, their method and a clear reason for pursuing their studies. Kaneko's book is an attempt to provide a foundation for Shin Buddhist Studies by analyzing its object, its methodology and the reason for engaging in this particular field of inquiry.

Kaneko begins from the third point—why—and argues that there is only one genuine reason for pursuing Shin Buddhist Studies: to achieve release from the cycle of birth-and-death. The study of Shin Buddhism is not a dispassionate analysis of ancient texts, but the existential quest for buddhahood. Traditionally, this has been expressed, using the phrase frequently employed by the eighth Honganji abbot Rennyo 蓮如 (1415–1499), as the quest for the solution to the problem of "the great matter of the afterlife" (*gose no ichidaiji* 後世の一大事). However, Kaneko argues that this phrase sounds old-fashioned and irrelevant to the people of his age, inasmuch as it suggests that salvation is a matter of being physically reborn after we die in a Pure Land. Such substantialist understanding of birth in the Pure Land, Kaneko declares, is no longer acceptable to people influenced by modern ways of thinking. Hence, he suggests that we must try to understand the feeling this phrase evoked in the minds of the people of the past. In Kaneko's view, this phrase symbolized the great gap between the everyday world in which we live and anguish and the ideal world for which we all yearn. Ordinarily, we believe our everyday world is real while the ideal world is an illusion. However, when our everyday world is perceived to be empty and devoid of ultimate meaning, it is radically negated, and the ideal world comes to have an overwhelming reality for us. Such radical negation of the everyday world is, in Kaneko's view, the fountainhead of religion and the feeling that the phrase "the great matter of the afterlife" evoked in the minds of the people of the past. And, Kaneko concludes, we must proceed in our study of Shin Buddhism with the determination to confront and resolve this matter.

Next, Kaneko asserts that its object of study in Shin Buddhist Studies must be "the true words of the Great Sage, in other words, the words of Śākyamuni Buddha." To be more specific, it is the *Sutra of Immeasurable Life*, which Shinran declares in the *Kyōgyōshinshō* to be the "true teaching." Here Kaneko disagrees with the common assumption that the object of Shin Buddhist Studies is the *Kyōgyōshinshō* itself, that is, the systematic outline of the Shin Buddhist teaching by the school's founder. Instead Kaneko argues "from now on, Shin Buddhist Studies should not be defined as the study of Shinran's writings, but the study of how Shinran studied." In other words, it must be the study of the teaching presented in the *Sutra of Immeasurable Life*, specifically Amida Buddha's forty-eight vows presented in this sutra, which is the ultimate source of Shinran's faith.

But here lies an important problem. Mahāyāna Buddhist texts repeatedly insist that the truth is inexpressible. As Kaneko himself declares, words are merely conventional designations and cannot express reality just as it is. However, Shinran declared the *Sutra of Immeasurable Life* to be Śākyamuni Buddha's true words and developed his religious thought from such a perspective. But if the truth is beyond linguistic expression, how can the sutra express the truth which Śākayamuni realized? This is the problem that Kaneko felt compelled to address in the *Prolegomena*. Hence, in chapters 4 and 5 of this volume, Kaneko makes a long detour to discuss the relationship between the truth (*shinri* 真理), the person who teaches the truth (Buddha or awakened person; *setsunin* 説人) and the teaching (or words; *kyōbō* 教法).

Kaneko begins by reviewing the Buddhist assertion that all things are inexpressible. Words, Kaneko notes, are concepts and cannot express the reality that we experience directly. Citing the well-known Buddhist metaphor, he notes that words are like fingers pointing to the moon and are not the moon itself. However, Kaneko continues, once we awaken to the truth, we realize that it is the truth within ourselves that awaken to the truth. Hence, there is no distinction between the truth and the awakened person (buddha) because the latter is also none other than the truth itself. Then the truth manifests itself—or, to use Kaneko's own words, proclaims itself (*nanoru* 名のる)—in the words and teachings of the awakened person and works dynamically through the medium of language to lead beings to awakening. Taking up the example of an artist painting a flower, Kaneko states:

> Indeed, it's been said since long ago that to really draw a flower, the flower must draw itself. The artist does not draw the flower, but the flower must make the artist draw the flower. In such situations, the artist disappears and the flower itself draws the flower. . . . If that's true, then why isn't it possible for the unconditioned truth to act in the same way? . . . If we enter directly into the realm where the truth reveals itself—that is to say, in situations where

we have really awakened to the truth—we do not awaken to the truth but the truth becomes our self. Then the truth itself speaks and proclaims itself.

Citing Asaṅga's *Mahāyānasaṃgraha*, he calls this truth the teaching that "flows forth from the pure *dharmadhātu*." Furthermore, following Shinran's *Kyōgyōshinshō*, Kaneko states that the essence of the teaching is Amida's Name or Namu Amida Butsu. In Kaneko's view, the Name is none other than the self-proclamation of Amida Buddha or the truth proclaiming itself. Through the Name, Amida makes his presence known to the people of the world and calls them to awakening.

Finally, what is the methodology appropriate to Shin Buddhist Studies? Kaneko argues that it is to be found in the "the interpretations of the great patriarchs." As is well known, Shinran chose seven monks from the Buddhist tradition as patriarchs of Shin Buddhism. These monks are Nāgārjuna and Vasubandhu of India; Tanluan, Daochuo, and Shandao of China; and Genshin and Hōnen of Japan. According to Kaneko, these seven patriarchs all shared a common method for studying Buddhism, or, more specifically, for interpreting the *Sutra of Immeasurable Life*. Because, as noted earlier, Kaneko believed that the teaching of Amida's forty-eight vows presented in this sutra is the true object of study in Shin Buddhism, he maintained that the tradition of exegesis on this sutra transmitted by the seven patriarchs offers us the most appropriate methodology for Shin Buddhist Studies.

In two lengthy chapters (chapters 8 and 9) comprising one third of the *Prolegomena*, Kaneko takes up the question of how this sutra has been studied by Pure Land scholars in the past. As noted previously, he argued in the earlier chapters that the true teaching (and the object of study) of Shin Buddhist Studies is the *Sutra of Immeasurable Life*, which describes how Amida Buddha's Pure Land came into being and outlines how we can attain birth there. But, he argues, there are two possible ways in which to study of this sutra. One is to describe the circumstances (*jiyū* 事由) which led to its composition, whereas the second is to clarify the reason (*riyū* 理由) behind its appearance. Although it is not always clear what Kaneko meant by the terms circumstances and reason, it appears that the former refers to the specific historical circumstances that led the creation of this sutra, whereas the latter refers to the deeper spiritual yearning that the sutra expresses. Needless to say, it is Kaneko's assertion that the latter is the true cause or reason why the sutra came into existence.

Kaneko explains the circumstances why the *Sutra of Immeasurable Life* arose within the Buddhist community with reference to the notion of the decline of the Dharma. According to this theory, during the age when Śākyamuni Buddha resided in the world, anyone could attain enlightenment by listening to the Buddha, thanks to his extraordinary pedagogic skills. But once the Buddha passed away and his influence began to dissipate, the world became increasingly evil and less and less conducive to attaining enlightenment. In such an evil world, people began to feel that it is impossible to attain enlightenment by their own powers. Hence, they began to seek birth in the Pure Land, where they could encounter an enlightened being and receive spiritual instructions for attaining buddhahood quickly and effortlessly.

In Kaneko's view, most Pure Land scholars have been preoccupied with describing the circumstances (i.e., the specific historical circumstances) why the sutra came into existence. However, when they tried to prove the reality of Amida Buddha and the Pure Land from such an objective (or positivistic) historical perspective, they fell into serious difficulties. Indeed, Kaneko maintains that all attempts to provide rational proofs for the existence of Amida and the Pure Land inevitably ring hollow and remain unconvincing. To truly understand why human beings have been drawn to seek the Pure Land over the centuries, it is necessary to perceive the fundamental reason, or the profound human yearning for spiritual contentment and the Buddha's compassionate desire to fulfill their yearning, lying behind the genesis of the Pure Land teachings.

But, as Kaneko says, that reason can only be discovered by introspection, that is, by looking inwardly within ourselves. In his view, the Pure Land is a subjective reality that emerges when we hear the voice of the Buddha summoning us to awaken to our evil-ridden selves and, through such awakening, are made to seek an ideal realm in which we are free from all our limitations. Hence the reason for the Pure Land is to be found in the voice of the Buddha calling to us to become aware of our profound desire to seek a world in which all of our hopes and spiritual aspirations can be fulfilled. In the concluding chapter of the *Prolegomena*, Kaneko says:

> The truth found in the teachings echoes only in the hearts of those who reflect inwardly on themselves. In other words, for those who adopt the attitude of inward reflection, the truth is revealed through the true words of the Great Sage. People who seek to prove things logically will choose as their object of study those teachings that present various theories. People who are attached to their self-centered beliefs may study sutras that are most convenient in defending their positions. However people who reflect inwardly on the

reason are compelled to listen to the Great Sage's direct and spontaneous words of truth.

These words succinctly summarize Kaneko's understanding of the genuine method for studying Shin Buddhism. Through attentive introspection, we can hear the true words of the Great Sage constantly calling to us from the innermost depths of our being, urging us to awaken to our true selves. Shin Buddhist Studies must be our response to that call.

Notes

1. Standard biographies of Kaneko include Kikumura 1975, and Hayata and Tatsudani 1993.
2. For a translation of the first chapter of the *Jōdo no kannen*, see Yokoyama 1995, 127–38.
3. On Nonomura and the controversy surrounding *Jōdokyō hihan*, see Kigoshi 2004b.
4. Abe 1997, 139.
5. KDC 3: 185.
6. Kaneko's analysis of this passage is found in Kaneko 1927, 7–25. For an English translation, see Yokoyama 1995, 129–38. Interestingly, in support of his argument that the Pure Land arises in faith, Kaneko refers to William James' famous essay, "The Will to Believe." Kaneko paraphrases the argument of the essay as follows: "Although we do not know if God exists or not, human life will be improved and made more valuable by believing in His existence. That is to say, the will to believe brings the God one believes into existence." Kaneko 1927, 98.
7. *The Collected Works of Shinran* 1997, 1:85, slightly amended.
8. Kikumura 1975, 76–90 and Hataya and Tatsudani 1993, 286–88.
9. Hayata and Tatsudani 1993, 296–97. On the response of Pure Land Buddhist thinkers of both the Higashi and Nishi Honganji to wartime policies, see Ikeda 1997, 128–71.
10. This volume constitutes the fourth volume of the supplement (*bekkan* 別巻) of the *Kaneko Daiei chosakushū* (Collected Writings of Kaneko Daiei).
11. Yamabe and Akanuma 1913; most recent reprint 2008.

Chapter 11

Prolegomena to Shin Buddhist Studies*

Kaneko Daiei

Translated by Robert F. Rhodes

I. Study

Shin Buddhism teaches us to go to the Pure Land by saying the nenbutsu. That's all. Since that's all there is to the teaching of Shin Buddhism, is there any need to study it academically? This, I heard, was the question once posed by a person connected with the government's educational policies. The same matter came up among my colleagues: Can Shin Buddhist Studies really be a valid field of study? To be sure, we have long been engaged in academic studies. However, the meaning of the academic study of Shin Buddhism practiced so far, and the meaning of the Shin Buddhist Studies to be pursued academically from now on in the context of a college setting, seem to me quite different.[1] Hence, the question arose among the faculty, "Can such a discipline as Shin Buddhist Studies really exist?" In this way, both from within and outside the university, the question was posed as to whether it is possible for Shin Buddhist Studies to be an academic enterprise. This is an important question that the professors of Ōtani and Ryūkoku universities must answer together with ordinary scholars

---

*(Tr.—The text used for this translation is Kaneko 1966. As some of the paragraphs in the original essay were quite long, I have sometimes taken the liberty of dividing them into smaller paragraphs. Footnotes found in the original text are translated without any comment. Footnotes added by the translator begin with the notation "Tr." and are surrounded by parentheses.)

of Shin Buddhism. Now, as for the question, "Can such a discipline as Shin Buddhist Studies really exist?" To be sure, Shin Buddhism has been studied academically a lot until now, but today we must answer this question by establishing Shin Buddhist Studies as a field of study in a novel sense. This is not something that just one or two people can accomplish. It's something we all have to do together. My talk is a prolegomena to this task.[2] That's the meaning of the title of my talk. The word *prolegomena* immediately brings Kant's *Prolegomena*[3] to mind, but I haven't thought through the problem like Kant. But I wish to talk about my ideas with a spirit like his.

Generally speaking, what does it mean to study? Before we ask whether or not there can be such a thing as Shin Buddhist Studies, we must ask what "studies" in general means. This is how we must approach the problem, but this is such a big matter. In a broad sense, all research can be included within the term "studies." However, it can be understood in a narrow sense as well. The inquiry of one's life, that is to say, what all humans must study once they have been born as a human being: this is what "studies" must mean. This is something we have to consider in detail. But let's leave that for later. Here I would first like to focus on the old word *gakumon* 学問 (academic study).

What does this word *gakumon* mean? I not sure about its etymology, but it's made up of two Chinese characters, *gaku* 学 (study) and *mon* 問 (question). When I see this word, I can't help but focus on the second character, *mon*. Here, study (*gaku*) means to question (*mon*). When we have a question, that is to say, when we confront a problem, that's when we study. No one can engage in academics without having a question. What is the most fundamental question that we human beings have? I think it's made up of three parts: the question of *what*, the question of *why*, and the question of *how*. In other words, we must first ask what it is that we study. For example, when we consider the various types of academic disciplines found in the world, we first ask, "What are they studying?"[4] They're all studying something. Likewise, we must all observe and clarify the thing that we're studying. Next we have to think about how to study it. This *how* is the question of method. In the case of scientists, they engage in experiments. Finally, there is the question of *why*. Since the question *why* is one that inquires into the reason (*riyū* 理由) for undertaking the study, it is something that requires thinking. Our rationality is at work here. It's impossible to understand something just by observing it, or by doing various experiments and observing the results. Scientists have to ask why the experiment had a certain result. They have to think about why something happened. In this way, the object of study derives from asking *what*, its method derives from asking *how*, and the ground for engaging in an academic study develops from the question *why*.

The fact that we have these three questions is very suggestive. These three questions exist in every field of academic study. These three questions must be firmly related to the self. We can't just ask how and why we study something. I myself must have clearly formulated these questions. At the very least, the fact that we exist here means that these three questions hold sway over us. However, these three questions seem to imply that, fundamentally, they all come down to one question. When we ask ourselves from the depth of our heart what we should do, the question of *how* arises. Next, concerning *what*. This question arises when we come to ask why we exist. What are we humans? And what is the ground of our existence? When we ask such questions, it indicates that, even while we humans are individual existences, we are seeking for something objective. We humans are not just individual beings, but we sense something universal in us. Moreover, in addition to the questions of *what* and *how*, we also ask the question *why*. This really shows that humans are rational beings. The fact that we have these three questions reveals the nature of human existence.

II. The Significance of Shin Buddhist Studies

I think that the significance of Shin Buddhist Studies must be discussed from the perspective of the three questions. However, let us return to the beginning for now, and ask if such a thing as Shin Buddhist Studies is possible. First, some people say that religion is nothing more than faith. We feel this faith directly. We, so to speak, intuit the Buddha's saving power. Because it concerns intuition, there is no need to study it academically. There is no place for academic study in the world of intuition. This is the first objection concerning Shin Buddhist Studies. Other people say that the characteristic feature of Shin Buddhism lies in the recitation of the nenbutsu, which is a very simple practice. Each of us individually recites Namu Amida Butsu and experiences something in it. There is nothing else to Shin Buddhism. To take up anything else and treat it academically is actually a hindrance. For this reason, academic study is unnecessary in Shin Buddhism. That's what these other people say.

However, as I have said before, all humans have three questions. Moreover, the fact that we have these three questions defines us as human beings. For this reason, even though it is true that faith or practice is the only important thing in Shin Buddhism, a certain realization, that is to say a certain kind of rationality, must be working in the depth of faith and practice. No matter how much a human observes an object with a microscope, if he has no brains, it's impossible to discover any scientific truth. In just the same way, even if it is said that we should just believe or just practice, neither faith nor practice is possible as long as we have not been readied by our rational faculties. Thus, a certain kind of rationality must be working in the depth of faith and practice. Seen in this way, both practice and faith can be included within study. This certain rationality lies at the basis of Shin Buddhist Studies.

My explanation is becoming quite complex, but let me here discuss the three questions as they relate to Shin Buddhist Studies. Now, what is the object of Shin Buddhist Studies? What do we study? We must first begin by discussing the object of Shin Buddhist Studies. Once we establish what it is that we study, we must next discuss how we study it (i.e., its method). Finally, there is the question of why we study it, but in my opinion this *why* is the deepest and most fundamental question in Shin Buddhist Studies.[5]

So, why do we have to engage in Shin Buddhist Studies? This is a very broad way of putting it. From the standpoint of Buddhism in general, the traditional answer is to gain release from the cycle of birth-and-death. It's true that the words "the great matter of gaining release from the cycle of birth-and-death" (*shōji shutsuri no ichidaiji* 生死出離の一大事) sound old-fashioned to us today. People in olden times spoke of "the great matter of the afterlife" (*gose no ichidaiji* 後世の一大事) or "the great matter of life-and-death" and these words undoubtedly made a far greater impression on them than they do on us. They sound irrelevant to people like us who have been influenced by modern thought. But when people first began to use these words, what feelings did they evoke in them? If we approach these words in this way, maybe we can understand what they mean.

For example, if Rennyo's[6] words "the great matter of the afterlife" are understood to mean that this world is not important and that the important thing is that we will be led to the Land of Supreme Bliss after we die, these words may sound very remote to people like us who are attached to the actual world. To clarify the meaning of this phrase "the great matter of the afterlife," we can contrast it with the phrase "the great matter of this life" (*konoyo no ichidaiji* この世の一大事). If the words "great matter of the afterlife" are no good, let's use the words "the great matter of this life." When we consider what is evoked in our minds by the words "the great matter of this life," it's always something materialistic, something actual. In any case, it's always something connected with our daily lives. Then let's contrast the words "the great matter of this life" with "the great matter of the afterlife" and consider the feelings evoked by the words "the great matter of the afterlife." Because the word "afterlife" refers to the life after death, most people would understand this to mean that this world is not important. However, these words evoke in us something very profound. It concerns something that you have totally forgotten, the great problem of the spirit. It is the problem of your soul. It is the problem of your fundamental spirit. This is what it evokes. We're being too hasty when we only pay attention to the surface meaning of words and say that, just because it says "the afterlife," this world doesn't matter. When we reflect deeply on the nuance of the words "great matter of the afterlife," we realize that they evoke the problem of our soul or the problem of your spirit.

The phrase "the great matter of life-and-death" has the power to overturn reality as we understand it from the bottom up. These words reveal the contrast between the actual world and the ideal world. We ordinarily live in the actual world. As long as we are living in the actual world, worrying about food and clothing or worrying about love and desire, religion does not exist. From such a point of view, any thought about the ideal world is slighted as illusory. It's often said that religion concerns the world of nothingness. It's said that problems of food, clothing or love and desire are real problems, but that problems of faith in the gods or buddhas, concern the world of nothingness. However, words like "the great matter of the afterlife" or "the great matter of life-and-death," end up overturning such a commonsense view of the world. The world that we until now thought was illusory somehow comes to have a powerful significance, whereas the conception of reality that we actually held until now becomes empty. What was most actual then becomes most empty. I think this is something that everyone experiences at some time or another.

We were begotten between the Heaven and Earth and we worry over various matters concerning our bodies and minds. What does it all mean? We claim to exist in the actual world, but is it really so? What does it mean to exist? This may appear to be a very strange question, but it is actually a question that has the power to attack us from our very roots. When we are confronted with this question, everything we had taken to be real until now comes to seem empty like dreams or illusions, whereas things that we had set aside as empty and illusory press on us with great urgency. Although we too experience this reversal, I think that people of the past felt it much more strongly. I think the people of the past perceived the ideal world much more clearly and perceived the actual world as dreams or illusions to the same degree that we now consider the actual world to be real. When we experience this reversal, when this "floating world"[7] becomes empty, we perceive that there is something to the ideal world which we have taken to be empty. Furthermore, we come to perceive that we are fulfilled only in that ideal world. Without such a reversal, I think religion would not exist. It is only when we experience such a reversal that religion, in the true sense, arises. This is what has been expressed since olden times by the words "the great matter of birth-and-death" and "the great matter of the afterlife."

This "great matter of birth-and-death" is a matter that concerns our entire being. It is imperative to proceed in our studies with such a problem in mind. In other words, we must proceed in our studies with the vow to confront and resolve this great problem of birth-and-death. Unless it's done in this way, it's impossible to engage in Shin Buddhist Studies. But does this mean that we must totally forsake the actual world? Of course not! That is to say, once we enter the ideal world, we are revived and brought back to the actual world by the power of the ideal world. The worldly realm, so to speak, is revived by the trans-worldly realm. In any case, we have considered "the great matter of gaining release from the cycle of birth-and-death," "the great matter of the afterlife" or the need to realize the impermanence of human existence to be irrelevant to us for a long time. But that's really not the case. The feeling of impermanence is the feeling that human life is transitory, and it has the power to overturn our values from the very foundation. The significance of Shin Buddhist Studies lies in the fact that it seeks to think through and resolve this great matter.

So, what then is the object of Shin Buddhist Studies, and what is its method? Although I spoke of the object and method as if they were two different things, in reality, the method will be determined as a matter of course once the object is clarified. In the same way, the object of study arises naturally once the method is determined. In this way, the object of study and method cannot be separated. However following the standard academic procedure, I first establish the object of Shin Buddhist Studies and then turn to its method.

III. The Object of Study: The True Words of the Great Sage

The object of study in Shin Buddhism is the true words of the Great Sage, in other words, the words of Śākyamuni Buddha. The phrase "true words of the Great Sage" appears in the "Chapter on Practice" of Shinran's *Kyōgyōshinshō*. There, Shinran speaks of the "true words of the Great Sage" (*daishō no shingon* 大聖の真言) and the "interpretations of the great patriarchs" (*daiso no geshaku* 大祖の解釈).[8] The "true words of the Great Sage" here reveals the object of Shin Buddhist Studies, whereas the "interpretations of the great patriarchs" shows the method to be employed. This is my general idea.

The *Kyōgyōshinshō* begins with the "Chapter on Teaching," which indicates the true teaching of Buddhism. Śākyamuni's teachings are quoted prominently throughout the entire *Kyōgyōshinshō*, and they are followed by the interpretation of these words by the seven patriarchs of Shin Buddhism.[9] In other words, the *Kyōgyōshinshō* does not exist apart from the true words of the Great Sage and the interpretations of the great patriarchs. So, to begin with, I wish to establish that the object of study is the true words of the Great Sage. To be more concrete, the object of Shin Buddhist Studies is the true teaching, the *Sutra of Immeasurable Life*.

However, some people may say that this is incorrect. They would say that the object of the academic study of Shin Buddhism is not the *Sutra of Immeasurable Life* but the *Kyōgyōshinshō* itself. Moreover, there are other texts, like Rennyo's *Ofumi* (*Letters*)[10] and the works of the seven patriarchs of Shin Buddhism, which deserve to be studied as well. So, if the *Kyōgyōshinshō* by Shinran, the founder of the school, is the fundamental text of Shin Buddhism, this text should be the object of Shin Buddhist Studies. This is the first objection that many people would have. For this reason, we must first determine what the purpose of Shin Buddhist Studies is. Does it consist of research into Shinran's writings? Or should we consider Shinran himself as a student of Shin Buddhism? If it is the latter, this means that we are heirs to Shinran's studies, and we have to clarify how Shinran studied Shin Buddhism. This may seem like a minor point, but it is of considerable importance for Shin Buddhist Studies.

As for myself, I don't know what it was like before. However, from now on, Shin Buddhist Studies should not be defined as the study of Shinran's writings, but the study of how Shinran studied. This is the point I want to make. This is a significant point. If Shin Buddhist

Studies is the study of Shinran's writings, we should begin from the standpoint that Shinran is the founder of the Shin school and study his doctrines diligently, like it was done during the Tokugawa period. However, from now on we should study the way in which Shinran studied. Shinran too engaged in the study of Buddhism, and our task now is to study how Shinran studied. That is Shin Buddhist Studies. In my opinion, this is the only way that we can open up Shin Buddhist Studies to the world. It's not that Shin Buddhist Studies was not accessible to everyone before, but it will become even more accessible in this way. To study, as I said before, is to question with all of one's powers. What kinds of questions engaged Shinran's attention? What did he study and how did he study them? If we focus on Shinran's questions, Shin Buddhist Studies will become a broader field of study. In other words, Shin Buddhist Studies will become accessible to all sentient beings in the ten quarters of the universe. Seen in this way, the *Kyōgyōshinshō* is not the object of our study. The *Kyōgyōshinshō*'s object of study should itself become the true object of Shin Buddhist Studies. If that is the case, it follows that the *Sutra of Immeasurable Life*, in other words the true words of the Great Sage as revealed in the *Kyōgyōshinshō*, is the object of Shin Buddhist Studies.

However, other people may present the following question: "I agree with what you say. However, we do not wish to study the expositions found in the sutra. Instead we wish to study how the doctrines of the Shin school were created and what lies in their background. Shouldn't such historical problems be the object of Shin Buddhist Studies?"[11] Others may ask whether our faith should not be the object of Shin Buddhist Studies.[12] They hold that we should conduct research into the contents of our faith from various angles, that we should concern ourselves more with the theoretical study of faith, or with our actual experience of faith. Such people would find it impossible to believe that the true words of the Great Sage should be the object of study. Of course, we must respond to these questions, but I think these questions will be resolved naturally as we proceed. So for now, I would like to clarify a little bit more what I mean when I say that the true words of the Great Sage (i.e., the teachings of Śākyamuni) are the object of study.

IV. The Teacher and the Teaching

Now we have to confront two questions, the relation between the teacher and the teaching and that between the teaching and the truth.

When we study the teaching, at least three things are involved: the teaching (words), the person who teaches (the teacher), and the truth pointed out by the teaching. How are these three related? I think this is a very important problem in considering the object of Shin Buddhist Studies. We had been led astray for a long time because the relationship between them was unclear. Are these three totally different or are they in a certain sense one while remaining different? Unless this point is clarified, we shall become totally confused.

First, the teacher and the teaching. Some people may say that, when we study texts, we must first understand the text's author before we can understand what the text teaches. We can't understand a text just by reading it. We can't understand a text until we read its author's biography and know what kind of life he lived. That's what some people say. But other people may disagree. They say that, even if we don't know anything about the author, if we only read the text, we can understand it because the author is clearly reflected in the text. What's a biography, anyway? It's something in which a later person traces the path tread by an earlier person, in order to show how great the traces left by that earlier person are. That's how a biography tries to bring a person to life. But is it really possible to bring a person to life in this way? I don't think its possible for any biography to truly show us that earlier person. But that's not the case with a person's writings. A person's writings are in themselves that person's biography. A person's real-life story appears in that person's writings.

Take Shinran, for example. Do we understand the *Kyōgyōshinshō* after we gradually come to understand Shinran's life? Or can we understand him just by reading the *Kyōgyōshinshō*, even if we don't know anything about his life? That's the question that I have always asked myself. Some people may say it doesn't make any difference one way or the other. However, unless this matter is firmly settled, it would mean that we cannot determine the value of the *Kyōgyōshinshō* unless we can establish whether or not Shinran was Hōnen's disciple, or whether or not Shinran is actually the author of this text. However, when we read the *Kyōgyōshinshō* itself, we can find Shinran in it. Shinran's whole person is clearly alive in the words that make up the *Kyōgyōshinshō*.

So there are two ways of thinking about the relationship between the teaching and the person that taught it. The first is that, because the teaching and the person who taught it are different, it is first necessary to know the person to understand the teaching. The second is that the teaching itself reflects the person who taught it.

What is a teaching? I don't know much about logic or mathematics, but to study these subjects, I think we have to distinguish between texts of logic and mathematics and the life of the person who wrote them. If you have really penetrating insight, you may be able to grasp the personality of the author when you read books on logic and mathematics, even if you don't undertake research into that person's life. But that's impossible for most people. But sometimes in the case of people who have experienced profound self-awakening, later biographies tend to hide that person from us. So, in such cases, I think that a person's writings are his true biography. It may only be a matter of degree, but I think it's something well worth pondering over.

From such a perspective, the first way of thinking—that the teacher and the Dharma that is taught are different—arises. The true teacher must have awakened to some truth. However, by nature, enlightenment cannot be expressed in words. Enlightenment is something we sense (*kantoku* 感得), a kind of self-realization. It's not something you can explain. Words can never express the world apprehended through sense or self-realization. Words are all concepts; they can never express what is truly apprehended through our senses. When we say that fire is hot, it is something we sense. But you don't get burned just by shouting, "Fire is hot!" A word is just one concept, and it doesn't express the truth. Teachings are something inexpressible that humans express using concepts. Because it's impossible to make people understand what we have sensed by remaining silent, we are forced to use concepts to express it. When a teaching is expressed in words, it has already been conceptualized. A teaching is like a finger pointing to the moon. It's not the moon itself. Because the moon of enlightenment is something that words only point to, the realization of the person who preached the teaching and the words used to preach it are quite different.

So one fundamental problem is language. I am planning on discussing this problem in greater detail elsewhere,[13] but I want to share my ideas briefly with you. In any case, I think I have to investigate the nature of language a little more. It's for this reason that I want to investigate linguistic philosophy, but I haven't had time for it yet.

But how is language treated in Buddhism? First, there is a theory that a word is not a dharma itself. This is found in Vasubandhu's *Abhidharmakośa*.[14] This thing that I hold in my hand is called a rosary. But the word "rosary" is not something belonging to the rosary itself. The word "rosary" does not belong to the rosary itself. The word "rosary" belongs to us. It is us who call this thing a "rosary." When we perceive this rosary directly, we have no way of calling it, so we grasp it with the name "rosary." It doesn't mean that it has the name rosary. The *Laozi* says, "The nameless is the beginning of Heaven and Earth; the name is the mother of the myriad things."[15] That's really interesting. In the beginning, Mother Nature was nameless. Human life came into existence when names were given to things. Human life becomes meaningful only at this point. Buddhism speaks of "perfuming through words" (*myōgon kunjū* 名言薫習).[16] This means that human life begins with names. What we have are signs and the name does not belong to the thing itself.

Why do we give names to things that have no name? According to the *Chengweishilun* 成唯識論 (*Treatise on Mere Consciousness*), things have two characteristics: their individual characteristic (Jpn. *jisō* 自相, Skt. *svalakṣaṇa*) and the common characteristic (Jpn. *gūsō* 共相, Skt. *sāmānya-lakṣaṇa*).[17] The individual characteristic is something that reveals that dharma itself, while the common characteristic is something that reveals the common characteristic possessed by a group of things. Our words cannot express the thing itself. For this reason, our words grasp at some common characteristic and give it a name. For example, the word "flower" refers to all flowers, not to one particular flower. Even if we say "this flower," "this" is a common characteristic. Hence, the word "this flower" is a concept. No matter what expression we employ, as long as we use words, we are just playing with concepts. The true characteristic of the thing itself is beyond our knowledge. It is beyond what Kant calls understanding (*Verstand*). Our thoughts are a kind of judgment. "Flower" is a judgment. To speak of "this" or "that" is a judgment. Such judgment, in other words, is a kind of concept. It's never the form of the thing itself. So what we express in words is not really the wisdom of self-realization gained through sensing something. What we express in words is not something we sense as "hot." Through an expedient, provisional wisdom, we grasp the concept of "hotness." That's what the *Chengweishilun* says. However, because we are accustomed to using language, we think that language expresses the thing itself. We fall into delusion through "perfuming through words," especially through the perfuming of the word "self." From such a perspective, even the Buddhist teaching differs from the world of sense and self-realization. Śākyamuni's true realization, what he really realized, is impossible to express in words. In so far as it is expressed, it has already been conceptualized. We must say that the words are already far away from the thing itself.

However, there is a problem here. Buddhism speaks of individual characteristics and common characteristics. However, can there be a individual characteristic apart from the common characteristic? An individual characteristic is already a common characteristic. As long as we conceive of the common characteristic as something existing in opposition to the individual characteristic—that is to say, as long as we consider the common characteristic as a concept—it can be said that the individual characteristic is also a concept. But when we cast away all of our knowledge, saying that they are nothing but common characteristics, will there remain something called the individual characteristic? I think this is the point that we really must think about. Rather I think that the individual characteristic unifies common characteristics, and that the individual characteristic gives rise without end to common characteristics. I think that is what the individual characteristic is in the true sense. I believe it was Cohen[18] who said that the Idea (Jpn. *rinen* 理念; German Idee) is the self-consciousness of concepts.[19] I think this is very interesting. We can't get rid of concepts just because they are concepts. There must be something there at the basis of a concept. Some Idea must be the basis of a concept, and that Idea appears in the form of a concept. If we consider all concepts to be bad and throw them aside, doesn't this mean that we lose the subsistent Ideas? In any case, I have reservations concerning the distinction between individual characteristics and common characteristics. Where did such distinction come from, anyway? Who first began using such terms? If the realization of the thing itself and our words are in totally different realms, where did such words like individual characteristic and common characteristic come from? There is no end to questions like these.

Let us, on the other hand, say that enlightenment and words are not different. Of course, even though enlightenment and words are not different, they are not identical either. But let's say for now that it's possible to express enlightenment in words. If we say that we cannot truly express the realm of enlightenment, does this mean that the world of enlightenment can never be expressed using words? Or does it mean that, even though we really and truly want to express our enlightenment, it's impossible to express it in words because enlightenment contains an infinite number of words? In this way, there are two possibilities when we say that enlightenment cannot be expressed in words. Even though we want to explain it, there is just no way of expressing it. That's one possibility. Or it can also mean that our realization has not deepened to the point where we can explain it in words. We have to consider these two possibilities when we say that the world of enlightenment cannot be expressed in words.

If it is impossible to express enlightenment in words, should we blame the words or should we blame the person who is unable to express it in words? Although it's possible to say that the words are at fault, I'm not convinced that it's so. I want to stress the other view, that we cannot find the words to express it or that our enlightenment cannot deepen it enough to express itself in words. Therefore, when we say that enlightenment cannot be expressed in words, it is because it is infinite in content. No matter how many words we use to express it, it still cannot be fully expressed. Even when we express it by saying that enlightenment is inexpressible, that in itself is an expression.

Language is one form of expression. However, even before words, we use our hands and bodies to express ourselves. Physical actions are forms of expression. People say that actions speak louder than words. Hence they belittle words and put more weight on a person's actions. I think that is unwarranted. In our commonsense world, we say that a certain fellow says some interesting things or that he is quite articulate, but that his actions leave much to be desired. In other words, we say that actions genuinely express a person, but his words do not. But I don't think that's really the case. If our words can be false, our actions can be false too. Both can lie. It's of course possible for us to say that, even though a person acts correctly, he is really no good because what he says is actually worthless. But that's not what we usually say. We usually say, although he is not very articulate, what he does is right. Or we say, well, although his words are splendid, his actions can't be trusted. It seems to me that, along with sincere criticism, there is some self-serving motive behind these words. We can be false in both our words and actions. Or, although people may say that it's hard to put our thoughts into action, it's also possible to say that it's easy to express what is in our minds. For example, when we are really embarrassed, our faces turn red and we cover them with our hands. In such case, our physical expression reveals our thoughts directly. In that sense, it's easy to express what's in our minds.

It's not easy to express profound experiences in words. Let's consider the bodhisattva's vows and practices in the ten stages of his progress to buddhahood. At the first Stage of Joy (*shokangiji* 初歓喜地), the bodhisattva discovers the truth and experiences joy. In the second stage, the truth he has discovered is put into action. Reaching the third stage, the bodhisattva hears the true teaching for the first time. He then continues his practices until he reaches the eighth and ninth stages. At these stages, he is finally able to preach the Dharma. This shows how difficult it is to express oneself in words. Although some people say that actions speak louder than words, in the world of true self-awakening, I think that words are to be valued over action. Seen in this way, it must be said that words do not necessarily hide a person, but that a person really appears in his most truthful words. A Buddhist treatise speaks of both "the dharma-body of realization" (Jpn. *shōtoku hosshin* 証得法身, Skt. *prajñapti dharmakāya*) and "the dharma-body of preaching" (Jpn. *gonsetsu hosshin* 言説法身, Skt. *vyavahāra dharmakāya*).[20] The latter refers to the dharma-body as words. In other words, one's entire person appears in one's words. I am convinced that the way to really encounter someone is through his most truthful words.

V. The Teaching and the Truth

Next, let's go on to the relationship between the teaching and the truth. It's generally believed that the teaching and the truth are different. But this is open to question. First, if it's argued that the truth is different from words, let me ask, "What is truth?" Truth is beyond words. We say that it is inexpressible. We call it "truth" or "suchness" (*shinnyo* 真如). What then is the truth that is beyond all words? This is a major problem.

In thinking about the problem of the relationship between the truth and the teaching, we must first consider the relationship between the truth and enlightenment. What is the wisdom of enlightenment? And what is truth itself? Is the truth itself and the wisdom through which we awaken to the truth two different things? Or are they the same? This has long been a point of debate in Buddhism. One group of Buddhist scholastics maintained that truth is an unconditioned (*asaṃskṛta*) dharma, and hence is an eternal and changeless dharma. But the wisdom through which we awaken to this dharma is a human possession and hence is a conditioned (*saṃskṛta*) dharma. For this reason, it was argued that the wisdom of enlightenment and the truth itself must be strictly distinguished.

However, why is it necessary to maintain that the truth is unconditioned? When we say that the truth is unconditioned, we make the truth into some cold principle, into something cold and empty. Truth, of course, is infinite in content. That truth awakens to itself. Truth itself is what attains enlightenment. This is the argument of the second group of scholastics.

Indeed, it's been said since long ago that to really draw a flower, the flower must draw itself. The artist does not draw the flower, but the flower must make the artist draw the flower. In such situations, the artist disappears and the flower itself draws the flower. This, I've heard, describes the way in which the most accomplished artists paint their pictures. If that's true, then why isn't it possible for the unconditioned truth to act in the same way? To say that it's impossible is only what humans have decreed. If we enter directly into the realm where the truth reveals itself—that is to say, in situations where we have really awakened to the truth—we do not awaken to the truth but the truth becomes our self. Then the truth itself speaks and proclaims itself. It is here that the teaching is found. Hence, the truth and the teachings are not two separate things. When the truth strives to reveal itself as the truth, it becomes the teaching. When it's impossible for the truth just to remain as the truth, when it is necessary for the truth to reveal itself as the truth, then the truth becomes a person's words. Here the truth manifests itself as the teaching. Emphasizing this point, Buddhist scholars call this the teaching that "flows forth from the pure *dharmadhātu*."[21]

Long ago, students of the Veda maintained that speech is eternal. Buddhist texts say that it's impossible for speech to be eternal, but that's because the authors of these texts wish to criticize this idea from the standpoint of Buddhist philosophical texts. But what arguments should we use to oppose those people who criticize the notion that speech is eternal? The words revealed in the Veda are true, and these words, they say, are eternal. But to such people, we can say that what the Veda teaches is not true. It's easy to say that what the Veda teaches is not true. But we cannot oppose the form of the Vedic expression "speech is eternal." That's because it's the truth proclaiming itself. The Veda is the story of the god Brahma. It's the manifestation of the truth itself. Because it's argued in this way, it has an authority that we cannot deny. For this reason, it's the same as the teaching that "flows forth from the pure *dharmadhātu*." In the *Mahāyānasaṃgraha*, we find words to the effect that the truth flows forth to become self-realization, or that self-realization flows forth to become the teaching.[22] The teaching is the truth itself.

Let us consider the terms "to give name to" (*nazukeru* 名づける) and "to proclaim oneself through a name" (*nanoru* 名のる). When we give names to things, they are concepts. But can we resist when a flower proclaims itself as a flower? Because the flower incessantly insists on proclaiming itself as a flower, I can do nothing but listen to the flower proclaiming itself. In struggling to proclaim itself, the truth becomes our self-awareness, and this self-awareness finally becomes the teaching. What does it mean to discover the truth apart from the teaching? Such a thing may be possible in a world that looks down on words, but that's impossible in the realm of truth. Rather, when we understand the real meaning of words, then we can discern the whole truth in the true teaching set forth by the teacher.

So far, I have pointed out that there are two ways of looking at words. One is to see the true meaning of words, while the other is to see the conventional meaning of words. However, it is possible for the Buddha's true words to be understood in a conventional way. Moreover, there are some teachings taught by the Buddha on the level of conventional understanding. Neither, however, is the true teaching. But it does not mean that we must understand what kind of person Śākyamuni was in order to apprehend the true teaching. Rather by listening to the teaching as it is expressed, we discover both Śākyamuni and the truth in the teaching. Such teaching is the true teaching. From among the various Buddhist teachings, Shinran selected the *Sutra of Immeasurable Life* as the true teaching. That is the object of Shin Buddhist Studies.

In the "Chapter on Teaching" in the *Kyōgyōshinshō*, Shinran says that "the true teaching is the *Sutra of Immeasurable Life*."[23] Furthermore, he summarizes the contents of the sutra with the words, "to teach the Tathāgata's original vow is the true intention of this sutra; the name (*myōgō* 名号) of the Buddha is its essence."[24] The name of the Buddha here refers to Namu Amida Butsu, which are the words in which the Buddha proclaims himself. The name refers to the Buddha proclaiming "I am the Buddha!" and "Here I am!" upon hearing the import of enlightenment. The proclamation "I am!" by the Buddha himself lies at the source of his teachings.[25] The name is enlightenment proclaiming itself. As long as there is no proclamation, there can be no truth. As long as there is no proclamation, it is impossible for the Buddha to be described as "Immeasurable Light" or "Immeasurable Life." At the same time that the Buddha proclaims "I am" and proclaims himself as Amida, he wishes to make this fact fully known to all the beings in the universes of the ten directions. In his wish to make his presence fully known to all beings lies his vow to actualize himself. From the fundamental self-awareness that "I am" arises the vow to actualize himself. This vow to actualize himself is none other than the forty-eight vows. The original vows are not our private endeavors. When the truth awakens to itself—that is to say, when suchness (*tathā*) came forth (*āgata*)—the truth actualized itself as the forty-eight vows. For this reason, the forty-eight vows are the essence of the name. From the proclamation that "I am," there arises the forty-eight vows to actualize himself. And the vow to actualize himself makes possible the proclamation "I am."

When we listen to the name closely, we hear the Buddha proclaiming, "I am." From his profound wish to actualize himself, the Buddha set forth the forty-eight vows, and, as Dharmākara Bodhisattva, worked to realize the name that proclaims "I am." Hearing these original vows, Śākyamuni preached the *Sutra of Immeasurable Life*.

Even Śākyamuni was unable to preach the true world from which the proclamation came forth, and he preached just as he heard. The teaching that "flows forth from the pure *dharmadhātu*" refers to Śākyamuni's teaching that he expressed just as he heard. From this perspective, it is meaningless to assert, "It is impossible to understand the teaching unless we understand Śākyamuni the person," or "It is impossible to understand the teaching unless we understand the truth to which the teachings refer." The teaching itself has an independent meaning. The teaching itself that possesses an independent meaning is the real object of Shin Buddhist Studies.

VI. The Method Determined Naturally from the Object of Study

Once we understand what it is that we must study, the method for studying it will be determined as a matter of course. First of all, the dogmatic authoritarianism that has long characterized Shin Buddhist Studies is not the true method of study. I am not opposed to recognizing the authority of the teachings. However, I'm not sure whether it was the teaching, or the teacher, that was considered authoritative until now. Instead of recognizing the teaching itself as authoritative, the teacher was considered the source of authority. Because it was said by someone who never lies, it must be truthful, they said. However, we don't know if that's right unless we study the teachings closely. Although people may say that Śākyamuni's teaching is correct because he never lies, how can we know that unless we rely on the teachings? We shall never know. People who think like this only recognize the authority of the teacher, and fail to recognize the authority of the teaching itself. We must not focus on the teacher but must clarify the significance of the teaching. If we just say that a teaching must be true because it was preached by an outstanding person and fail to study its significance, we cannot grasp the fundamental truth. It's only dabbling with words, and for his reason, it's not the true method of Shin Buddhist Studies.

At the same time, it is incorrect to understand the teaching simply as a finger pointing to something else. For example, some people have preached that Amida is some substantial reality or that the Pure Land refers to our own minds. In other words, they have asserted that Amida is nothing but the manifestations of our minds (*yuishin no mida* 唯心の弥陀) or that the Pure Land resides in our own mind (*koshin no jōdo* 己心の浄土).[26] These are just two examples, but people who hold these views do not grant any meaning to the words of the teachings themselves. They turn their backs on the teaching, claiming that it is a symbol for something else. In my opinion, this is not the proper method of study either.

The genuine method for apprehending the teaching of the Awakened One is to approach it as a voice calling to us.[27] What, then, should be our attitude in approaching that object? This is the second important question concerning the method. Neither dogmatic authoritarianism nor the way of thinking that asserts that the truth must be sought outside the teaching are correct methods. On the contrary, we must grant true authority to the teaching. We must treat the teaching with utmost respect and recognize that the teaching itself is the truth proclaiming itself. Because the teaching is itself the teaching of the Awakened One, we must begin our analysis of the method of Shin Buddhist Studies by reflecting on how the teaching echoes in our ears and how our spirits are impressed by the teaching.

VII. The Method: The Interpretations of the Great Patriarchs

Following the structure of modern academic studies that distinguishes between the object of study and the method for studying it, I have so far generally discussed the former—the object. However, is it really necessary to discuss both the object of study and the method in order to study something academically? It is of course important to reflect on what we mean by "study" in a fundamental way. To repeat what I have said before, we cannot live without asking about the meaning of our existence. The fact that we have this question reveals something about our existence. This question, moreover, necessarily contains three further questions. Hence, I thought it would be possible to set up the object and method of Shin Buddhist Studies. That's why I took them up for consideration. For this reason, I borrowed Shinran's own words in order to discuss the object and method of Shin Buddhist Studies, and have stated that the object of Shin Buddhist Studies is the "true words of the Great Sage," while the method for studying it is to be found in the interpretations of the Great Patriarchs. But it may be clearer to employ Shinran's own words from the *Kyōgyōshinshō* and state that the object of Shin Buddhist Studies is the *Sutra of Immeasurable Life*. And since the forty-eight vows constitute the core of the *Sutra of Immeasurable Life*, it must be said that the Tathāgata's forty-eight original vows must be the object of study in the Shin school. The *Tannishō* says,

(All the various sacred writings that clarify the significance of the truth of other-power state that) anyone who believes in the original vow and says the nenbutsu will attain Buddhahood. Other than this, what learning (*gakumon*) is necessary for birth? Truly, the person confused about this should by all means engage in learning (*gakumon*) and understand the significance of the original vow.[28]

The significance of Shin Buddhist Studies is clearly described here. In any case, it may be more precise to say that the Buddha's original vows taught in the *Sutra of Immeasurable Life* is the object of Shin Buddhist Studies.

Why did Shinran consider the *Sutra of Immeasurable Life* to be the fundamental sutra of the Shin school? It is because it is the true words of the Great Sage. Since this sutra corresponds to the Idea of the true words of the Great Sage, Shinran selected the *Sutra of Immeasurable Life* as the true teaching. But I think there is a point that must be further clarified here. That is to say, can it be that there is absolutely no other sutra which can be called the true words of the Great Sage? In fact, Shinran came to the conclusion that the *Sutra of Immeasurable Life* is the true words of the Great Sage as a result of his studies. He didn't know it was so from the beginning. Shinran, so to speak, first discerned the true words of the Great Sage and only later discovered that the *Sutra of Immeasurable Life* was none other than the true words of the Great Sage. If that's the case, Shinran didn't make the *Sutra of Immeasurable Life* the object of his study from the beginning. He began by studying Buddhism as a whole and as he deepened his study, he discerned the *Sutra of Immeasurable Life* to be the true Buddhist teaching. Hence, it's jumping to conclusions to claim from the outset that this sutra is the object of Shin Buddhist Studies. By studying all of the teachings that the Buddha taught during his lifetime using one particular method and with a certain attitude, we come to the conclusion that the *Sutra of Immeasurable Life* is what we must truly study. In this way, we can say that the object of study was determined on the basis of the method. Thus, the method and object of study are mutually related. Although I have distinguished the object from the method for the sake of convenience, in order to determine that something must be studied, we must devote ourselves wholeheartedly to one method.

What is the method for studying the *Sutra of Immeasurable Life*, or, to use a phrase I employed earlier, the method for studying Buddhism as a whole? There are unquestionably many such methods. A scholar of literature may come up with a book with a title like *The Spirit*

Coursing through the Sutra of Immeasurable Life upon reading this sutra. A classicist may read it to understand the various philosophies that have influenced this sutra. In these ways, although the object of study may be the same *Sutra of Immeasurable Life*, the significance we discover in the sutra differs depending on the method we use to study it.

Let us look at it from another angle. Buddhism as a whole is the object of a Buddhist's study. All the Indian, Chinese, and Japanese monks famous as scholars and commentators had to confront the question of how to study Buddhist texts. Hence, there is no problem in saying that monks who became founders of Buddhist schools were all people who studied Buddhism using his own particular method. Seen in this way, there is no question that there are many ways to study Buddhism. A moment ago, I gave just two ways of studying the *Sutra of Immeasurable Life*, and there are of course many more ways of studying it. But as for myself, I study it from the standpoint of the *Kyōgyōshinshō*. Shinran recognized that the seven patriarchs of India, China, and Japan all had their own special method for studying the Buddhist teachings, by means of which they all unerringly expressed the true words of the Great Sage. Shinran composed the *Kyōgyōshinshō* by paying utmost respect to them.

Since long ago, many theories have been set forth as to why Shinran chose these seven eminent monks from India, China, and Japan and praised them as the seven Pure Land patriarchs. Let me review the main theories here. One theory holds that there is no special reason for it. It was only because these seven monks appeared one after another to transmit the teachings. Tanluan's *Jingtulunzhu* 浄土論註 (Commentary on the Pure Land Treatise) begins, "Respectfully reflecting on Nāgārjuna Bodhisattva's *Daśabhūmikavibhāṣā* (Treatise on the Ten Stages), it says, 'There are two path by which a bodhisattva may seek non-retrogression.' "[29] Although Tanluan's work is a commentary on Vasubandhu's *Pure Land Treatise*, Tanluan accords Nāgārjuna an important place in it. Hence the first three patriarchs became Nāgārjuna, Vasubandhu, and Tanluan. Daochuo converted to Pure Land Buddhism after reading the inscription on a stone monument praising Tanluan found at the Xuanzhong Temple 玄中寺.[30] Shandao is Daochuo's disciple. Furthermore, in Japan, Hōnen became a follower of Shandao after reading Genshin's works. It was in order to show that the teaching was passed down in this way that Shinran especially selected these seven monks as the patriarchs. That is one opinion.

However, there is different theory. This theory holds that Shinran selected these seven monks in particular because they all had the same faith. Moreover, they all left behind texts explaining their faith, and each of these texts have their own distinctive character. It's for these two reasons that the seven monks were chosen as Pure Land patriarchs.

In these ways, since long ago many teachers have set forth their theories concerning this matter. They are, of course, all quite meaningful. But I believe that Shinran chose the seven patriarchs for one reason only. In Shinran's view, all of the seven patriarchs share one common method for studying Buddhism. And although there were many other great scholar-monks in the past, such as Zhiyi 智顗 (538–597), the founder of the Tiantai (Jpn. Tendai) school, or Fazang 法蔵 (643–712), the founder of the Huayan (Jpn. Kegon) school, in Shinran's view, this distinctive method for studying Buddhism was limited to these seven monks. Of course, only Shinran, with his keen religious insight, could have perceived this. It's not very clear to us. Only when we listen to Shinran's teaching can we realize that the seven patriarchs share one common method. From our standpoint, it's rather hard to see. It's only when we have it explained in this way that we become convinced that the seven patriarchs all have this consistent method. We can't understand it easily by reading a few pages of their writings. Shinran thought that all the seven patriarchs had a common method for understanding the sutras. Moreover, he himself believed that he had inherited the same method from the patriarchs and used it to understand the true words of the Great Sage in the same serious manner. This is what I secretly believe. Now I want to focus on the seven patriarchs, and consider the method they used to study Buddhism, particularly the Buddhist teaching as represented by the *Sutra of Immeasurable Life*.

VIII. The Method for Demonstrating the Circumstances

As many people have noted since long ago, the content of the first fascicle of the *Sutra of Immeasurable Life* clearly differs from that of the second fascicle. The first fascicle describes the Tathāgata, his Pure Land and how it came into existence, whereas the second explains how sentient beings can achieve birth in that land.[31] In other words, the first fascicle describes how, eons ago in the past, Dharmākara Bodhisattva set forth his forty-eight vows. These vows can roughly be divided into three groups. The first group of vows concerns the *dharmakāya*. These vows express both Dharmākara's desire to be a great buddha whose light and life are infinite and whose name is heard throughout the ten directions of the universe, and his resolve not to become a buddha until these conditions are fulfilled. The second group concerns the sentient beings that are born in the Pure Land. These vows express Dharmākara's resolve to save and teach all beings without exception. The third concerns the Pure Land itself, and expresses, in addition to Dharmākara's desire to save sentient beings and become a buddha himself, his desire to create a pure, beautiful world, that is to say, a true world. These three constitute the forty-eight vows.[32] Besides these, there is no other vow. In order to fulfill these forty-eight vows, Dharmākara practiced for innumerable aeons, and, as a result, became a buddha called Amida ten kalpas ago. This is what is found in the first fascicle of the sutra. Simply put, I think it's sufficient to say that it describes the Tathāgata and how he came to be. Or it can be said to describe the Buddha's vow to adorn the Pure Land. The Pure Land is created when the Buddha attains buddhahood and fulfills his vow to save all sentient beings. In other words, an authentic world is created when Dharmākara attains buddhahood by saving all beings. Hence, it may be said that the path to enlightenment described in the first fascicle of the *Sutra of Immeasurable Life* is the path to adorn the Pure Land. In other words, it reveals the bodhisattva path. A great bodhisattva is someone who arouses an indomitable spirit to save, not only himself, but all beings, and practices ceaselessly on the basis of this indomitable spirit. This practice naturally leads to the adornment of a pure land.

The second fascicle describes how sentient beings can achieve birth in that land. It describes how, now that Dharmākara Bodhisattva has created the Pure Land and has become Amida Buddha, we can be sure of attaining birth in that land by hearing Amida Buddha's name, by wishing to go to that land, by single-mindedly vowing to be born in that land, and by undertaking various practices. Therefore, if the first fascicle can be said to describe the path for adorning the Pure Land, the second fascicle describes the path for achieving birth in that land.

This briefly is the content of the *Sutra of Immeasurable Life*. If we survey the Buddhist teachings as a whole from the standpoint of the *Sutra of Immeasurable Life*, we can see that all of Buddhism is contained within this sutra. Zhanran 湛然 (711–782), the sixth patriarch of the Tiantai school, says, "Many sutras praise Amida Buddha."[33] As this shows, many sutras preach the path for attaining birth in the Pure Land. It's not only the *Contemplation Sutra* or the *Amida Sutra* that preach this path. Since long ago, many scholars have read through the Buddhist canon and have compiled lists of passages taken from various sutras describing how we can achieve birth the Pure Land.

But what about such sutras as the *Huayan* or the *Prajñāpāramitā*, which actually do not teach us to seek birth in the Pure Land? What do they teach? The answer is that they teach the path for adorning the Pure Land. Although the name of Dharmākara Bodhisattva does not appear in these sutras, they generally teach the necessity of resolving to become great bodhisattvas and creating an authentic world (i.e., the Pure Land). Therefore, it is possible to divide Buddhist sutras into two in terms of what they teach: those teaching the adornment of the Pure Land, and those teaching birth in the Pure Land. I believe these two approaches are skillfully brought together in the *Sutra of Immeasurable Life*. For this reason, if we can truly understand the *Sutra of Immeasurable Life*, we can naturally understand the meaning of Buddhism as a whole.

How, then, are these two paths—those of the adornment of the Pure Land and birth in the Pure Land—related to each other? Perhaps they are not related to each other at all. To study this matter, I believe there are two methods. One is to inquire into the circumstances (*jiyū* 事由) under which the sutras came into being. We often employ this method. In order to study the development of Buddhist doctrine, in particular how Pure Land teachings developed within Buddhism, we cannot help but inquire into the circumstances that led to its development. So, along with the reason, I want to think about the circumstances.

The second method is to study the reason why Pure Land Buddhism developed. The reason refers to the basis on which something came to be. It refers to the true principle underlying an action or event. When we are asked "why"—for example, when I am asked why I did such and such a thing—it's possible to answer in two ways. One is to answer by explaining the specific reason for my action. For example, I may answer, "I really don't want to do it, but I have to because of such and such circumstances." Or else, if I am asked, "Why did you do such and such," I could answer by saying, "My action has such and such a meaning." Or I could say, "My work has such and such significance. Even if I do nothing else, I am commanded by a voice within me to do this." In the second case, I do not explain the circumstances under which I did something. I give the principle underlying my action. This is why I especially want to emphasize the reason. Although people may sympathize when we answer with the circumstances, it is not the royal road. Even though it may be very rare for a person to act according to the reason, it is the royal road. Everyone must take it. We do not sympathize with it, but spontaneously bow our heads down before it. Philosophically speaking, it may be possible to speak of the reason and circumstances as the idealistic explanation and realistic explanation. The particular circumstances are realistic, in that it says, "I do this for this reason" or rather, "I do this because of such a situation." This is a very important point in the study of Buddhism. There is an important meaning in the fact that I have clearly distinguished between the reason and circumstances.

Let me first begin by thinking about the circumstances.[34] When a bodhisattva practices the great path of adorning the pure land, he not only attains awakening himself, but he also works to save all people and to construct an authentic world. We cannot but follow in his footsteps. Therefore, we must listen to the great bodhisattva's original vows to adorn the pure land and arouse the aspiration for enlightenment. It is an exceedingly noble thing to arouse the aspiration for enlightenment. To arouse the aspiration for enlightenment is to listen unerringly to the Buddhist teachings and devote oneself wholly to its practice. But once we have aroused this aspiration, can we progress along the path to enlightenment as set forth in the sutras without stumbling? Many difficulties will appear in our path. Once we have aroused the aspiration for enlightenment and have vowed to save all sentient beings and attain awakening for ourselves, how can we progress along the path to enlightenment without stumbling? We won't understand anything if we keep our eyes closed imprudently, saying that it is a matter that pertains to awakening.

When we study, it is first of all important to choose where and with whom to study. That's only common sense. Some people may say that it's possible to study anywhere, pointing to the fact that there was a person who studied in a brothel long ago. Theoretically it's possible. But practically speaking, it's very difficult. In order to really study, we need to choose a special setting, such as a quiet place or an excellent school. But it's not enough just to choose the place to study. We must also choose someone who can teach us, that is to say, our masters. In all fields of learning, it's really important to choose where and with whom to study. Before undertaking the practice to attain buddhahood, it's extremely important to choose the right setting and the right teacher carefully.

For example, when that great person called Śākyamuni was alive, anyone who entered his order could progress toward buddhahood. This was true no matter how evil a person may have been. Because Śākyamuni was such a great person, anyone who encountered him could progress towards buddhahood. While Śākyamuni was alive, it was possible to arouse the aspiration for enlightenment, keep the precepts and follow the Buddha's instructions exactly. But after the Buddha passed away, the world gradually changed and wise sages disappeared. Buddhists began to lament that both the environment and the people had turned evil. Although their grief may not have been so profound in the beginning, the further away from the time of the Great Sage it became, the deeper it must have become.

Although I referred to Śākyamuni's age earlier, nowadays, it has come to the point where we can no longer simply remain nostalgic for the time when Śākyamuni's order existed. To begin with, the world we live in is entirely evil. Our world, after all, is the *sahā* world, "the world in which we must endure various forms of anguish." Although we earnestly seek to follow the path to enlightenment, the world we live in is evil. It was when people were confronted with such a world that the desire for the Pure Land arose. These are the circumstances under which the desire for birth in the Pure Land arose. As I stated before, because this does not reveal the reason, we do not bow our heads in reverence to it. But when we understand the circumstances that gave rise to this desire, we cannot help but sympathize with it. In fact, we who live in the actual world cannot help but sympathize with it. The Pure Land teachings arose out of our desire to get away from this defiled evil world and to practice the Buddhist path in some other pure world. People may ask what use there is in casting aside this world and going to another world. But people who ask this question feel no grief concerning the conditions of the actual world. They don't understand anything at all.

Actually, I don't believe that a person as dull-witted as I really understands anything. But even I see that the world is full of shameful things when I keep my eyes open. There are people who are loudly clamoring for reconstruction (*kaizō* 改造),[35] but what are they doing anyway? Politicians should devote all their efforts to running the country, but in fact they don't seem to be thinking seriously about such things. It's really sad! Everywhere we look, our society is rapidly falling into evil ways, and no one apparently has any idea as to what will happen. People say that the world will gradually evolve into a better place. However, I can't help but think that they are only deluding themselves. Claiming to create something new, they are only destroying what we have. We are laboring with the hope that some day our world will turn into a perfect, beautiful place. But this hope is always sadly crushed. Can we really create the kind of world we long for?

When we begin to think along these lines, we begin to want to turn our backs on society as a whole. We begin to want to conclude that this *sahā* world is an evil place corrupted by the five defilements, that it is obstructed by evil karma, that it is characterized by suffering, and that it is utterly impossible to really gain self-awakening here. The first of the five defilements is the defilement of kalpas. It means that we are in an evil age. The second is the defilement of views. It means that our opinions differ. Nowadays, people all have different opinions. If you ask five people about something, you are bound to get five different answers. If you ask ten people, you'll get ten different answers and we're at a loss as to which course of action we should take. The third is the defilement of evil passions, which refers to the fact that greed, anger, and hatred fill the world. The fourth is the defilement of life span, meaning that this is a delusion-filled world in which suicide and murder are common. The fifth, defilement of sentient beings, refers in general to the fact that humans are lacking in sincerity. When we survey human life in this way, it is only natural that we would want to cast aside the actual world and seek another world in the future. Disappointed with the conditions of this world, we feel that it is not worth living in and that it is utterly impossible to gain salvation in this world. It is for this reason that the desire for the Pure Land arose.

Next, the people. Humans are truly noble creatures, and for this reason the tie between a teacher and a student was very strong in the past. If you had a good teacher, you followed him to the ends of the earth. People nowadays say there is no need for such a teacher–student relationship. But is it really unnecessary? I don't think so. No one can remain satisfied by keeping their thoughts to themselves. We want to convey our thoughts to others. Or rather, we look for someone who has apprehended more clearly what we ourselves have only vaguely understood, with the hope that he would let us understand clearly what we see only dimly. I think that, without the help of such a person, we cannot progress along the path of Buddhist practice. But such a person cannot be found in the world today, as we are in the age of the five defilements, when the Buddha is no longer in the world. No matter how hard we look, there is no one like Śākyamuni in the world today. Hence we seek birth in the Pure Land, where a truly awakened person resides. By attaining birth in the Pure Land, we hope to fulfill our aspiration for enlightenment and truly achieve self-awakening. It was due to this sort of sentiment that the Pure Land teachings arose.

We can truly sympathize with such sentiments. To begin with, a sentiment is meaningful only when it elicits sympathy. For example, it's like the case where an elderly person seeks birth in the Pure Land at death. A young person, who still has high hopes for the future, does not recognize the world beyond. But an elderly person may have no more hope for the "floating world" of transmigration and only live in the hope of achieving birth in the Pure Land. People who summarily ridicule such a person are truly lacking in compassion. Similarly, we live in an age when the world has lost all meaning and we feel totally lost. Who will not fully sympathize with people who seek for the Pure Land far away, hoping to arouse the aspiration for enlightenment and practice the Buddhist path there?

In this way, at least the circumstances behind the rise of the Pure Land teachings have become clear. I do not presume to deny the need for arousing the aspiration for enlightenment and practicing the bodhisattva path to achieve buddhahood. However, nowadays it's practically impossible follow the bodhisattva path for adorning a pure land. For this reason, people have sought to undertake practices for gaining birth in the Pure Land.

However, as this is one particular interpretation of the rise of the Pure Land teachings, we have to demonstrate that it is a valid interpretation. The desire to seek the Pure Land is an understandable cry that wells up from the depths of our hearts. However, how do we know that a peaceful and undefiled Pure Land exists? And how do we know that a wise and compassionate Buddha exists? We have to demonstrate their existence and show the grounds for making this assertion.

When we look to Chinese Buddhist texts in order to do this in a way that is faithful to the Buddhist tradition, we find that these texts discuss these points in great detail. Although I had assumed that such questions as whether or not buddhas and pure lands exist would not prove problematical, I found that it was not necessarily so. These Chinese texts try to prove the existence of buddhas and pure lands in various ways. Reading the *Abhidharmakośa*,[36] for example, we see that Indian scholars argued over whether or not Śākyamuni is the sole buddha in the universe. On the one hand, some people say that Śākyamuni is the only buddha in the universe. Of course, Maitreya Buddha may appear in the future, but there is only one buddha at any time. This is because, since the buddha's powers are infinite and absolute, he can, if he desires, even save people living in the world of another buddha, infringing on the latter's powers. For this reason, there is only one buddha in the universe. This is how the argument goes. Against this assertion, other scholars argue as follows. Of course, within a certain area of the universe, Śākyamuni is the only buddha. However, because the universe is vast, there must be an infinite number of buddhas even now. Even now there are innumerable people who have vowed to become buddhas and are practicing to reach this goal. For this reason, it's impossible to deny that someone may be attaining buddhahood at this very instant somewhere in this vast universe. Such arguments also are frequently found in Buddhist texts written much later in China to defend the Pure Land teachings. Originally, to say that something "cannot be said not to exist" is quite different in meaning than saying that it "exists." Although it's possible to say that pure lands "cannot be said not to exist," it doesn't necessarily mean that pure lands actually "exist." However, many proofs for the existence of pure lands offered in the past have taken these two to be the same thing. The same is true of the arguments for the existence of buddhas.

To begin with, what kind of buddha is required by the Pure Land teachings? Let me begin by taking Śākyamuni as an example. Nowadays, when we try to understand something, we all try to understand it from our own particular perspectives. Hence, even when we try to understand someone like Śākyamuni, we try to understand him using our own selves as yardsticks. Śākyamuni was human just like us; just like us, he must have been tormented by various passions (*kleśa*), we say. But we must think more deeply than that. If we treat this problem in a perfunctory way, we shall make many mistakes.

For example, physically I am very sickly, so I have a weak constitution. But I can't assume that, just because they are human like me, people who are physically fit like sumo wrestlers also have a weak constitution. By training ourselves physically and practicing austerities, we can change ourselves physically. Likewise, as Śākyamuni himself clearly says, through spiritual practices, he came to the realization that "I am a buddha." He declared that things destined to pass away will inevitably pass away and that "I have been liberated from delusion." We want to take these words literally and believe that Śākyamuni was a great person. If we can believe in Śākyamuni in this way, for the same reason, we can believe that, not only Śākyamuni, but other beings such as Mahāvairocana or, in the case of Pure Land Buddhism, Amida, became buddhas by practicing austerities. There are, or there seems to be, many such buddhas in this universe. Or rather, there should be many such buddhas, we think. However, although there seem to be a number of buddhas in the universe, we can't be satisfied just by saying that there seem to be, or that there should be, a number of buddhas in the universe. I mentioned this point already, so I won't discuss it any further.

What I would like to consider here is the extent of the merits or abilities the Buddha attained through his practices. Through our discussion so far, we have been able to conceive of Śākyamuni as a person far greater than ourselves. But no matter how hard we try, we cannot conceive of Śākyamuni as someone who is, physically speaking, an illusory manifestation, as someone with unlimited supernatural powers, or as someone who can do anything he wants. No matter how much we may esteem Śākyamuni, we can't accept that he is an all-powerful god like the God of the non-Buddhists. That is to say, the Buddha is not a unique omnipotent God, possessing absolute power and having the ability to do anything he wants with the universe. The Buddha is someone who has attained awakening, and we must not attribute to him the powers of an all-powerful creator God. It is necessary to make this clear if we wish to elucidate the Buddha's character as an awakened person. Buddhism holds that neither gods nor souls exist. Śākyamuni started from the position that there is neither a god nor a soul. Hence it became possible to be free from all the problems that arise from accepting the existence of gods and souls. We can free ourselves from the difficult problem of whether or not God exists when we recognize that neither gods nor souls exist.

How, then, is the Buddha understood in Buddhism? It's easy to understand that he became an awakened person after a long period of practice. We can understand that he practiced and became a great person. But why were powers similar to those of an all-powerful god attributed to this awakened person? This was the result of an emotional leap. Although Buddhism says there are neither gods nor souls, it was thought that powers similar to those attributed to an all-powerful god were required if the awakened person were to save us. This is a point that must be carefully considered when treating the particular circumstances behind the birth of the Pure Land teachings.

Let's go back to my earlier point: that even if we say something "cannot be said not to exist," it doesn't mean that it "exists." Something cannot be said to exist—for example, we can't say that there is no one living on Mars. We can't say that there is no life on Mercury and Jupiter. But that's a little different from saying that there *is* life on those planets. How, then, are we to understand the words that the Pure Land exists? Many explanations have been offered but they all basically make the same argument. In the final analysis, the Pure Land texts all just say that the Buddha's words cannot be false. Because the Buddha said that the Pure Land exists in the west, it must be true. But they never start from the argument that the Buddha never lies. They begin from the argument that the Pure Land cannot be said not to exist. It is only when the defect of this argument becomes clear that they try to prove the existence of the Pure Land by asserting that the Buddha's words can never be false. For example, in the *Jingtuwen*

浄土文 (*Passages on the Pure Land*),[37] Wang Rixiu 王日休 argues as follows. Because Śākyamuni preached the principle of cause and effect—in other words, because he preached something that is unmistakably true like the principle that good actions bring about good results—Śākyamuni's teaching that the Pure Land exists in the west must also be true. This is a very interesting proof, but I feel that it is still not free from skepticism. Wang says that the principle of cause and effect is unmistakably true, but what's the significance of the principle of cause and effect for me? That, to begin with, is the problem. Moreover, just because the principle of cause and effect is unmistakably true, it doesn't necessarily mean that the Pure Land exists. Problems like these arise one after another.

I must further mention that there is an even more difficult problem in demonstrating the circumstances in such way. Let us suppose that we can determine that the Pure Land and Amida Buddha exist. How, then, can we go to the Pure Land? How can we gain birth in the Pure Land? This is the problem.

According to the general rule of Buddhism, we are born as the result of two things: passions and action (karma). When the water of passions is sprinkled on the soil of good and evil actions, karma gradually grows and we are reborn into our next lives. We are never reborn into the six realms of transmigration—the realms of hell, hungry ghosts, animals, *asura*s, humans, and heavenly beings—solely through our actions. Nor are we reborn solely through our passions. Only when the water of our passions is sprinkled on our actions are we reborn into the realms of transmigration. Similarly, to be born in the Pure Land the appropriate action is needed. What are the actions for birth in the Pure Land? Master Shandao has picked them out from the *Contemplation Sutra*.[38] Likewise Jiacai 迦才 lists many such actions in his *Jingtulun* 浄土論 (Pure Land Treatise).[39] In these works, the recitation of the nenbutsu, the reading of the sutras, paying reverence to the Buddha and other acts are described as leading to birth in the Pure Land. The practice of the nenbutsu—in other words, the recitation of Amida's name—is the action for birth. However, it is not enough just to recite the name. It is also necessary to aspire for birth in the Pure Land. You must aspire to go to the Pure Land. If you recite the nenbutsu with the wholehearted desire to be born in the Pure Land, you will surely be born there.

In order for us to have been born in the human world, we must have had the appropriate karmic conditions. According to the sutras, the observance of the five precepts[40] and the practice of the ten good actions[41] lead to birth in the human realm. If we have not fulfilled these conditions completely, then we end up near-sighted or hard of hearing like me. So in order to be born in the Pure Land, we must recite the nenbutsu with the sincere desire to be born there. This sincere desire is none other than the aspiration for enlightenment. With the desire for enlightenment as our fundamental spirit, we must desire to be born in the Pure Land and recite the nenbutsu. The *Contemplation Sutra* distinguishes nine grades of birth in the Pure Land and describes the practices corresponding to each grade.[42] They include many different kinds of practice, including caring for one's parents, attending to one's teachers and elders, and so forth. But although it's possible to be born in the Pure Land through such actions, they're not enough to gain serene conviction (*anjin* 安心) concerning our birth. That's where Amida's original vows come in. Not only do we desire to be born in the Pure Land, but Amida himself also vows to take us to his land. His vow becomes the decisive condition (Jpn. *zōjōen* 増上縁, Skt. *adhipatipratyaya*), or the most powerful condition, for our birth. On our side, we undertake practices for birth in the Pure Land, while the Buddha, on his side, helps us with the power of his vows. This is how our birth in the Pure Land is realized.

However, there is a major problem here too. This is the hotly debated problem of the so-called "birth in the land of recompense" (*hōdo ōjōron* 報土往生論).[43] This concerns the type of Pure Land into which we can be born. It's said that, once we are born there, we can attain enlightenment naturally. But we must admit that the world into which we can gain birth through our practices is only slightly better than the triple realms of transmigration.[44] In no way can such a realm be called the realm of enlightenment. It is the realm created through Amida's vow-power. But even so, doesn't it still resemble the world of delusion? If Amida's realm is not just the highest point in the realm of delusion, but is truly the realm of enlightenment, how is it possible for us to get there? This question is also solved with reference to Amida's vow-power. The fact that we can be born in the Pure Land through the power of Amida's vow is due to the teaching of the good person. In this way, whenever we come to an impasse, we always bring up the teaching of the good person. However, as I have already pointed out before, someone is called a good person because he sets forth the good teaching. From the discussion here, I believe it has become pretty clear how Buddhists have worked hard for a long time at demonstrating the circumstances that gave rise to the Pure Land teachings and also how useless this attempt has been.

IX. On the Method for Reflecting Inwardly on the Reason for the Pure Land

Many Pure Land exegetes have appeared in China. In various ways, they have sought to provide proofs for the path for achieving birth in the Pure Land. When they discuss the circumstances, they are quite persuasive, but when it comes to proving the fundamental reason for the Pure Land path, they all fall into inconsistencies. For this reason, we have to change our approach if we are to provide convincing proof of the reason for the Pure Land path.

Here, I am reminded of Kant's so-called "Copernican revolution." An upperclassman once tried to convince me of the truth of the geocentric view of the universe. I don't really understand the heliocentric view either, but I've heard that it's not impossible to maintain that the sun and moon revolve around the earth. After hearing some complicated arguments for around two hours, I came to think that maybe it is possible that the earth is at rest and the heavenly bodies are in motion around the earth. When I think about this, I realize that the geocentric view of the universe before the Copernican revolution must have been very complicated. The more complicated it becomes, the harder it gets to understand, and finally they had to change their perspective.

I really don't understand Einstein's new theory of relativity, which is in vogue today, but I find it quite interesting. He first thought that it was impossible to explain the phenomena of light unless he postulated the existence of ether. But in postulating its existence, many new problems arose. It was possible to explain these problems away, but he found that the answers were not very convincing. The more he tried to explain away these problems, the less sense the entire theory began to make. So he finally decided to do away with the ether hypothesis and start anew. A scholar would laugh and say that Einstein spent a lot of time thinking in vain. But seen from a broader perspective, the fact that he spent much time thinking about something that proved ultimately useless is actually meaningful. Scholarship may be like this. Even though a line of thought may come to nothing, it's not wasted. From a broader perspective, it's not wasted, because it helps you discover the need to change your perspective. One person who discovered the need for such a change in perspective was Shinran. But Shinran set forth his new method by relying on the seven patriarchs. He stopped explaining the circumstances, and began to reflect inwardly on the reason for the Pure Land. That was his method. Here I must explain what "introspection" (*naikan* 内観) on the fundamental reason means.

As I stated before, "reason" means "necessity." Therefore, in order to discover it, we have to reflect inwardly on our actions. For example, why do we place our palms together and pay reverence to the Buddha? When we are asked this question, we may give the circumstances that led to this act and answer as follows. As long as we are in this world, we are unable to progress along the path to enlightenment. Therefore, we desire to gain birth in the Buddha's realm in the future. That's why we pay reverence to the Buddha. That's how we answer. However, in order to give the reason for our action, we have to explain what meaning is contained in our act of putting our hands together, that is to say, why we feel the necessity to pay reverence to the Buddha. When we answer by giving the circumstances, we clarify things from the perspective of the external situation determined by fate. In contrast, the reason recognize the true nature of a thing by means of its internal logic. When we place our palms together in nenbutsu, we truly know that this is the "command of the original vow calling to and summoning us."[45] This is because we have discovered the reason for taking this action. We discover the ground (*iware* いわれ) for our need to place our palms together and our need to seek birth in the Pure Land in the realm of our fundamental subjectivity. The ground can only be discovered in the realm of subjectivity.

Let me digress a bit here and explain the meaning of necessity in terms of the theory of cause and effect. Generally speaking, cause and effect are separated in time. Because I was not careful of my health yesterday, I became ill today. This is cause and effect. But is there a necessary relationship between cause and effect that is separated in time? In the *Madhyamakakārikā*, Nāgārjuna argues that, for A to be the cause of B, A must simultaneously both exist and not exist within B. Because this is a contradiction, causation itself becomes problematic.[46] In our common sense, we strictly distinguish between cause and effect and maintain that the cause brings about the effect. The relationship between the cause and effect is valid only within the world of common sense. To explain in this way is only giving the circumstances. The necessary connection between cause and effect cannot be understood from the standpoint of realism.

However, I think it can be understood from the standpoint of self-awakening. From the standpoint of self-awakening, cause and effect are simultaneous. That is to say, when we perceive the fundamental source of some actually existent thing, we perceive that it has a cause. When we reach that point, we find both cause and effect there, as well as the necessary connection between them. In the world of Ideas, things that exist are existent, and things that don't exist are nonexistent. When they are laid out side by side in a commonsense way, existence is unobtainable, nonexistence is unobtainable, and we are not sure whether causation exists or not. But in the world of self-awakening, it is clear whether or not they exist. When, from the standpoint of our self-awakening, we intuit that the self does not exist, the fact that it does not exist is the truth. But if a person should cry out that the self exists, we can't reject that either. Similarly, the true necessity for causation can only be realized from the standpoint of self-awakening. Therefore the commonsense view of cause and effect is nothing but the shadow of the true cause and effect. We are only gazing at the shadow of cause and effect, and hence there is no necessary connection between cause and effect. The truth of things only exists as the contents of fundamental self-awakening.

Let me go back to what I was saying earlier. Why do we have to recite the nenbutsu? Why do we have to take refuge in the Buddha? Why do we have to go to the Pure Land? Let's not seek a firm ground for our aspiration in our psychological situation. Let us seek its universal, necessary basis within ourselves. When we truly seek for the reason of our birth in the Pure Land, we make a discovery. We discover the world of the adornment of the Pure Land.

In one sense, we may say the nenbutsu because it is unavoidable. But what does it mean to say the nenbutsu? When we are urged to "just say the nenbutsu," are we to recite it out loud or are we to focus our minds on Amida Buddha? When we recite "Namu Amida Butsu" out loud, are we really focusing our minds on the Buddha? We must reflect inwardly on such questions, gradually deepening our reflection. Some people say that there is no need to recite the nenbutsu out loud, and that it's enough to just focus our minds on Amida Buddha. But are we really focusing our minds on the Buddha at such times? We must really reflect deeply on such questions. By reflecting deeply on such questions, we can enter into the nenbutsu perfectly. But how does such pure nenbutsu arise? Confronted with this question, we cannot help but experience immediately the bodhisattva spirit adorning the Pure Land at the source of the path leading to birth in the Pure Land. The path for adorning the Pure Land and the path for birth in the Pure Land are actually the same. In both paths, the Buddha's vow-power makes itself manifest to us. In other words, we do not say the nenbutsu, but the Buddha says it. When we believe in the Buddha and his original vows, it is not we who believe in them. Rather the Buddha's wisdom or the Buddha's original vow itself manifests itself as our faith. We believe when the Buddha's wisdom manifests itself in us. To make us have faith—that is the Buddha's work. In fact, we can truly take refuge in the Buddha only through the working of the Buddha.

It is at this point that genuine necessity first appears. As we gradually reflect inwardly on the realities of daily life, we immediately experience the Buddha's original vows. Put differently, to immediately experience the Buddha's original vows means that the original vows manifest themselves in us. There is a necessary connection between the two. This is the theme that underlies Shinran's *Kyōgyōshinshō*. People before Shinran urged us to recite Namu Amida Butsu. In contrast, Shinran says that we must listen to Namu Amida Butsu. As long as we are saying the nenbutsu consciously, we are not really saying it. Shinran says, "As for myself, I just say the nenbutsu."[47] When Shinran says, "I just say the nenbutsu," this does not mean that an individual called Shinran is consciously saying the nenbutsu. "Just saying" is itself Shinran. The nenbutsu becomes the person saying the nenbutsu. Hence, as long as we are conscious that we are saying the nenbutsu, it is not the true nenbutsu. What does "just saying the nenbutsu" mean? Although it may seem that we are saying the nenbutsu, the voice saying the nenbutsu becomes, without our being aware of it, the self-proclamation of Amida Buddha. We are hearing the voice of the buddhas witnessing to Amida. This is necessarily so. I think it cannot be otherwise.

I limited myself to the act of saying the nenbutsu above, but if I were to inquire into it further, faith is also transferred from other-power (*tariki ekō* 他力廻向). This is something that is taught only in Shinran's Shin Buddhism. What, then, is this teaching of transference from other-power? When we speak of the Buddha who saves and myself who is saved, it's common sense to think both that the one who has faith in the Buddha is myself and the person who is saved is myself. But Shin Buddhism says that this is not so. Faith and salvation are entirely other-power. People say that the teaching of Shin Buddhism is outrageous. If we accept other-power, then it would mean that we don't have to do anything. We can be saved even if we just take naps, they say. But this is totally wrong. This is not what other-power means. The original vow that is other-power can be known only when we genuinely reflect inwardly on the reason. The reason can never be understood from the level of common sense. Transference of merit by other-power and other-power as commonly understood are totally different. Let's say that the Buddha and ordinary beings are placed side by side as objects of the same consciousness, and that the Buddha will save the ordinary being even if the latter sits still, doing nothing. Not only is this meaningless, but it ultimately means that religion makes no difference one way or the other.

People who criticize Spinoza's pantheism argue that, if gods can be found throughout nature, there should be no harm or evil in the world. Similar criticism is directed toward the other-power teaching. But this is a mistake deriving from a one-dimensional misunderstanding of other-power. It is not enough just to place the Buddha and ordinary being side by side and demonstrate their relationship, that is to say, the circumstances. We can understand the original vows only by going back to our selves, our true selves. Only then can we immediately experience the Tathāgata's original vows. Only because there is such fundamental reason, can our religious actions become pure. Thus the other-power faith is rare and difficult to achieve. It's rare because it's other-power. Self-power faith is much easier to achieve. That's because you can say, "This is what I believe" and stick with it no matter what other people may say. Although it may appear difficult, achieving self-power faith is easy because all you have to do is stick to your opinion. But it seems that such an uncritical faith arises from a mind afflicted with doubt.

Of course, it may be all right for there to be some doubt in faith because one may become more passionate as a result. But when will we become free of such doubt and be saved by the truth? Looking into ourselves in this way, we gradually enter the realm of inward reflection. At that point, the Buddha's vow-power is transferred to us. The bodhisattva's great spirit of adorning the Pure Land manifests itself in our hearts. Thus, by reflecting inwardly on the reason, I believe a way is opened for understanding those points that could not be elucidated just by demonstrating the circumstances for birth in the Pure Land.

Note: Needless to say, I focus here on the method of inwardly reflecting on the fundamental reason. I do not suppose that it suffices to cover all of Shin Buddhist Studies. I must leave for the future the question of how the spirit of the *Sutra of Immeasurable Life* should be studied.

X. The Object of Study Determined Naturally from the Method

Because I have already explained how the object of study will be determined naturally once the method of study is settled, I only add a few words here.

Even when we tried to determine the truth of the Pure Land teachings by explaining how they arose, we ultimately had to fall back on "the words of a good person." In other words, we finally come to the authoritative teaching (Jpn. *shōgyōryō* 聖教量) or proof based on the teaching (*kyōshō* 教証). But what is this "teaching"? What does "the words of a good person" mean? We are not able to provide a satisfactory answer as long as we only give the circumstances. This is because it is impossible to distinguish between the true and provisional teachings by this method.

The truth found in the teachings echoes only in the hearts of those who reflect inwardly on themselves. In other words, for those who adopt the attitude of inward reflection, the truth is revealed through the true words of the Great Sage. People who seek to prove things logically will choose as their object of study those teachings that present various theories. People who are attached to their self-centered beliefs may study sutras that are most convenient in defending their positions. However people who reflect inwardly on the reason are compelled to listen directly to the Great Sage's spontaneous words of truth.

Notes

1. Since long ago, "study" in Buddhism and Confucianism has meant "to mentally apprehend and physically practice something." But nowadays studies are divided into things like the sciences and philosophy, or into natural science and normative science. Be that as it may, the important point is that a field of study is required to be organized systematically. Thus, in thinking about whether Shin Buddhist Studies can become a valid field of study, we must consider whether it can be organized systematically. However, I believe that a kind of system can be developed on the basis of Shinran's *Kyōgyōshinshō*, and that the significance of Shin Buddhist Studies can be clarified from this perspective.

2. Of course, each person must pursue his own study by himself. But for a discipline to truly be universal and valid, it requires that like-minded people study the topic together. According to an old saying, "When three people get together (to think about a problem), they're equal to Mañjuśrī in wisdom." A solution that results from Mañjuśrī's wisdom is never a compromise worked out between conflicting positions. His wisdom is not based on individual guesses but is based on insight into genuine universal principle. In this sense, I would be honored if this prolegomena were to be understood as a suggestion for us to work together to create a field called Shin Buddhist Studies.

3. (Tr.—Immanuel Kant, *Prolegomena to Any Future Metaphysics*)

4. Is not the fact that we have these three questions—in particular the fact that one individual has these three questions—the source from which arises the thing that can be systematized as a field of study? Furthermore, science works through observation, experimentation, and thoughtful consideration of the results. These three steps, I believe, correspond to the three questions of "what," "how," and "why." Hence, if these three questions are fundamentally constitutive of our being, they may provide openings from which to think about the so-called "primacy of practical reason."

5. I have said that the question *why* leads to the object of Shin Buddhist Studies, whereas the question *how* leads to its method. However, concerning the question *why*, I have not argued that it leads to anything, but that it concerns the significance of undertaking any study. This is because I believe that the question of *why* is the most fundamental problem. In other words, it is on the basis of this fundamental *why* that both the object and the method are determined. Therefore, any discussion of the object of Shin Buddhist Studies ultimately comes back to this fundamental question of *why*. Likewise, the truth of the method also begins from this fundamental question.

6. (Tr.—Rennyo played a pivotal role in spreading Shin Buddhism during the Muromachi period. In his efforts to popularize Shinran's teachings, he frequently employed the expression "the great matter of the afterlife.")

7. (Tr.—The world of transmigration.)

8. (Tr.—SSZ 2:43. Cf. CWS 1:69.)

9. (Tr.—The seven patriarchs are Nāgārjuna [c. 150–250], Vasubandhu [c. 400–480], Tanluan [476–542], Daochuo [562–645], Shandao [613–681], Genshin [942–1017], and Hōnen [1133–1212].)

10. (Tr.—A collection of Rennyo's pastoral letters. For an English translation, see Rogers and Rogers 1991.)

11. Of course, this is something that should be established as a field of study. But it is a way of studying from the "outside," so to speak, and is not the pure Shin Buddhist Studies that we seek. But the proper method for such study is also probably to be discovered on the fundamental Idea of Shin Buddhist Studies.

12. Shinran, who stated that the content of the true teaching are the Tathāgata's original vows, would say that the object of Shin Buddhist Studies is the Tathāgata's original vows. However, I believe that the Tathāgata's original vows cannot be limited to being the object or the method of study. On the teachings and the original vows, see my "Shinshū-gaku no san mondai" 真宗学の三問題 ("Three Problems of Shin Buddhist Studies") in the journal *Kenshin* 見真 (*Seeing the Truth*), vol. 1. (October 6, 1922), pp. 18–40. (Tr.—This article is Kaneko 1922a. It was later included in Kaneko's volume of essays entitled *Shinrankyō no kenkyū* 親鸞教の研究 [*Studies in Shinran's Teachings*]. See Kaneko 1925. This book was reprinted in KDC, volume 3. The article in question is found on pp. 43–51 of this volume.)

13. See my article "Kyōbō no honshitsu" 教法の本質 ("The Essence of the Teaching") in *Kenshin*, vol. 2. (October 23, 1922, pp. 17–34). (Tr.—This

article is Kaneko 1922b. It also was included in *Shinrankyō no kenkyū* (Kaneko 1925). See also KDC 3:23–33.

14. Fascicle 5, "(Phonemes, words and phrases) belong to sentient beings. They belong to the person who speaks, not to the things that they designate." (Tr.—This translation is taken from la Vallée Poussin 1998, 1:253.)

15. (Tr.—This is found in the first chapter of the Laozi. For an alternate translation, see Chan 1963, 139.)

16. (Tr.—A term taken from the Yogācāra, or mere consciousness, philosophy. The Yogācāra school maintains that all phenomena arise from the *ālayavijñāna* ["storehouse consciousness"], which corresponds to the eighth and deepest level of human consciousness. The arising of phenomena is due to the maturation of the various *bīja* ["seeds"] that were "perfumed" [or "planted"] in the *ālayavijñāna*. The *bīja* are planted in two ways: through the effects of past actions [karma] and through hearing words, such as the teaching of an enlightened person. The term "perfuming through words" refers to this second type of perfuming.)

17. "'Reality' means the individual characteristic (*svalakṣaṇa*), it is not the object of conventional knowledge and expression. That is, conventional knowledge and expression do not reach the individual characteristic of the thing. They only function with regard to common characteristics (*sāmānyalakṣaṇa*) of dharmas." (Tr.—These lines are found in the *Chengweishilun*. See T 31, 7b. The translation is taken from Cook 1999, 42.)

18. (Tr.—Hermann Cohen [1842–1918], the founder of the Marburg school of Neo-Kantianism.)

19. (Tr.—This passage is found in Cohen's *Logik der reinen Erkenntniss*. See Cohen 1914, 15. It is possible that Kaneko consulted the Japanese translation of Cohen's work by Fujioka Zōroku 藤岡蔵六. For the Japanese translation, see Cohen 1921, 13.)

20. (Tr.—This is found in the *Vajracchedikāsūtraśāstra* (*Treatise on the Diamond Sūtra*) by Asaṅga. The Japanese text of the *Prolegomena to Shin Buddhist Studies*, on which this translation is based, has "*shōtoku hosshin*" 正得法身 and "*shōsetsu hosshin*" 正説法身, which are clearly mistakes. In the *Vajracchedikāsūtraśāstra*, the "dharma-body of realization" refers to the dharma-body gained by sentient beings through practice, whereas the "dharma-body of preaching" refers to the scriptures itself. See T 25, 757b. However, in later Buddhist tradition, the "dharma-body of preaching" comes to refer to the dharma-body as expressed through language.)

21. Asaṅga, *Mahāyānasaṃgraha*, fascicle 1, etc. (Tr.—T 31, 136a. Cf. Keenan 1992, 31.)

22. Vasubandhu's commentary on the *Mahāyānasaṃgraha*, translated by Paramārtha, fascicle 10. (Tr.—T 31, 222b.)

23. (Tr.—SSZ 2:2. Cf. CWS 1:7.)

24. (Tr.—SSZ 2:3. Cf. CWS 1:7.)

25. "Honganron: Ware nashi, ware ari, ware to naran" 本願論—我なし、我あり、我とならん ("On the Original Vow: I Am Not, I Am, I Will Be I"),

Kenshin, vol. 4 (December 6, 1922, pp. 17–31). (Tr.—This article, Kaneko 1922c, was later included in *Shinrankyō no kenkyū*. See KDC 3:43–51.)

26. (Tr.—These ideas are taken up and criticized by Kakunyo 覚如 in his *Gaijashō* 改邪鈔 [*Reforming Heretical Views*]. See SSZ 3:84.)

27. Here arises the question of how to hear and accept the teaching "just as it is." On this point, see "Oshie no mama" 教えのまま ("The Teachings Just as They Are") in my short book, *Shukyōteki risei* 宗教的理性 (*Religious Rationality*). (Tr.—This collection of essays was originally published in 1922. It was later reprinted in volume 2 of KDC. For this essay, see KDC 2:264–67.)

28. (Tr.—SSZ 2:780. Cf. CWS 1:668.)

29. (Tr.—T 40, 826a. For an alternate English translation, see Inagaki 1998, 121.)

30. (Tr.—The temple at which Tanluan resided.)

31. (Tr.—This is a free translation of this passage. Kaneko actually says, "The first fascicle explains the cause and effect of the Tathāgata's Pure Land, while the second fascicle explains the cause and effect of sentient beings' birth in the Pure Land.")

32. (Tr.—This threefold division of the forty-eight vows was first proposed by Huiyuan 慧遠 of Jingying Temple 浄影寺 [523–592] in his *Wuliangshoujing yishu* 無量寿経義疏 [*Commentary on the Sutra of Immeasurable Life*]. See T 37, 103b.).

33. (Tr.—T 46, 182c.)

34. The circumstances I have given mostly derive from the following words found at the beginning of Tanluan's *Jingtulunzhu*: "It is difficult to seek the stage of non-retrogression in the age of the five defilements when no buddha dwells in this world." I have used these words to represent the thought of many commentators. But even while giving these circumstances, Tanluan consciously does not attempt to prove the Pure Land teachings. Instead he reflected deeply within himself for the fundamental reason for the Pure Land. In his sure grasp of reality, I discover Tanluan's greatness as a patriarch of Shin Buddhism. In as much as it arises from actual emotions, the circumstances should not be rejected. But it is necessary to internalize this feeling. Hence, what should be avoided are not the circumstances themselves but the attempt to prove them. (Tr.—Tanluan's words cited above is found at T 40, 826b. For an alternate English translation, see Inagaki 1998, 121.)

35. (Tr.—*Kaizō* was originally a name of a journal that began publication in 1919. The term was subsequently used to refer to programs for restructuring Japan along socialist lines.)

36. *Abhidharmakośa*, fascicle 12. (Tr.—The passage in question is found at T 29, 64c–65a. For an English translation, see de la Vallée Poussin 1988, 2:484–86.)

37. *Jingtuwen*, fascicle 1, sections 7 and 8 of "Jingtu qixin" 浄土起信 ("Arising of Faith in the Pure Land"). (Tr.—Jodoshū zensho kankōkai 1906, 6:843–44.)

38. According to the section on the "Non-meditative Good Actions" (*sanshanyi* 散善義), the actions leading to birth in the Pure Land are reading

and reciting the sutras, contemplation, paying obeisance to the Buddha, reciting the nenbutsu, and praising and venerating the Buddha. (Tr.—This is found in the section dealing with the "Non-meditative Good Actions" constituting the fourth fascicle of Shandao's *Guanwu liangshufojing shu* 観無量寿佛経疏 [*Commentary on the Sutra on the Contemplation of the Buddha of Immeasurable Life*]. See T 37, 272b.)

39. Jiacai's *Jingtulun* gives the following: recitation of the nenbutsu, paying obeisance to the Buddha, praising the Buddha, arousing the aspiration for enlightenment, contemplation, and transferring merit. (Tr.—This can be found at T 47, 89b)

40. (Tr.—Not to kill, not to steal, not to engage in sexual misconduct, not to lie, and not to drink intoxicants.)

41. (Tr.—Not to kill, not to steal, not to engage in sexual misconduct, not to lie, not to speak harshly, not to engage in backbiting, not to engage in frivolous speech, not to covet, not to harbor malice, and not to have false views.)

42. (Tr.—*The Contemplation Sutra* distinguishes nine levels of birth into the Pure Land, from the highest level of the highest grade to the lowest level of the lowest grade. See Inagaki 1994, 339–348.)

43. (Tr.—Shandao argued that (a) Amida's Pure Land was a "land of recompense," which this Buddha obtained as the result of his practice over innumerable kalpas to attain buddhahood and (b) that ordinary unenlightened beings can gain birth there. Shandao is here criticizing the views of Shelun 摂論 scholars, who, even though they accepted that Amida's Pure Land is a land of recompense, denied that ordinary unenlightened beings can be born there. On this debate, see Mochizuki 1975, 184–88.)

44. (Tr.—The triple realms refer to the realms of desire, form, and formlessness).

45. (Tr.—SSZ 2:22. Cf. CWS 1:38.)

46. (Tr.—Nāgārjuna's analysis of causality is discussed at length in Murti 1955, 132–35.)

47. (Tr.—This passage is found in the second chapter of the *Tannishō*. See SSZ 2:774. Cf. CWS 1:662.)

Yasuda Rijin

At age 77. (Courtesy of Sōō Gakusha, dated 1978)

Chapter 12

Yasuda Rijin
Shin Philosopher of Self-Awareness

Paul B. Watt

Yasuda Rijin 安田理深 (1900–1982) inherited the legacy of the Shin leaders introduced in the preceding chapters, but he had a special relationship to his teacher Soga Ryōjin. Soga's emphasis on the Yogācāra School of Mahāyāna philosophy in interpreting the Shin tradition gave direction to Yasuda's scholarship throughout his adult life. Indeed, one of Yasuda's students suggested that he should be viewed in a lineage that extends from Soga Ryōjin to Shinran, the founder of Shin Buddhism, and on to Asaṅga and Vasubandhu, who established the Yogācāra School in the fourth century CE.[1] For Yasuda, perhaps the defining feature of Shin Buddhism is the possibility it offers to karma-bound human beings of a transformation of consciousness and the realization of a true awareness of both self and reality. A second salient feature of Yasuda's thought is the constructive engagement he sought between Shin Buddhism and Western philosophy.[2] His interest in Western philosophy in part reflects the tradition of modern Shin scholarship within which he stood, beginning with Kiyozawa Manshi, the founder of that tradition. However, Yasuda's exploration of modern European thought in particular was also stimulated by his contacts with the influential Kyoto school of philosophy led by Nishida Kitarō, Tanabe Hajime 田辺元 (1885–1962) and Nishitani Keiji 西谷啓治 (1900–1990), all scholars who drew on Western, especially modern Continental, thinkers as well as Buddhist sources.

Yasuda's Life

Yasuda was born in 1900 in the town of Umigami 海上 in Hyōgo Prefecture and was given the personal name Kameji 亀治. His father, Tsuruzō 鶴造, had married into the Yasuda family, which for generations had provided the local *shōya* 庄屋 or village headman. A brother, Takuji, was born in 1901. At age six, Yasuda was placed in a Christian kindergarten. His parents divorced when he was seven and, thereafter, he was raised by his mother. After completing primary school in 1913, he attended a private night school from 1914 to 1916 studying morals, classical Japanese and Chinese, history, math, English, and maritime affairs.[3] During these years, he developed an interest in Buddhism and he received the precepts from Hioki Mokusen 日置黙仙 (1847–1920), a Sōtō Zen master who in 1916 became head of Eiheiji, the Sōtō center established by the sect's founder Dōgen in the thirteenth century. While working at a bank in 1917 and 1918, he continued his study of English and also read books on Christianity as well as Buddhism. In 1919, he encountered Kaneko Daiei's *Bukkyō gairon* 仏教概論 (*Survey of Buddhism*), a book that left a profound impression on him both for its style and for what he judged to be the depth of its treatment of Buddhist thought.

After the death of his mother in 1920, Yasuda moved from his native prefecture to Kyoto. For a short time he worked at the water purification plant at Keage 蹴上, but his real interests lay in the study of Buddhism. His attraction to Zen Buddhism continued; he listened to sermons and lectures at the famous Kyoto Zen temples of Shōkokuji and Nanzenji. When he asked the Nanzenji Zen monk Nisshu Jōzan 日種譲山 (n.d.) about how he might pursue his study of Buddhism, he was referred to Sasaki Gesshō, a professor at Ōtani University. However, instead of contacting Sasaki, Yasuda wrote to Kaneko Daiei and he received a tentative but encouraging reply about the possibility of studying at Ōtani. Around this time, Yasuda also became aware of Soga Ryōjin's writings. As a result, in his early twenties Yasuda appears to have reached the conclusion that the Shin understanding of the Buddhist tradition was personally the most persuasive, despite his interests in Zen. In a diary entry from 1923, he cites approvingly Soga Ryōjin's criticism of the path of self-realization (*jishō* 自証) as overly "individualistic and idealistic." Soga praised, instead, "the eternal practice of the bodhisattva."[4] These references suggest that the attraction of Shin Buddhism for Yasuda was its commitment to giving expression to Mahāyāna Buddhist teachings in the context of daily life. Also in 1923, Yasuda read Vasubandhu's *Pure Land Treatise* (Jōdoron

浄土論), a central text in the Pure Land tradition, and decided to make it and Yogācāra scholarship the focus of his studies from that point on.

With the aid of Kaneko, Yasuda became an auditor at Ōtani University in 1924. In 1925, Soga joined the faculty and Yasuda attended his lectures. Yasuda remained a student at Ōtani until 1930, and during his student years he began to publish his own writings in small circulation publications.

However, the late 1920s were a time of academic turmoil at Ōtani. Sasaki Gesshō, who had become the president of Ōtani in 1924 and who had sought to foster a new era of rigor and openness in Shin scholarship, died suddenly in 1926. In 1928, the highest organ overseeing doctrine within the Ōtani branch, the Jitōryō, successfully pressured the university to dismiss Kaneko for his demythologizing interpretation of Shin Buddhism. Furthermore, in 1929 Kaneko's name was removed from the registry of Ōtani school priests. Soga, who had also been a target of criticism, then resigned from the school in 1930 in solidarity with his colleague.[5] A few students who wished to continue their studies with Kaneko and Soga formed a private academy called the Kōbō Gakuen 興法学園 or "Academy for Raising Up the Dharma," where the two scholars lectured. Yasuda served as head of the academy, and the students associated with it both studied and lived together. Although the academy was disbanded in less than three years, Yasuda published a number of philosophical essays in the group's journal, *Kōbō* 興法 (*Raising Up the Dharma*), two of which have been translated here.

By 1933, Yasuda seems to have established his intellectual identity, and for years he made his living as an independent Shin scholar. His income came chiefly from lectures he would give at temples in the Shin heartland of Niigata and Toyama Prefectures, where Shinran had spent time in exile, or to Ōtani students. The focus of his lectures was usually one or another of the Yogācāra texts or the writings of Shinran. In 1935, he established another private academy with which he was chiefly identified for the rest of his life, the Sōō Gakusha 相応学舎 or the School of Conformity [to the True Practice]. Soga chose the name for the school, drawing on a line from Vasubandhu's *Pure Land Treatise*. Over the course of Yasuda's life, the school was moved several times and often no more than a small group of individuals would attend his talks. However, it became the focal point for a small community of Shin followers who were dedicated to Yasuda and to his contemporary restatement of Shin teachings.

Yasuda married Nakai Ume 中井梅 in 1938 and they had a son later that year. In 1943, Yasuda formally entered the Shin clergy and received the name Rijin from Soga. From 1944 on, Yasuda held a number of mostly part-time or irregular appointments at Ōtani University. In 1959, he joined the translation committee headed by Suzuki Daisetsu (1870–1966) that was charged with rendering into English Shinran's *Kyōgyōshinshō*, which was eventually published in 1973 under the title *The Kyōgyōshinshō: The Collection of Passages Expounding the True Teaching, Living, Faith, and Realization of the Pure Land*.[6] In 1960, Yasuda had the opportunity to have a meeting with the German theologian Paul Tillich, which inspired Yasuda to present the lecture "A Name but Not a Name Alone" (Na wa tan ni na ni arazu 名は単に名にあらず), which is translated here.

Yasuda had the first of his bouts with tuberculosis in 1967. Constant dedication to his scholarship and to lecturing, both in and outside of Kyoto, contributed to recurrences of the disease in 1969 and 1975. On February 19, 1982, Yasuda died in Kyoto of heart failure at Kyōgokuji 京極寺, his home and the last location of his private academy. It is worth noting that, although Yasuda's life spanned the rise of Japan's militarism and imperialism in Asia, Yasuda never lent his support to those efforts.

Writings from the Kōbō Years (1930–1933)

As noted earlier, the formation of the Kōbō Gakuen in 1930 came after Kaneko Daiei had been dismissed from Ōtani University and Soga Ryōjin had resigned under pressure. These were dark years for the scholars and students at Ōtani who viewed these men as leaders of a movement to bring Shin Buddhism into the modern era. The thrust of Kaneko's and Soga's scholarship was to shift the focus of Shin belief from a Pure Land and an Amida conceived of as actually existing in some other world to an internalized understanding of the Pure Land and, as Soga argued, to a new understanding of the bodhisattva Dharmākara—who according to the *Sutra of Immeasurable Life* had become Amida through the fulfillment of his bodhisattva vows—as a representation of the deepest layer of one's own consciousness, the *ālayavijñāna*. Although both Kaneko and Soga would later return to Ōtani University and become leaders there, the repression of their views in the late 1920s caused the founding members of Kōbō Gakuen to live with a sense of urgency about their times and about the need to preserve and explore further the fresh understandings of Shin Buddhism that these scholars had articulated.

One of the consequences of the new interpretations that Kaneko and Soga advanced was to put Shin Buddhism in a closer dialogue with the larger Buddhist tradition, which had often viewed Shin as existing on the margins. No longer concerned merely with passing on sectarian tradition, Kaneko, Soga, and the young students they inspired were engaged in a debate about the fundamentals of Mahāyāna Buddhist teachings. This character of their scholarship is reflected in the first two essays by Yasuda translated here. Neither essay appears to be explicitly concerned with Shin Buddhism, although one encounters in them themes that recur in his later writings on Shin. In the first essay, "The Practical Understanding of Buddhism" ("Bukkyō no hōhōteki ha'aku" 仏教の方法的把握), Yasuda begins by distinguishing between Buddhism as an existential path to understanding the true nature of the self and reality and Buddhism as an object of academic or cultural study. The former alone interests him, because in his view only Buddhism as "practical understanding" leads human beings beyond a false reification of things to insight into their true empty character and, ultimately, to an understanding of the Dharma or Buddhist truth as something that can only be lived in the present reality. In the second essay, "The Mirror of Nothingness" ("Mu no kagami" 無の鏡), Yasuda explores the related theme of the meaning of self-realization in a world that is fundamentally empty. It is through the realization of the emptiness of things, he argues, that the ordinary, limited self is negated and self-transcendence is possible. Thus, through absolute negation the true nature of sentient beings is revealed and, from a new perspective, their world is affirmed as "the Complete One, the One Dharma Realm." Both essays represent well Yasuda's dense philosophical style.

"A Name but Not a Name Alone"

In contrast to the first two essays translated here, the third piece deals explicitly with a subject at the heart of Shin Buddhism, the correct understanding of the name of Amida Buddha. In 1960, Yasuda had the opportunity to have an extended discussion with the German theologian Paul Tillich (1886–1965). In the summer of that year Tillich visited Japan and expressed the desire to meet with Buddhist leaders. Yasuda actually met Tillich twice that summer. The first meeting took place in Kyoto and was a brief encounter, along with other scholars, at the Shingon temple, Tōji 東寺. Because there was not sufficient time for a conversation on that occasion, another meeting was arranged at a hotel in Karuizawa 軽井沢 in early July. In addition to Tillich and Yasuda, Nobukuni Atsushi 信国淳 (1904–1980), then president of Ōtani Senshū Gakuin 大谷専修学院, a school that trained Shin priests, and Richard DeMartino, a Zen scholar and a professor at Temple University in Philadelphia, joined the discussion. DeMartino served primarily as an interpreter. Yasuda's encounter with Tillich spurred him to present a lecture at the Kyoto temple Sennyūji 泉涌寺 on the occasion of the celebration of his sixtieth birthday in September of that year. The title he chose for the lecture was "A Name but Not a Name Alone," words that, as Yasuda explains at the beginning of his talk, Tillich wrote on a *tanzaku* 短冊—a narrow strip of paper intended for short poems or calligraphy—as a memento of their meeting.

A record of the Karuizawa discussion remains and sheds light not only on the lecture translated here, but also on Yasuda's thought as a whole.[7] The discussion ranged over a number of topics, but it is clear that Yasuda was concerned that Tillich understand that, contrary to popular treatments of Shin Buddhism, it is not based on a belief in an other-worldly buddha and the experience of his grace. In the exchanges that Yasuda and Tillich had on the topics of "destiny and freedom," for example, Yasuda takes up the Buddhist teaching of karma, noting in particular that "I myself create my destiny, not a deity." He goes on to characterize the related topic of "transmigration" as a "mythic" and "ancient expression." For modern people, "the significance of karma is that one has a sense of responsibility for one's existence," a sense of responsibility that is expressed within the historical and social conditions of one's life.[8] In their conversation about the nature of Amida, Yasuda explains that Amida has no form. "Amida is sentient beings themselves, human beings themselves. [Amida] is one and the same (*ichinyo* 一如) with human beings. He has no form. Rather, through human action, the Tathāgata who has no form becomes form or takes form."[9] When pressed by Tillich to expand on what it means to say that Amida is without form, Yasuda describes Amida as "the origin (*honrai* 本来) of form, not an other (*tasha* 他者),"[10] and by the basis of form, it become clear, Yasuda means suchness or emptiness, the true nature of reality. The name of Amida is what allows human beings to awaken to the true nature of reality and of themselves, not in any magical way, but by achieving a transformation of consciousness.[11] Through this transformation of consciousness, one not only gains a new and true self-awareness, but one is also able to participate in the work of Amida's original vow to save all sentient beings. "Through the name, sentient beings are awakened. The Tathāgata himself is realized in the mind of awakened sentient beings."[12]

Yasuda used the occasion of his lecture at Sennyūji to elaborate on these ideas. Readers familiar with Mahāyāna thought will be able to pick up on his line of argument most easily beginning about one quarter of the way into the lecture. Drawing on the thought of both the Mādhyamika School of emptiness associated with the second- and third-century scholar, Nāgārjuna, and Asaṅga and Vasubandhu's Yogācāra School, Yasuda portrays ordinary individuals as unaware of the true empty nature of reality and of the false and mentally constructed character of the world they inhabit. They are like silkworms, bound up in worlds of their own creation; human worlds are constructed through mental discrimination and the creation of names. On the one hand, human beings have no alternative but to construct mental worlds in this way; however, when they fail to see that such mentally constructed worlds are empty and have only a provisional character, they generate the attachments and passions that characterize the lives of the unenlightened. In a world of provisional names, the name of Amida Buddha is also a provisional name, but within the context of Yasuda's interpretation of the Shin tradition, it is more than a name. It is the name that negates the relative human world of provisional names, while at the same time affirming the world of provisional names and empowering the individual to work in it. It is the name that makes it possible for people to abide in the place of non-abiding or in the realm of mere consciousness. As he noted in his conversation with Tillich, here too he points out that Amida has no form. The call Namu Amida Butsu is directed to no being; rather it is a manifestation of a transformed consciousness, an awareness of "the relationship between that which has form and that which does not." The individual who has this awareness, Yasuda argues, "just as he or she is, is the Tathāgata."

While Yasuda situates his understanding of the name of Amida Buddha and of the call Namu Amida Butsu within the context of the major schools of Mahāyāna thought, he begins the lecture with references to several texts and figures that have special significance within Shin Buddhism. In setting up his discussion of the name, Yasuda seeks in particular to clarify the relationship that exists between the *Sutra of Immeasurable Life*, an Indian text usually dated to the first or second century CE and the central sutra of Shin Buddhism, and the *Pure Land Treatise* by Vasubandhu, as that relationship was understood by Shinran and expressed in his *Kyōgyōshinshō*. In the course of this opening discussion, Yasuda refers to yet another important text in the Shin tradition, the *Commentary on the Pure Land Treatise* (Ch. *Jingtulunzhu*, Jpn. *Jōdoron-chū* 浄土論註) by the Chinese master Tanluan.

The *Sutra of Immeasurable Life* is brought into the discussion almost immediately when Yasuda refers to the fact that "the name of the Tathāgata is the name of the original vow." In the tradition of modern Shin scholars out of which Yasuda emerged, the *Sutra of Immeasurable Life* is commonly regarded as myth, but myth with a deep religious significance. Yasuda's thought may be understood as his attempt to articulate that deep meaning.

As Yasuda points out, it is necessary to keep the *Sutra of Immeasurable Life* in mind, because it was from the perspective of the original vow that Shinran read Vasubandhu's *Pure Land Treatise*.[13] Shinran's reading of the *Pure Land Treatise* in this way led to a new understanding of Pure Land practice and of the significance of the name. Inagaki Hisao describes Vasubandhu's *Treatise* as "the first systematic presentation of the Pure Land teachings in India that centers on contemplation of Amida and his Pure Land."[14] In writing the *Treatise*, it is unclear whether Vasubandhu was interpreting one or more of the Pure Land sutras. He embraced Pure Land practice in a non-exclusive way and identified five practices—the *gonenmon* 五念門 or five gates of mindfulness—for attaining birth in the Pure Land. The five gates of mindfulness are:

1. *raihai* 礼拝, worshipping Amida,
2. *sandan* 讃歎, praising Amida,
3. *sagan* 作願, making the vow to be born in the Pure Land,
4. *kanzatsu* 観察, contemplating Amida and the Pure Land, and
5. *ekō* 回向 or transferring one's merits to other sentient beings.

Vasubandhu conceived of this course of practice within the framework of the bodhisattva path, which always aims at benefiting both self and others. Hence, the first four gates of mindfulness were understood as leading to enlightenment and entrance into the Pure Land, whereas the fifth signaled the acceptance of the bodhisattva's mission to serve others.[15] However, Shinran radically reinterpreted Pure Land practice. As a result of his own experiences and his independent reading of Pure Land sources, especially the *Sutra of Immeasurable Life*, Shinran saw the entirety of the Pure Land way embedded in the name. In his view, the name, or the nenbutsu, encompassed both the practice that leads to the Pure Land—which for Shinran is, in the first place, a transformed state of mind—*and* transference or the life of service to others. It is because of the transformative power of the name, correctly understood, that Yasuda speaks early on in his lecture of the capacity of the name to address in a fundamental way the problem of human existence.

Notes

1. Honda 1993, 239.

2. A sense of his interest in Western philosophy can be gained from *Yasuda bunko yōsho mokuroku* 安田文庫洋書目録 (Kyoto: Ōtani daigaku toshokan, 1987), a bibliography of Yasuda's collection of Western books now held at Ōtani University. Pages 62–382 of this 390-page bibliography are devoted to philosophy, with books by or about German and Austrian authors covering nearly two-hundred pages.

3. YRS Supplementary Volume: 366.

4. Ibid., 370.

5. Accounts of these developments can be found in Ōtani Daigaku Hyakunenshi Hensan Iinkai 2001, 338–41, and in Terakawa 2001, 151–55.

6. Suzuki 1973.

7. YRS 1:482–512.

8. Ibid., 489.

9. Ibid., 497.

10. Ibid., 500.

11. Ibid., 504–07.

12. Ibid., 507.

13. Inagaki Hisao has translated into English Vasubandhu's *Pure Land Treatise* as preserved in Chinese and Tanluan's commentary on it; see Inagaki 1998.

14. Ibid., 54.

15. On the five gates of mindfulness, see ibid., 59–60 and 205–16.

Chapter 13

The Practical Understanding of Buddhism*

Yasuda Rijin

Translated by Paul Watt

It goes without saying that to study within the Buddhist path and to study the Buddhist path have different standpoints. To study within the Buddhist path is to study the self within the Buddhist path. The standpoint of studying the self within the Buddhist path already presupposes that to study the Buddhist path in regard to the self is the reason for study. For that reason, studying within the Buddhist path constitutes the standpoint that the Buddhist path studies the self and signifies practical understanding. That we here take up the problem of the practical understanding [of Buddhism], distinguishing it from the standpoint that takes Buddhism as the object of academic analysis, is because we want to consider the meaning that the Buddhist worldview has for practice or the meaning of the realization of the Dharma.

When we say that we study the self within the Buddhist path, the concepts of path and self must first have a clear definition. Moreover, as long as the exploration of the self itself is the proper object of study within the Buddhist path, there can be no path apart from the study of

---

*YRS 1: 122–27; originally published in *Kōbō*, 1931, No. 2. The words "practical understanding" translates the Japanese *hōhōteki haaku* 方法的把握. Although a literal translation of these words would result in a title such as "The Methodological Understanding of Buddhism," or perhaps more freely, "The Method for Understanding Buddhism," Yasuda's remarks in this essay indicate that he has the applied or practical understanding of Buddhism in mind.

the self. At the same time [we may ask] what sort of thing the self is before [it is seen in relation to] the path. Our inquiry, therefore, cannot depart from the present existence of the self that exists in relation to the path. Through exploring the self that can be gained through reflection on the present and [through exploring] the Dharma that causes the self to be the self, we hope to be able to ground the self in the realization of the Dharma. Through reflection on the present, [it becomes clear that] the self [understood] within the Buddhist path is that which makes the Dharma real and the Buddhist path [seen] in relation to the self is the method for self-understanding.

The important point [that should be made] in distinguishing the practical understanding of Buddhism [that entails] study within the Buddhist path from an exam-like comprehension [that entails] study of the Buddhist path is that the former has a relationship to the present existence of the self that has everyday life problems; thus, it rests on the demands [that arise in conjunction with] the unification and systemization of the actual self, in other words, its rests on the practical demands of the realization of the Dharma. In contrast, the latter [approach] treats [the Buddhist path] as the object of analytical interest or of cultural studies. The difference [between the two approaches] is based on the totally different demands of those associated with a worldview[1] and those [arising from] cultural interests. As long as one treats Buddhism as the object of an exam-like comprehension, that which is given [as the object of study] can only be static and fixed teachings and theories, but the Buddhism that is demanded as practical (*hōhōteki* 方法的) is the Dharma that functions as reflection on the sublation[2] and systematization of everyday life experiences. Of course, even though we speak of static teachings, it goes without saying that they constitute a worldview that has an historical status. Thus, even though we take the standpoint of exploring the Dharma as practical understanding, in terms of procedure, we regard historical teachings as a medium [for the study of the Dharma]. [Yet] to the end, they are systems that have historical limitations or thought that has been systematized with everyday life experiences as its content; they cannot be the systems or the thought of this age or of our everyday life experiences. Furthermore, they have the significance of mediums [that point to] the existence that causes history to be history. In that case, [when we study them,] we do not travel backwards to the past, but rather we enter the basis of present reality. To return to the basis of present reality is nothing other than [to discover] the Dharma that causes the past to be the past as functioning, in a practical way, in the present.

As long as teachings and theories, no matter of what kind, cannot be found in the Dharma that is discovered in relation to the self's problems of everyday life, they cannot, at their core, be teachings [that provide] practical guidance, nor can they have the meaning of theories of a worldview. In a word, as long as they are that kind of thing, they don't even become the classics and teachings that have [taken on] the significance of materials for study. Teachings in the classical sense, even if they are responses to certain problems of everyday life, for the present, can be spoken of as something given. As long as they are something given, for the self they are something "other," something "distant." As long as they are something other and distant, one cannot find the Dharma that systematizes experiences or the Dharma that sublates present reality. Teachings that cannot be expressions of the Dharma, in the strict sense, cannot be called teachings. Therefore, that which causes teachings to be teachings is the Dharma that causes the self to be the self, and the Dharma that causes the self to be the self is something discovered in the given problems of everyday life. In other words, the eternal Dharma that is discovered in the given problems of everyday life is truly that which causes one to discover the present Dharma in the given teachings.

Ultimately, as long as the Dharma is the Dharma, it must be something eternal and present. It is for that reason that it causes this to be this and that to be that. Before this was this and that was that, this could not be this and that could not be that. In the present reality, that which causes the present reality to be the present reality is indeed the path that can be called Mahāyāna and the Buddhist path; it is the Dharma that is called the *dharmakāya* and the *dharmadhātu*.[3] That it cannot be grasped as the name of a particular fixed and thus historical [body of] thought or teachings signify that it is the Dharma of the eternal present. Moreover, because it is eternally present, it also can be particular and historical. This is because the universal that cannot be particular, in the end, is nothing more than a general, abstract concept. That which cannot be validated as having a systematizing function in a particular present reality cannot be called something universal; in short, it cannot be called the Dharma. Of course, given teachings, unless they have already functioned in some present reality as a Dharma that systematized experience, would not have reason to have an historical status as teachings. However, that would pertain to some present reality and not this present reality. One cannot replace this particular present reality with that particular present reality. That is because the theories about the Dharma manifested in that particular present reality, in regard to this present reality, become, just as they are, given teachings that are the object of an exam-like comprehension.

Reflection that sublates present reality and systematizes experience in Buddhism is called the view that accords with reality (*nyojitsukan* 如実観). As long as we think of the Dharma as that which causes the self to be the self, the self is something reflected upon in relation to the Dharma, and the Dharma is reflection related to self-understanding. Therefore, apart from the view that accords with reality, there cannot be that which we call the self or the Dharma. It is because it is reflection in which one is aware of the original nature of the self and in which one understands the transcendental nature of experience that we can speak of it as reality. Prior to that, the self can be nothing more than the content of something one has intellectually discerned. At the same time, as long as the Dharma cannot be the realization of this kind of reflection, it is nothing more than mere abstract conceptual existence. Therefore, that which we call the view that accords with reality clearly views the self and realizes the Dharma. By clearly viewing the self, we mean that the view that accords with reality naturally takes on itself the problems of present reality. The view that accords with reality gives to itself the problems of the given present reality and through exploring their original nature manifests and realizes the Dharma. By the manifestation of the Dharma, we mean that the present reality is the present reality and the self is the self. It is the understanding of the self as that which unifies and that which gives. This is the systematization of the true present reality and the establishment of the self. In a word, the view that accords with reality is reflection that transforms that which is given into that which gives.

When we say that the view that accords with reality functions by transforming the given present reality, what meaning does transform have? That which is given is that which is given in relation to the view that accords with reality. What does it mean to say that something is given in relation to the view that accords with reality? Here the function of negation associated with the view that accords with reality has an important meaning. To be given in relation to the view that accords with reality negates the standpoint prior to the view that accords with reality that has the presupposition of the given. The structure that depends on this negation must have the meaning of transformation or contemplation. In Buddhism, that the view that accords with reality is explained as the contemplation on conditioned arising that negates the standpoint of intellectual discernment, I think, has this meaning. The standpoint of intellectual discernment is the standpoint of abstract reflection on existence, nonexistence, arising and perishing. Abstract reflection, regardless of whether or not it is commonsensical or academic, has the presupposition of substance and real existence at its base. The standpoint that sees the Dharma, regardless of whether it is experiential reflection or abstract reflection, negates the substantial and real nature that that reflection presupposes. With regard to that which is given, as long as its existence is clung to, it becomes impossible for the giving [to take place]. The present reality cannot have meaning as the present reality. As long as one has that standpoint, the world is fixed and static, and the self exists within the inevitable limitations of the external and mechanical. In a view of the world as fixed and in a view of life as externally limited, the possibility of the life of practice cannot exist. The view that accords with reality, by negating such a fixed nature and external inevitability, causes experience to conform to reality. The world that exists as the unification of the Dharma, and the practice that is the realization of the Dharma are realized through the medium of negation.

The view that accords with reality is something that takes present reality as given and that negates abstractness and realness in relation to the given. Thus, [we may ask] what kind of meaning does systematization in regard to negation have. The systematization that has negation as its medium can be thought to cause the internalization of the external. In other words, in regard to the view that accords with reality, the Dharma that systematizes experience is investigated internally. However, "internally" cannot mean "individualistically" and "subjectively," because individualistic subjectivity, as before, can only be a kind of external thing. Therefore, it must be that the internal that stands in contrast to experiential phenomena understands those phenomena in their original nature and in their totality and concreteness. External investigation seeks that which causes things to be themselves outside of those things. The internal investigation of those things sees them in their original nature. It is said that one who sees conditioned arising see the Tathāgatas, Those Who Come from Suchness.[4] Suchness is the suchness of those things. Beyond suchness there cannot be the original concrete form of those things. By "concrete" we mean experience based on suchness. The Dharma, in contrast to experience, transcends experience, but as long as it is that which makes experience possible, it is the original nature of experience. To transcend does not mean to make abstract, but rather it signifies the unifying systematization that makes experience possible. There cannot be an unconditioned Dharma apart from the conditioned. The unconditioned that is separate from the conditioned can only be the abstract concept of transcendence. That which truly causes the conditioned to be the conditioned and causes experience to be experience cannot be the object of abstract reflection. That the systematization of experience is discussed using a negative term like "emptiness," it can be thought, is because it [involves] the concrete concepts of self realization and inner realization. That it is spoken of with such representational language as "Tathāgata" and "*dharmakāya*," it can be thought, [is because] it has the meaning of total nature or concrete nature.

In regard to the view that accords with reality, we have considered the fact that we have that which is given, that it is mediated through negation, and that thereby that which is given is structured as that which gives. Here the Dharma that unifies and systematizes is truly something discovered through the view that accords with reality. Because it is something discovered, it has the power to unify. However, that which has been discovered can also be thought to actually be that which discovers. Through the view that accords with reality, the Dharma was discovered. That is because the view that accords with reality is the Dharma's realization as Dharma. The fact that the self is caused to be the self would not be possible without the logic of the Dharma being the Dharma. The process of discovery through the view that accords with reality, if it is not at the same time the unfolding of the Dharma, [means that] the reflection [involved in that] discovery is subjective and not objective and that the Dharma discovered is representational and not real. The Dharma is said to be quiescent and eternally abiding—doesn't that mean that it is objective? It is precisely because it is objective that it is possible for it to be real in relation to all things. Such self-understanding that is objective and real is what is said to be the study of the self in the Buddhist path and the practical understanding of the Buddhist path.

Notes

1. Yasuda uses worldview or *sekaikan* 世界観 here as a technical term to indicate a unified understanding of the world as a whole.
2. "Sublation" renders the Japanese *shiyō* 止揚, which is a translation of the German *aufheben*. As used by Hegel, the term indicates the negation but also the preservation in an altered form of an element in a dialectic process.
3. *Dharmakāya* is literally, "the body of the Dharma," which refers to the true nature of reality. In Mahāyāna, the true nature of reality is known by various names, including thusness, suchness and emptiness. *Dharmadhātu* (*hokkai* 法界) also refers to this same reality.
4. Here and elsewhere in his writings and lectures, Yasuda occasionally draws on the meaning of *Nyorai* 如来 or Tathāgata as "One Who Has Come from Suchness" (i.e., one who embodies the true nature of reality).

Chapter 14

The Mirror of Nothingness*

Yasuda Rijin

Translated by Paul Watt

That which is called the Complete One, the One *Dharmadhātu*[1] is the ultimate object of questing of sentient beings as self-aware existences. As long as the problem of sentient beings remains within the bounds of a problem of knowledge or a problem of realism, it is like an object that cannot yet [properly] become a problem. It can be said that everything that is the product of the rational labor of sentient beings limits the meaning of the existence of those sentient beings. Thus, the objective world that is the product of those sentient beings can be thought of as an interpretation at the stage or within the realm of the sentient beings who produced it. Therefore, in accord with the respective perspectives of the quests of sentient beings who are physical and historical existences, the states of their understanding are formed. However, from these perspectives, can sentient beings themselves or the ultimate state of sentient beings be completely understood? Is it possible, at least, from such perspectives, to call into question sentient beings themselves or the ultimate state of sentient beings? That which is called the Complete One, the One *Dharmadhātu* is the understanding of the realm of sentient beings as a complete unity or as a unified *dharmadhātu*. At this point, we may call [sentient beings] into question not as sentient beings [who exist] as a fixed aspect of the limited world of possible limitations, but rather as [beings] who embrace all limitations and who, therefore, are also self aware, as

---

*YRS 1: 128–32; originally published in *Kōbō*, May 1931, No. 3.

finite living things, of the totality of possible limitations and of the total structure [of existence]. The reason that sentient beings take on such a quest as their own is nothing other than that they want to become sentient beings in reality. They want to become sentient beings who are self-aware existences. Thus, the interpretation of such a structure is not a mere [matter of] understanding, nor does it stop at mere practice, in as much as one stands within the quest. That is [because] it is a problem of sentient beings as self-aware existences, a problem of the self itself. Until one attains the Complete *Dharmadhātu*, a sentient being cannot establish the self itself. That which is called a religious quest, in the end, is summed up in this. And because it concerns the fundamental structure of understanding, it can also be said to be a philosophical quest.

That sentient beings can be human beings in reality depends on their basing the self on that which causes the self to be the self, while at the same time transcending the self. However, to base the self on the transcendent is not to form a union between the transcendent and sentient beings. This is because, as long as the transcendent exists over against sentient beings, the union of the two is impossible. Thus, to base [the self on the transcendent] must mean the discovery of the self within the transcendent or the discovery of sentient beings as the self-determination of the transcendent. Therefore, the transcendent is the structural unifier of sentient beings with respect to the self. Through this unification, the self can establish the self as the self while at the same time transcending the self. That which is the Complete One is, in short, this unification. It is the totality that is the unifier and the unified, the understanding of the self as the self-expression of the transcendent. To truly transcend opposition must mean to encompass opposition within that [totality]. An absolute that stands in opposition to the relative is still relative and can only be an abstraction. True transcendence unifies opposition; the true absolute encompasses the relative as the systematic totality of parts. Therefore, to base the self on the transcendent is not to add to the self a transcendent that exists outside of the self but to understand sentient beings with respect to the transcendent as abiding in the nature of self-nature. For the transcendent, this is self-manifestation or self-delimitation, but for sentient beings it is the self's return to its self-nature. To return to the transcendent that is the foundation upon which the self is realized is, in reality, for the self to return to the self itself. As long as the quest for the transcendent and the understanding of the self are not the same, the transcendent is "other" and, as long as it is other, it must be unrelated to the self. However, for the self to be the self, the self must rely on the transcendent. For the self to be the self, even if the transcendent is the transcendent, it cannot be the transcendent unless it realizes itself in the moment when it is related to sentient beings who are selves. Thus, [we can ask] what does it mean when we say that [sentient beings] depend upon the transcendent and [the transcendent] is related to sentient beings.

That sentient beings are sentient beings and as such are dependent on the transcendent means that sentient beings negate sentient beings themselves. That sentient beings can achieve unification of the self through dependence on the transcendent, not by the addition of a transcendence that is other, means that everything that is given as possible is given as things associated with sentient beings, as non-transcendent things. Thus, that sentient beings achieve unification of the self through the transcendent is nothing other than sentient beings achieving a self-awareness of their limited world as sentient things, in other words, their achieving self-delimitation. Self-delimitation as sentient beings is the negation of the self of sentient beings. The dharmas of the five skandhas that constitute the existence of sentient beings are dharmas that arise through dependent origination, that is, are conditioned dharmas. It is for this reason that their self-nature is negated. Moreover, just as there is the unconditioned that transcends the five *skandha*s through the negation of the self-nature of the five *skandha*s, so transcendence is realized through the negation of the self of sentient beings. It is not that there is the realization of the transcendent after the negation of sentient beings; rather it is the absolute negation of sentient beings itself that is the unification of the self of sentient beings, that is, the realization of the transcendent. Therefore, the unifier of sentient beings in this sense cannot be a substantive existence. [Rather] it is emptiness itself that signifies absolute nothingness, that is, absolute negation. It can be said that that which makes possible all existence is absolute nothingness. If one thinks of existence as infinitely discriminated unique [phenomena], that which actually makes possible those unique [phenomena] is the emptiness that is the ultimate universal. The world of sentient beings can truly be realized as the world of sentient beings through the unification that depends on that sort of absolute negation. It goes without saying that, just as we think that the absolute is not something that stands in opposition to the relative, we cannot think of this sort of emptiness as something that stands in opposition to existence or as emptiness as an actually existing thing. In the fact that negation is absolute negation lies the significance of emptiness. In other words, it must be the case that emptiness, because it is empty, encompasses existence. At the same time that sentient beings are sentient beings through self-negation, emptiness manifests itself as sentient beings through the self-delimitation of emptiness itself. There can be no significance to emptiness beyond its manifestation as sentient beings. Emptiness is not an empty, abstract concept; [rather] it can be thought of as a function that empties [all things] infinitely. Through this function, there is the unification of the realm of sentient beings. The self-manifestation of emptiness is, at the same time, the unification of sentient beings.

The emptiness [that functions] as the negating unifier of sentient beings is a mirror that reflects sentient beings within it and through it. A mirror itself contains nothing, yet it reflects all things in itself. The ultimate basis [of things] must be the basis that has no basis. It is precisely because of that, that it is able to provide a foundation for the realm of sentient beings. That we regard ignorance as the last condition for the realization of the realm of sentient beings can be understood to mean that the realm of sentient beings has no ultimate conditions, in other words, that it has the nature of having no basis. But it is in the nature of having no basis that, on the contrary, one can find ultimate unification. Thus, through absolute nothingness, it is not that the realm of sentient beings is rejected, but rather that its original nature is made manifest. A mirror through its quiescence and purity reflects sentient beings. What we call original nature is of course not an experiential existence, but the fundamental state of experiential existence. It can be said to be the existent with marks within the nature of emptiness, the worldly truth within the absolute truth. Perhaps it can be said to be movement that has been quieted or purity that has been sullied. That which can encompass the sullied and cause it to exist is itself original purity. The sullied that exists through original purity is truly the originally sullied. A mirror causes all things to exist within itself and manifests all things within it. In that sense, it can be said that a mirror is able to store all things. It is said, "All sentient beings exist within the Tathāgata's wisdom." Just as the truly absolute encompasses the relative within it, so sentient beings, with respect to their true state, take the Tathāgata as the place of realization. "All sentient beings never depart from the state of suchness." True sentient beings are reflected in the mirror of the Tathāgata's wisdom; in other words, they are sentient beings that exist as the object of the absolute's self-realization and the content of the absolute's self-awareness. Doesn't the ultimate structure of sentient beings lie in the fact that sentient beings exist within the Tathāgata's womb? Isn't it too that those whom we call "religious sentient beings" are sentient beings who are reflected in the mirror of nothingness? If we regard philosophical reflection as distinct from enlightened reflection, don't we have to imagine something like the self-aware wisdom of nothingness? The Complete One that stores and is stored, that unifies and is unified, if we regard this as the deepest root of sentient beings, then the various interpretations of sentient beings can be thought of, as it were, as delimited aspects of the Complete One.

Notes

1. These words translate the phrases *zen'ichi naru mono, ichihokkai to iwaruru mono* 全一なるもの、一法界といわるゝもの. Both *zen'ichi* and *ichihokkai* refer to absolute reality.

Chapter 15

A Name but Not a Name Alone*

Yasuda Rijin

Translated by Paul Watt

I

I have put forth the title "A Name but Not a Name Alone," but that was simply a last resort. When world-famous scholar Professor Paul Tillich came to Japan in early July (of 1960), I had the opportunity to have a conversation with him through the efforts of people at Higashi Honganji and Tōji. As a memento [of that meeting], I had Professor Tillich write something for me on a tanzaku. What he wrote were the words, "A name but not a name alone." I have taken those words for the title of today's talk.

Now the name I mention here is the name of the Tathāgata.[1] However, having had the experience of the conversation [with Professor Tillich], I [became aware] of the problem that, while the name of the Tathāgata has a deep meaning, it is not easy for us to understand how that deep meaning is expressed in the name. Hence, we are made to rethink the name.

It is said that the name of the Tathāgata is the name of the original vow. That the name is not just any name is indicated [by the fact that] it is the name of the original vow. However, in his *Kyōgyōshinshō*, Shinran says that this name, the name of the Tathāgata, is practice. "The great practice is to say the name of the Tathāgata of Unobstructed Light."[2] I wonder if, with this statement alone, this isn't

---

*YRS 1:318–45.

difficult to understand. The name is the name and practice is practice. Even if one says that the name is practice, this is not something that can be immediately understood. The meaning of [the line] "a name but not a name alone" is that the name [also] has the meaning of practice. In order to indicate that [point], we speak of it as the name of the original vow. The name is the name of the Tathāgata, but when we speak of it as practice, it is the practice of sentient beings. The name is always the name of the Tathāgata. The name indicates the Tathāgata. Yet although that is the case, at the same time, it also has been given the meaning of the practice of sentient beings. In other words, the name is the Tathāgata, but because of the Tathāgata, the name of the Tathāgata is not just the name of the Tathāgata; it is also responding to sentient beings. Therein lies the meaning [of the line], "A name but not a name alone."

The name of the original vow, it goes without saying, is Namu Amida Butsu, but its fundamental significance is that it responds to human existence. That sort of thing in general is the problem of religion. When it comes to responding in a fundamental way to the problem of human beings, it is necessary to transcend human beings by [simultaneously] negating and embracing them. [Through] the negation and affirmation of human beings, in that sense, the problem of human beings is responded to in a fundamental way. The problem of religion can be expressed in this form. When [religion] takes on that kind of meaning, then as regards the Buddhist way of the original vow, the name has religious meaning. In other words, the name is not just a name. It has religious meaning. To indicate that religious [meaning], the name is used. The name may be a common thing, but it has a unique significance. Therefore, the name is not just any name. It is a unique name.

Regarding the problem of religion, without using anything else, the name in particular was chosen. That which tells us that is the original vow. This original vow is called the selected original vow (*senjaku hongan* 選択本願).[3]

That which the Tathāgata used to delimit itself is the name. The Tathāgata delimited itself as the name. Without delimiting itself using anything else, it delimited itself as the name. That is because names are not incidental to human beings, but have an essential relationship to them. In other words, the name is the name of the Tathāgata, but originally the Tathāgata had no name. However, that the Tathāgata defines itself with the name is because names are peculiar to human existence itself. In other words, the name is the Tathāgata's definition of itself as sentient beings. It manifested itself in the form of sentient beings. That by which the Tathāgata becomes sentient beings is the name. Therefore, sentient beings return to the Tathāgata through the name.

Names are peculiar to human beings. From that perspective, I think that the name must be considered once again from the standpoint of Buddhist ontology.

As I said earlier, in the *Kyōgyōshinshō*, the name is used to indicate the great practice. There it says, "[The great practice] is to say the name of the Tathāgata of Unobstructed Light." Of course, these are Shinran's own words, but if we go back, [we can see that] they are based on Vasubandhu's words in the *Pure Land Treatise*. In the *Pure Land Treatise*, the practice of the Pure Land is indicated as being the five gates of mindfulness. In the second gate, that of praise, the calling of the name appears as the content of the practice of praise [in the line], "[One should] say the name of that Tathāgata." The Great Teacher Tanluan interpreted that [line] as "One should say the name of the Tathāgata of Unobstructed Light." Here he added the words "Unobstructed Light." Whether one says "say the name of that Tathāgata" or "say the name of the Tathāgata of Unobstructed Light," the meaning does not change, but Shinran takes as his own the words of the *Commentary on the Treatise* that interprets the *Pure Land Treatise*. That he uses these words in particular has a deep meaning.

When the *Commentary on the Treatise* interprets the *Pure Land Treatise*, in the background of the *Treatise* is the *Sutra of Immeasurable Life*. The *Sutra of Immeasurable Life* explains the Tathāgata's original vow. That which determines the meaning of the *Treatise* is not one's personal impression. Simply because "one thinks so," one cannot determine the meaning of the *Treatise*. In interpreting the *Treatise*, one views the *Treatise* by transcending it. In this way, an interpretation can be formed. In other words, by viewing it in the light of Amida Buddha's original vow, the meaning of the name was determined. Thus, although the *Pure Land Treatise* describes practice as the five gates of mindfulness, when one returns to the original vow of Amida Buddha, [there] it talks about "up to ten [moments of] mindfulness." Therefore, if one looks at the *Treatise* on its own, apart from the *Sutra*, one interpretation may be possible, but when one views the *Pure Land Treatise* as that which clarifies the meaning of the original vow of the *Sutra of Immeasurable Life*, one can not view the "mindfulness" of [the phrase] "up to ten [moments of] mindfulness" as different from "the five gates of mindfulness."

The phrase "up to ten [moments of] mindfulness" refers to the nenbutsu. . . .[4]

[The *Sutra of Immeasurable Life* speaks of the nenbutsu, being mindful of or saying the name of Amida Buddha, as an "act," but it may also be spoken of as practice.] However I wonder if practice doesn't have a deeper meaning. Rather than just being an act, practice implies a loftier concept. After all, in the *Pure Land Treatise* there is mention of "practice that accords with reality." When we consider [practice] with that point [in mind], it is the practice of the Tathāgata, the One Who Has Come from Suchness.[5] Suchness, as suchness, just as it is, practices. Without suchness, there is no practice. Suchness is a word that indicates the original meaning of all existence. Existence—things, just as they are, practice.

[The words] "One Who Has Come from Suchness" can be restated as suchness comes; however, unless one adds the stipulations of from where and how [suchness comes] the concept does not become clear. [But] "the where" is suchness, "the what" is suchness, and "the how" is suchness. Suchness comes from suchness as suchness. If it doesn't have that meaning, I think that we can't speak of genuine practice. Practice transcends merely individual acts.

From that perspective, the name of the original vow is the practice of sentient beings, but the practice of sentient beings is, in fact, the practice of the Tathāgata itself. The practice of the Tathāgata itself, without losing its identity, is the practice of sentient beings. It is the so-called bodhisattva practice. That meaning is indicated through the five gates of mindfulness. When viewed from [the perspective of] the original vow, [that practice] is the nenbutsu, but that nenbutsu was chosen as the practice of sentient beings. And, at the same time, it is the practice of the Tathāgata. . . .[6]

If one looks only at the *Pure Land Treatise*, the central practice of the five gates of mindfulness is not clear. The *Pure Land Treatise* is a Yogācāra treatise and the practice of Yogācāra is cessation and contemplation. In the *Pure Land Treatise* as well, mention is made of "contemplation on the marks of that world" and "contemplation on the power of the Buddha's original vow"; hence, it is natural that when we speak of practice we mean Yogācāra practice. Viewed in that way, the gate of contemplation is the center. [Or] the two gates of making the vow and contemplation become the center. [Yet] it is customary [to think] that contemplation, understood as the system of practice of cessation and contemplation and as the practice of cessation and contemplation [focused on] the original vow, is central.

While not negating that [view], when one looks at the five gates of mindfulness in the light of the original vow, the center [of the practice] shifts. This is a complicated problem, but when the five gates of mindfulness are viewed from the standpoint of the original vow, there are two centers. Those are the second gate of praise and the fifth gate of transference. In the second gate of praise, the name appears. In the fifth gate, transference appears. Transference refers to the fact that the Tathāgata, without losing its identity as the Tathāgata, becomes the practice of sentient beings. It is transferred by means of the name. That which we call the name is the name [understood] within the broad [context of] religion. In the Buddhist path of the original vow, the name is not just the name; rather it is the name that has religious significance. The name responds to the problem [addressed by] religion. Although it is responding to the problem of religion rather than [merely] that of Buddhism, it responds by means of the name. There, the problem of human beings transcends human beings and the transference of the Tathāgata is fulfilled. That the name has a deep meaning is because it has the meaning of transference.

When expressed in Chinese, [the term "transference"] is made up of the two characters [read in Japanese as] *e* 回 and *kō* 向. One can talk about what each character means, but simply speaking, the concept of *e* is especially important. *E* means "to turn or revolve." It refers to the fact that something turns from something toward something. Hence, the character *kō* (to face forward) emerges naturally [in this context]. Talking about the separate meanings of *e* and *kō* is a Chinese style of interpretation. The critical thing is that the concept of "turning or revolving" is important; it refers to the turning of suchness. The suchness that transcends names returns as the name. In the form of the return of the Tathāgata, the problem of human beings is responded to by transcending human beings and further, without human beings becoming the humanistic [standard], by transcending human expectations. This is what is knows as the fulfillment of transference.

The solution to [the problem of] human beings is not for humans to become just as they think they should be; the problem of human beings is deeper than we human beings think. Hence, that which responds to the problem of human beings before humans do so [themselves] is the original vow. Thus, the problem of human beings is responded to by transcending human expectations. That is what is meant by the fulfillment of the original vow. The problem of human beings is responded to [in the form of] the Tathāgata. It is precisely because it has the meaning of transference that the meaning of the name is profound. Herein lies the significance of Shinran having spoken of the True Pure Land way, rather than simply the Pure Land way. The unique significance of the Buddhist teaching of the original vow is made manifest in the concept of transference. It is the name that embraces that transference, the name that has [within it that] transference.

From that perspective, the five gates of mindfulness have the two centers of the name of the second gate of praise and the name of the fifth gate of transference. Apart from the name that is transferred that I was just discussing, the name appears in [the section on the] second gate of praise. When one simply looks at the *Pure Land Treatise* apart from the original vow, the practice is contemplation, but when one views [the matter] through the original vow, the name is practice. And it is not just a name, but the name of the Tathāgata. To say that name is the praise [of the second gate of mindfulness]. When one asks how [the name] should be said, it should be said according to its *myōgi* 名義, the object to which it refers. In other words, broadly speaking, the name refers to the object of the name. The name is something that stands in relation to its object; it is that which expresses its object. And that which is intended by the name is its object.

In the teachings of the Yogācāra [school], *myōgi* holds an important place. The term *myōgi* may be understood to mean "concept." The myōgi of Amida Buddha is the concept of Amida Buddha. *Myōgi* is something that has a very profound and great significance for human existence.

In the *Pure Land Treatise*, it appears briefly, but when one takes the standpoint of the doctrines of Vasubandhu's Yogācāra [school], one sees that, as regards the problem of human existence, myōgi holds an important place. Myōgi expresses the idea of [mental] discrimination or conceptualization. It is also spoken of as the discrimination of objects and the discrimination of names.

We experience "reality" and speak about "reality," but we can not directly conceptualize "reality" itself. We think that we are experiencing reality, but [that which we experience] becomes human experience through names. Reality itself is not a name. However, by establishing names, reality is conceptualized as an object. Therein lies the secret of human experience. As I said earlier, names are not associated with the Tathāgata; rather names are associated with human beings. Hence, human experience is not the direct experience of reality itself or the Tathāgata itself; rather the Tathāgata becomes human experience as a concept (*myōgi*). Of course, even if the Tathāgata becomes human experience, it does not exist apart from the Tathāgata. However, the Tathāgata ceases to be the Tathāgata [itself]; it is there that the world of human beings is established through conceptualizations. Although the world of human beings does not exist apart from the Tathāgata, the Tathāgata is transformed by humans into a concept. If I use provocative language, [I might say that the relationship between the Tathāgata and human beings] is turned upside down.

Human beings do not exist in reality itself; rather they function within the context of their interpretation [of reality]. Humans are able to function in and be concerned about the human world alone; they cannot function in a world that transcends humans. We are like silkworms who make cocoons and who live within the cocoons we ourselves make. We do not live in a world of direct experience. Discriminating among names and objects is the basis of human existence. If that were not so, there would be no way for the passions and the like to arise in a world of direct experience. Human beings function within the world they construct. In that sense, humans are beings of the world. It is not that humans would exist whether or not there were names. In a sense, humans are beings who, through names, are deluded by names. In order to awaken those human beings, the only alternative was to rely on names. Because humans are beings deluded by names, to awaken humans [the Tathāgata] could not help but use names.

To be deluded by names is to regard them has having a real substance. Our experience is formed [on the basis of] the substantiation of names. However, substantiated names, originally, are provisional names (*kemyō* 仮名) rather than real things. The fact that names are provisional is important; they are established provisionally in contrast to objects. Without objects, there are no names. That is the point I want to speak about today. Don't we think of names as "real names"? But names are originally provisional. When we refer to the name of the original vow, you may think it is a "real name," but even the name of the original vow is a provisional name.

II

The character for *ke* 仮 (provisional) has the meaning of something "temporarily established." Something that is "constructed" is also referred to as *ke*. The German word is *setzen*. In other words, [*ke* refers to] something that did not originally exist. Hence in contrast to something that is original [that existed from the beginning], it is something that is contingent. Therefore, it is also called an "incidental name" (*kakumyō* 客名). The concept of provisional names is not made clear in Theravada Buddhism. Even if the Abhidharma of the Theravādins speaks of "no-self," it refers [only] to the no-self of the *pudgala,* the no-self of persons. In contrast, in Mahāyāna teachings, [phrases such as] "all dharmas are mere consciousness" and "all dharmas are empty" are intended to make clear the emptiness of all things. It is in that connection that provisional names are given so much attention.

Provisional names are clearly discussed not only in the teachings of Vasubandhu, but also in Nāgārjuna's *Madhyamakakārikā*.[7] According to the Tiantai interpretation of the *gāthā* on the three truths contained in the well-known chapter on the Four [Noble] Truths, [a distinction is made between] the empty, the provisional, and the middle aspects of truth, but there too that which is empty is indicated to be a provisional name.[8] It further says that "this is the middle way." In the opening chapter of Vasubandhu's *Thirty Verses on Mere Consciousness* (Ch. *Weishisanshisong*, Jpn. *Yuishiki sanjūju* 唯識三十頌), it says, "Because they are provisional, the Buddha explained them as the self and dharmas." The self and dharmas, existent things, are merely names. All existing things are referred to as the self and dharmas, but the self and dharmas are merely those things that have names. In Chinese perhaps the phrase [indicating their nature] would be "To have a name but no substance." Speaking from that perspective, the essence of names is fundamentally that they are provisionally established. I believe that this is a point worthy of [special] consideration.

The Great Teacher Tanluan has said that the name of the Tathāgata is different from ordinary names in that it has the function of saving sentient beings. As an example—one that probably comes out of Daoist texts—is the view that if one calls the name [of the Tathāgata], illnesses will be cured. This is probably a misinterpretation that arises from over-enthusiasm for the name, but if that were the case, the name would become a magical spell or incantation. This is one of the great dangers that the name possesses and is a great pitfall.

When Namu Amida Butsu becomes a magical incantation, the name no longer fulfills its religious function. [Indeed] it obstructs its religious function. By destroying the human being in a fundamental way, religion thereby provides a foundation for the human being. If that doesn't happen, it cannot be called a religion. If [the name becomes] an incantation, it obstructs the absolute negation that destroys human beings. When it is substantiated, the world of religion becomes something magical. This is a danger inherent in religion. When one thinks about that, the fact that names are only provisional has great significance. To regard names as real is not to respect names, but rather is to be deluded by names. By understanding names as provisional, one becomes able to use names without being deluded by them.

Because we use [the term] provisional names, one may think that it refers to something of little value, but using the term provisional names is correct. [Viewing] names as representing reality is completely delusional. In Buddhist ontology, names have a special significance. For example, in Yogācāra treatises, names exist in contrast to objects. Names are established in contrast to objects and objects are established in contrast to names. In the *Treatise on Mere Consciousness* (Ch. *Weishilun*, Jpn. *Yuishikiron* 唯識論), there are the well-known words, "names and objects are incidental to one another." This [passage] refers to the [concept of] incidental name that I mentioned previously. These are probably the words that first revealed the key [to understanding] concepts.

For us human beings, there are two fundamental arbitrary views. Philosophically speaking, [the first] is called "naïve realism." By [the first] arbitrary view, I refer to the position that [holds that] there is some object of consciousness and that we become conscious of that object. [In this view,] consciousness is something that represents the object of consciousness. For example, [according to this view,] a flower exists before there is consciousness of it. We think that by coming into contact with the flower, the content of "flower" is formed in the previously contentless consciousness. This content is the representation of the flower. [Believing that] the representation of the flower reflects the flower just as it is is one great arbitrary view.

When we are conscious of a flower, we think that the flower exists outside of consciousness. [But] we cannot say that the object itself exists. An object does not exist apart from consciousness. In the realm of consciousness, all things are objects. It is not that existing things alone become objects. Nonexisting things also become objects. In as much as there is the consciousness of nothingness, in the realm of consciousness both existing and nonexisting things become objects. Therefore, we cannot say an object called a flower exists unless we presuppose consciousness.

The second arbitrary view is that we think that there is a flower itself and that it is indicated with the concept of flower, or [we think that] the concept of flower transmits the flower itself, without losing its essence, or [we think that] the word flower, that word itself, indicates the actual existence of the flower. We think that the concept of flower transmits the flower that actually exists without losing its true nature. This is the second arbitrary view.

In this way, for human beings there are two arbitrary views. The [world of] human naturalistic experience is based on such arbitrary views. [In Buddhism,] this type of experience is called delusion. It is not that there is something that deludes us; [rather] without there being something that causes delusions, humans are deluded about the fundamental structure [of consciousness]. That being the case, [it is as though] the name "flower" is something the flower itself originally spoke. That would be a "real name." [But] that is something that cannot be; names are constructed things. Therefore, the words "names and objects are incidental to one another" are the first to reveal these arbitrary views that have existed from the beginningless past.

Even the name of the original vow is not a special name. It is the fundamental nature of names that, in the end, they are [all] provisional names. Therefore, we can refer to [the original vow] as a *shingon* 真言 or "true word." The name is a word, a word about the true nature of reality; in other words, it is a true word. The true word of esoteric Buddhism is called a *dhāraṇī*. Now [I am discussing] the true word of exoteric Buddhism. The name of the original vow is the true word of exoteric Buddhism. In that case, it might be called the word about the true nature of reality, but when we use these words, we are not contrasting real names with the provisional names mentioned earlier; [rather] provisional names are true words. It is not that one abandons provisional names for true words; provisional names are themselves true words.

Within Mahāyāna teachings, from the perspective of a purely religious standpoint, human beings are existences that are affirmed in an absolute way after passing through an absolute negation. If that is not the case, human beings cannot [in fact] become human beings. That [understanding of] the human being is the human being seen from the standpoint of religion. Human beings are existences that carry a great contradiction within them. To speak of human beings as existences of absolute contradiction is something that can be said on the basis of religious self-awareness; apart from religion, that probably cannot be said. In Buddhism, that sort of deep, fundamental self-awareness is expressed through words like "faith" or "awakening." In short, those words refer to the wisdom of nondiscrimination.

Whether we speak of common sense or philosophy or science, it is undeniable that all [transmit a kind of] wisdom, but the difference between them and religious wisdom (*jñāna/prajñā*) lies in [the idea of] awakening. Awakening is not rational or objective understanding. Even if one speaks of it as truth, it refers to a truth to which one has awakened. Consciousness that is in conformity with the truth is called understanding. It is not the kind of truth that, once experienced, [allows one] to remain just as one was. Even though we may attain a scientific understanding [of things], there is no need to cease being the type of human being we were because of that understanding. [Indeed] the fact that we are human beings is further reinforced. [But] as regards understanding to which one has become awakened, once that sort of understanding has been attained, one can not return to the human being one was before. It represents a kind of truth that transforms human beings. That kind of truth is truth to which one has become awakened. The awakened human being is the Tathāgata. The human being, just as he or she is, is the Tathāgata. That sort of wisdom is called the wisdom of nondiscrimination. When one thinks about this in relation to the problem of names I have been discussing, it takes on some interesting dimensions.

According to Asaṅga,[9] when a bodhisattva achieves the wisdom of nondiscrimination, that is, when people attain that understanding, sentient beings who existed as ordinary people are transformed into bodhisattvas. In that state, they abide among names among which no discrimination of objects is made. Here [the concept of] *myōgi* or names and objects appears. In other words, [Asaṅga] describes the state of our having achieved the wisdom of nondiscrimination [with the words,] "they abide among names among which no discrimination of objects is made." The word "abide" means "to abide with ease"; in other words, they abide with ease [in the realm] of names. The ordinary person abides [in the realm of] discrimination. When discrimination is negated, one becomes a bodhisattva. [Asaṅga's words] are a response to the problem of where those bodhisattvas abide.

Perhaps it is hard to follow what I am saying when I use words like bodhisattva and ordinary person. Those who are deluded are ordinary people; those who are awakened are bodhisattvas. A bodhisattva is not an especially eminent person. A true human being [who] exists with a self-awareness of human existence—that is a bodhisattva. Human beings live but they [also] exist with an awareness of the fact that they are living. Dogs and cats live, but they are not aware of their existence. It is only human beings that, while they are alive, live with an awareness of their existence. Therefore, speaking from the perspective of existence, among all living things, the opportunity to have a self-awareness of existence exists only in the case of human beings. To live with an awareness of oneself—the being who lives in that fashion is called a bodhisattva. An ordinary person exists without a self.

To define an ordinary person is a matter of discriminating among names and objects; that is the realm in which an ordinary person abides. In contrast, the realm in which a bodhisattva abides is [the realm of] the nondiscrimination of names and objects. To abide among names which do not discriminate among objects means to abide in the realm where there is no place to abide, to abide in the place of nonabiding. To have no place in which to abide, that is the realm where self-aware beings abide. This is the type of expression one finds in the Prajñāpāramitā [sutras].[10] To abide in the realm of nonabiding is a paradox. In the teaching of Yogācāra, paradoxical expressions are presented analytically.

Vasubandhu expresses this [idea] with the words "to abide in the true nature of mere consciousness." This refers to the mind at ease (*anjin* 安心). "To abide" means "to abide with ease." The nature of mere consciousness refers to the original nature of consciousness; consciousness is at ease with the original nature of consciousness itself. I think that [the term] "a mind at ease" is a Chinese phrase. It probably arose in connection with the Chan (Zen) and nenbutsu [schools]. I don't think there is such a word in the languages of India, but if we were to look for [a parallel], it would probably be "to abide in the nature of mere consciousness." The phrase mentioned earlier, "to abide among names among which no discrimination of objects is made," refers to the mind at ease. The method for bringing to light the mind at ease is "observation of the mind" (*kanjin* 観心). That so much attention is given to observation of the mind is because it is the method for attaining a mind at ease. To have one's mind be at ease with itself is only possible when the mind returns to its original nature. When the mind arises as names and objects, it takes on a form that negates its original nature; when the mind returns to its original nature, that is awakening (*satori* 悟り). The *sato* of *satori* has the meaning of original nature. To recover one's original nature (*satotoru* さととる)—until one returns to one's original nature, the human mind cannot be at ease. When one asks what kind of original nature it is [that one recovers], it is the original nature of an uneasy mind.

When we say that the mind of faith[11] is a mind at ease, as far as Pure Land Buddhism is concerned, there are three minds associated with the ease of mind attained through the nenbutsu. It was the Great Teacher Shandao who first established [the concept of] a mind at ease as a precise and technical term. In the Great Teacher Tanluan's [works] as well, the words "a mind at ease" appear, as in the line, "The Pure Land is the abode of the mind at ease [attained through] practice." But it was from Shandao on that it became established as a precise, technical term. [The line] "The mind of faith is a mind at ease" [is true] in so far as "faith" has the meaning of "awakened." "Awakened" means "realized." In as much as faith has the meaning of realization, faith leads one to a mind at ease. Generally speaking, faith [is viewed] as the beginning of realization; [the stage before] one has yet to achieve realization is spoken of as faith. But faith in that case has the meaning of unease.

That faith can be spoken of as realization is because faith itself has the meaning of realization. Faith is not just the beginning of realization. Realization is said to be the end point, but it [actually] begins from the end point. The customary idea is that faith is faith and realization is realization; but at the same time that faith reaches its conclusion in realization, faith begins from the realization that has been reached. That faith and realization have [this] circular relationship is something that cannot be said apart from the original vow. It cannot be said apart from the name.

III

That which we call names are provisional; things that are temporarily established, this is the original meaning of names. In other words, this is [the meaning of] names to which one is awakened. Therefore, [the phrase] "names and objects are incidental to one another" exposes the profound arbitrariness associated with names. This arbitrariness exists when we regard names as real. Names are something temporarily established. Originally, that which we call "real" has the meaning of "that which itself proclaims its own existence," but provisional names are incidental. In other words, this means that their relationship to objects is incidental.

That "the name is not just a name" also means that the name is simply a name. In that sense, it indicates that it is not just a name. Although it is a complicated matter, the name is originally just a name; hence it indicates that it is not a name. [Yet] we are not saying, therefore, that it [represents] a reality that denies provisional names. Even if we refer to it as a real name, we are not denying that names are things that are temporarily established and [asserting that] the name itself is real. [Rather] we are saying that that which has been temporarily established is reality. I wonder if this isn't the fundamental character of names.

Asaṅga indicates the wisdom of nondiscrimination through the words "to abide among names among which no discrimination of objects is made." The wisdom of nondiscrimination is Buddhist wisdom or *prajñā*. When a consciousness characterized by faith [becomes] the wisdom of nondiscrimination, it can be spoken of as characterized by a pure faith. In other words, when we say the name of the original vow, through the name, the wisdom of nondiscrimination is aroused. That the name was originally taken up is because it is related to discrimination. Through names, human beings discriminate among names and objects. [The phrase] "names and objects" indicates discrimination. Because it is related to discrimination, the name causes discrimination to be transformed and nondiscrimination to be aroused. If the name itself is not [related to] discrimination, then it would be impossible to indicate nondiscrimination through the name.

An object is a concept. [The term] "object" in the line "to abide among names among which no discrimination of objects is made" in Sanskrit is *artha*. In Chinese translations it is [rendered with the character] *yi* 義 (Jpn. *gi*). Along with [the sense of] "meaning," *gi* also indicates an object of consciousness. In the present case, it is perhaps correct to refer to it as "object" rather than "meaning." [The term] "abide" in the line "to abide among names among which no discrimination of objects is made" [means] "to abide with ease." In this case, it [means] to abide in the *dharmatā*, the true nature of all things. From the perspective of noesis, it constitutes nondiscrimination; from the perspective of noema, it is the true nature of all things or their original nature. In a certain treatise, there is the line, "to abide in the true nature of the mind." In other words, the mind abides in the true nature of the mind. [Or] the mind is at ease when it discovers the original nature of mind itself. In that situation, Asaṅga indicates that [in the line] "to abide among names," using the work "name." This is an interesting expression. One abides [in the consciousness] that all things are provisional names.

Discrimination is [also related to] concepts. With [discrimination], for the first time, an object [of consciousness] is formed. Therefore, our consciousness is fundamentally related to objects; it [consists] of the discrimination of objects. By making our own selves an object, we are conscious of that which has been objectified. We cannot be conscious of anything that is beyond consciousness; consciousness is conscious of consciousness. In that case, the consciousness of which we are conscious can be cognized by making the self an object. That is the structure of discrimination. However, in that case, the mind is not at ease. From that standpoint, there can be no human consciousness without objects. It is not that there are objects and that we then become conscious of them. This [view] is based on the idea that consciousness is from the start consciousness of something. From that perspective, all existent as well as nonexistent things are objects of consciousness.

Consciousness has no objects beyond consciousness; whether it be existent or nonexistent things that [appear to be] beyond consciousness, both in the end are expressed as objects within consciousness. That is consciousness as we usually think about it. Therefore, consciousness expresses itself as an object and is [then] conscious of that object which is its self-expression. In connection with that structure [of consciousness], various emotions arise. Consciousness arises as the consciousness of some object. It is not that there [first] are flowers of which we become conscious; [rather] the consciousness of flowers arises. Because we are conscious of objects of consciousness, consciousness is bound by those objects. Therefore, that which binds consciousness is consciousness itself.

In this sense, consciousness in fact is manifested in a form that is not itself. The consciousness that ordinarily arises conceals consciousness itself. When consciousness arises, consciousness itself is manifested in a way that negates its original nature. Therefore a consciousness that has objects cannot be at ease in consciousness itself. Consciousness is constantly being changed by the objects of consciousness. It moves from [one moment of] discrimination to the next. Therefore, in that situation, there is no way for the unconsciousness of faith (expressed as wisdom) to form.

From this standpoint, the consciousness of faith that is manifested as the wisdom of nondiscrimination is a consciousness without objects. When that is the case, for the first time, the consciousness of faith can be distinguished from all other instances of consciousness. That which we call the consciousness of faith, if expressed generally as a concept in the philosophy of religion, is consciousness of the eternal. The eternal is not something that can be made into an object. One cannot think of the eternal as an object. A consciousness that expresses the eternal as an object is not a religious consciousness. In a form that is not religious consciousness, religion is made manifest. If one is conscious of the eternal, then that is the same as saying that one is conscious of something that can be represented as an object. I think that, even as regards the Tathāgata or the Pure Land and the like, if one grasps them as objects, one does not have a religious consciousness. Even as regards [such acts as] meditating on the buddha or having faith in the buddha, if one's consciousness [is concerned with] thinking about the buddha or if the buddha himself is [treated as] an objective existence, I doubt that one's consciousness can be said to be a religious consciousness.

[To have] the consciousness of a buddha, one must be a buddha. The consciousness that has faith in the buddha must be the mind of a buddha. One cannot hold up the buddha as an object [of consciousness]. Therefore, in Buddhism, [this idea] is expressed in the concept of emptiness. In the teachings of the Prajñāpāramitā [school], they speak of "emptiness as the nature [of all things]." In the Yogācāra [school], they speak of "the nature that is made manifest through emptiness." In teachings such as these, there are some differences. Things that are not emptiness [are empty], how much more so are things that are not existing things—[the teachings] indicate that sort of thing. In any event, the concept of emptiness expresses pure negation. In the case of the Prajñāpāramitā [school], although emptiness is initially [understood as] negation, it also is [understood as indicating] wondrous existence. It is not simply a negative concept. *Prajñā* is a concept that expresses simultaneous negation and affirmation. In any event, the fact that a concept expressing negation is used [indicates] that speculation about the eternal is forbidden. Seeking the eternal as an object [of consciousness] is [to follow] a path that takes one away from eternity. Instead, by abandoning the search one may find [the eternal] at one's feet.

In short, to express the eternal through the concept of emptiness is [to indicate] that the eternal is not an objective existence and [further] that it is [part of] the original nature. The mind that seeks the eternal is the original [mind]. That is the eternal. The mind that seeks the eternal is itself the eternal. Because people don't understand that, they seek the eternal outside of themselves. If one does not awaken to the mind that seeks the eternal itself, nowhere can one find that point that distinguishes [Buddhist] religious consciousness from that of other religions.

[In the passage under consideration,] Asaṅga indicates "the empty nature" [of things] through names. This is an approach unique to him. Nāgārjuna uses "emptiness," which is the same as the provisional. In the Tiantai interpretation, [the three concepts of] the empty, the provisional, and the middle are established, but in Nāgārjuna's *Mahyamakakārikā* itself, the empty and the provisional are synonyms. Emptiness is also a provisional name. In this sense, [the line] "to abide among names among which no discrimination of objects is made" is the same as abiding in the empty nature [of things]. "The empty nature [of things]" is already a name, but as long as it is expressed as emptiness, it is not emptiness. In other words, the ideal of the eternal and the eternal itself are different. The representation of the eternal and the eternal itself are different. The eternal transcends time, but the representation of it exists in time. The eternal itself does not enter time. The Tathāgata, the Pure Land and the like, they are eternal. But if one tries to express the eternal in time, there is no alternative to expressing it as the future. We say that "we will be born [in the Pure Land] in the future," expressing the eternal as an extension of time.

We indicate the eternal as an infinite extension of time. By so doing, we have the [concept of] the future.

However, one cannot put one's mind at ease in a future Pure Land represented in that way. As long as consciousness has objects, one cannot be at ease in consciousness itself. Once cannot be at ease unless one returns to the place of one's departure. One cannot be at ease along the way. Because being at ease makes contact with the origins of delusion, one is able to be at ease. The mind that has made contact with the origins of delusion and that has clarified the real character of delusion will no longer be deluded. Once the origins of delusion have been identified, going to the trouble of negating delusion is unnecessary.

The term of negation, "emptiness," indicates something that is not empty. It indicates the original nature that is not a negation. Hence, that which is provisional is something temporarily established. There are the concepts of the "established" and the "nonestablished" truths; the term "the empty nature [of things]" [belongs to the category of] established truth. However, the name "the empty nature [of things]" does not indicate emptiness. Emptiness itself cannot have even the name of "emptiness." In other words, something that is not a name is being indicated by a name. That [consciousness] is the self-awareness of names. People may think that the meaning of "provisional names" is shallow and that of "real names" is profound, but in fact that is not the case. There are no "real names." That fact that all things that exist are nothing other than names brings one into contact with the awakened [state] by transforming the perspective that sees real things as objects. The awakening [that involves seeing] the things one sought as objects as originally [a matter] of self-awareness is indicated by names. When we say that existent things exist as names, the things we made into objects become subjective [consciousness].

As I said previously, it is impossible to grasp the original nature of things as an object; rather they exist as [a matter of] subjective self-awareness. As regards consciousness as well, it is first a consciousness of objects. However, as Descartes says, we can be conscious of consciousness. We are conscious of things as objects, but we can also be conscious of the function of consciousness. In that sense, we can speak of self-awareness, but with that sort of self-awareness, the self-awareness that is faith will not take form. If one stops at the point of knowing the function of consciousness, that cannot be called the self-awareness that is faith. Consciousness can see its function as an object [but] if consciousness stops there, it is absolutely the case that awakening will not take form in consciousness.

By coming into contact with its origin, consciousness becomes aware of itself. If it is not the case that consciousness can awaken from dreams, then no matter how humans may seek to gain awakening, they cannot become awakened. We can say that, even in dreams, not only can we become conscious of things as objects, but we can also be conscious of consciousness. That which can awaken us from such a consciousness is consciousness. Therefore, the self-awareness that is faith is the empty nature of the mind or the self-awareness that is consciousness returned to its source. If it is not that sort of consciousness, if one [only] vaguely refers to self-awareness, [the sort of consciousness I am referring to] is not made clear. The Zen master Dōgen used [the phrase] "To shine the light back on oneself." [Usually] when we shine a light on something, we shine it in a forward direction. If we are only conscious of [the things before us], human beings can never escape delusion. However, consciousness shines both forward and backward. It can shine light on the dream [that arises from only] shining one's light forward. In that way it returns to the [true] nature of the mind.

[In that state of mind,] even if one sees various things, one does not see them as objects. However, that doesn't mean that one has abandoned consciousness. There is a contradiction in the term "the wisdom of nondiscrimination." If it is nondiscrimination, it is not wisdom, and if it is wisdom, then there is discrimination. In expressing the wisdom of nondiscrimination, Asaṅga asks whether wisdom is something associated with the mind or something that is not mind (i.e., matter). If wisdom is associated with the mind, in other words, if it is associated with consciousness, then it must be said that wisdom [involves] discrimination. Since making discriminations is the essence of the mind, if wisdom has to do with the mind, how can we speak of nondiscrimination. If [wisdom is associated with] nondiscrimination, then it is other than mind. In other words, it is matter. If it is the same as matter, then how can we say that it is wisdom? Therefore, the wisdom of nondiscrimination neither affirms nor abandons discrimination. The consciousness that is faith is not unconsciousness.

When the consciousness that is faith is called the wisdom of nondiscrimination, there is a conceptual contradiction. [It is] nondiscriminating yet it is wisdom. It is not that consciousness has been abandoned. While conscious, one has nevertheless abandoned the clinging [nature] of consciousness. While conscious, one has nevertheless abandoned the form of consciousness. Although seeing the self itself as an object is consciousness, while conscious, one has abandoned that object. That is the original self-awareness of consciousness itself. Consciousness is incomprehensible. As long as it is comprehensible, a mind at ease will not form. Consciousness is incomprehensible to itself. [By realizing that,] at that point, consciousness becomes at ease. If it is not that way, the consciousness that is faith cannot be distinguished from all other [types of] consciousness.

Therefore, the wisdom of nondiscrimination is indicated by names. Hence, names are forms or phenomena. When we call them phenomena, there are no longer things. Existence is a phenomenon. It is not that things exist as objects. They are phenomena. They are not objects. When we refer to names, they are the names of nameless things. They are wordless words. That is the real character of words.

It is not that words express something. If something is indicated by a name—in other words, if something expresses itself through a name—then [that something] would be an object. Consciousness expresses itself as an object and takes an interest in that object that has been expressed. What we call the passions is having an interest in things. As a result, the consciousness that is conscious [of objects] is bound by the things of which it is conscious.

Hence humans are fettered without fetters. Because that is the case, Asaṅga, commenting on the problem of names, spoke of "abiding among names among which no discrimination of objects is made."

[In his *Mahāyānasaṃgraha*, Asaṅga] established the ten names to encompass all names, expressing [the idea] in a verse. [In his list,] both dharmas and objects are names. Through the ten names he encompasses all existing things, but he calls the tenth and last name the ultimate name. Both the previous nine names and the tenth name are names; and there is no difference among them in that regard. In this case, it is not that they are special names. Even in the world of the original vow, names are provisional names. When one thinks of them as special names, that constitutes the substantiation of names. In other words, Namu Amida Butsu becomes a magical incantation. If it is a magical incantation, it cannot be a provisional name. That constitutes not an awakening to [the nature of] names, but the fact of being deluded by names. It constitutes not the consciousness of objects, but objects on a grand scale. Therefore, human beings are not deluded merely by the things of the secular world, but also by the name of the Tathāgata. They are also deluded by the Tathāgata. In other words, they make an object of the Tathāgata. Therefore, both that which is not ultimate is a name and that which is ultimate is a name. [Asaṅga] says that all things are names. To indicate that which is ultimate through a name that can indicate that which is not ultimate—that [is the meaning of the phrase] "names among which no discrimination of objects is made" mentioned previously; among the ten names, it is the ultimate name.

When sentient beings arouse the wisdom of nondiscrimination, that constitutes abiding in the ultimate name. It is a name that indicates that which is ultimate or eternal. Temporal things are expressed through names and the eternal is expressed through names. Because whether it is temporal or eternal it is just a name, a name is just a name. It is not the case that a name is not just a name. A name is only a name. That fact indicates that it is not just a name.

In his *Mahāyānasaṃgraha*, Asaṅga says that "cherry tree" is a name, "desk" is a name. "Amida" is also a name. But Amida is something that indicates that which is ultimate. The name of the Buddha is an ultimate name. There is not only the example of the *Mahāyānasaṃgraha*; even if one thinks of Vasubandhu's *Pure Land Treatise*, he speaks of the abridged explanation of entrance into the phrase One Dharma[12] in contrast to the unabridged explanation of the twenty-nine phrases. "Phrase" and "name" are similar concepts. Therefore the phrase One Dharma mentioned in the *Pure Land Treatise* is an ultimate name. The "One" is not one among twenty-nine. Twenty-nine is a number; the One that is contrasted with twenty-nine is not a number. It is the one of the One Dharmadhātu. Rather than a number, it indicates totality. It is the One, the phrase One Dharma, that indicates all-encompassing totality.

The name of the original vow has the meaning of the ultimate name or the phrase One Dharma. Whether it is the phrase One Dharma or the twenty-nine phrases, if one takes the name as an object—in other words, if one substantiates the name—the world that one experiences is the defiled land. If the name is just a name, then [the world that one experiences] is the Pure Land. The world that is indicated by phrases such as the phrase One Dharma and the twenty-nine phrases is the Pure Land. They are phrases [that indicate] that even as regards the Pure Land, there is no particular such object.

[In his *Commentary on the Pure Land Treatise*,] the Great Teacher Tanluan says, "The abode of the Pure Land is the so-called seventeen phrases." Beyond "phrases" there is no Pure Land. In this case as well, the One, the ultimate, is not something one speculates about as an object. If one applies the translations [used in the *Mahāyānasaṃgraha*] to such terms as the phrase One Dharma and the ultimate, they would be "the all-pervading dharma" or "the all-encompassing dharma;" in other words, [they indicate] the totality [of all things]. "One" indicates something that is ultimate and all-encompassing; that which is all-encompassing is not an object. Because "pervading" [indicates] the comprehensive or the extreme, [it refers to] the most comprehensive, the comprehensivenss that is nothingness. If it is made into an object, it becomes an existing thing.

That which is comprehensive cannot exist as an object. That which is comprehensive is something that exists subjectively (although in fact even the word "subjective" is insufficient). It is not a subjective that merely negates the objective. [It refers to something that] cannot be objectified in terms of subjective and objective. Because subjective and objective can be made objects [of consciousness], that which cannot be objectified in any sense, that is the self. Only by the self knowing the self, or by the self returning to its original self, can one grasp the absolute or eternity. It is not something that can be established as an object apart from oneself. That which has the function of turning an objective name into a non-object is the ultimate name referred to here.

IV

Consciousness is not only something that can reflect [on itself]; it is also something that can [achieve] awakening. In other words, that which can awaken from a dream is consciousness. If it is not that sort of self-awareness, one cannot indicate religious self-awareness. Reflective self-awareness is merely subjective self-awareness. That is, it is objectified as a subject and stands in contrast to the objective. As long as [consciousness] is objectified, it will not return to the self. Consciousness that does not return to the self is not at ease. The self-awareness that is faith—if we use the language of the *Awakening of Faith*—is self-awareness similar to "the original awakened [state]" (*hongaku* 本覚). *Gaku* is the awareness (*kaku* 覚) of self-awareness, but it is also an awareness contrasted with illusion.

Names are incidental names. Even if it is the name of the Tathāgata, it is an incidental name. Although a name is just a name, the self-awareness that is it just a name is not just a name. The awareness of religious self-awareness has two meanings. In other words, to be aware is not to know things. Although it has the meaning of the self-consciousness of knowing that one knows, at the same time, it also has the meaning of "to awaken," which is contrasted with delusion.

If it stops at only knowing that one knows something, that would be a limited concept. No matter how much one traces back the subjective, it only remains a limited concept. It can only remain as cognition of the subjective. In that case, it is discrimination; one cannot [achieve] a mind at ease. It is the subjective self-awareness of the ego that is contrasted with the objective. It is still subjective. However, at the same time, awareness has the meaning of "to open one's eyes." It is not that which simply knows the self; it is that which is awakened. If it is that which can be known, it is no different than the ego. The self cannot be the self just as it is in its deluded [state]. The self is that which is awakened; it is self-awareness that is awakened. If it is not that, one cannot indicate the self-awareness that is faith.

Things that are not ultimate are names, but ultimate names are also names. A name is just a name. However, as regards ultimate names, it is not that there is something, as named, that exists. All that exists is the name alone, and thereby that which is not just a name is symbolized. If that is not clear, I wonder if the name of the original vow too won't give rise to infinite misunderstandings. Therefore, the following representation of [the name] is perhaps best: ~~name~~

This [manner of expression] follows Heidegger. The line [through the name] does not signify the nullification [of the name]; rather here the name indicates that which is not the name. When we think about this in relation to Tanluan's [concept of] the *dharmatā*, that which nullifies is the *dharmatā* and the name is the *upāya* (*hōben* 方便) or means. It is the name that is the sole method for bringing us into contact with that which is not the name. Names are things that do not originally exist in the *dharmatā*. They exists among deluded sentient beings. Sentient beings objectify things through [the use of] names. Consciousness then becomes restricted by the objectified consciousness. Names belong to human beings. If those who are deluded by names are human beings, then there is no way other than names to cause them to awaken [from that delusion].

The name of the original vow is the *dharmakāya* of means (*hōben hosshin* 方便法身).[13] The Tathāgata has no form; suchness has no form. Even if one speaks of the name of the Tathāgata, the One Who Has Come from Suchness, by the time [the Tathāgata] has come, [the Tathāgata] is already a name. The "of" in "[the name] of the Tathāgata" is unnecessary. [The name of the Tathāgata] does not have the meaning of "the name that the Tathāgata has." It is not the name that indicates the Tathāgata. The Tathāgata is the name. The word "Namu" [reverence] is also attached to the name of the original vow. Therefore, adding "reverence," we call [the entire phrase] the name. It is not that Amida alone is the name. It is not that there is Amida Buddha to which "reverence" was later added. That which we cannot help but "reverence" is Amida.

In that way, "reverence" is [part of] the ultimate name of the original vow. Whether it is the name of the Tathāgata or the name of Amida, they are words that prohibit the viewing of Amida as an object. It is not that there is the Amida Buddha to which we attach a name. There is no Amida beyond the name. It is not that the name of the original vow indicates an objective thing. There is no form to Amida itself. However, not only that, at the same time that it is the name of something without form, "reverence" is added. Because it is a name that encompasses "reverence," it is not that a thing without form is [actually] something with form that is static.

The *dharmatā* is something static. Through "reverence," that which has been static becomes dynamic. In other words, when something without form takes forms, it does not simply remain quiescent. Because it has the function of transforming deluded sentient beings and returning them to their origin, it has the significance of "calling."

Amida is something without form; when something without form becomes a name, that which is without form calls to that which has form. No matter how much it may call, that does mean that there is something that is calling. Rather we receive the call at that place where there is no thing that calls. It is the voiceless voice. It is not that, having been called, I exist. Rather I myself take form as the call. I am transformed as the call. It is not that the call exists outside of us and that we listen to it and are moved. I take form as the call.

The name of the original vow does not indicate a thing. It is a name that indicates a relationship. It indicates the relationship of I and Thou, not the existence of something. However, that relationship is not the relationship of one thing to another; it is the relationship between that which has form and that which does not. It indicates the relationship of time and eternity. The relationship is always mutual. It is not one-sided. To be called is to have heard, is to have responded. It is not that there is the call and then, later, one responds.

The call is something that exists only for those who have heard it. It does not exist for those who have not heard it. If we say that it exists for those who have not heard it, that kind of call would be an objective thing. Therefore, the call is at the same time a response to it. The relationship in this case is a mutual relationship. It is the name that indicates a relationship of call and response between that which has form and that which does not. If we express this idea using the unique language of the Chinese people, it would be "the mutuality of receptivity and response" (*kannō dōkō* 感応道交) [between sentient beings and the buddhas]. In today's language it would be a "mutual relationship." When the existing mind [of sentient beings] is receptive, the no mind [of the Buddha] responds. It is not a relationship of one thing to another. It is a relationship of existence and nonexistence. Just as we call the totality [of all things] the "all-encompassing dharma" or the "all-pervading dharma," this too is not an objective thing. Because it prohibits objectification, it is called emptiness. We also may call it absolute nothingness. In that way, that which indicates the mutual relationship of existence and nonexistence is that which we call the name. That which is without form, through the name, takes on a relationship with that which has form.

The name of Amida Buddha is not simply referring to Amida. As I explained earlier, [the problem of] sentient beings is being responded to. Through Namu Amida Butsu, human beings are being responded to in a fundamental way. They are not responded to according to human ideas. This is something much deeper than humans [merely] reflecting on themselves. In other words, humans are responded to as Tathāgatas. But because of that, it is not that humans have become something other than humans. Rather, because of that, humans become humans for the first time. Therefore, Namu Amida Butsu is the means whereby humans are caused to return to their origin. And it is also the term that indicates that return. That which causes the return refers to the words of the original vow, but that which has returned refers to the words of the mind of faith. In the sense that [Namu Amida Butsu] brings about the mind at ease, it is Dharma and it is also the person who gains the mind at ease.

When the Tathāgata becomes the name—that is, when we speak of saying the name—that the word "reciting" is expressly added to the name of the original vow indicates that anyone can do it. It is the way by which anyone, anytime, anywhere can return to his or her origin. The word "to say" symbolizes the fact that anyone can do it. This is not just raising one's voice. It symbolizes the fact that no effort is required. That it does not require our own effort is because it [embodies] the true effort that transcends our effort. That is because it is practice. Through the name, the Tathāgata is practicing.

Our attainment of the wisdom of nondiscrimination, or the attainment of the believing mind, or again the realization of [the stage of] non-retrogression, all exist as practice. The name is practice. That which we call the name is the name that is the practice of sentient beings. It is the name of the Buddha, but the name of the Buddha does not indicate the Buddha; rather, it is that name that is the practice of sentient beings. It is the name that causes the Tathāgata [to reveal itself] as sentient beings; in other words, it causes suchness as non-suchness to return to suchness. It is that kind of practice. To attain the mind of faith or to realize birth [in the Pure Land] is for sentient beings to return to [their original nature], and it is the name that causes that return. In that sense, the name of the Buddha is the name that causes sentient beings to become buddhas; therefore, when we refer to the name of the original vow, it is the Dharma, the Buddha Dharma. The name of the Buddha is the Buddha Dharma. The name of Amida Buddha is the Buddha Dharma. In that sense, Dharma is language that stands in contrast to human beings. To say that it is Dharma is to say that it does not need human beings.

That the Tathāgata was made known in the form of the name expresses the fact that it is the Tathāgata on which we can rely and in which we can attain a mind at ease. That is the name. If that which is without form were only without form, we could not rely on it nor could we be saved by it. When it becomes the name, it is not that the Tathāgata exists in a personified form. It is not thought to be a personified existence; rather it is Dharma. To take refuge in Namu Amida Butsu is to conform to the Dharma. When the name is made into a thing, it becomes a persona; in other words, [in that case] we establish Amida Buddha as an objective absolute or as a personified existence that stands over against us as the other. If we regard Christianity as directed toward the other, then Buddhism is directed to the origin. The Tathāgata is the original nature of sentient beings, not the other [that stands over against] sentient beings. The other has form, but there is no form to original nature. That which does not require the power of the other is Dharma. When there is no Dharma, we have no choice but to set up the other. When there is Dharma, in other words, when there is the name, there is no need to set up an other. This is the reason that it is said that one should rely on the Dharma and not rely on an other.

In summary, what I wanted to say to you is that the name is originally a name, a provisional name. The name is just a name; however it is the form and the dynamic working of that which is not just a name; it is also the practice that causes one to return to it. It is not that we negate provisional names and arrive at the true reality. Provisional names are the true reality. True reality, in the words of the Great Teacher Tanluan, is the *dharmatā*. It is not that the *dharmatā* is manifested by negating means. The means, just as they are, are the *dharmatā*.

Appendix A

The five gates of mindfulness is not an analysis of the nenbutsu, but rather it tells of the history of the nenbutsu from the perspective of the nenbutsu. In the "Chapter on Practice," it says that "the name of the original vow is the established act"; [hence] when we speak of the nenbutsu [we should understand that] it has the meaning of act. That which we call an act is, in fact, practice. Acts and practice are similar things. The nenbutsu may be called either a practice or an act. However, [when we speak of] practice, I think that there is a problem that must be considered in a more focused way. When we regard the nenbutsu as promised in the original vow as an act, the meaning it has of "being developed in five [ways]" [indicates] practice. I think that it was the Treatise that made that meaning clear.

Should we speak of acts, we refer to the three acts in the *Pure Land Treatise* [where] it speaks of the "three acts and the two benefits." These acts are performed at some time, at some place, and by some one. That is, someone, at some time and at some place performs some sort of act.

Appendix B

At that point, mindfulness is divided into five aspects. This is not simply an analysis of the concept of the nenbutsu; rather [it indicates] how, through the nenbutsu or through being mindful of the Tathāgata, the entire history of suchness is formed within one who is mindful. In this sense, the five gates of mindfulness were established.

Notes

1. More specifically, the name of the Tathāgata Amitābha, or Amida.
2. The passage cited here appears near the beginning of the "Chapter on Practice" of the *Kyōgyōshinshō*.
3. This term was used by Shinran's teacher, Hōnen, to signify the special effectiveness of the nenbutsu as indicated in Dharmākara's eighteenth vow.
4. See Appendix A for a translation of the passage omitted here.
5. On "One who has Come from Suchness," see "The Practical Understanding of Buddhism," n. 5.
6. See Appendix B for a translation of the passage omitted here.
7. A basic text of the Mādhyamika, Chūgan 中観 or Emptiness school.

8. The reference is to Zhiyi's (538–97) interpretation of Mādhyamika teachings; Zhiyi was the third partriarch of the Chinese Tiantai school.

9. In this lecture, Yasuda refers frequently to Asaṅga's *Mahayānāsaṃgraha* or, in Japanese, *Shōdaijōron* 摂大乗論.

10. That is, the *Perfection of Wisdom Sutras*, which began to appear around the first century BCE and which mark the rise of Mahāyāna Buddhism.

11. "Mind of faith" translates the Japanese *shinjin*, a key term in Shin Buddhism. In some translations, the Japanese term itself is used. *The Collected Works of Shinran*, published by the Jōdo Shinshū Hongwanji-ha, says of *shinjin*, "It denotes the central religious experience of Shin Buddhism, and literally means man's 'true, real and sincere heart and mind' (*makoto no magokoro*), which is given by Amida Buddha" (CWS 2:206).

12. The expression "phrase One Dharma" renders the Japanese *ippokku* 一法句. *The Collected Works of Shinran* adopts a similar translation (CWS 2:301). Inagaki translates this term as the "One Dharma Principle." In discussing the twenty-nine adornments of Amida's Pure Land, the Tathāgata himself, and his bodhisattvas, Vasubandhu explains that they are part of the phrase One Dharma: "The phrase One Dharma is the purity phrase; the purity phrase is so called because it is the unconditioned *dharmakāya* of True Wisdom." For the original Chinese, see Inagaki 1998, 266. Inagaki's translation of this passage differs from the one provided here; see ibid., 265.

13. The means by which the true nature of reality or the *dharmakāya* expresses or communicates itself.

Combined Glossary

- Amida Sutra (*Amituojing* 阿弥陀経 *Amidakyō*)

The Japanese name for the *Smaller Sukhāvatīvyūhasūtra* in its Chinese translation by Kumārajīva (T No. 366). One of the so-called threefold Pure Land Sutras that form the basis of all forms of Pure Land Buddhism in Japan since Hōnen selected them out of the many that contribute to the belief in Amida Buddha. It expounds a message focusing on the splendor of the Pure Land, how one achieves rebirth in that realm by holding the sacred name of Amida Buddha with focused attention, and how a multitude of buddhas in other realms testified to the reality of Amida's Pure Land.

- anjin 安心

A peaceful and tranquil mind, a mind of firm faith, or a mind in which doubts have been resolved. It often is frequently as a synonym for *shinjin* in Shin Buddhism, but also is used as a general term in East Asian Buddhism as a whole for an enlightened or liberated state of mind.

- Birth/birth in the Pure Land (*ōjō* 往生)

To gain birth in Amida Buddha's Pure Land at death by relying on the power of Amida's vows and practicing the nenbutsu. Traditionally, it was believed that birth in the Pure Land depended on whether one can concentrate one's mind on Amida Buddha and his Pure Land at the moment of death. In contrast, Shinran argues that the moment one gains faith, one is assured of gaining birth in the Pure Land.

- buddha lands (*butsudo* 仏土)

The locale of a buddha; that is, wherever a buddha resides is a buddha land (*buddhakṣetra*). In Mahāyāna Buddhism, buddhas generally are conceived of as eternally present, each in his own land. These lands are accessible by living beings through the process of rebirth, and form an idealized postmortem goal contrasted with this world because a buddha is present to teach and directly assist individuals there reach final liberation. Some are part of *saṃsāra*, such as the Tuṣita heaven where Maitreya resides, some are constructed by bodhisattvas who make vows concerning their creation and signify leaving saṃsāra, some are associated with directions, and generally all have names. In East Asia, buddha-lands were traditionally called "pure lands" as each is purified by a buddha's presence. The so-called Pure Land of Amida Buddha is called Sukhāvatī; it was promised by that buddha as a bodhisattva prior to attaining buddhahood, and is located in the western direction.

- Contemplation Sutra (*Guanjing* 観経 *Kangyō*)

Abbreviated title of *Guanwuliangshoujing* 観無量寿経 *Kanmuryōjukyō*, translated by Kālayaśas (T No. 365). One of the three so-called Pure Land Sutras (see *Amida Sutra*). Against the setting of the "palace tragedy" taking place at that moment when Prince Ajātaśatru murdered his father Bimbisāra to usurp the throne, Śākyamuni preaches to the mother Vaidehī who also is incarcerated and facing death herself. The discourse presents Vaidehī achieving a vision of Amida's Pure Land, a sixteen-step program of visualization meditation, and a categorization of living beings into nine grades of spiritual ability with practices specific for each. The sutra also is known for teaching that a person of the lowest grade, that is, someone who has committed serious crimes, does not understand the teachings, and is unable to concentrate, can still attain rebirth in the Pure Land of Amida by reciting the buddha's name on his or her deathbed.

- defiled land (*edo* 穢土)

Contrasted with the idealized Pure Land, this term represents this world, rife with corruption, pollution, and defilement. It also implies the dimension of reality in which there are concerns over karma (absent in the realm of buddhas) and hence karmic rebirth in *saṃsāra* as well.

- dharmadhātu (*hokkai* 法界)

The phenomenal world when seen as infused with the sacred. Here "dharma" means phenomena, and thus the term may be used to designate the object of human perception, all forms of existence, or the universe as a whole, but always as a sacred presence. Essentially, it is a way of designating reality as truth. Generally understood to represent the perspective of the *Kegon Sutra*, *dharmadhātu* in fact appears in many Mahāyāna sutras.

- Dharmākara (Hōzō 法蔵)

The name of Amida Buddha when he was still a bodhisattva. According to the *Sutra of Immeasurable Life*, Dharmākara set forth his forty-eight vows in the presence of Lokeśvararāja Buddha, promising to create a splendid Pure Land when he attained enlightenment. Having acquired enlightenment after fulfilling his vows, he now resides in his Pure Land in the west called Gokuraku (the Land of Supreme Bliss; Sukhāvatī in Sanskrit).

- dharmakāya (*hosshin* 法身)

Literally, "dharma body," this refers to the truth of buddhahood in its essence. Here "dharma" means truth. There are various conceptions of multiple "bodies" associated with buddhas in the Mahāyāna, the most universal being a contrast between a buddha in a physical body (*rūpakāya*) and a buddha in a dharma body (*dharmakāya*). But there is a wide variety in how *dharmakāya* is used in the scriptures, at times as the essence of a buddha prior to any physical manifestation, at times as the body of teachings, at times as the body of the buddha standing before an assembly and preaching. The Kegon tradition has a fivefold division of *dharmakāya*, for example. In the Shin tradition, there are two aspects or forms of *dharmakāya* based on Tanluan, manifested (*hōben hosshin*) and unmanifested (*hosshō hosshin*).

- eighteenth vow (*jūhachigan* 十八願)

The most important of Dharmākara Bodhisattva's forty-eight vows. This vow promises that anyone who sincerely remains mindful of Amida for at least ten instants in faith and seeks birth in the Pure Land will be born there after they die.

- forty-eight vows (*shijūhachigan* 四十八願)

The forty-eight vows which Dharmākara Bodhisattva made in the presence of Lokeśvararāja Buddha, promising to undertake various practices in order to create a perfect Pure Land. The *Sutra of Immeasurable Life* states that the bodhisattva actually did fulfill his vows and now resides as Amida Buddha in his Pure Land called Gokuraku (the Land of Supreme Bliss; Sukhāvatī in Sanskrit) in the west.

- gakuryō/gakurin 学寮/学林

Seminaries established by Japanese Buddhists schools. A number of such educational institutions were established, especially in the Edo period. *Gakuryō* is the term used by the Higahsi Honganji to refer to its seminary. In the Nishi Honganji, it was called a *gakurin*.

- hō 法 and ki 機

Hō refers to the Buddha's teaching, while *ki* originally refers to the innate potential within sentient beings to respond to the Buddha's teachings. Later, *ki* comes to refer both to the different abilities that sentient beings possess (in this context, the distinction often is made between superior, middling and inferior abilities) and to the sentient beings themselves. In the Pure Land tradition, the terms *hō* and *ki* are used to refer to Amida Buddha and sentient beings. Moreover, the nenbutsu (Namu Amida butsu) is interpreted to refer to the unity of *ki* (namu=sentient beings) and *hō* (Amida butsu=Buddha).

- Honganji 本願寺

One of the many sectarian lineages to emerge after Shinran who took him as their founder. it claims a blood lineage as well as a dharma lineage. Beginning with a mausoleum built at the site of Shinran's grave by his daughter Eshinni, its institutional history as a religious order really begins with with Kakunyo (1270–1351), Shinran's great-grandson. It became the largest and most dominant branch of the Shin tradition under Rennyo (1415–1499). Politically, it had become the most dominant Buddhist sect by the Sengoku period, and was split into two institutions by Tokugawa Ieyasu in the early seventeenth century. Although some splitting has occurred in the postwar period, Honganji remained dominated by the two institutions dating to Ieyasu's time. Today they are known as Jōdo Shinshū Hongwanji-ha and Shinshū Ōtanhi-ha.

- jātaka (*honshō* 本生)

Stories of the previous lives of Śākyamuni Buddha, they illustrate what he did to build up his store of virtue, merit, and good karmic roots that prepared him karmically (morally) to attain buddhahood. The stories themselves are quite imaginative and contain many elements of popular didactic fiction in India.

- kalpa (*kō* 劫)

A long period of time in Indian myth. Reckoned at times as short, medium, and long in Buddhist sutras, the word *kalpa* frequently appears without the actual duration of time being clarified. There are various figurative explanations, however. In one description of a long kalpa, if a forty-square kilometer were filled with mustard seeds and one were removed every one hundred years, a kalpa would be the amount of time it would take to remove all the seeds.

- Kegon (Ch. Huayan 華厳)

The name of a long Mahāyāna sutra as well as a sectarian tradition based on that sutra dating from the seventh century in China. This is one of the most influential intellectual traditions in East Asian Buddhism, and its impact on Chan/Zen thought was particularly strong.

- Kyōgyōshinshō 教行信証 (Teaching, Practice, Faith, and Enlightenment)

Shinran's main work and the fundamental text of Shin Buddhism. The full title is *Ken jōdo shinjitsu kyōgyōshō monrui* 顕浄土真実教行証文類 (Passages Revealing the True Teaching, Practice and Realization of the Pure Land). It consists of six chapters: "Teaching," "Practice," "Faith," "Realization," "True Buddha and Land," and "Transformed Buddha and Land." The majority of the text consists of passages taken from Buddhist sutras and writings of authoritative Buddhist masters, occasionally interspersed by Shinran's own comments.

- Larger Sutra. *See* Sutra of Immeasurable Life

- Latter Dharma.

The benighted age after the Buddha's parinirvāṇa in which it is impossible to practice the Buddhist teachings and attain enlightenment. The notion of the Latter Dharma is part of a deeply pessimistic Buddhist interpretation of history. According to this theory, the time after the Buddha's passing is divided into three periods, the ages of the True Dharma, Counterfeit Dharma and Latter Dharma, in which holds that the spiritual conditions of the world inexorably decline. During the age of the True Dharma, the Buddhist teachings, their practice and the attainment of enlightenment can all be found in the world. However, in the Counterfeit Dharma, although the Buddhist teachings and their practice exist, there is no one who can attain enlightenment. Finally, during the age of the Latter Dharma, the spiritual conditions of the world deteriorates to the point where only the Buddha's teachings remain, and neither the practice of the Buddhist path nor the attainment of enlightenment is possible.

- Meiji Restoration (Meiji Ishin 明治維新)

The Meiji Restoration, which occurred in 1868, toppled the Tokugawa shogunate that had ruled Japan for more than two and a half centuries and created a new government centered on the emperor. The Meiji government pursued a policy of rapid modernization, importing new technologies and knowledge from Western countries in order to create "a rich country and strong military" (*fukoku kyōhei*). As a result, Japan was thoroughly transformed, politically, socially, and economically, within a few decades.

- naikan 内観

Introspection. The practice of contemplating the workings of one's mind. Kiyozawa Manshi employed this practice as a means to investigate and destroy attachment to deluded thoughts that arise in his mind. Kiyozawa sometimes refers to his Seishinshugi as *naikan-shugi* ("introspection-ism").

- nenbutsu 念仏

Literally, to remain mindful of the Buddha. Typically, it is a practice directed toward Amida Buddha as a means of gaining birth in his land at death. There are two types of nenbutsu: the contemplative and recitative. The contemplative nenbutsu refers to the practice of entering *samādhi* (meditative absorption) and visualizing the figure of Amida. The recitative nenbutsu refers to the practice of reciting the phrase "Namu Amida Butsu" (I take refuge in Amida Buddha). The latter became the most widely practiced form of nenbutsu in East Asia.

- nine grades of people (*kubon* 九品)

A doctrine found in the *Contemplation Sutra*, which divides all people who are born in Amida's Pure Land into nine levels. According to the sutra, they can be divided into three ranks, each of which are further subdivided into three grades, resulting in nine grades, from the upper rank of the upper grade to the lowest rank of the lowest grade.

- ōbō-buppō 王法仏法

Literally, "the king's law and the Buddhist law." They refer to the secular laws of the land and the Buddhist teachings. In the medieval period, Japanese Buddhists created an ideology in which these two "laws" were considered dependent on each other, with one reinforcing the other.

- original vow (*hongan* 本願)

The vows, forty-eight in number according to the *Sutra of Immeasurable Life*, which Amida Buddha set forth while he was still a novice bodhisattva called Dharmākara, promising to create an ideal Pure

Land if and when he attained Buddhahood. It is said that Dharmākara fulfilled these vows and now resides as Amida Buddha in his Pure Land in the west.

- other-power *(tariki* 他力)

The salvific power of Amida Buddha. In Pure Land discourse, it is declared possible to attain birth in the Pure Land by entrusting oneself to other-power. Other-power is contrasted to self-power *(jiriki)*; people who rely on self-power seek to gain enlightenment by relying on one's own abilities and power without relying on the salvific power of a Buddha like Amida.

- pure land 浄土

The realm of a buddha. In Pure Land, it refers specifically to the Pure Land of Amida Buddha called Sukhāvatī (Japanese: Gokuraku), or the Realm of Supreme Bliss. Since Amida's Pure Land provides an ideal environment for practicing the Buddhist path, people who are born there can attain complete Buddhahood quickly and effortlessly. In the *Kyōgyōshinshō*, Shinran describes the Pure Land as a realm of infinite light and equates it with nirvāṇa itself.

- Pure Land Treatise (*Jōdoron* 浄土論)

A short text on the Pure Land attributed to the Yogācāra philosopher Vasubandhu (fifth century). The first half of the text is written in verse, while the second half consists of Vasubandhu's own comments on the verses in prose. It describes Amida's Pure Land in terms of twenty-nine kinds of adornments. Note that there is another treatise by Jiacai with the same name.

- samādhi *(sanmai* 三昧)

The original Buddhist usage was "concentration" and thus is a frequently used term in pre-Mahāyāna literature for meditation in general. But in most Mahāyāna contexts *samādhi* designates unusually deep states of meditative trance where religious experience often occurs, and many *samādhi* states are described in some detail and given names; the names of some sutras are nothing more than the names of *samādhis*, at times reflecting the samādhi of Śākyamuni experienced just prior to giving the discourse. The attainment of samādhi is considered crucial to higher states of achievement on the path in all Mahāyāna traditions, and one of the ways in which Hōnen justified nenbutsu practice was that it produced *samādhi* for the devoted practitioner.

- Seishinkai 精神界

A journal published by the Kōkōdō, a Buddhist community that gathered around Kiyozawa Manshi. It was begun in 1901 and continued until 1919. Kiyozawa published numerous essays in this journal to describe and spread his philosophy of Seishinshugi. It was one of the most widely read religious journals of the Meiji period.

- Seishinshugi 精神主義

Kiyozawa Manshi's religious philosophy, which he popularized through his essays in the journal *Seishinkai* (*Spiritual World*). In the first issue of *Seishinkai*, Kiyozawa published an essay entitled "Seishinshugi," setting for the general outline of his Seishinshugi philosophy. The Seishinshugi philosophy proved extremely important in the subsequent development of Shin Buddhist thought, influencing virtually all of the major figures of the denomination, including Soga Ryōjin, Kaneko Daiei, and Yasuda Rijin.

- self-power (*jiriki* 自力)

Contrasted with the power outside the self in the term other-power (*tariki*), self-power refers to the belief or presumption that religious attainment is solely the result of one's own efforts without any intervention by bodhisattvas or buddhas.

- selected vow (*senjaku hongan* 選択本願)

This is Hōnen's term for the *hongan* in the *Sutra of Immeasurable Life*. It implies that there is a special authority in the practice of nenbutsu because it was chosen or selected by Amida Buddha for those seeking birth in his Pure Land. Also translated as "chosen vow."

- Seven patriarchs (*shichiso* 七祖)

Seven monks whom Shinran perceived as being the authoritative masters of the Pure Land teachings. They are Nāgārjuna (c. 150–250) and Vasubandhu (c. 400–480) of India, Tanluan (476–542), Daochuo (562–645) and Shandao (613–681) of China, and Genshin (942–1017), and Hōnen (1133–1212) of Japan.

- shinjin 信心

The spiritual attainment of entrusting oneself to the original vows of Amida Buddha. In Shin Buddhism, this entrusting is considered to be, not something that one acquires through one's diligence and practice, but something turned over to oneself from Amida. Once one attains unwavering *shinjin*, one is assured of attaining birth in the Pure Land.

- Shinran 親鸞 (1173–1262)

The founder of Jōdo Shinshu school, popularly known as Shin Buddhism. He became novice at the age of nine and studied for twenty years at Enryakuji on Mt. Hiei, the head temple of the Tendai school. However, at the age of twenty-nine, he joined Hōnen's (1133–1212) nembutsu community in the city of Kyoto. When Hōnen's movement was outlawed in 1207, Shinran was exiled to Echigo (modern Niigata prefecture). After being pardoned, he moved to the Kanto, where he proselytized the nenbutsu teaching, only returning to Kyoto at the end of his life. Shinran wrote many works, among which the *Kyōgyōshinshō* is the most well-studied.

- Shōshinge 正信偈 (Hymn of True Faith)

Full title, Shōshin nenbutsuge 正信念仏偈 (Hymn of True Faith and the Nembutsu). A hymn of 120 lines, found at the end of the Chapter on Practice of Shinran's *Kyōgyōshinshō*. Shinran states that he composed the hymn in order to express his gratitude to Amida Buddha. The first half of the hymn consists of verses in praise of the teaching of liberation through the nenbutsu as found in the *Sutra of Immeasurable Life*, while the second half recounts the teachings of the seven patriarchs of the Pure Land tradition.

- Suchness

Tathatā in Sanskrit and *shinnyo* 真如 in Japanese. The nature of reality or the true state of things. Mahāyāna Buddhism holds that all things are empty, and from this perspective, maintain that all things are one. Suchness refers to this absolute oneness.

- shūgaku 宗学

The tradition of sectarian scholarship in Japan that was established in the seminaries (*gakuryō/gakurin*) of the major Buddhist schools during the Edo period. When Japan entered the tumultuous Meiji period after more than two hundred years of *shūgaku,* the momentum of the way in which this particular form of education defined the doctrinal, linguistic, and artistic traditions for each sect for institutional Buddhism, as well as the authoritative role it played in giving meaning to its rituals and forms of practice proved extremely persuasive. As a result, *shūgaku* continued through the modern period and remains influential today.

- Sutra of Immeasurable Life (*Wuliangshoujing* 無量寿経 *Muryōjukyō*)

The Chinese translation of the *Larger Sukhāvatīvyuha Sūtra*, attributed to Saṃghavarman. Of the five extant Chinese translations of the *Larger Sukhāvatīvyuha Sūtra*, this is the most popular in East Asia. Along with the *Contemplation Sutra* and the *Amida Sutra*, the *Sutra of Immeasurable Life* is counted in Japan as one of the so-called three Pure Land sutras, the central texts of the Pure Land tradition. It describes how Dharmākara bodhisattva set forth his forty-eight vows to create an ideal Pure Land, and how, after eons of practices, succeeded in creating such a land.

- Takakura Gakuryō 高倉学寮

A seminary of the Higashi Honganji, founded in 1665. Its name derives from its location at the corner of Takakura and Uodana streets in Kyoto, a few blocks from the Higashi Honganji. It is the precursor of the present Ōtani University.

- Tannishō 歎異抄 (*Tract Lamenting Differences*)

A short work by Shinran's disciple Yuien (1222–1289), written to counter various views diverging from Shinran's teaching that had become prevalent after the latter's death. The first part consists of Shinran's teachings taken down by Yuien, whereas the second part is taken up with criticism of various interpretations of Pure Land teachings that diverged from Shinran's position.

- tathāgata

One of the appellations of the Buddha, meaning one who has come (*āgata*) from Suchness (*tathā*). This is used essentially as a synonym for buddha, and often is the way the Buddha refers to himself in sutra discourses.

- two truths theory/doctrine (shinzoku nitaisetsu 真俗二諦説)

The two truths refer to the absolute truth (*paramārtha-satya*) and conventional truth (*samvṛti-satya*). The former refers to the ultimate truth about existence, namely that all things are empty, while the latter refers to the world as conventionally experienced by ordinary people. In modern Shin Buddhist discourse, these two truths were reinterpreted to indicate the two goals that a Shin Buddhist believer should strive to achieve: the goal of birth in the Pure Land, equated with the absolute truth, and adherence to secular morality, equated with the worldly truth.

- Vasubandhu 世親

There were at least two people in Indian Buddhism with this name, the most famous being the author of the influential treatise known as the *Abhidharmakośa,* and some believe this to be the same person also wrote the Yogācāra essays called *Triṃśīkā* and *Viṃśatikā*, and his dates are guessed at 400–480. In the Pure Land tradition in East Asia, the most authoritative śāstra (treatise) to come out of India is a commentary on the *Sutra of Immeasurable Life* by a Vasubandhu, known as the *Jingtu lun* or the *Wangsheng lun*. In East Asian Buddhism, the Abhidharma, Yogācāra, and Pure Land Vasubandhus were all accepted without question as the same person, which raised interesting doctrinal questions. But today many scholars question whether the Jingtu lun Vasubandhu was the same person.

- Yogācāra ('consciousness only' 唯識)

A school of Mahāyāna Buddhism known for its focus on the operations of consciousness, similar but critical approach to Buddhist doctrine as seen in the analytic tradition of Abhidharma literature, and theories of "consciousness only" (*yuishiki* 唯識) in analyzing how we process and make sense of sensory experience.

Bibliography

Abe, Masao. 1997. *Zen and Comparative Studies*. Honolulu: University of Hawai'i Press.
Akamatsu Tesshin 赤松徹真. 1977. "Kindai Nihon shisōshi ni okeru seishinshugi no isō: Kiyozawa Manshi no shinkō to sono kansei 近代日本の思想史における精神主義の位相—清沢満之の信仰とその陥穽." In *Bukkyō shigaku ronshū* 仏教史学論集, edited by Futaba hakase kanreki kinen-kai 二葉博士還暦記念会, 519–22. Kyoto: Nagata bunshōdō.
Akamatsu Toshihide 赤松俊秀 and Kasahara Kazuo 笠原一男, eds. 1963. *Shinshūshi gaisetsu* 真宗史概説. Kyoto: Heirakuji shoten.
Akegarasu Haya 暁烏敏. 1909. *Kiyozawa sensei no shinkō* 清沢先生の信仰. Tokyo: Mugasanbō.
———. 1911. *Tannishō kōwa* 歎異抄講話. Tokyo: Mugasanbō.
———. 1979. *Akegarasu Haya zenshū* 暁烏敏全集. 27 vols. Mattō: Ryōfū gakusha.
Andō Shuichi 安藤州一, ed. 1904. *Kiyozawa sensei shinkō zadan* 清沢先生信仰座談. Tokyo: Mugasanbō.
Andō Fumio 安藤文雄, Yasutomi Shin'ya 安冨信哉, Ichiraku Makoto 一楽真, Kaku Takeshi 加来雄之 and Ōshiro Kuniyoshi 大城邦義. 1983. "Yasuda Rijin sensei ni nani o manabuka 安田理深先生に何を学ぶか." *Shinran kyōgaku* 親鸞教学 42:61–85.
Andreasen, Esben. 1998. *Popular Buddhism in Japan: Shin Buddhist Religion and Culture*. Richmond: Japan Library.
Bandō, Shōjun. 1969. "Soteriology in Shin Buddhism and Its Modern Significance." *Japanese Religions* 6-1:24–32.
Bandō Shōjun 坂東性純, Itō Emyō 伊東慧明 and Hataya Akira 幡谷明. 1993. *Jōdo Bukkyō no shisō 15: Suzuki Daisetsu, Soga Ryōjin, Kaneko Daiei* 浄土仏教の思想15 鈴木大拙 曽我量深 金子大栄. Tokyo: Kōdansha.
Bandō, Shōjun, and Harold Stewart, trs. 1980. "*Tannishō*: Passages Deploring Deviations of Faith." *The Eastern Buddhist* 13-1:57–78.
Bellah, Robert. 1957. *Tokugawa Religion*. Glencoe, Illinois: Free Press.
Bloom, Alfred. 2003. "Kiyozawa Manshi and the Revitalization of Buddhism." *The Eastern Buddhist* 35-1/2:1–5.
Blum, Mark L. 1988. "Kiyozawa Manshi and the Meaning of Buddhist Ethics." *The Eastern Buddhist* 21-1: 61–81.

———, tr. 1989. "The Relationship between Religious Morality and Common Morality." *The Eastern Buddhist* 22-1:96–110.

———. 2000. *The Origins and Development of Pure Land Buddhism*. Oxford: Oxford University Press.

———. 2003. "Truth in Need: Kiyozawa Manshi and Søren Kierkegaard." *The Eastern Buddhist* 35-1/2: 57–101.

———. 2007. "Biography as Scripture: Ōjōden in India, China, and Japan." *Japanese Journal of Religious Studies* 34-2: 329–50.

Blum, Mark L., and Shin'ya Yasutomi, eds. 2006. *Rennyo and the Roots of Modern Japanese Buddhism*. Oxford: Oxford University Press.

Chan, Wing-tsit. 1963. *A Source Book in Chinese Philosophy*. Princeton: Princeton University Press.

The Collected Works of Shinran. 1997. 2 vols. Kyoto: Jōdo Shinshū Hongwanji-ha.

Cohen, Hermann. 1914. *Logik der reinen Erkenntniss*. Berlin: Bruno Cassirer.

———. 1921. *Kōen junsui ninshiki ronrigaku* コーエン純粋認識の論理学. Translated by Fujioka Zōroku 藤岡蔵六. Tokyo: Iwanami shoten.

Cook, Francis H., tr. 1999. *Three Texts on Consciousness Only*. Berkeley: Numata Center for Buddhist Translation and Research.

Cooke, Gerald. 1978. "The Struggle for Reform in Ōtani Shin Buddhism." *Japanese Religions* 10-2: 16–41.

Dobbins, James. 2006. "The Origins and Complicated Development of Shin Buddhism as an Area in Religious Studies." *The Pure Land* 22:1–27.

Dōbō daigaku Bukkyō gakkai 同朋大学仏教学会, ed. 2002. *Shinshū no kyōka to jissen* 真宗の教化と実践. Kyoto: Hōzōkan.

Earhart, Byron. 1997. *Religion in the Japanese Experience: Sources and Interpretations*, 2nd ed. Belmont, Albany: Wadsworth Publishing Company.

Fujiwara Masatoshi 藤原正寿. 2004. "Naikan no Butsudō: Seishinshugi no gendaiteki igi 内観の仏道—精神主義の現代的意義." *Gendai to Shinran* 現代と親鸞6:37–52.

Fujinaga Seitetsu 藤永清徹. 1976. "Shinzoku nitairon 真俗二諦論." *Shūgakuin ronshū* 宗学院論輯26:1–43.

Fujita Masakatsu 藤田正勝, ed. 1997. *Nihon kindai shisō o manabu hito no tameni* 日本近代思想を学ぶ人のために. Kyoto: Sekai shisōsha.

———. 2003. "Kiyozawa Manshi and Nishida Kitarō." *The Eastern Buddhist* 35-1/2:42–56.

———. 2004. "Nihon ni okeru seiyō tetsugaku no juyō to Kiyozawa Manshi 日本における西洋哲学の受容と清沢満之." *Shinran kyōgaku* 親鸞教学 82/83:114–30.

———. 2004. "Nihon ni okeru seiyō tetsugaku no juyō: Kiyozawa Manshi to Ōnishi Hajime 日本における西洋哲学の受容—清沢満之と大西祝." *Gendai to Shinran* 現代と親鸞 6:150–91.

Fujita Masakatsu 藤田正勝 and Yasutomi Shin'ya 安冨信哉, eds. 2002. *Kiyozawa Manshi: Sono hito to shisō* 清沢満之—その人と思想. Kyoto: Hōzōkan.

Fukazawa Sukeo 深沢助雄. 1991. "Tetsugakushika to shite no Kiyozawa Manshi sensei 哲学史家としての清沢満之先生." *Shinran kyōgaku* 親鸞教学 58:92–130.

Fukuda Masaharu 福田正治 and Kiyozawa Manshi shi seitan hyakunen kinenkai 清沢満之師生誕百年記念会, eds. 1963. *Kiyozawa Manshi no tetsugaku to shinkō* 清沢満之の哲学と信仰. Nagoya: Reimei shobō.

Fukuma Kōchō 福間光超. 1986. "Kinsei kōki Shinshū no sezoku ronri ni tsuite: 'okite' kara 'kyōgi' e 近世後期真宗の世俗論理について—「掟」から「教義」へ." *Ryūkoku daigaku ronshū* 龍谷大学論集 429:46–59.

Fukushima Eiju 福島栄寿. 2003. *Seishin shugi no gudōsha tachi: Kiyozawa Manshi to Akegarasu Haya* 精神主義の求道者達—清沢満之と暁烏敏. Kyoto: Kōka joshi daigaku Shinshū bunka kenkyūsho.

———. 2003. *Shisōshi to shite no "seishin shugi"* 思想史としての「精神主義」. Kyoto: Hōzōkan.

Fukushima Hirotaka 福嶋寬隆. 1986. " 'Kindai Bukkyo' no rekishi-teki naijitsu: 'Seishinshugi' ni tsuite 「近代仏教」の歴史的内実—「精神主義」について." In *Nihon Bukkyōshi ronsō* 日本仏教史論叢, edited by Futaba Kenkō hakase koki kinen ronshū kankōkai 二葉憲香博士古希記念論集刊行会, 725–43. Kyoto: Nagata bunshōdō.

Fukushima Hirotaka 福嶋寬隆 and Akamatsu Tesshin 赤松徹真, eds. 1991. *Shiryō Kiyozawa Manshi* 資料清沢満之. 3 vols. Nagoya: Dōbōsha.

Fukushima Kazuto 福嶌和人. 1996. "Shinshū kyōgakusha no naka no shizenkan o yomu: *Tannishō chōki* 真宗教学者の中の自然観を読む—歎異抄聴記." *Shinshū kyōgaku kenkyū* 真宗教学研究 18:68–81.

Futaba Kenkō 二葉憲香, ed. 1979. *Kokka to Bukkyō* 国家と仏教. 2 vols. Kyoto: Nagata bunshōdō.

Futaba Hakase Kanreki Kinenkai 二葉博士還暦記念会, ed. 1977. *Bukkyō shigaku ronshū* 仏教史学論集. Kyoto: Nagata bunshōdō.

Gómez, Luis O., tr. 1996. *The Land of Bliss: The Paradise of the Buddha of Measureless Light*. Honolulu and Kyoto: University of Hawai'i Press and Higashi Honganji Shinshū Ōtani-ha.

Hanada Shuho 花田衆甫. 1902. "Hai-Seishinshugi: *Seishinshugi* o nanjite Kōkōdō shoshi no kotae o nozomu 排精神主義『精神主義』を難じて浩々洞諸氏の答を望む." *Shin Bukkyō* 新仏教 3-2:75–78.

Harootunian, Harry. 1988. *Things Seen and Unseen: Discourse and Ideology in Tokugawa Nativism*. Chicago: University of Chicago Press.

Hase, Shōtō. 2008. "In Memory of Jan Van Bragt." *The Eastern Buddhist*, 39-1:135–38.

Hashida Takamitsu 橋田尊光. 2003. "Kiyozawa Manshi to Shinshū Ōtani-ha kyōdan: Shirakawa-tō shūmon kaikaku undō o megutte 清沢満之と真宗大谷派教団—白川党宗門改革運動をめぐって." *Shinran kyōgaku* 親鸞教学 80/81:62–75.

Hashimoto Mineo 橋本峰雄, ed. 1970. *Kiyozawa Manshi, Suzuki Daisetz* 清沢満之・鈴木大拙. Tokyo: Chūō kōronsha.

———. 2003. "Two Models of Modernization of Japanese Buddhism: Kiyozawa Manshi and D. T. Suzuki." *The Eastern Buddhist* 35-1/2:6–41.

Hataya Akira 幡谷明. 1977. "Jikken no kyōgaku: Kindai Shinshū kyōgaku ni tsuite no oboegaki 実験の教学—近代真宗教学についての覚書." *Shinran kyōgaku* 親鸞教学 31:18–31.

Hataya Akira 幡谷明 and Tatsutani Akio 龍渓章雄. 1993. "Kaneko Daiei: Monshi no kyōgakusha 金子大栄—聞思の教学者." In *Jōdo Bukkyō no shisō 15: Suzuki Daisetsu, Soga Ryōjin, Kaneko Daiei* 浄土仏教の思想15 鈴木大拙 曽我量深 金子大栄, edited by Bandō Shōjun 坂東性純, Itō Emyō 伊東慧明 and Hataya Akira 幡谷明. 263–388. Tokyo: Kōdansha.

Higuchi Shōshin 樋口章信. 1998. "R. H. Lotze to Kiyozawa Manshi: *Metaphysik* to *Junsei Tetsugaku* o hikaku shite R. H. Lotzeと清沢満之—*Metaphysik*『純正哲学』を比較して." *Ōtani daigaku kenkyū nenpō* 大谷大学研究年報 50:53–101.

———. 1995. "Amerika ni watatta Kiyozawa Manshi no seishin: Noguchi Zenshirō sanka no 1893 Chicago World Parliament of Religion o tōshite アメリカに渡った清沢満之の精神—野口善四郎参加の1893 Chicago World Parliament of Religionを通して." *Ōtani gakuhō* 大谷学報 75-2:13–27.

———. 1992. "Kiyozawa Manshi no 'shinnen' ni tsuite 清沢満之の「信念」について." *Shinran kyōgaku* 親鸞教学 59:67–82.

———. 1995. "Kiyozawa Manshi no bunka, bunmei kan 清沢満之の文化・文明観." *Shinran kyōgaku* 親鸞教学 65:33–49.

———. 1999. "Henshō suru shinshō no kanzatsu: Kiyozawa Manshi ni okeru 'ōyō shinrigaku' kaikō no imi 変象する心性の観察—清沢満之における「応用心理学」開講の意味." *Shinran kyōgaku* 親鸞教学 73:17–30.

Hino Kenryū 日野賢隆, ed. 1987. *Kindai Shinshūshi no kenkyū* 近代真宗史の研究. Kyoto: Nagata bunshōdō.

Hirose Takashi 廣瀬杲. 1963–64. "Waga shinnen no naikei (1, 2) 我が信念の内景（一・二）." *Shinran kyōgaku* 親鸞教学 3:39–47; 4:45–57.

———. 1977. "*Kōrinshō* o haidoku shite『光輪鈔』を拝読して." *Shinran kyōgaku* 親鸞教学 30:27–60.

———. 1983. "Shinshūgaku to wa nanika: Kaneko Daiei sensei no gakuon o shasu 真宗学とは何か—金子大栄先生の学恩を謝す." *Shinran kyōgaku* 親鸞教学 42:111–38.

Hisaki Yukio 久木幸男. 1993. "Muichibutsu no kyōikusha: Kiyozawa Manshi no kyōiku ron 無一物の教育者—清沢満之の教育論." *Shinran kyōgaku* 親鸞教学 61:72–94.

———. 1995. *Kenshō Kiyozawa Manshi hihan* 検証清沢満之批判. Kyoto: Hōzōkan.

Honda Hiroyuki 本多弘之. 1978. "Kindai Shinshū kyōgaku no konpon kanshin 近代真宗教学の根本関心." *Ōtani gakuhō* 大谷学報 58-2:15–26.

———. 1983. "Naikan no daijōbu 内観の大丈夫." *Shinran kyōgaku* 親鸞教学 42:38–52.

———. 1988. *Shinran kyōgaku: Soga Ryōjin kara Yasuda Rijin e* 親鸞教学—曽我量深から安田理深へ. Kyoto: Hōzōkan.

———. 1992. *Shinran no kōmyaku: Kiyozawa Manshi* 親鸞の鉱脈—清沢満之. Shikaidō: Sōkōsha.

———. 1993. *Shinran no shinnen to shisō ni ikiru: Waga shi Yasuda Rijin no michi* 親鸞の信念と思想に生きる—わが師安田理深の道. Shikaidō: Sōkōsha.

———. 1995. *Kindai Shinran kyōgakuron* 近代親鸞教学論. Shikaidō: Sōkōsha.

———. 2002. "Shinran e no kaiki to Shinran kara no shuppatsu 親鸞への回帰と親鸞からの出発." *Shinshū kyōgaku kenkyū* 真宗教学研究 23:23–41.

———. 2004. "Shinran kyōgaku no hōin: Manshi no shinkō kadai no tenkai 親鸞教学の法印—満之の信仰課題の展開." *Gendai to Shinran* 現代と親鸞 6:2–17.
Honda, Patricia A. 1990. "Kiyozawa Manshi and the Revitalization of Shin Buddhism." *The Pure Land* 7:80–91.
Honda Shizuyoshi 本多静芳. 1991. "Shinzoku nitai kanken (sono 2): Shinzoku nitai to Kiyozawa Manshi no 'Shūkyōteki dōtoku (zokutai) to futsū dōtoku to no kōshō' 真俗二諦管見（その2）—真俗二諦と清沢満之の「宗教的道徳（俗諦）と普通道徳との交渉." *Musashino joshi daigaku Bukkyō bunka kenkyūsho kiyō* 武蔵野女子大学仏教文化研究所紀要 9:61–71
Hosokawa Gyōshin 細川行信. 1965. "Meiji-ki ni okeru Shinshū kyōgakushi no sobyō 明治期における真宗教学史の素描." *Shinran kyōgaku* 親鸞教学 7:47–62.
Hōzōkan 法蔵館, ed. 1986. *Kindai no shūkyō undō:* Seishinkai *no kokoromi* 近代の宗教運動—『精神界』の試み. Kyoto: Hōzōkan.
Hurvitz, Leon, tr. 1976. *Scripture of the Lotus Blossom of the Fine Dharma*. New York: Columbia University Press.
Ikeda Gyōshin 池田行信. 1997. *Shinshū kyōdan no shisō to kōdō* 真宗教団の思想と行動. Kyoto: Hōzōkan.
Ikeda Yūtai 池田勇諦. 2003. "Shinshū kyō 'gaku'" 真宗教「学」." In *Bukkyō kara Shinshū e: Uryūzu Ryūshin hakase taishoku kinen ronshū* 仏教から真宗へ—瓜生津隆真博士退職記念論集, edited by Uryūzu Ryūshin sensei taishoku kinen ronshū kankōkai 瓜生津隆真先生退職記念論集刊行会, 209–221. Kyoto: Nagata bunshōdō.
Imadate Tosui 今立吐酔, tr. 1886. *Bukkyō mondō* 仏教問答. Tokyo: Bussho shuppankai.
Imamura Hitoshi 今村仁司. 2002. "Kiyozawa Manshi to shūkyō tetsugaku e no michi 清沢満之と宗教哲学への道." *Shisō* 思想 943:26–45.
———. 2003a. *Kiyozawa Manshi no shisō* 清沢満之の思想. Kyoto: Jinbun shoin.
———. 2003b. "Kiyozawa Manshi ni okeru engi no gainen 清沢満之における縁起の概念." *Shinran kyōgaku* 親鸞教学 80/81:46–61.
———. 2004a. *Kiyozawa Manshi to tetsugaku* 清沢満之と哲学. Tokyo: Iwanami shoten.
———. 2004b. "Kiyozawa Manshi ni okeru *Shūkyō tetsugaku gaikotsu* no shisōteki igi 清沢満之における『宗教哲学骸骨』の思想的意義." *Gendai to Shinran* 現代と親鸞 6:53–100.
Imamura Hitoshi 今村仁司, Takeuchi Seiichi 竹内整一 and Honda Hiroyuki 本多弘之. 2004. "Shinkō to risei: Kiyozawa Manshi wa gendai ni nani o katari uruka 信仰と理性—清沢満之は現代に何を語りうるか." *Gendai to Shinran* 現代と親鸞 6:192–244.
Inaba Masamaru 稲葉昌丸. 1928. *Rennyo Shōnin gyōjitsu* 蓮如上人行実. Kyoto: Ōtani daigaku shuppanbu.
———. 1937. *Rennyo Shōnin ibun* 蓮如上人遺文. Kyoto: Hōzōkan.
Inaba Shūken 稲葉秀賢. 1963. "Kiyozawa sensei no shinzoku nitai ron 清沢先生の真俗二諦論." *Shinran kyōgaku* 親鸞教学 3:14–25.
Inagaki, Hisao, tr. 1994. *The Three Pure Land Sutras: A Study and Translation*. Kyoto: Nagata bunshōdō.

———, tr. 1998. *T'an-luan's Commentary on Vasubandhu's Discourse on the Pure Land*. Kyoto: Nagata bunshōdō.

Inoue Tetsujirō 井上哲次郎. 2003. *Inoue Tetsujirō shū* 井上哲次郎集. 9 vols. Edited by Shimazono Susumu 島薗進 and Isomae Jun'ichi 磯前順一. Tokyo: Kuresu shuppan.

Ishida Mizumaro 石田瑞麿. 1984. *Nihon Bukkyōshi* 日本仏教史. Tokyo: Iwanami shoten.

Ishida Yoshikazu 石田慶和. 1990. "Shinran rikai no suii ni tsuite 親鸞理解の推移について," *Shinshūgaku* 真宗学 82:46–70.

Itō Emyō 伊東慧明. 1993. "Soga Ryōjin: Shinchi no shizenjin 曽我量深—真智の自然人." In *Jōdo Bukkyō no shisō 15: Suzuki Daisetsu, Soga Ryōjin, Kaneko Daiei* 浄土仏教の思想15 鈴木大拙 曽我量深 金子大栄, by Bandō Shōjun 坂東性純, Itō Emyō 伊東慧明 and Hataya Akira 幡谷明, 127–260. Tokyo: Kōdansha.

———. 1994. "Hōzō bosatsu: Soga Ryōjin sensei no shōgai o tsuranuku mono 法蔵菩薩—曽我量深先生の生涯を貫くもの." *Shinran kyōgaku* 親鸞教学 64:76–93.

Jaffe, Richard M. 2001. *Neither Monk nor Layman: Clerical Marriage in Modern Japanese Buddhism*. Princeton: Princeton University Press.

Jodoshū zensho kankōkai 浄土宗全書刊行会, ed. 1906. *Jōdoshū zensho* 浄土宗全書. 23 vols. Tokyo: Kaji Hōjun.

Johnston, Gilbert L. 1966. "Kiyozawa Manshi: A Shinshu Buddhist View of Stoic Self Reliance." *Japanese Religions* 4-4:31–44.

———. 1991. "Morality Versus Religion in Late Meiji Society." *Japanese Religions* 16-4:32–48.

Kaku Takeshi 加来雄之. 1991a. "Shinshū kindai kyōgaku ni okeru yuishikigaku kenkyū: Soga Ryōjin/Yasuda Rijin no kyōgaku no igi 真宗近代教学における唯識学研究—曽我量深/安田理深の教学の意義." *Shinshū sōgō kenkyūsho kenkyūsho kiyō* 真宗総合研究所研究所紀要 9:69–89.

———. 1991b. "Naikan no keifu 内観の系譜." *Shinran kyōgaku* 親鸞教学 58:19–33.

———. 1998a. "Shinshū no daini no saikō: Soga Ryōjin no Rennyo kan 真宗の第二の再興—曽我量深の蓮如観." In *Rennyo no sekai* 蓮如の世界, edited by Ōtani daigaku Shinshū sōgō kenkyūsho 大谷大学真宗総合研究所, 242–272. Kyoto: Bun'eidō.

———. 1998b. "Shūkyōteki jinkaku no tankyū: Soga Ryōjin ni okeru Hōzō bosatsuron 宗教的人格の探究—曽我量深における法蔵菩薩論." *Shinran kyōgaku* 親鸞教学 72:52–75.

———. 2004. "Kiyozawa Manshi ni okeru shūkyō gensetsu no toinaoshi 清沢満之における宗教言説の問い直し." *Shinran kyōgaku* 親鸞教学 82/83:19–49.

———. 2006. "Rennyo's Position in Modern Shin Buddhist Studies: Soga Ryojin's Reinterpretation." In *Rennyo and the Roots of Modern Japanese Buddhism*, edited by Mark L. Blum and Shin'ya Yasutomi, 150–63. Oxford: Oxford University Press.

Kamei Kō 亀井鑛. 2001. *Chichi to musume no Kiyozawa Manshi* 父と娘の清沢満之. Tokyo: Daihōrinkaku.

Kanbe Kazumaro 神戸和麿. 1991. "Shinshū no sanga o motomete 真宗の僧伽を求めて." *Shinran kyōgaku* 親鸞教学 57:77–114.

———. 1989. "Seishin shugi no teishō 精神主義の提唱." In *Shinran ni deatta hitobito* 1 親鸞に出遇った人びと1, 39–47. Kyoto: Dōbōsha.

———. 1992. "Jōdo no sanga: Kenja no shin o kikite 浄土の僧伽—賢者の信を聞きて." *Shinran kyōgaku* 親鸞教学 60:1–22.

———. 2000. *Kiyozawa Manshi no sei to shi* 清沢満之の生と死. Kyoto: Hōzōkan.

———. 2003. "Kiyozawa Manshi no myōgōron 清沢満之の名号論." *Shinran kyōgaku* 親鸞教学 80/81:1–30.

Kaneko Daiei 金子大栄. 1922a. "Shinshūgaku no san mondai 真宗学の三問題." *Kenshin* 見真 1:18–40. Reprinted in KDC 3:11–22.

———. 1922b. "Kyōbō no honshitsu 教法の本質." *Kenshin* 見真 2:17–34. Reprinted in KDC 3:23–33.

———. 1922c. "Honganron: Ware nashi, ware ari, ware to naran 本願論—我なし、我あり、我とならん." *Kenshin* 見真 4:17–31. Reprinted in KDC 3:43–51.

———. 1922d. *Shukyōteki risei* 宗教的理性. Kyoto: Chūgai shuppan.

———. 1925. *Shinrankyō no kenkyū* 親鸞教の研究. Tokyo: Ōmura shoten.

———. 1927. *Jōdo no kannen* 浄土の観念. Kyoto: Bun'eidō.

———. 1943. *Kōkoku to Bukkyō* 皇国と仏教. Kyoto: Ōtani shuppan kyōkai.

———. 1944. "Kōkoku Bukkyōgaku josetsu 皇国仏教学序説." *Ōtani daigaku kenkyū nenpō* 大谷大学研究年報 3:1–58.

———. 1955–1963. *Kaneko Daiei senshū* 金子大栄選集. 23 vols. Tokyo: Zaike Bukkyō kyōkai.

———. 1965. "The Meaning of Salvation in the Doctrine of Pure Land Buddhism." *The Eastern Buddhist* 1-1:48–63.

———. 1966. *Shinshūgaku josetsu* 真宗学序説. Reprint. Kyoto: Bun'eidō.

———. 1971–1977. *Kaneko Daiei kōwashū* 金子大栄講話集. 5 vols. Edited by Nishimura Akira 西村明. Kyoto: Hōzōkan.

———. 1972–1974. *Kaneko Daiei zuisōshū* 金子大栄随想集. 10 vols. Kyoto: Yūkonsha.

———. 1977. "Kaneko Daiei sensei ryakureki, chosaku mokuroku 金子大栄先生略歴・著作目録." *Shinran kyōgaku* 30:142–150.

Kashiwahara Yūsen 柏原祐泉. 1958. "Myōkōninteki shinkō no shisōshiteki keifu: Akunin shōki no jikaku no rekishi 妙好人的信仰の思想史的系譜—「悪人正機」の自覚の歴史." *Ōtani gakuhō* 大谷学報 38-1:1–18.

———. 1967. "Kindai ni okeru kyōdan ron no yōtai 近代における教団論の様態." *Shinran kyōgaku* 親鸞教学 11:74–88.

———, ed. 1989. *Shinran taikei, rekishi hen (dai 10 kan) kindai no Shinshū* 親鸞大系、歴史篇(第10巻)近代の真宗. Kyoto: Hōzōkan.

———. 1995–2000. *Shinshūshi Bukkyōshi no kenkyū* 真宗史仏教史の研究. 3 vols. Kyoto: Heirakuji shoten.

Katō Chiken 加藤智見. 1968. "Kiyozawa Manshi ni kansuru ichi kōsatsu 清沢満之に関する一考察." *Philosophia* フィロソフィア 53:223–38.

———. 1990. *Ikani shite 'shin' o eruka: Uchimura Kanzō to Kiyozawa Manshi* いかにして「信」を得るか—内村鑑三と清沢満之. Kyoto: Hōzōkan.

Katō Hisatake 加藤尚武, ed. 2003. *Tasha o owasareta jigachi: Kindai Nihon ni okeru rinri ishiki no kiseki* 他者を負わされた自我知—近代日本における倫理意識の軌跡. Kyoto: Kōyō shobō.

Kawanami Akira 河波昌. 1969. "Kindai Jōdokyō ni okeru ga no jikakushi 近代浄土教における我の自覚." *Tōyōgaku kenkyū* 東洋学研究 3:133–47.

Keenan, John, tr. 1992. *The Summary of the Great Vehicle*. Berkeley, Numata Center for Buddhist Translation and Research.

Ketelaar, James. 1990. *Of Heretics and Martyrs in Meiji Japan: Buddhism and its Persecution*. Chicago: University of Chicago Press.

Kigoshi Yasushi 木越康. 1991. "Shinshū kyōdanron: Yasuda Rijin ni okeru kyōdanron no tenkai 真宗教団論—安田理深における教団論の展開." *Indogaku Bukkyōgaku kenkyū* 印度学仏教学研究 40-1:233–36.

———. 1993. "Shinshū kyōdanron: Yasuda Rijin ni okeru kyōdanron no tenkai 真宗教団論—安田理深における教団論の展開." *Shinran kyōgaku* 親鸞教学 61:55–71.

———. 2000. "Posutomodan to Shinshū: 'Anoyo' o futatabi koete ポストモダンと真宗—「あの世」を再び超えて." *Ōtani gakuhō* 大谷学報 79-2:22–38.

———. 2004a. "Shinshū kyōgaku no kindaika to genzai: Jōdo rikai no hensen o tōshite 真宗教学の近代化と現在—浄土理解の変遷を通して." *Shinran kyōgaku* 親鸞教学 82/83:50–68.

———. 2004b. "Shin Buddhist Doctrinal Studies and Modernization: A Dispute over the Understanding of the Pure Land." In *Buddhismus und Christentum vor der Herausforderung der Sakularisierung*, edited by Hans-Martin Barth, Ken Kadowaki, Ryo Minoura and Michael Pye, 89–101. Schenefeld: EB-Verlag.

Kikumura Norihiko 菊村紀彦. 1975. *Hito to shisō: Kaneko Daiei*. 人と思想—金子大栄. Tokyo: Yomiuri shinbunsha.

Kiyota, Minoru. 1978. "Buddhist Devotional Meditation: A Study of the *Sukhāvatīvyūhôpadeśa*." In *Mahāyāna Buddhist Meditation: Theory and Practice*, edited by Minoru Kiyota, 249–96. Honolulu: The University Press of Hawaii.

Kiyozawa Manshi 清沢満之. 1902. "Seishinshugi to sanze 精神主義と三世." *Seishinkai* 精神界 2-2:2–4. Reprinted in KMZ 6:91–3.

———. 1913–14. *Kiyozawa zenshū* 清沢全集. Edited by Tada Kanae 多田鼎, Sasaki Gesshō 佐々木月樵 and Akegarasu Haya 暁烏敏, 3 vols. Tokyo: Mugasanbō.

———. 1928. *Kiyozawa bunshū* 清沢文集. Tokyo: Iwanami shoten.

———. 1934–35. *Kiyozawa Manshi zenshū* 清沢満之全集. 6 vols. Edited by Kōkōdō 浩々洞. Tokyo: Yūkōsha.

———. 1935a. *Zettai tariki no shinkō: Kiyozawa sensei yuikō* 絶対他力の信仰—清沢先生遺稿. Edited by Inaba Masamaru 稲葉昌丸. Kyoto: Kiyozawa sensei tsuionkai.

———. 1935b. *Teihon Kiyozawa Manshi bunshū* 定本清沢満之文集. Edited by Inaba Masamaru 稲葉昌丸 and Andō Shūichi 安藤州一. Tokyo: Daiichi shobō.

———. 1936. *Selected Essays of Manshi Kiyozawa*. Translated by Kunji Tajima and Floyd Shacklock. Kyoto: Bukkyō bunka kyōkai.

———. 1953–1956. *Kiyozawa Manshi zenshū* 清沢満之全集. 8 vols. Edited by Akegarasu Haya 暁烏敏 and Tada Kanae 多田鼎. Kyoto: Hōzōkan.
———. 1963a. *Seishinshugi: Kiyozawa Manshi bunshū* 精神主義 清沢満之文集. Edited by Nishimura Kengyō 西村見暁. Kyoto: Hōzōkan.
———. 1963b. *Kiyozawa Manshi bunshū* 清沢満之文集. Edited by Ōtani daigaku 大谷大学. Kyoto: Ōtani daigaku.
———. 1971. *Waga shinnen: Kaisetsu Kiyozawa Manshi bunshū* 我が信念—清沢満之文集. Edited by Terakawa Shunshō 寺川俊昭. Kyoto: Bunmeidō.
———. 1972. "The Great Path of Absolute Other Power and My Faith by Kiyozawa Manshi." Translated by Shōjun Bandō. *The Eastern Buddhist* 5-2:141–52.
———. 1979. *Teihon Kiyozawa Manshi bunshū* 定本清沢満之文集. Edited by Matsubara Yūzen 松原祐善 and Terakawa Shunshō 寺川俊昭. Kyoto: Hōzōkan.
———. 1982. "The Great Path of Absolute Other-Power" Translated by James W. Heisig. In *The Buddha Eye: An Anthology of the Kyoto School*, edited by Fredrick Franck, 232–35. New York: Crossroad.
———. 1984. *December Fan: The Buddhist Essays of Manshi Kiyozawa*. Translated by Nobuo Haneda. Kyoto: Higashi Honganji.
———. 1999. *Kiyozawa Manshi seishinkai ronbunshū* 清沢満之精神界論文集. Edited by Ōtani daigaku Shinshū sōgō kenkyūsho 大谷大学真宗総合研究所. Kyoto: Ōtani daigaku Shinshū sōgō kenkyūsho.
———. 2000. *Tariki kyūsai no daidō: Kiyozawa Manshi bunshū gendaigo yaku* 他力救済の大道 清沢満之文集現代語訳. Translated by Honda Hiroyuki 本多弘之. Shikaidō: Sōkōsha.
———. 2001a. *Gendaigoyaku Kiyozawa Manshi goroku* 現代語訳清沢満之語録. Translated by Imamura Hitoshi 今村仁司. Tokyo: Iwanami shoten.
———. 2001b. *Kiyozawa Manshi "Tetsugaku gaikotsu" shū* 清沢満之「哲学骸骨」集. Edited by Ōtani daigaku Shinshū sōgō kenkyūsho 大谷大学真宗総合研究所. Kyoto: Ōtani daigaku Shinshū sōgō kenkyūsho.
———. 2002. *Gendaigoyaku shūkyō tetsugaku gaikotsu* 現代語訳宗教哲学骸骨. Translated by Fujita Masakatsu 藤田正勝. Kyoto: Hōzōkan.
———. 2003. *Gendaigoyaku tarikimon tetsugaku gaikotsu* 現代語訳他力門哲学骸骨. Translated by Fujita Masakatsu 藤田正勝. Kyoto: Hōzōkan.
———. 2004. *Gendaigoyaku seishinshugi* 現代語訳精神主義. Translated by Fujita Masakatsu 藤田正勝. Kyoto: Hōzōkan.
Kodama Gyōyō 児玉暁洋. 1997. "Mirai o hiraku hito Kiyozawa Manshi: Fukuzawa Yukichi no keimō shisō o sanshōshitsutsu 未来を開く人清沢満之—福沢諭吉の啓蒙思想を参照しつつ." *Shinran kyōgaku* 親鸞教学 69:66–93.
———. 2002. *Kiyozawa Manshi ni manabu: Gendai o Shinshū ni ikiru* 清沢満之に学ぶ—現代を真宗に生きる. Tokyo: Jushinsha.
Kōgatsuin Jinrei 香月院深励. 1899. *Tannishō kōgi* 歎異抄講義. Kyoto: Gohōkan.
Kōkōdō 浩々洞, ed. 1915. *Kiyozawa sensei no kyōkun* 清沢先生の教訓. Tokyo: Mugasanbō.
Komori Tatsukuni 小森龍邦. 1993. *Shukugōron to seishin shugi* 宿業論と精神主義. Sakai: Kaihō shuppansha.

Koshmann, J. Victor. 1987. *The Mito Ideology: Discourse, Reform and Insurrection in Late Tokugawa Japan 1790–1864*. Berkeley: University of California Press.

Kyōka kenkyūsho 教化研究所, ed. 1957. *Kiyozawa Manshi no kenkyū* 清沢満之の研究. Kyoto: Kyōka kenkyūsho.

——, ed. 2004. *Kiyozawa Manshi: Shōgai to shisō*. 清沢満之—生涯と思想. Kyoto: Higashi Honganji shuppanbu.

Kyōgaku kenkyūsho Tokyo bunshitsu 教学研究所東京分室, ed. 1963. *Gendai Shinran kōza* 現代しんらん講座. 3 vols. Tokyo: Futsūsha.

la Vallée Poussin, Louis de. 1988. *Abhidharmakośabhāṣyam*. 4 vols. Translated by Leo M. Pruden. Berkeley: Asian Humanities Press.

Marra, Michele F., tr. 2007. *The Poetics of Motoori Norinaga: A Hermeneutical Journey*. Honolulu: University of Hawai'i Press.

Maruyama, Masao. 1974. *Studies in the Intellectual History of Tokugawa Japan*. Tokyo: University of Tokyo Press.

Matsubara Yūzen 松原祐善. 1962. "Kōkōdō no ayumi: Kiyozawa Manshi o chūshin ni 浩々洞の歩み—清沢満之を中心に." In *Kōza kindai Bukkyō* 講座近代仏教, edited by Hōzōkan 法蔵館, vol. 6, 83–106. Kyoto: Hōzōkan.

——. 1962. "Kiyozawa Manshi no zokutaigi ni tsuite 清沢満之の俗諦義について." *Shinran kyōgaku* 親鸞教学 1:22–33.

——. 1963. "Kiyozawa Manshi ni taisuru futatsu no gimon 清沢満之に対する二つの疑問." *Shinran kyōgaku* 親鸞教学 3:26–38.

——. 1967. "*Tannishō* to Manshi to Kanzō 歎異抄と満之と鑑三." In *Tannishō no kenkyū* 歎異抄の研究, edited by Ōtani daigaku Shinshū gakkai 大谷大学真宗学会, 55–72. Kyoto: Bun'eidō.

——. 1971. "Soga Ryōjin sensei o tsuioku shite: Hōzō bosatsu no shutsugen 曽我量深先生を追憶して—法蔵菩薩の出現." *Ōtani gakuhō* 大谷学報 51-2:129–33.

——. 1972. "Kōkōdō no hitobito: Kiyozawa Manshi to Soga Ryōjin 浩々洞の人々—清沢満之と曽我量." *Shinran kyōgaku* 親鸞教学 20:28–40.

——. 1977a. "Kaneko Daiei sensei o shinobu: Kaneko Daiei sensei no wakakihi o shinobite 金子大栄先生を偲ぶ—金子大栄先生の若き日を偲びて." *Ōtani gakuhō* 大谷学報 57-1:67–78.

——. 1977b. "Kaneko Daiei sensei o tsuioku shite: Kaneko sensei to *Kyōgyōshinshō* 金子大栄先生を追憶して—金子先生と『教行信証』." *Shinran kyōgaku* 親鸞教学 30:1–11.

——. 1988. "Soga Ryōjin sensei o shinobite 曽我量深先生を偲びて." *Shinran kyōgaku* 親鸞教学 51:75–94.

Matsumi Tokunin 松見得忍. 1985. "Ki to gūzen 機と偶然." *Shinshū kyōgaku kenkyū* 真宗教学研究 9:26–31.

Mibu Taishun 壬生台舜, ed. 1975. *Bukkyō no rinri shisō to sono tenkai* 仏教の倫理思想とその展開. Tokyo: Daizō shuppan.

Miharu Toshiaki 三明智彰. 1990. "Shōwa shonen Soga Ryōjin/Kaneko Daiei Ōtani daigaku tsuihō jiken 昭和初年曽我量深/金子大栄大谷大学追放事件." *Shinshū sōgō kenkyūsho kenkyūsho kiyō* 真宗総合研究所研究所紀要 8:1–28.

——. 1995. "Soga Ryōjin no Hōzō bosatsu ron no keisei katei to sono genri 曽我量深の法蔵菩薩論の形成過程とその原理." *Shinshū sōgō kenkyūsho kenkyūsho kiyō* 真宗総合研究所研究紀要 12:1–84.

Mizushima Ken'ichi 水島見一. 2004. "Kindai Shinran kyōgaku no kihonteki shiza 近代親鸞教学の基本的視座." *Shinran kyōgaku* 親鸞教学 82/83:69–98.
———. 2005. "Kiyozawa Manshi no sanga ron (1, 2) 清沢満之の僧伽論 (上・下)." *Ōtani gakuhō* 大谷学報 83-3/4:1–28; 84-1:1–24.
———. 2007. *Ōtaniha naru shūkyōteki seishin* 大谷派なる宗教的精神. Kyoto: Shinshū Ōtaniha shūmusho shuppanbu.
———. 2010. *Kin gendai Shinshū kyōgakushi kenkyū josetsu: Shinshū Ōtaniha ni okeru kaikaku undō no kiseki* 近・現代真宗教学史研究序説―真宗大谷派における改革運動の軌跡. Kyoto: Hōzōkan.
Mochizuki Shinkō 望月信亨. 1975. *Chūgoku Jōdo kyōrishi* 中国浄土教理史. Kyoto: Hōzōkan.
Moriya Tomoe 守屋友江. 1997. "Kiyozawa Manshi ni okeru *Shiagon*: *Kyōkai jigen* to no kankei o chūshin ni 清沢満之における『四阿含』―『教界時言』との関係を中心に." *Shinran kyōgaku* 親鸞教学 69:55–65.
Murti, T. R. V. 1955. *The Central Philosophy of Buddhism*. London: George Allen and Unwin.
Myōon'in Ryōshō 妙音院了祥. 1909. *Tannishō monki* 歎異抄聞記. Tokyo: Hōwakai shuppanbu.
Nishimura Kengyō 西村見暁. 1951. *Kiyozawa Manshi sensei* 清沢満之先生. Kyoto: Hōzōkan.
Nishitani Keiji 西谷啓治. 1952. "Kiyozawa sensei no tetsugaku 清沢先生の哲学." *Kyōka* 教化 14-2:15–32.
———. 1963. "Kiyozawa sensei no 'seishin' 清沢先生の「精神」." *Shinran kyōgaku* 親鸞教学 3:70–82.
———. 1971. "Soga Ryōjin sensei o shinobu: Soga sensei no koto 曽我量深先生を偲ぶ―曽我先生のこと." *Ōtani gakuhō* 大谷学報 51-2:126–29.
———. 1973. "Soga sensei no jidai to sono shisō 曽我先生の時代とその思想." *Shinran kyōgaku* 親鸞教学 22:77–94.
Nobutsuka Tomomichi 延塚知道. 1992. "Shinshū daigaku no tokushitsu: Kiyozawa Manshi hisshō no negai 真宗大学の特質―清沢満之畢生の願い." *Shinran kyōgaku* 親鸞教学 60:23–45.
———. 1995–99. "Shinshū daigaku no tokushitsu: Keiō gijuku daigaku tono taihi (1, 2, 3) 真宗大学の特質―慶応義塾大学との対比（上・中・下）." *Shinran kyōgaku* 親鸞教学 66:1–15; 67:18–36; 74:1–25.
———. 2001. *Tariki o ikiru: Kiyozawa Manshi no gudō to Fukuzawa Yukichi no jitsugaku seishin* 他力を生きる―清沢満之の求道と福沢諭吉の実学精神. Tokyo: Chikuma shobō.
———. 2003. "Shinshū daigaku kaigaku no seishin 真宗大学開学の精神." *Shinran kyōgaku* 親鸞教学 80/81:76–102.
Nosco, Peter. 1984. *Confucianism and Tokugawa Culture*. Princeton: Princeton University Press.
———. 1990. *Remembering Paradise: Nativism and Nostalgia in Eighteenth-century Japan*. Cambridge, MA: Council on East Asian Studies, Harvard University.
Ōe Osamu 大江修. 1988. "Soga Ryōjin no shisō 曽我量深の思想." In *Kindai Shinshū shisōshi kenkyū* 近代真宗思想史研究, edited by Shigaraki Takamaro 信楽峻麿, 201–56. Kyoto: Hōzōkan.

Ogawa Ichijō 小川一乗. 2003. "Ōtani daigaku no yakuwari: Manshi ni okeru kindaika 大谷大学の役割—満之における近代化." *Shinran kyōgaku* 親鸞教学 80/81:103–26.

Ōkōchi Ryōgo 大河内了悟 and Sasaki Hasumaro 佐々木蓮麿, eds. 1963. *Kiyozawa Manshi sensei no kotoba* 清沢満之先生のことば. Kyoto: Nagata bunshōdō.

Olcott, Henry Steel. 2004. *Buddhist Catechism*. In *Buddhism in the United States 1840–1925*. Vol. 5. London: Ganesha Publishing.

Ono Renmyō 小野蓮明. 1988. "Nyorai ware to naru: Hōzō bosatsu (1, 2) 如来我となる—法蔵菩薩（上・下）." *Shinran kyōgaku* 親鸞教学 51:1–17; 52:15–30.

———. 1988. "Shinran no Hōzō bosatsukan 親鸞の法蔵菩薩観." *Indogaku Bukkyōgaku kenkyū* 印度学仏教学研究 36-2:21–28.

———. 2004. "Kiyozawa Manshi no shinnen: Sono gensen to naijitsu 清沢満之の信念—その源泉と内実." *Shinran kyōgaku* 親鸞教学 82/83:1–17.

Ōshiro Kuniyoshi 大城邦義. 1990a. "Kindai Shinshūgaku to wa nanika: Soga Ryōjin no Nichirenkan 近代真宗学とは何か—曽我量深の日蓮観." *Shinshū kenkyū* 真宗研究 34:62–81.

———. 1990b. "Kyōgakusha to wa nanika: Soga Ryōjin no kyōgaku no shuppatsuten 教学者とは何か—曽我量深の教学の出発点." *Shinran kyōgaku* 親鸞教学 56:31–46.

Ōtani daigaku hyakunenshi hensan iinkai 大谷大学百年史編纂委員会, ed. 2001. *Ōtani daigaku hyakunenshi* 大谷大学百年史. Kyoto, Ōtani daigaku.

Ōtani daigaku kanshōsha 大谷大学観照社, ed. 1951. *Kiyozawa Manshi* 清沢満之. Kyoto: Ōtani daigaku kanshōsha.

Ōtani daigaku toshokan 大谷大学図書館, ed. 1987. *Yasuda bunko yōsho mokuroku* 安田文庫洋書目録. Kyoto: Ōtani daigaku toshokan.

Piovesana, Gino K. 1968. *Recent Japanese Philosophical Thought, 1862–1962: A Survey*. Tokyo: Enderle Bookstore.

Rogers, Minor L., and Ann T. Rogers. 1991. *Rennyo: The Second Founder of Shin Buddhism*. Berkeley: Asian Humanities Press.

Sagara Tōru 相良亨, ed. 1993. *Chōetsu no shisō: Nihon rinri shisōshi kenkyū* 超越の思想—日本倫理思想史研究. Tokyo: Tokyo daigaku shuppankai.

Sakaino Kōyō 境野黄洋. 1902. "Ruijaku shisō no ryūkō [Niiche-shugi to Seishinshugi] 羸弱思想の流行 [ニイッチェ主義と精神主義]." *Shin Bukkyō* 3-2:64–70.

Sekimori, Gaynor. 2005. "Paper Fowl and Wooden Fish: The Separation of Kami and Buddha Worship in Haguro Shugendō, 1869–1875." *Japanese Journal of Religious Studies* 32-2:197–234.

Serikawa Hiromichi 芹川博通. 1989. *Kindaika no Bukkyō shisō* 近代化の仏教思想. Tokyo: Daitō shuppansha.

Shigaraki Takamaro 信楽峻麿. 1982. "Shinshū ni okeru shinzoku nitairon no kenkyū (sono 2) 真宗における真俗二諦論の研究（その二）." *Shinshūgaku* 真宗学 65:1–34.

———, ed. 1988. *Kindai Shinshū shisōshi kenkyū* 近代真宗思想史研究. Kyoto: Hōzōkan.

Shimaji Daitō 島地大等. 1969. "Meiji shūkyōshi 明治宗教史." In *Meiji shūkyō bungakushū I* 明治宗教文学集 I, of *Meiji bungaku zenshū* vol. 87 明治文学全集, edited by Yoshida Kyūichi 吉田久一, 373–90. Tokyo: Chikuma shobō.

Soga Ryōjin 曽我量深. 1913. "Chijō no kyūshu: Hōzō Bosatsu shutsugen no igi 地上の救主—法蔵菩薩出現の意義." *Seishinkai* 精神界 13-7:16–24. Reprinted in SRS 2:408–21.

———. 1922. *Kyūsai to jishō* 救済と自証. Kyoto: Chōjiya shoten.

———. 1924. *Chijō no kyūshu* 地上の救主. Kyoto: Chōjiya shoten.

———. 1927. *Nyorai hyōgen no hanchū to shite no sanshinkan* 如来表現の範疇としての三心観. Kyoto: Shinshūgaku kenkyūsho. Reprinted in SRS 5:151–216.

———. 1933. *Hongan no butchi* 本願の仏地. Tokyo: Daitō shuppansha, 1933. Reprinted in SRS 5:217–384.

———. 1935. *Shinran no Bukkyōshikan* 親鸞の仏教史観. Kyoto: Bun'eidō. Reprinted in SRS 5:385–471.

———. 1938. *Denshō to koshō* 伝承と己証. Kyoto: Chōjiya shoten.

———. 1938. *Naikan no Hōzō* 内観の法蔵. Kyoto: Chōjiya shoten.

———. 1947. *Tannishō chōki* 歎異抄聴記. Kyoto: Ōtani shuppan kyōkai. Reprinted in SRS 6.

———. 1947. *Soga Ryōjin ronshū* 曽我量深論集. 4 vols. Kyoto: Chōjiya shoten.

———. 1954. *Bunsuirei no hongan* 分水嶺の本願. Kyoto: Shinjinsha shuppanbu. Reprinted in SRS 11:245–339.

———.1961. "Shin ni shishi gan ni ikiyo 信に死し願に生きよ." *Kyōka kenkyū* 教化研究 33:12–22. Reprinted in SRS 12:74–89.

———. 1963. *Kyōgyōshinshō "shin no maki" chōki* 教行信証「信の巻」聴記. Kyoto: Hōzōkan. Reprinted in SRS 8.

———. 1965. "Dharmakara Bodhisattva." *The Eastern Buddhist* 1-1:64–78.

———. 1968–1970. *Soga Ryōjin sensei kōwashū* 曽我量深先生講話集. 5 vols. Toyama: Gatsuaien.

———. 1975. *Soga Ryōjin sekkyōshū* 曽我量深説教集. 10 vols. Edited by Nishitani Keiji 西谷啓治. Kyoto: Hōzōkan.

———. 1977. *Soga Ryōjin sekkyō zuimonki* 曽我量深説教随聞記. 4 vols. Edited by Fujishiro Toshimaro 藤代聡麿. Kyoto: Hōzōkan.

———. 1978. *Soga Ryōjin kōgishū* 曽我量深講義集. 15 vols. Edited by Gyōshin no michi henshūsho 行信の道編集所. Tokyo: Yayoi shobō.

———. 1984. "The Core of Shinshū." Translated by Jan Van Bragt. *Japanese Journal of Religious Studies* 11-2/3:221–42.

Sueki Fumihiko 末木文美士. 2002. "Uchi e no chinsen wa tasha e mukai uruka: Meiji kōki Bukkyō no teiki suru mondai 内への沈潜は他者へ向かいうるか—明治後期仏教の提起する問題." *Shisō* 思想 943:8–25.

———. 2004a. *Kindai Nihon to Bukkyō* 近代日本と仏教. Tokyo: Transview.

———. 2004b. *Meiji shisōka ron* 明治思想家論. Tokyo: Transview.

Suwa Gijō 諏訪義譲. 1976. "Kiyozawa, Sumita ryō sensei no deai: Sono tsuioku to shūgaku 清沢・住田両先生の出遇い—その追憶と宗学." In *Kyōgyōshinshō keshindo makkan no kenkyū* 教行信証化身土末巻の研究, edited by Dōbō daigaku Bukkyō gakkai 同朋大学仏教学会, 269–74. Nagoya: Dōbō daigaku kenkyūshitsu.

Suzuki Daisetsu 鈴木大拙. 1963. "Kiyozawa Manshi wa ikiteiru 清沢満之は生きている." *Shinran kyōgaku* 親鸞教学, vol. 3:83–96.

Suzuki, Daisetz T. 1972. "What is Shin Buddhism? (Posthumous)." *The Eastern Buddhist* 5-2:1–11.

———, tr. 1973. *The Kyōgyōshinshō: The Collection of Passages Expounding the True Teaching, Living, Faith, and Realizing of the Pure Land.* Kyoto: Shinshū Ōtaniha.

———. 1993. "Kiyozawa's Living Presence." *The Eastern Buddhist* 26-2:1–10.

Suzuki, Daisetz, Ryōjin Soga, Daiei Kaneko, and Keiji Nishitani. 1985–86. "Shinran's World (Parts I and II)," *The Eastern Buddhist* 18-1:105–19; 19-2:101–17.

Takeda Kiyoko 武田清子 and Yoshida Kyūichi 吉田久一, eds. 1977. *Niijima Jō shū, Uemura Masahisa shū, Kiyozawa Manshi shū, Tsunashima Ryōsen shū* 新島襄集、植村正久集、清沢満之集、綱島梁川集. Tokyo: Chikuma shobō.

Takeda Mikio 武田未来雄. 2001. "Shin no kyōdōtai: Jōdo kensetsu no seishin 真の共同体—浄土建設の精神." *Shinshū kyōgaku kenkyū* 真宗教学研究 20:39–54.

———. 2002. "Shinran ni okeru toki no mondai: Soga Ryōjin no jikanron o chūshin to shite 親鸞における時の問題—曽我量深の時間論を中心として." *Shinshū kyōgaku kenkyū* 真宗教学研究 23:74–88.

Takeuchi Seiichi 竹内整一. 2001. "Nihonjin no chōetsu kankaku 日本人の超越感覚." *Shinran kyōgaku* 親鸞教学 78:58–80.

Tamamuro Fumio 圭室文雄. 1987. *Nihon Bukkyōshi: Kinsei* 日本仏教史—近世. Tokyo: Yoshikawa kōbunkan.

Tamura Akinori 田村晃徳. 2000. "'Shin no jiriki' to shite no shinnen: Nishitani Keiji no Kiyozawa Manshi kan「真の自力」としての信念—西谷啓治の清沢満之観." *Shinran kyōgaku* 親鸞教学 76:36–49.

———. 2002. "Kiyozawa Manshi ni okeru 'jiriki' no hyōgen ni tsuite 清沢満之における「自力」の表現について." *Ōtani gakuhō* 大谷学報 81-3:16–27.

———. 2004. "Reizon to shite no jiko: Gojin no kachi wa ikan 霊存としての自己—吾人の価値は如何." *Gendai to Shinran* 現代と親鸞 6:18–36.

Tanaka Junshō 田中順照. 1982. "Kaneko Daiei sensei 金子大栄先生." *Bukkyō gakkaihō* 仏教学会報 8:26–28.

Tatsudani Akio 龍渓章雄. 1983. "Kaneko Daiei cho *Jōdo no kannen* no ichikosatsu 金子大栄著『浄土の観』の一考察." *Indogaku Bukkyōgaku kenkyū* 印度学仏教学研究 32-1:152–53.

———. 1993a. "Kōshō, Kaneko Daiei (1) Yōshōnen jidai (1) Seichi Takada no kankyō 考証・金子大栄（一）幼少年時代(1)生地高田の環境." *Ryūkoku daigaku ronshū* 龍谷大学論集 442:73–94.

———. 1993b. "Kōshō, Kaneko Daiei (2) Yōshōnen jidai (2) Seika Saikenji 考証・金子大栄（二）幼少年時代(2)生家最賢寺." *Ryūkoku daigaku ronshū* 龍谷大学論集 443:132–149.

———. 1994. "Kaneko Daiei no chichi Yūei ni tsuite: Kaneko Daiei kenkyū nōto 金子大栄の父勇栄について—金子大栄研究ノート." In *Bukkyō to ningen: Nakanishi Chikai sensei kanreki kinen ronbunshū* 仏教と人間—中西智海先生還暦記念論文集, edited by Nakanishi Chikai sensei kanreki kinen ronbunshū kankōkai 中西智海先生還暦記念論文集刊行会, 613–28. Kyoto: Nagata bunshōdō.

———. 1995a. "Kōshō, Kaneko Daiei (3) Yōshōnen jidai (3) Katei kankyō (1) Chichi Yūei 考証・金子大栄（三）幼少年時代（3）家庭環境㊀父勇栄." *Ryūkoku daigaku ronshū* 龍谷大学論集 445:197–236.

———. 1995b. "Kaneko Daiei no *Kyōgyōshinshō* kenkyū: Tokuni saishoki o megutte 金子大栄の『『教行信証』研究—特に最初期の研究をめぐって." *Shinshūgaku* 真宗学 91/92:299–332.

———. 1995c. "Kōshō, Kaneko Daiei (4) Yōshōnenjidai (4) Katei kankyō (2) Haha Sada, kazoku kōsei, keizai jōkyō 考証・金子大栄（四）幼少年時代（4）家庭環境㊁母貞・家族構成・経済状況." *Ryūkoku daigaku ronshū* 龍谷大学論集 446:218–61.

———. 1995d. "Kōshō Kaneko Daiei (5) Yōshōnen jidai (5) Tanjōbi, yōmei, tokudo 考証・金子大栄（五）幼少年時代（5）誕生日・幼名・得度." *Ryūkoku daigaku ronshū* 龍谷大学論集 447:111–38.

———. 1982. "Kyōgaku ni oite 'dentō' towa nanika 教学において「伝統」とは何か." *Shinshū kenkyūkai kiyō* 真宗研究会紀要 15:62–114.

———. 1984. "Shinshū kyōgakusha ni okeru rekishi to sekinin: Kyōgakusha no sensō sekinin o megutte 真宗教学者における歴史と責任—教学者の戦争責任をめぐって." *Shinshū kenkyū* 真宗研究 29:76–93.

Terada Masakatsu 寺田正勝. 1977. "Tsuibo Kaneko Daiei sensei 追慕金子大栄先生." *Shinran kyōgaku* 親鸞教学 30:12–26.

Terakawa Shunshō 寺川俊昭. 1970. "Kiyozawa Manshi no 'seishin' ni tsuite 清沢満之の「精神」につい." *Ōtani daigaku kenkyū nenpō* 大谷大学研究年報 22:1–50.

———. 1973. *Kiyozawa Manshi ron* 清沢満之論. Kyoto: Bun'eidō.

———. 1978. "Kindai Shinshūgaku no ayumi 近代真宗学の歩み." *Shinshū kyōgaku kenkyū* 真宗教学研究 2:20–31.

———. 1980. "Shin Buddhism in Modern Japan: An Examination of the Thought of Manshi Kiyozawa." In *Studies in the History of Buddhism*, edited by A. K. Narain, 339–42. Delhi: B. R. Publishing Corporation.

———. 1994. "Ganshō no hito Kiyozawa Manshi: Jōtaku myōyū no jikaku kara hiaku shūzen no iyoku e 願生の人清沢満之—乗托妙用の自覚から避悪就善の意欲へ." *Shinran kyōgaku* 親鸞教学 63:78–102.

———. 1994a. "Soga Ryōjin ni okeru Hōzō bosatsu no tankyū 曽我量深における法蔵菩薩の探究." *Ōtani gakuhō* 大谷学報 73-2:1–17.

———. 1994b. "Soga Ryōjin ni okeru Hōzō bosatsu no tankyū 曽我量深における法蔵菩薩の探究." *Shinran kyōgaku* 親鸞教学 64:56–75.

———. 2001. *Nenbutsu no sanga o motomete: Kindai ni okeru Shinshū Ōtaniha no kyōdan to kyōgaku no ayumi* 念仏の僧伽を求めて—近代における真宗大谷派の教団と教学の歩み. Kyoto: Hōzōkan.

———. 2004. "Dōrishin to shūkyōteki shinnen: Kiyozawa ni okeru tetsugaku to shūkyō 道理心と宗教的信念—清沢における哲学と宗教." *Gendai to Shinran* 現代と親鸞 6:101–49.

Terakawa Shunshō 寺川俊昭 and Ōkōchi Ryōgo 大河内了悟, eds. 1980. *Ware, tariki no kyūsai o nenzuru toki: Kiyozawa Manshi ni manabu* 我、他力の救済を念ずるとき—清沢満之に学ぶ. Kyoto: Higashi Honganji shuppanbu.

Totman, Conrad. 1993. *Early Modern Japan*. Berkeley: University of California Press.

Ueda Katsumi 上田勝美, ed. 1990. *Katō Hiroyuki bunshū* vol. 3 加藤弘之文集第三巻. Kyoto: Dōbōsha.

Wakimoto Tsuneya 脇本平也. 1967. *Kindai no Bukkyōsha: Shutsujō gogo (Tominaga Nakamoto), Waga shinnen (Kiyozawa Manshi)* 近代の仏教者—出定後語（富永仲基）・我が信念（清沢満之）. Tokyo: Chikuma shobō.

———. 1968. "Kiyozawa Manshi to Ōtaniha kyōdan: Zenhansei no shinri bunseki kara 清沢満之と大谷派教団—前半生の心理分析から." *Shinran kyōgaku* 親鸞教学13:78–96.

———. 1968. "Manshi Kiyozawa and Otani Sect of Shinshu Buddhism: A Study of His Early Life." In *The Sociology of Japanese Religion*, edited by Kiyomi Morioka and William H. Newell, 73–83. Leiden: Brill.

———. 1982. *Hyōden Kiyozawa Manshi* 評伝清沢満之. Kyoto: Hōzōkan.

———. 1985. "Kiyozawa Manshi ni okeru 'jiko'" 清沢満之における「自己」." *Shinran kyōgaku* 親鸞教学 45:65–81.

———. 1986. "Meiji no shūkyō teki fūdo 明治の宗教的風土." In *Kindai no shūkyō undō: Seishinkai no kokoromi* 近代の宗教運動—『精神界』の試み, edited by Hōzōkan 法蔵館, 3–37. Kyoto: Hōzōkan.

———. 1995. "Kiyozawa Manshi 清沢満之." In *Iwanami kōza Nihon bungaku to Bukkyō* 岩波講座日本文学と仏教, edited by Konno Tōru 今野達, Satake Akihiro 佐竹昭広 and Ueda Shizuteru 上田閑照, vol. 10, 235–253. Tokyo: Iwanami shoten.

Wakimoto Tsuneya 脇本平也 and Kawanami Akira 河波昌. 1992. *Jōdo Bukkyō no shisō 14: Kiyozawa Manshi, Yamazaki Ben'ei* 浄土仏教の思想 14 清沢満之・山崎弁栄. Tokyo: Kōdansha.

Ward, Ryan. 2005. "Meiji, Taishōki Ōtaniha ni okeru ianjin mondai 明治・大正期大谷派における異安心問題." *Tōkyō daigaku shūkyōgaku kenkyūshitsu nenpō* 東京大学宗教学研究室年報 22:129–156.

Yamabe Shūgaku 山辺習学 and Akanuma Chizen 赤沼智善. 1913. *Kyōgyōshinshō kōgi* 教行信証講義. 3 vols. Tokyo, Mugasanbō.

Yamada Ryōken 山田亮賢. 1972. "Yuishikikan no keiki: Soga Ryōjin sensei no yuishikigaku e no kanmei 唯識観の契機—曽我量深先生の唯識学への感銘." *Shinran kyōgaku* 親鸞教学 20:76–81.

Yamamoto Nobuhiro 山本伸裕. 2011. *"Seishinshugi" wa dare no shisō ka* 「精神主義」は誰の思想か. Kyoto: Hōzōkan.

Yasuda Rijin 安田理深. 1958–1972. *Ganshōge chōki* 願生偈聴記. 18 vols. Fukui: Keitokuji.

———. 1961. *Kyūsai no chie to jikaku no chie: Jōdo Shinshū no chūshin mondai* 救済の智慧と自覚の智慧—浄土真宗の中心問題. Kyoto: Ōtani shuppansha.

———. 1962. *Jinen no jōdo* 自然の浄土. Kyoto: Bunmeidō.

———. 1963a. *Engi to shōki* 縁起と性起. Kyoto: Nagata bunshōdō.

———. 1963b. *Waga kokoro no kokyō* わが心の故郷. Kyoto: Bunmeidō.
———. 1966a. *Gon no kyōgaku* 言の教学. Kyoto: Bunmeidō.
———. 1966b. *Hongan no rekishi: Shōshinge jokō* 本願の歴史—正信偈序講. Kyoto: Bunmeidō.
———. 1967. *Ganshō jōdo* 願生浄土. Kyoto: Nagata bunshōdō.
———. 1968. *Jiko ni somuku mono* 自己に背くもの. Kyoto: Bunmeidō.
———. 1969. *Ningenzō to ningengaku* 人間像と人間学. Kyoto: Nagata bunshōdō.
———. 1971. *Yume to shisaku* 夢と思索. Kyoto: Bunmeidō.
———. 1972a. *Kan no kyōgaku* 感の教学. Kyoto: Bunmeidō.
———. 1972b. *Shimofusa tayori* 下総たより. Kyoto: Bunmeidō.
———. 1972–1986. *Keshindo no maki: Kyōgyōshinshō kōgi nōto* 化身土巻—教行信証講義ノート. 23 vols. Yokkaichi, Mie: Tōkai monpō gakushūkai.
———. 1974. *Tariki no shinjin* 他力の信心. Kyoto: Bunmeidō.
———. 1975a. *Shinkōteki jitsuzon: Rakuzai serumono* 信仰的実存—落在せるもの. Kyoto: Bunmeidō.
———. 1975b. *Jinen to ningen* 自然と人間. Kyoto: Bun'eidō.
———. 1975c. "Tamawaritaru shutai たまわりたる主体." *Shinran kyōgaku* 親鸞教学 26:12–29.
———. 1977. *Daijō no tamashii* 大乗の魂. Kyoto: Daichi no kai.
———. 1978–1986. *Yuishiki sanjūju chōki* 唯識三十頌聴記. 17 vols. Fukui: Fukui sōō gakusha.
———. 1982a. *Hō ni yorite hito ni yorazare* 法に依りて人に依らざれ. Kyoto: Bun'eidō.
———. 1982b. *Hongan no seikatsusha: Nyūshutsu nimonge* 本願の生活者—入出二門偈. Kyoto: Sōō gakusha.
———. 1983. *Shōgon to ekō* 荘厳と回向. Kyoto: Bun'eidō.
———. 1984. *Tamawaritaru shinjin* 賜りたる信心. Kyoto: Sōō gakusha.
———. 1986. *Shinran ni okeru ningengaku* 親鸞における人間学. Toyokawa, Aichi: Tōkai sōō gakkai kenkyūsho.
———. 1988. *Inni no ganshin* 因位の願心. Komonochō, Mie: Konzōji kaki kōshūkai yonjū shūnen kinen shuppan iinkai.
———. 1988–1994. *Shinran ni okeru kyūsai to jishō* 親鸞における救済と自証. 10 vols. Toyokawa, Aichi: Tōkai sōō gakkai.
———. 1994a. *Shinran no sekaikan: Fuan ni tatsu* 親鸞の世界観—不安に立つ. Shikaidō: Sōkōsha.
———. 1994b. *Jishō jikaku no shin* 自証自覚の信. Kyoto: Daichi no kai.
———. 1996–1997. *Kyōgyōshinshō shō no maki chōki* 教行信証証巻聴記. 3 vols. Kyoto: Bun'eidō.
———. 1997a. *Kyōgyōshinshō shinbutsudo no maki* 教行信証真仏土巻. 2 vols. Kyoto: Bun'eidō.
———. 1997b. *Shinkō ni tsuiteno taiwa* 信仰についての対話. 2 vols. Shikaidō: Sōkōsha.
———. 1998. *Shōdaijōron chōki* 摂大乗論聴記. Kyoto: Bun'eidō.
———. 1999. *Honjō to myōgon* 本生と名言. Kyoto: Bun'eidō.
———. 2000. *Yasuda Rijin kōgishū* 安田理深講義集. 6 vols. Tokyo: Yayoi shobō.

Yasuda Rijin 安田理深 and Motai Kyōkō 茂田井教亨, *Fuan ni tatsu: Shinran, Nichiren no sekai to gendai* 不安に立つ―親鸞・日蓮の世界と現代. Tokyo: Tokyo shinbun shuppan kyoku.

Yasuda Rijin sensei sankaiki hōyō jimukyoku 安田理深先生三回忌法要事務局, ed. 1984. *Honji Yasuda Rijin* 本師安田理深. Kyoto: Bun'eidō.

Yasumaru Yoshio 安丸良夫. 1988. *Shūkyō to kokka* 宗教と国家. Tokyo: Iwanami shoten.

Yasutomi Shin'ya 安冨信哉. 1991. "Kiyozawa Manshi no banbutsu ittai ron 清沢満之の万物一体論." *Shinran kyōgaku* 親鸞教学 58:69–91.

―――. 1993. "Meiji chūki no shinzoku nitairon to Kiyozawa Manshi 明治中期の真俗二諦論と清沢満之." *Shinran kyōgaku* 親鸞教学 62:1–17.

―――. 1994. "Shinkō to jiritsu: Kiyozawa Manshi ni okeru 'shūyō' no ichi 信仰と自律―清沢満之における「修養」の位置." *Ōtani gakuhō* 大谷学報 73-2:18–30.

―――. 1995. "Nōdōteki jiko 能動的自己." *Shinran kyōgaku* 親鸞教学 65:50–75.

―――. 1997. "Shūkyōteki 'ko' no ronri: Kiyozawa Manshi to seishin shugi 宗教的「個」の論理―清沢満之と精神主義." *Ōtani daigaku kenkyū nenpō* 大谷大学研究年報 49:71–122.

―――. 1998. "Kiyozawa Manshi to seishin shugi: Sono 'ko' no isō 清沢満之と精神主義―その「個」の位相." *Shinran kyōgaku* 親鸞教学 72:1–15.

―――. 1999. *Kiyozawa Manshi to ko no shisō* 清沢満之と個の思想. Kyoto: Hōzōkan.

―――. 2003. "The Way of Introspection: Kiyozawa Manshi's Methodology." *The Eastern Buddhist* 35-1/2:102–14.

―――. 2004. "Koritsu to kyōdō: Sekisuiki Kiyozawa Manshi o tegakari to shite 個立と協同―石水期清沢満之を手懸かりとして." *Shinran kyōgaku* 親鸞教学 82/83:97–113.

Yokoyama Hisayasu 横山久安. 1983. "Shōshi Yasuda Rijin sensei 正師安田理深先生." *Shinran kyōgaku* 親鸞教学 42:53–60.

Yokoyama, W. S. 1995. "Two Thinkers on Shin: Selections from the Writings of Soga Ryōjin and Kaneko Daiei." *The Eastern Buddhist* 28-1:123–54.

―――. 1998. "Editing Epictetus: Kiyozawa Manshi's *Rōsenki* and Long's *Discourses of Epictetus*." *Hanazono daigaku bungakubu kenkyū kiyō* 花園大学文学部研究紀要 30:59–90.

Yoshida Kyūichi 吉田久一. 1961. *Kiyozawa Manshi* 清沢満之. Tokyo: Yoshikawa kōbunkan.

―――. 1962. "'Shinbukkyō,' 'Seishinkai,' 'Muga no ai' 「新仏教」「精神界」「無我の愛」." *Shisō* 思想 456:111–12.

―――. 1975. "Shinkō to fukushi: Kiyozawa Manshi to Uchimura Kanzō 信仰と福祉―清沢満之と内村鑑三." In *Bukkyō no rinri shisō to sono tenkai* 仏教の倫理思想とその展開, edited by Mibu Taishun 壬生台舜, 243–69. Tokyo: Daizō shuppan.

―――. 1992. *Nihon kindai Bukkyōshi kenkyū* 日本近代仏教史研究. Tokyo: Yoshikawa kōbunka; Yoshida Kyūichi chosakushū 4 吉田久一著作集4. Reprint of 1959 edition.

―――. 1996. "Kiyozawa Manshi, Shinkō to shakai: Shinkō keisei 100 nen o kinen shite 清沢満之 信仰と社会―信仰形成100年を記念して." *Shinran kyōgaku* 親鸞教学 67:65–81.

Yoshinaga Shin'ichi 吉永進一, ed. 2007. Hirai Kinza and the globalization of Japanese Buddhism of Meiji era, a cultural and religio-historical study (Hirai Kinza ni okeru meiji bukkyō no kokusaika ni kansuru shūkyōshi–bunkashiteki kenkyū). Japan Ministry of Education, Culture, Sports, Science and Technology Report no. 16520060.

Index

Abe Masao, 161, 279
Abhidharma, 58, 89n, 134, 182, 199, 245, 277
Abhidharmakośa, 182, 199, 212n, 277, 288
afterlife, 6, 8, 10, 147, 167, 176–178, 210
Āgamas/Ahan jing/Agongyō, 35, 36, 40, 57, 59
Akanuma Chizen, 61, 166, 294
Akegarasu Haya, 36, 37, 59, 61, 107, 117, 279, 281, 286, 287
Akṣobhya, 120, 130
ālayavijñāna, 103, 211, 220
Amida/Amitābha, 3, 10, 37, **42–43**, 51, 57, 91, **102**, 105, **107**, 110, 112, 114, 117–18, 120, 123, 124, 128, **130–33**, 141–46, **148**, **163–64**, 169–170, 175, 188, 189, 194, **206**, 207, 222, 244, **260–63**, 265, 267, 269, 272–275
  as origin of Śākyamuni, 130, 133
  as original nature of living beings, 263
  career of, 102, 107n, 110, 117n, 123, 129, 146, 151, 193–94, 200, 220, 269
  compassion of, 142
  existence/reality of, 102, 112, 202, 220, 267
  expressing gratitude or praise of, 130, 135, 224, 275
  form/formlessness of, 118n, 222, 223, 261
  light from, 102, 112, 131, 141
  mindfulness/contemplation of, 42, 154n, 224, 242, 267, 269, 270
  name of, 118n, 138, 143, 169, 194, 202, 221, 222, 223, 242, 258, **261–63**, 267, 270
  voice of, 136
  vows of, 42, 91, 102, 105, 129, 130–33, 135, 141–45, 153, 154n, 164, 168–69, **203**, 222, 241, 267, 272, 274–75
  power of, 3, 10, 43, 57, 118n, 154
  pure land of. *See* pure land, of Amida Buddha
  viewing of, 261, 268
  visualizing of, 154, 272
  working of, 145
Amida Sutra, 51, 194, 267, 268, 276
Anesaki Masaharu, 28
anjin, 43, 83, 91n, 203, 250, 262, 267
Asaṅga, 169, 211n, 217, 223, 249, 251–252, 254, 256–58, 265n
Avataṃsakasūtra, 18
Awakening of Faith (*Qishinlun*), 75n, 259

Bhaiṣajyaguru, 130
bodhicitta. *See* enlightenment, aspiration for
Bōfūshiu, 108, 117
bonbu. *See* common mortals
buddha lands, 124, 267–268
Buddhist Catechism, 23, 50n, 290
Buddhist history, 4, 40, 104–105, 119–138

299

Buddhist Studies, ix, 27, 32, 48, 50n, 120, 121, 125, 126, 134
Bukkyō (journal), 23
Bukkyō gairon, 160, 218

characteristic (in Yogācāra)
  common, 183–84, 211n
  individual, 183–84, 211n
Chengweishilun, 211n
Chijō no Kyūshu, 102–103, 107–118, 291
Chikazumi Jōkan, 36, 59
Christ, 110
Christianity, viii, ix, 3, 5, **16**, 20, **22**, 28, 110–111, 218, 263
  Buddhist reactions to Christianity, viii–ix, 14, 16, **21–22**, 28, 29, 65
  Christian reactions to Buddhism, 17, 21
Cohen, Hermann, 161, 184, 211n, 280
Commentary on [Vasubandhu's] Pure Land Treatise (by Tanluan), 117n, 134, 154n, 192, 212n, 224, 225n, 241, 258, 284
Commentary on the Contemplation Sutra (by Shandao), 143, 145, 154n, 155n, 202, 213n
common mortals/ordinary people (*bonbu*), 74, 78, 112, 115–116, 118, 132, 135, **140**, **144**, 249, 277
Comte, Auguste, 91n
Confucianism, 7–8, 72–73, 76n, 209n, 289
Contemplation Sutra (*Guanwuliangshoujing*), 51n, 91n, 140, 143–44, 154n, 194, 202, 203, 213n, 268, 272
Critique of Pure Land Buddhism, 161
Critique of Pure Reason, 162

Daikyōin, 13, 23, 24
daikyō senpu, 13
danka seido, 10
Daochuo, 117n, 138, 169, 192, 210n, 274

Daodejing, 118n, 129
Daśabhūmikavibhāṣā, 192
Dazai Shundai, 10
defiled/evil world (*edo*), 149, 170, 197, 258, 268
DeMartino, Richard, 222
dharma, 17, 62, 69, 70, 78, 89, 93, 105, 108, 114, 120, 125, 136, 142, 145, 148, 165, 182, 183, 185–86, 219, 221, 227, **228–32**, 258, **262– 63**, 268, 270
  body (*dharmakāya*), 118n, 185–86, 211n, 269
  nature (*dharmatā*), 51n, 118n, 232n
  hearing of, 91n
  Hindu concept of, 10
  latter age of, 72, 138n, 169, 271
  One, 258, 265n
  storehouse, 128
  three periods of, 71–72, 75n, 134
  true/right (*saddharma*), 71–72, 118n, 138n, 271
  unconditioned (*asaṃskṛta*), 186, 231
dharmadhātu, 41–42, 50n, 70, 126, 169, 187, 189, 229, 232n, 233–34, 258, 268
Dharmākara, 102–4, 106n, **107–116**, 117n, 118n, 123, 126, 128–131, 136, 137n, **146**, **148–52**, 153–54, 188, 193–94, 195, 220, 269, 272, 276, 291
Dōgen, 7, 75, 218, 256
dōtoku, 20, 77n, 283

Edo period, vii, ix, 1, 5–16, 18, 21, 24–27, 29, 34–36, 40, 49n, 57, 59, 65n, 74n, 89n, 155n, 166, 269, 275
ego, 144, 146, 147, 152, 260
eighteenth vow, 91n, **113–15**, 118n, 155n, 264, 269
Eiheiji, 218
Ekū, 166
Eminent Conduct Bodhisattva, 150, 155n

emptiness, 62, 124, 221–23, 232, 232n, **235–36**, 246, **254–55**, 262, 264n
Enjōin Senmyō, 166
enlightenment, 71, 102, 109–11, 114, 118n, 128, 130, 137n–38n, 142, 170, 194, 203, 205, 224, 269, 271, 273
  and the sacred name, 188
  and truth, 186
  and words, **182**, 184–85
  aspiration for (*bodhicitta*), 196, 198–99, 203, 213n
  sudden, 71
entrusting, 97, **113–16**, 118n, 128, 155n, 273, 275
Epictetus, 36, 57–59, 296
esoteric Buddhism, 22, 71, 72, 78, 248
ethics, 2, 6, 9–10, 13, **19–20**, 23, **30–31**, 35, 39, 61–62, 78–80, 83, 89, 89n
  Auguste Comte on, 91n
  criticism of Kiyozawa on, 62–63, 68, 75n
  Inoue Enryo on, 61
  Inoue Tetsujirō on, 20
  Katō Hiroyuki on, 18–20
  Kiyozawa on, 39, **41–42**, **46–47**, 58, 61–63, 64–65, **77–91**, 97
  Kōnyo on, 30–31
  Shimaji Mokurai on, 23
existence of the Pure Land, 164, 201–203
evil. *See* good and evil, defiled/evil world

faith, 2, 26, 30, 35, 39, 43, 44, 50n, 57, 62, 65, 81–84, 86, **93–97**, 102–3, 106, 109, **112–13**, 115, 118, 120, 141, 142, 151, 163, 171, 175, 177, 207–8, 250, 253, 267, 269, 279
  as believing subject's true self, 112–115
  as cause of birth in Pure Land, 113
  as *namu* in nenbutsu, 118n
  as object of Shin Buddhist Studies, 180
  as realization, 250–51
  as religious attainment, 30, 40, 43, 62, 80, 82, **83–84**, 90n, 102, 113, 134, 263
  as other-power transferred, 207–8
  as self-awareness, 114, 116, 145–46, 151, 163–64, 248, 255–56, 259–60
  as voice of Dharmākara, 102
  as wisdom of nondiscrimination, 251, 253, 256
  and doubt, 208
  and history, 2, 63, 128, 136
  and liberation, 107n
  and the orginal vow, 104, 109, 113–114, 206
  and practice, 26, 35, 80, 83–84, 134, 176
  and *shinjin*, 80, 85, 265n
  and seven patriarchs of Shin, 192
  benefits of, 81, 94, 96
  in *Kyōgyōshinshō*, 90n, 106, 108, 117n, 136, 163, 220, 271, 275
  one moment of, 114, 115–116
  in nenbutsu, 113, 136
  of Shinran, viii, 114, 145, 163, 168, 192
  deep faith, twofold doctrine of, 142, **145–46**, 148, **150–54**, 154n, 163–64
  three aspects of, 113, 118n, 151, 155n
fate, 101, 140–41, 205
Fazang, 193
five gates of mindfulness, 151–152, 155n, 224, 241–244, 264
forty-eight vows of Amida Buddha, 102, 112, 117n, 118n, 131, 133, 137n, 164, 168–69, 188, 190, 193–94, 212n, 269, 276
four immeasurables, 153
Fujimura Misao, 42, 91n

302 INDEX

Fujita Yūkoku, 9, 49n
Fujiwara Seika, 9
Fukuda Gyōkai, 30
Fukuma Kōchō, 30, 280

gakuryō/gakurin, 26, 34, 51n, 101, 159, 166, 269, 275–276
Genshin, vii, 7, 138n, 169, 192, 274
good and evil, 78–79, 90n, 95–96, 139–140, 144–45, 202

haibutsu kishaku, 12
haigōji, 12, 24
Hayashi Razan, 9, 73, 76n
Heidegger, Martin, 260
heresy, 7, 9, 35, 103, 161, 164
Hīnayāna, 28, 78, 120, 122, 126–27, 140
Hinduism, 10, 14
Hioki Mokusen, 218
Hirai Kinza, 23, 297
Hirata Atsutane, 8, 15, 17, 25, 49n, 73, 76n
Hisaki Yukio, 63
hōben hosshin, 260, 269
Hōnen, vii, 7, 35, 51n, 96, 113, 117n, 119–120, 138n, 142–43, 150, 169, 181, 192, 210, 267, 274–75
hongaku, 259
hongan. See original vow(s)
Honganji
 Higashi Honganji/Shinshū Ōtaniha, 4, 24–26, 31–33, 51n, 55–56, **60**–61, 63–64, 101, **103–4**, 106n, 155n, 164–65, 239, 276
 Nishi Honganji/Hongwanji-ha, 22–23, 26, 30–31, 47, 50n, 51n, 57, 161, 171, 269
honmatsu seido, 11
hontai, 42, 95
Huayan
 school, 193, 271. See also Kegon school
 Sutra, 18, 123, 126, 137n, 195, 271

Idea (in Kantian sense), 103, 160–62, **184**, 191, 205, 210n
Ideas of Reason, 162
Ienaga Saburō, 32
Imadate Tosui, 23, 50n
Imperial Rescript on Education (*kyōiku chokugo*), 19–20, 29, 45, 47, 63
Inaba Masamaru, 60, 103–4, 106n, 164
incidental name, 245, 247, 259
Inoue Enryō, 17, 56, 60–61, 64
Inoue Tetsujirō, 4, 20, 46
instinct, 141
Ippen, 7
Ishida Baigan, 14, 50n
Itō Jinsai, 10, 73
Iwagaki Matsunae (also, Iwagaki Tōen), 73, 76n

Jaffe, Richard, 7
jātakas, 123, 125, 137n, 270
Ji sect, 33, 51n
Jiacai, 202, 273
Jimmu, Emperor, 122, 136–37n
jinen hōni, 140
Jinrei. See Kōgatsuin Jinrei
Jingtulun (by Jiacai), 202, 213n
Jingtulunzhu. See *Commentary on [Vasubandhu's] Pure Land Treatise* (by Tanluan)
Jitōryō, 164, 219
jiriki. See self-power
Jiun, ix, 27
Jōdo no kannen 103, 160–62, 171n
Jōdokyō hihan. See *Critique of Pure Land Buddhism*
Jōdo Shinshū. See Shin Buddhism

Kakunyo, 143, 155n, 166, 212n, 270
Kaneko, Daiei, viii, ix, 17, 103, 106n, 117n, **159–171**
 and Kant, 160–62, 174
 and Huayan/Kegon thought, 159–160, 193, 195

on individual and common characteristic, 183–84
on *dharmadhatu*, 18, 169, 187, 189
on Dharmākara, 188, 193–95
on faith, 163–64, 171n, **175–176**, 177, 180, 192, **206–8**
on Idea, 160–62, 184, 191
and *Kyōgyōshinshō*, 165, 167–69, **179–80**, 181, 188–89, 192, 207, 209n
on the interpretations of the great patriarchs, 169, 179, 190
on nenbutsu, 173, 175, 191, 202–3, 205, **206–7**, 213n
on original vow(s), 188, 190–91, 196, 203, 205–8, 209n
on practice, 175–76, 179, 185, 196–99, 200–3
on the Pure Land, **160–64**, 167, 169–70, 171n, 173, 189, 193, 195–96, 198, 201–2, 205–6, 208
on Śākyamuni, 167–68, 170, 179–80, 183, 188–89, 196–202
on the seven patriarchs, 169, 179, 192–93, 204
on Shin Buddhist Studies, 167–69, 171, **173–81, 188–91**, 208
on the *Sutra of Immeasurable Life*, 168, 188, 192–95, 208
on true words of the Great Sage, 167, 170–71, 179–80, 190–93, 209
and *Tannishō*, 190–91
Kannon, 6, 10, 112
Kant, Immanuel, 18, 161–62, 174, 183, 209n
Kashiwahara Yūzen, 11–12, 16
karma, 2, 6, 90n, 111, 112, 139n, **140–51**, 153, 155n, 198, 202, 211n, 217, 222, 268
Katō Hiroyuki, 18–19
Kegon school, 41, 70–72, 75n, 126, 159, 160, 269, 271
Kegonkyō. See *Huayan Sutra* and *Avataṃsakasūtra*
Keichū, 8, 15n
Ketelaar, James, 7, 49n

ki (機), 93, 112–13, 142, 145–46, 148, 151–153, 154n, 270
relationship with *hō* (dharma), 118n, 148, 150
king's law–buddha's law (*ōbō-buppō*), 13, 22, 47, 272
Kiyozawa Manshi
and *Tannishō*, 36–37, 58–60
effort for educational reform, 4, 32–35, 60–61
on Buddhist clergy, **67–74**
on conventional truth, 77–78, 80–81, **82–89**
on ethics and morality, 39, **41–42, 46–47**, 58, 61–63, 64–65, **77–91**, 97
on practice, 31–35, 37, **39–40**, 45, 55, 59, **69–73**, 74n, 75n, **79–84**, 86, 90n, 95
on faith 35, **39–40**, 43, 57, **62**, 69, 80–82, **83–84**, 85–86, **93–97**
critiques of, 44–47, 62–63
Kōbō (journal), 219, 227n, 233n
Kōbō Gakuen, 104, 219, 220
Kōgatsuin Jinrei, 36, 65n, 142–143, 155n, 166
Kōkōdō, 23, 36, 51n, 61, 64, 101, 274
Konkōkyō, 15
Kōnyo, 30–31
Kudenshō, 143, 155n
Kūkai, 73, 76n
Kumazawa Banzan, 9
kunkogaku, 166
Kurata Hyakuzō, 32
Kurozumikyō, 15
Kyōgyōshinshō, ix, 59, 104, 120, 134, 163, 165, **166**, 169, 179, 181, 192, 207, 223, 239, 271, 273, 275
and Shin Buddhist Studies, 167–69, 179–81, 190, 209n
Chapter on Faith, 90n, 106, 117n
Chapter on Practice, 117n, 135, 179, 239
Chapter on Teaching, 128, 179, 188
Suzuki Daisetz translation of, 220

Kyōgyōshinshō kōdoku, 165
Kyōgyōshinshō kōgi, 166
Kyōkai jigen, 35, 60, 64
Kyūsai to jishō, 102

land of recompense/reward, 141, 144, 203, 213n
Land of Supreme/Utmost Bliss, 120, 176, 269, 273
language, 11, 14–15, 17, 22, 27, **38**, 40, 59, 85, 89n–91n, 159, 168, **182–83**, 185, 211n, 232, 245, 250, 289, 261, 263
Laozi, 129, 182
Larger Sutra. See *Sutra of Immeasurable Life*
Larger Sutra of Immeasurable Life. See *Sutra of Immeasurable Life*
Lotus Sutra, 28, 48, 123, 126–27, 129, 136n, 137n, 150, 155n
and *Sutra of Immeasurable Life*, 150

Madhyamakakārikā, 205, 246
Mādhyamika, 223, 264n, 265n
Mahāyānasaṃgraha, 169, 187, 211n, 257–58, 265n
Maitreya, 120, 130, 199, 268
mappō. See Dharma, Latter
meditative and nonmeditative practices, 139, 143, 154n
meibun (Ch. *mingfen*), 10
Meiji period, viii, 1, 3–7, 9, 12, 14, 15, 18–30, 32, 36, 44, 47, 48n, 62, 65, 73, 166, 271, 275–76
 anti-Buddhist government policies, 7, **12–14**, 15, 22, 25–26
 Buddhist reform movements, 21, 24, 32
 crisis within institutional Buddhism, 15, 21–22
 four stages of Buddhist rhetoric during, 21–23
 new issues for Buddhist communities, 26–29
Meiji Restoration, viii, 1, 5, 9, 15–16, 21, 24, 26, 55, 73, 271

mere consciousness/consciousness only, 164, 183, 211n, 223, 245–47, 250, 277
Miki Kiyoshi, 32
Mito (domain), 5, 6, 9, 12
Mitogaku, 9, 49n
modernism, 1–3, 5, 59
Monnō, 8
morality, 30, 42, 46–47, 49n, 62, 65, 68, **77–89**, 89n, 91n, 97, 227
Motoori Norinaga, 8
Mujintō, 108
Murakami Senshō, 28, 60
myth, 20, 28, 102, 116, 148, 224
myōgi, 244, 249
Myōnyo, 31

Nāgārjuna, 30, 62, 89, 127, 205, 213n, 223, 246, 254
 as Pure Land patriarch, 138n, 169, 192, 210n, 274
naikan, 41, 204, 272
naikan-shugi, 38, 43–44
Nakae Tōju, 9, 49n
name, 229
 and discrimination, 252
 and wisdom of nondiscrimination, 257
 as having religious significance, 243
 as incantation, 246, 257
 as practice, 240, 244, 262–63
 as self-proclamation of Amida, 169, **187–88**
 as *upāya*, 260
 conventional (provisional) name, 89n, 223, **245–46**, 248, 251, 254–55
 incidental name, 247, 251, 259
 of Amida (*myōgō*), 108–9, 130, 133, 135–36, 143, 169, 188, 193–94, 202, 221, 222–25, 242, 255, 262–63, 264n
 of the original vow, 224, 239–40, 242, 245, 248, 251, 258, 260, 263, 264

of the path, 128
of the Tathāgata, 239–42, 244, 246, 257, 259–61, 264n
process of naming, **182–84**, 187
saying (reciting) the name, 114, 118n, 138n, 202
ten names, 257–58
ultimate name, 258–61
Namu Amida Butsu, 118n, 135–36, 153, 169, 175, 188, 206–7, 223, 240, 246, 257, 262–63, 270, 272
Nanjō Bun'yū, 27, 33, 60, 64
nativism, 5
National Learning (*kokugaku*), 7–9, 11, 14, 48n, 49n, 76n, 89n
Natsume Sōseki, 43, 48
nenbutsu, 105, 113–14, 117n, 131, 142, 173, 175, 191, 205–7, 224, 241–42, 250, 264, 267, 270, 272, 274–75
of the original vow, 120, 136
history of, 133–36
recitation of, 153, 154n, 175, 202–203, 206, 213n
Neo-Confucianism, 7
Nichiren, vii, 7, 48, 150
Nichiren sect (Nichirenshū), 12, 24, 29
Nichirenshugi, 48
Nihon Bukkyō shikan, 165
nine grades, 140, 144, **154n**, 203, 268, 272
nirvāṇa, 18, 62, 160, 162, 273
Nishi Amane, 16
Nishida Kitarō, 17, 61, 217
Nishitani Keiji, ix, 217
Nisshu Jōzan, 218
Nobukuni Atsushi, 222
Nonomura Naotarō, 161, 171n

Oda Nobunaga, 6, 25
Ogyū Sorai, 10, 73
ōjōden, 10, 49n
Olcott, Henry Steele, 22–23, 50n
One Dharma, 221, 258, 265n

One *Dharmadhātu*, 233, 258
One Vehicle, 122, 128, 136n
original vow(s), 105, 108–9, 111–14, 116, 120, 124, 128–29, 132–33, 135–36, 141, 143–45, 153, 188, 190–91, 196, 203, 2058, 210n, 222, 224, 239–45, 248, 251, 257–58, 260–64, 272
Original Vow of Faith and Entrusting, 114
Ōtani University, ix, 2, 18, 26–27, 36, 64, 106n, 159, 164, 166, 218, 276
other-power (*tariki*), 3, 26, 34–36, 39, 46, 62, 83, 85–86, 111–12, 114, 116, 117n, 122, 143–45, 154n, 191, 207-08, 272, 274
absolute other-power, 42
other-power-ism, 38
other-power of the original vow, 141, 143

Pali, 27, 57, 89n
path of sages, 109, 117n
Perfection of Wisdom Sutras, 126, 205, 265n
perfuming through words, 183, 211n
Plato, 161–162
practice, **26**, 31–35, 37, 39, 40, 45, 55, 59, **69–73,** 74n, 75n, **79–84,** 86, 90n, 95, 102, 104, 108–10, 113, 117n, 118n, 121–23, **134–35,** 138n, 139–41, 143–44, 151, 154n, 155n, 175–76, 185, 194, 196–97, 202–3, 209n, 211n, 218, 220, **224,** 227, 231, 234, **239–43,** 244, 250, **262–64,** 268, 271, 272, 274–76
Dharmākara's, 115–116, 118n, 129, 151–52, 194, 213, 242, 262, 269, 276
five gates of. *See* five gates of mindfulness
nenbutsu. *See* nenbutsu
Śākyamuni's, 200–1
Shinran on, 135–36, 152, 179, 239–240, 264

Prajñāpāramitā Sutra. See *Perfection of Wisdom Sutras*
Prolegomena to Shin Buddhist Studies, 160, 166–167, 173, 211n
pure land(s), 17, 149, 150, 199–20, 268
  of Akṣobhya, 120
  of Amida Buddha, 34–35, 37, 51n, 91n, 102, 108, 110, 116, 117n, 118n, 120, 124–25, 131, 160–64, 167, 169–70, 171n, 173, 189, 193, 195–96, 198, 201–2, 205–6, 208, 212n, 220, 224, 250, 253–55, 258, 265n, 267–69, 273, 276
  with and without form, 131–32, 137n
  as Idea, 160–62
  as myth, 28
  as nirvāṇa, 18, 160
  birth in, 31, 39, 49n, 113, 140–42, 144–45, 153, 154n, 155, 194–95, 199, 203, 204, 212n, 213n, 263, 267, 269, 272, 274–75, 277
  types of, 203
Pure Land Buddhism, vii, 192, 195, 267
Pure Land path, 117n, 135
Pure Land sects (schools), 33
Pure Land sutras, 28, 33, 267, 276
Pure Land Treatise (by Vasubandhu), 117n, 134, 137n, 155n, 163, 192, 218–19, 224, 225n, 241–42, 244, 258, 264, 273

Rennyo, vii, 30, 32, 36, 58–59, 91n, 106n, 155n, 167, 176, 179, 210n, 270
Rokuyōshō, 166
Ryōshō, 36, 65n, 142–43, 155n, 166
Ryūkoku University, 26, 161, 173

Saitō Yuishin, 104
Sakaino Kōyō, 44, 51n
Śākyamuni, viii, 12, 22, 27–28, 35, 39, 43, 71, 120–25, 127–30, 132–33, 135, 137n, 155n, 167–68, 170, 179–80, 183, 188–89, 196–202, 270, 273
  and original vow 105
Saichō, 73, 76n
sakoku, 4–5
saṃsāra, 109–11, 115–16, 127, 141, 144–45, 151, 154n, 268
Sanskrit, 27, 50n, 57, 89n, 91n, 252, 269, 275
Sasaki Gesshō, 61, 64, 218–19
satori, 250
sectarian Buddhism (*buha Bukkyō*), 16, 21, 127
Seishinkai, 23, 31–32, 36–37, 44–45, 59, 61, 64–65, 77, 102, 117n, 160, 274
Seishinshugi, 3–4, 7, 15, 17–19, 24, 30–33, **36–38**, 40–48, 51n, 61, 101, 159–60, 272, 274
selected vow, 145, 274
self, 17, 43, 45, 58, 68, 71, 83–84, 109–16, 141, 148, 169, 187, 206, 221, 224, 227–32, 234–35, 246, 249, 252, 256, 259–60
self-awareness, 114, 116, 124–25, 127, 133, 142, 145–46, 151, 163–64, 187–88, 222, 235–36, 248–49, 255–57, 259–60
self-nature and mind-only, 109, 129
self-power (*jiriki*), 35–36, 83, 111, 139, 141, 144, 151, 154, 273–74
  path of, 117n
  nenbutsu, 136
  faith, 208
Sengoku period, 11, 59, 270
Sennyūji, 12, 222–23
seven buddhas of the past, 129, 135, 137n
seven patriarchs (in the Shin tradition), 134–35, 138n, 169, 179, 192–93, 204, 210n, 274, 275
seventeenth vow, 130–31, 135, 138n
Shandao, 113, 140, 143, 145, 154n, 155n, 163, 202, 213n, 250
  as Pure Land patriarch, 138n, 169, 192, 210n, 274
Shigaraki Takamaro, 62

Shimaji Daitō, 12, 47, 52n
Shimaji Mokurai, 17, 23, 50n
Shin Bukkyō (journal), 24, 43–44, 46n
Shin Bukkyō (movement,) 44
Shin Buddhism, vii, 2, 4, 26, 32,
    35, 46, 57, 63, 101–2, 105, 118n,
    160, 173, 176, 207, 210n, 212n,
    217–23, 267, 275
  in the Meiji period, viii
  and two truths, 77, 82
  study of, 166–67, 169, 171, 175, 179
Shin Buddhist Studies, viii, 32, 167–
    69, 171, **173–81**, **188–91**, 208,
    209n, 210n
shinbutsu hanzenrei, 12
Shingon (school), ix, 27, 30, 76n, 221
shingon ("true word"), 179, 248
shinjin, 30, 63, 80–81, 84–85, 91, 275
Shinran, vii–ix, 24, 26, 29, 34–36, 48,
    51n, 57, 59, 91n, 96, 104, 112–14,
    117n, 119–122, 126–28, 130–31,
    134–36, 142–45, 152, 160, 162–
    63, 166–69, 179–81, 188, 190–93,
    204, 207, 217, 219–20, 223–24,
    239, 241, 243, 275
  Shinran-ism, 32
  and other-power, 34–35
Shinshū University, 26, 36, 61, 64,
    101–2, 159–60
Shinshūgaku josetsu. See *Prolegomena
    to Shin Buddhist Studies*
Shinto, vii, 4, 6, 8–9, 12–15, 19,
    72–73, 76n
  Office (Ministry) of, 13
  State Shinto, 4, 13
Shōshinge, 108, 135, 275
Shōtoku Taishi, 165
shūgaku, 18, 21, 26, 29, **33–34**, 35,
    275–76
shugi, 32, 38, 40–41
shūgi, 34
Social Darwinism, 18, 29
Soga Ryōjin, viii–ix, 17, 59, 61, 64,
    101–6, 217–218, 220, 274
  and Kiyozawa Manshi, 101–2
  and Kōbō Gakuen, 104

on Mahāyāna, **120–22**, **124–27**,
    131, 134, 136
on *ālayavijñāna*, 103
on Buddhist history, **104–5**, 119–
    22, 125–28, 130, 135–36, 137n
on Buddhist Studies, 120–21, 126,
    134
on Christianity, 110–11
on Dharmākara, **102–3**, 106n,
    107–16, 123, 126, 128–31, 136,
    146, **148–54**
on karma, 111–12, **140–51**, **153**
on *ki* aspect of deep faith, 142,
    145–46, 148, **150–53**
on nenbutsu, 105, 113–14, 120,
    131, **133–36**, 142, 153
on original vow(s), 104–5, 108–9,
    111–14, 116, 120, 124, 128–29,
    132–33, 135–36, 141, 143–45, 153
on practice, 108–10, 113, 115–16,
    121–23, 129, 134, 139–41, 143–
    44, 151–52
on Śākyamuni, **105**, **120–25**, **127–
    30**, **132–33**, 135
on Sutra of Immeasurable Life/
    Larger Sutra of Immeasurable
    Life/Larger Sutra, 105, 123,
    126–29, 133, 150
Sōō Gakusha, 219
Sōtō, 24, 218
Spain, 5
sublation, 228, 232n
suchness, 17, 69, 126, 137n, 186, 188,
    222, 231, 132n, 236, 242–43, 260,
    263–64, 275
Sudhana, 123, 137n
Sueki Fumihiko, 19, 46, 63
Sutra of Immeasurable Life (*Larger
    Sukhāvatīvyūhasūtra*), 91n, 105,
    127–28, 133, 168, 188, 192–95,
    208, 220, 223–24, 241–42, 269,
    271–72, 274–75, 276–77
  and Dharmākara, 102, 106n, 117n,
    118n, 123, 126, 137n, 150
  and Shin Buddhist Studies, 167–
    69, **179–180**, 190–91

Suzuki Daisetsu, 220

Tada Kanae, 61
Taishō period, 18
Takayama Chogyū, 48, 51n, 52n
Tanabe Hajime, 217
Tanluan, 117n, 134–35, 212n, 224, 225n, 241, 246, 250, 258, 260, 263, 269
  as Pure Land patriarch, 138n, 169, 192, 210n, 274
Tannishō, 23, 36, 50n, 137n, 139, 141–43, 145, 151, 154, 155n, 190, 213n, 276
  and Kiyozawa Manshi, 36–37, **57–59**
Tannishō chōki, 105, 139, 155n
Takakura Gakuryō, 51n, 101, 155n, 166, 276
tariki. See other-power
tathāgata, 93–97, 107–9, 111–16, 118, 123, 129, 132–33, 163–64, 188, 190, 193–94, 208, 222–24, 231–32, 236, 239–46, 249, 253–54, 257, 259–64
Tathāgata of Unobstructed Light, 239, 241
Tendai (Tiantai), vii, 70–72, 75n, 76n, 126, 155n, 193–94, 246, 254, 265n, 275
tengu, 150, 155n
Tenrikyō, 15
ten stages of a bodhisattva, 185
Tetsugakkai, 56
Thirty Verses on Mere Consciousness, 246
The Nature of My Faith (*Waga shinnen*), 65, 93, 163
three aspects of faith, 113, 118n, 151, 155n
Tillich, Paul, 220–23, 239
Tibetan, 27, 57
Tōji, 221, 239
Tokiwa Daijō, 61
Tokugawa *bakufu*, 4–5, 9, 21, 25, 74n, 76n

Tokugawa Nariaki, 12
Tokyo Imperial University, 55
Tominaga Nakamoto, 16, 27
Tōyō University, 102
transference (*ekō*), 207, 224, 243–44
transformation of consciousness, 217, 222
Treatise on Mere Consciousness (*Cheng-weishilun*), 211n, 247
Tripiṭaka, 120
Tsuda Mamichi, 16
two-truths, **30–31**, 62, 74n, 77–78, 80, 83–84, 89n, 276

Uchimura Kanzō, 20, 51n
Uesugi Bunshū, 104
ultimate truth (*paramārtha-satya*), 62, 69, 74n, 81, 89n, 90n, 276
unconditioned dharma, 231, 265n
Unshō, 30
upāya, 260
Utilitarianism, 18, 29, 38

Vasubandhu, 134–35, 152, 182, 211n, 217, 223–24, 241, 246, 250, 265n, 277
  as Pure Land patriarch, 138n, 169n, 192, 210n, 274
  and *Pure Land Treatise*, 134, 137n, 155n, 163, 192, 218–19, 223–24, 225n, 258, 273–74
Vow of Birth by Nenbutsu, 113
Vow of Praise of Amida's Name by All the Buddhas, 135

Wang Rixiu, 202
Wang Yangming, 8–9, 49n
Western philosophy, 4, 16–18, 56, 58–59, 74, 217, 225n
wisdom of nondiscrimination, 248–49, 251–53, 256–58, 262
World Parliament of Religion, 23, 56
worldly truth (*saṃvṛtti-satya*), 30, 62, 69, 74, 75n, 90n, 91n, 236, 277

Xuanzhong Temple, 192

Yamabe Shūgaku, 61, 166
Yamazaki Ansai, 73, 76n
Yasuda Rijin, viii, ix, 33, 104, **217–220**
and Kōbō Gakuen, 219–20
and Kyoto school, 217
and *Pure Land Treatise* (by Vasubandhu), 218–19, 224, 241–42, 244, 258, 264, 273
and Sōō Gakusha, 219
and Tillich, Paul, 220–23, 239
and Western philosophy, 217
on *dharmadhatu*, 229, 233–34
on One *Dharmadhātu*, 233, 258
on provisional name, 223, **245–46**, 248, 251, 254–55
on self, 221, 224, 227–32, 234–35, 246, 249, 252, 256, 259–60
on self-awareness, 217, 222, 235–36, 248–49, 255–57, 259–60
on suchness, 236, 242–43, 260, 263–64, 275
on the view that accords with reality (*nyojitsukan*), 230–32
on transformation of consciousness, 217, 222
on wisdom of nondiscrimination, 248–49, 251–53, 256–58, 262
on Yogācāra, 217, 219, 223, 242, 244, 247, 250, 254, 273, 277
Yogācāra, 41, 211n, 217, 219, 223, 242, 244, 247, 250, 254, 273, 277
Yoshida Kyūichi, 12

Zen, vii, 23, 35, 55, 71–72, 75n, 126, 218, 222, 250, 256, 271
Zhanran, 194
Zhao Kuo, 72, 75n
Zhiyi, 193, 265n
Zhu Xi, 8–9, 49n
Zonkaku, 166

www.ingramcontent.com/pod-product-compliance
Ingram Content Group UK Ltd.
Pitfield, Milton Keynes, MK11 3LW, UK
UKHW041916140426
5217IPUK00013B/173